The Limits of Empire

The Limits of Empire

THE UNITED STATES AND SOUTHEAST ASIA SINCE WORLD WAR II

Robert J. McMahon

Columbia University Press

NEW YORK

Columbia University Press

Publishers Since 1893

New York   Chichester, West Sussex

Copyright © 1999 by Columbia University Press

Library of Congress Cataloging-in-Publication Data

McMahon, Robert J., 1949—

The limits of empire :   the United States and Southeast Asia since

World War II /   Robert J. McMahon.

p.   cm.

Includes bibliographical references (p.   ) and index.

ISBN 0-231-10880-X (alk. paper).

ISBN 0-231-10881-8 (pbk.   :   alk. paper)

1. Asia—Foreign relations—United States.

2. United States—Foreign relations—Asia.

3. United States—Foreign relations—1945–1989.   I. Title.

DS33.4.U6M33   1999

327.7305—dc21   98-19525

♾

Casebound editions of Columbia University Press books

are printed on permanent and durable acid-free paper.

Printed in the United States of America

c 10 9 8 7 6 5 4 3 2 1

p 10 9 8 7 6 5 4 3 2 1

To My Father, William J. McMahon

Contents

Preface

Over the past half century, few corners of the globe have experienced more conflict, turmoil, devastation, and change than Southeast Asia. And few have drawn more interest and attention from the United States—or more fevered bouts of activism and interventionism on its part.

Before World War II, Americans paid scant notice to Southeast Asia. U.S. officials viewed its mainland and insular territories largely as preserves of the European imperial powers. The colonial order presided over by the British, French, and Dutch did not conflict with America's minimal interests in the area; quite to the contrary, it ensured U.S. importers reasonable access to Southeast Asia's rubber, tin, and other important primary products while maintaining an overall structure of peace and stability throughout the region. The Americans, for their part, were busy readying the Philippines for independence prior to Pearl Harbor, a move that would have constituted a formal divestment of Washington's own modest prewar empire in Southeast Asia.

World War II, and the Cold War that followed so closely on its heels, changed all that, dramatically altering American perceptions about Southeast Asia's value and triggering broad-gauged American intervention in the affairs of the region. With surprising speed, the administration of Harry S. Truman came to identify Southeast Asia as a region of vital significance to the peace, stability, and prosperity of the world—and a region, consequently, that held vital importance to the national security interests of the United States. Truman and his successors gradually constructed a new empire across postcolonial Southeast Asia, a Cold War empire. In doing so, they aimed to keep a critical area within the boundaries of the so-called Free World. So obsessed did Americans become with Southeast Asia's presumed centrality to the global balance of power, and to their own exercise of world leadership, that they became embroiled, by the mid-1960s, in a shattering, self-defeating war there.

That conflict carried far-reaching consequences, not only for

America's position in Southeast Asia but for its broader role as global hegemon as well. And much more. Indeed, the Vietnam War probably affected Americans as profoundly as any event since their own Civil War a century earlier. The fighting that raged across the Indochina peninsula also left an indelible imprint on the political, economic, and geostrategic landscape of the region in which it was fought. Over 58,000 Americans perished in that agonizing conflict. The struggle left more than two million Vietnamese dead and, in one of its most savage aftershocks, claimed perhaps another two million Cambodians. And those grim casualty statistics barely hint at the war's broader impact.

Yet the Vietnamese communist triumph of 1975 brought few of the dreaded consequences long feared by U.S. policymakers. Nor did its humiliating defeat lead the United States to disengage completely from a region whose strategic worth it had so grievously exaggerated. As the twentieth century comes to a close, the United States remains a Southeast Asian power, though its role in the region is perforce much more modest and circumscribed than that of the recent past. The American empire in Southeast Asia has long since crumbled, along with the Cold War fears that originally brought it forth.

The wounds of the Vietnam War have now begun to heal. Even the war's principal combatants have taken tentative steps toward reconciliation and a new relationship. If Americans and Southeast Asians still live in the shadow of that harrowing conflict, they have also moved beyond it in manifold ways. They have managed to forge different bonds in recent years, bonds far less asymmetrical than those of the past. Those new bonds have been cemented especially by the dictates of commercial ambition, on both sides. And they have been made possible by the growing political assertiveness, economic maturation, and regional cohesiveness displayed by the nations of Southeast Asia—nations once caricatured by American strategists as helpless dominoes.

This book examines the ebb and flow of the U.S.-Southeast Asian relationship from the dawn of the postwar era to the end of the 1990s. It is the story, essentially, of the dramatic rise and precipitous decline of the American empire in Southeast Asia and, concomitantly, of the emergence of the indigenous peoples and states of postcolonial Southeast Asia as arbiters of their own destiny. The story parallels, and forms a critical part of, the broader narrative of global politics during the Cold War and early post-Cold War eras. Its principal themes rank among the predominant ones of the past half century: the vastness of America's postwar ambitions versus the limitations of U.S. power; the inadequacy of empires—European or American, territorial or informal—as a means for asserting control over non-Western peoples; the irresistible appeal of nationalist, anticolonial, and anti-Western currents to Asian and other so-called Third World peoples; the replacement of indigenous forms of regional order with externally imposed ones.

I develop other major themes in the narrative that follows as well. Strategic fears, I contend, especially those associated with globally derived Cold War visions and concerns, heavily influenced U.S. actions up through the end of the Vietnam War. Economic interests, the psychological underpinnings of global power, and the vagaries of domestic politics also played important, if secondary, roles in U.S. policy-making. Yet the strategic fears that proved so instrumental to the creation of America's Cold War empire in Southeast Asia seem, in retrospect, to have been grossly exaggerated; they rested more on illusory, worst-case scenarios about impending strategic and economic disasters than on careful calculations of the "real" interests and threats at stake in Southeast Asia. Since the mid-1970s, I argue, commercial considerations have achieved primacy in American policy-making. During that period, the Southeast Asian region has dramatically transformed itself into an economic dynamo while U.S. perceptions both about the area's strategic import and about the imminence of external threats to it have progressively faded.

This book also emphasizes the various ways that Southeast Asians have used—even manipulated—American power, ambitions, and fears for their own purposes. Further, I stress that it has been the unintended effects of U.S. actions that have frequently proven most consequential to developments within the region. Nationalism, ironically, has proven at one and the same time the greatest impediment to American designs in Southeast Asia and the greatest impetus for regional order, cohesion, development, and stability.

Now seems a particularly fitting time to offer a broadly focused, interpretive overview of America's post-World War II relationship with Southeast Asia. The passage of time has allowed for a greater degree of historical perspective on that tumultuous, contentious, and multifaceted relationship. Nearly a quarter century has now passed since the end of the Vietnam War, almost a decade since the demise of the Cold War that did so much to turn its localized flames into an international conflagration. Moreover, a rich array of secondary and primary sources pertaining to this subject are now available.

We remain very close to many of the events discussed herein, to be sure. As a charter member of the "Vietnam generation," I am hardly immune to the passions that still surround that era. I grew up with the war. Along with the civil rights movement, it constituted the dominant political—and moral—challenge of my young adult years. I saw friends go off to fight in a place that then seemed both remote and exotic, watched other friends seek to avoid service by virtually any means available to them, and observed (and occasionally joined) still other friends whose opposition to the conflict turned them into angry activists. All the while, my college years were charged, invigorated, and not infrequently disrupted by the intellectual ferment and societal disorder that the Vietnam War spurred within the United States. My interest in this subject doubtless stems in large measure from those formative years. Whatever biases it might possess likely stem from that personal history as well.

All scholarship builds upon, and benefits from, the work of others. That truism is particularly apt for one who seeks to make sense of a topic as broad as the present one. Without the impressive body of secondary literature that now exists on various aspects of the U.S. encounter with Vietnamese, Thais, Filipinos, Indonesians, Cambodians, and other Southeast Asians, I would quite simply not have been able to write this book. I draw liberally from that scholarship, and seek to synthesize it, in the pages that follow. I have supplemented the available secondary literature by tapping primary materials as well, especially those available in published form. That source material is unusually voluminous up through the end of the 1960s, especially on the American side. For the more recent period, governmental records remain largely closed to scholars. I have, consequently, drawn heavily from the public record in seeking to tell the story of U.S.-Southeast Asian relations since the end of the 1960s.

The first chapter sets the stage. It examines, in broad-brush fashion, the emergence of the European colonial order, the nature of the principal internal and external challenges to it, and the development of an American policy toward colonialism during the Second World War. Chapter 2 explores the crucial 1945–1950 period, a period that witnessed America's emergence as a full-fledged Southeast Asian power, and analyzes the links between the Southeast Asia policy of the United States and the Cold War. The following two chapters survey the ever-deepening U.S. involvement in the region during the 1950s, while chapters 5 and 6 focus centrally on the Vietnam War and its impact throughout the region. Chapter 7 offers an overview of the post-1975 period, emphasizing America's steadily declining strategic interests in the area and its steadily rising economic interests. It also stresses the growing importance of the Association of Southeast Asian Nations and the indigenous regional order it has been so instrumental in bringing about.

Acknowledgments

Numerous individuals and institutions have provided generous support during the preparation of this book. I am especially grateful to Gary R. Hess, Melvyn P. Leffler, and Robert H. Zieger, each of whom read the entire manuscript and offered valuable suggestions for its improvement. I thank George C. Herring and David Anderson, among others, for making incisive comments on early versions of different parts of this study. I am also indebted to Akira Iriye, with whom I first discussed the idea for this book several years ago and who, from the first, was extremely supportive and encouraging. And I am thankful to the knowledgeable librarians and archivists at the University of Florida, the National Archives, the Library of Congress, and the Truman, Eisenhower, Kennedy, and Johnson presidential libraries.

Jason Parker, Allison Taylor, and Mark Hove have each rendered invaluable research assistance over the past two-and-a-half years, while the superb staff at the University of Florida's history department, especially Kimberly Yocum and Betty Corwine, have proven as helpful as they have been cheerful and supportive. I thank them all.

I have had the opportunity to share some of the ideas contained in this book with audiences of fellow scholars at a variety of venues, including the Lyndon B. Johnson Library in Austin, Texas, the Contemporary History Institute at Ohio University, the Woodrow Wilson International Center for Scholars in Washington, D.C., the International Conference on Asian Democratization and Cooperation in Seoul, South Korea, and the Fulbright American Studies Conference at the University of Otago, in Dunedin, New Zealand. I thank the participants at those meetings for the numerous thoughtful suggestions and ideas that they offered and the intellectual stimulation that they provided.

I am particularly indebted to my superb editor at Columbia University Press, Kate Wittenberg, whose enthusiasm and support for this project never flagged.

Finally, I thank my family—for everything.

The Limits of Empire

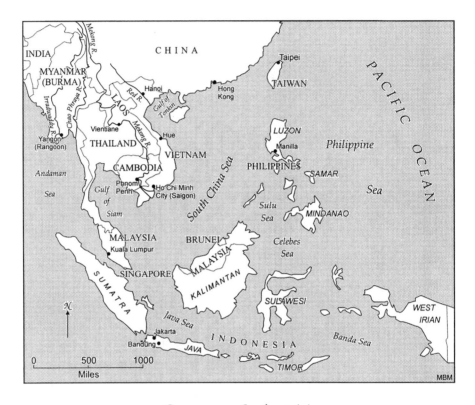

Contemporary Southeast Asia

The geographical designation "Southeast Asia" did not come into widespread use until World War II, and then largely as a by-product of Allied military planning. Before then, many Chinese writers referred to the area as Kun Lun or Nan Yang (Little China). British, French, and Indian scholars often called it Farther India, Greater India, or "L'Inde Exterieure."[1] For their part, French officials coined the term *Indochina* as a label for the portion of the region that they eventually conquered and colonized (Vietnam, Laos, and Cambodia). Those competing appellations reflected the tendency of outsiders to look at the southeastern quadrant of the Asian continent in relation to the two larger and more powerful political entities that flanked it. And, throughout history, China and India had indeed cast a long shadow over the weaker and less populous states of Southeast Asia, frequently dominating them.

The term *Southeast Asia* is commonly applied today, both inside the region and throughout the wider international community, to designate the area bounded by the modern nation-states of Burma, Thailand, Cambodia, Laos, Vietnam, Malaysia, Singapore, Brunei, Indonesia, and the Philippines. All ten of those countries currently belong (or, in the case of Cambodia, are slated soon to belong) to the Association of Southeast Asian Nations (ASEAN). In the three decades since its birth, that association has gone a long way toward forging a sense of common regional identity and purpose among Southeast Asians. ASEAN has, in the process, helped impart a meaning to the concept of Southeast Asia that goes beyond mere geographical shorthand.

But that, it bears emphasizing, is a very recent phenomenon. Before the contemporary era, Southeast Asians had not held any sense of regional identity or self-consciousness. The region never underwent the political consolidations that marked Chinese and Indian societies. Nor did it ever possess the common cultural heritage that characterized, at least relatively speaking, the historical experiences of both China and India. Scholars can speak, without undue distortion, of a Chinese or an Indian civilization existing across a long span of time; one cannot speak in a comparable sense of a Southeast Asian civilization. Rather, Southeast Asia has been notable more for its remarkable diversity and heterogeneity—cultural, historical, religious, ethnic, and linguistic—than for any distinctive unifying features.

All the Southeast Asian states, it is true, Thailand (Siam) excepted, eventually fell under the Western colonial yoke. Yet the superficially homogenizing effects of that experience were more than offset by the divergent policies pursued by the different imperial powers. Western methods of rule varied so widely that the colonial interlude, in some important respects, just further accentuated a sense of separateness among the region's various peoples.

The Emergence of a Colonial Order

Western control over Southeast Asia and the colonial order imposed on the region by the West are primarily phenomena of the nineteenth century. The Europeans had made their presence felt in maritime Southeast Asia much earlier, to be sure. The Dutch, through the vehicle of the privately owned Dutch East India Company, had established a firm commercial foothold on Java and on the Moluccas during the first half of the sixteenth century; they were drawn there, in particular, by the fabled spices of the Indies. The Portuguese and Spanish had arrived in insular Southeast Asia even earlier, the latter establishing suzerainty over a significant portion of the Philippine islands during the course of the sixteenth century. But as the nineteenth century opened, most of Southeast Asia still lay well beyond the reach of Western influence. At that point, only the trading centers of Penang and Melaka, major portions of the Philippines, some of the Moluccas, and much of Java were truly under European control.

Even as late as 1850, European encroachments were limited to a few additional British-controlled trading ports along the Malayan peninsula, the most important of which was Singapore (established in 1819), a British toehold in Burma, the beginning of a French presence in Indochina, and a modest extension of the Dutch imperial domain in the East Indian archipelago. At midcentury, the European colonial empire in Southeast Asia remained more commercial than territorial; it consisted primarily of titular claims to sovereignty, the right to collect certain revenues, and the exploitation of a set of specific economic privileges.

Between 1850 and 1880, dramatic changes swept both insular and mainland Southeast Asia. During those three decades, the European powers divided virtually the entire region into clearly demarcated spheres of influence, inaugurating what scholars now call the era of high colonialism. Only Thailand managed to maintain nominal independence, and not without paying a substantial price. Still, even by the end of the 1870s substantial parts of the Southeast Asian hinterland remained untouched by the European presence. Actual control over indigenous populations did not extend much beyond a handful of metropolitan centers.

Between 1880 and 1920, Western rule throughout Southeast Asia tightened appreciably. During those frenzied years of conquest and consolidation, the Western powers established centralized administrative-bureaucratic states in each one of their colonial dependencies. Those colonial state apparatuses possessed coercive capabilities far in excess of anything previously experienced in the long history of the region. Western functionaries now could, and did, reach into the lives of ordinary villagers to an unparalleled extent. Using superior military might when needed, diplomacy, the threat of force, administrative fiat, or native collaboration when one or more of those sufficed, the Western colonizers overwhelmed indigenous opposition, frequently destroying well-entrenched native political and legal structures. Whole political entities were obliterated in the process, including Aceh, Bali, and Sulu, making clear in each case the folly of armed resistance.

Great Britain, befitting its status as the predominant power in the region, took the lead. During this period the British consolidated their hold on the Malay states and completed, by 1885, their conquest of Burma, forcing the traditional rulers to flee and thereafter abolishing the Burmese monarchy. The French completed their conquest of Vietnam that same year, extending their empire to embrace Laos by 1893. Following a brief war with Spain in 1898, the United States, too, became a colonial power, by virtue of its seizure of the Spanish Philippines. American forces managed to secure outright control of the islands, but only after mounting a bloody counterinsurgency campaign against independence-minded Filipinos. The Dutch, for their part, extended their imperial domain in the East Indies during this period, succeeding, by 1914, in quashing Bali, the archipelago's last independent kingdom.

The administrative-bureaucratic states established by the Western powers intruded upon the lives of indigenous peoples in unprecedented ways. Colonial administrators aimed systematically to order, control, and "improve" the lives of their subjects, using modern methods of dispassionate bureaucratic management and economic efficiency. Their resulting policies brought sweeping changes in a number of areas, including tax collection, legal processes, policing powers, land management, economic enterprise, public health and sanitation, and the construction of roads, bridges, public build-

ings, and transportation networks. Taxation proved a particularly ubiquitous, and onerous, by-product of the new regimes. In French Cochinchina
tax revenues swelled from 5.7 million piastres in 1913 to 15.7 million in
1929; in the Netherlands East Indies they rose from 57.3 million guilders in
1900 to 361 million in 1928; and in the Philippines, the value of the revenue
collected by American authorities rose 170 percent between 1900 and 1916.[2]

The era of high colonialism spurred massive changes in the underlying
social and economic structures of Southeast Asian societies. This period witnessed burgeoning urbanization, incipient industrialization, massive in-
migration, soaring birth rates, and a tremendous spurt in productive economic activity. In order to increase the profitability of their dependencies, the
Western colonizers encouraged the systematic development of large-scale
economic enterprises geared to the export market. Those enterprises were
generally capital-intensive, privately financed, and corporately managed.
They concentrated on the development and export of a wide variety of commodities, including rubber, tin, petroleum, coal, timber, sugar, coffee, and
tea. Rice, the region's most essential crop, was also produced for export,
though in most areas its cultivation remained a small-scale activity. The population movements and alterations in traditional patterns of work necessitated by the new extractive industries took a heavy toll on the region's labor
force. To take but one grisly statistic from this era, in 1927 fully one out of
every twenty rubber plantation workers in Vietnam perished.[3]

The new colonialism that burst forth in Southeast Asia during the late
nineteenth century was coterminus with the European powers' partition of
Africa and their aggressive search for spheres of influence in China. Similar
forces were impelling the Western powers to seek an expansion of their commercial and territorial holdings at this time. The profit motive, without
doubt, was paramount. Rapidly industrializing, and increasingly competi-
tive, Western economies displayed an insatiable appetite for new markets,
investment outlets, and sources of raw materials. Strategic considerations
often reinforced commercial motives. Great Britain, for example, established
control over Burma and the Malay states for a mixture of economic and
strategic reasons. Those included, most prominently, the felt need to protect
the eastern flanks of British India, the desire to safeguard existing maritime
trade routes to China, and the search for new inland trade links between
India and the Chinese mainland. The French conquest of Indochina derived
in large measure from their belated search for a reliable window on the
Pacific. France believed that by carving a colonial empire out of the Indochinese territories it could indirectly facilitate its penetration of the lucrative
China market, profit directly from the development of local extractive enter-

prises, and at the same time enhance its international stature as a great power. The American decision to hold on to the Philippines derived from a similar mix of motives; the United States saw value in the possession of a Pacific colony that offered commercial benefits and promised future base sites for its Pacific fleet.

Humanitarian and idealistic motives often intersected with these more concrete economic and strategic calculations, at times exerting an independent influence on policy decisions. Tellingly, every imperial power developed, by at least the beginning of the twentieth century, its version of what the French glorified as "la mission civilisatrice" and the British called the "white man's burden."

The great disparity between the military power and technological prowess of the West, on the one hand, and that possessed by indigenous polities, on the other, encouraged and conditioned Western expansion. By the late nineteenth century, the Western powers possessed the *means* to dominate Southeast Asia, means not fully available to them a generation earlier. The relative weakness of indigenous states during the latter part of the nineteenth century, and the divisions within and among traditional ruling elites, greatly facilitated the Western conquest as well. Southeast Asians were not, of course, simply the helpless—and hapless—victims of an inexorable Western advance, as a previous generation of scholars tended to depict them. They helped make their own history in numerous ways, exercising the full array of options that were available to them. A process of accommodation plainly took place on both sides; and influence moved in a multidirectional rather than a unidirectional manner. Yet, if modern scholarship has corrected old stereotypes and rightly focused on indigenous peoples as actors in their own right, it bears emphasizing that Southeast Asians operated from the late nineteenth century onward in a highly constricted environment. The boundaries of that environment were manipulated and controlled by those who possessed a monopoly on the coercive powers of the state—namely, the British, French, Dutch, and American colonial authorities. By the early decades of the twentieth century, they had forged a colonial order in Southeast Asia that appeared virtually impregnable.[4]

Challenges—From Within and Without

Although Southeast Asia's colonial order may, on the surface, have appeared impregnable, the Western imperialists had already begun sowing the seeds of their own demise. To the extent that colonialism, by its very nature, undermined traditional political and social structures, exploited local labor forces, and caused, in most parts of the region, a decline in standards of living, it inevitably bred resentment and rebellion. To hold power, the imperial powers needed to use force, or the threat of force, to bend indigenous peoples to their will. They also needed to gain the passive acquiescence of the vast majority of their subjects, while selecting and nurturing a small group of elites to serve as collaborating functionaries. Yet local populations always vastly outnumbered the relative handful of resident Western civil and military representatives. At no point during the era of high colonialism, in fact, did the Western presence in any Southeast Asian colony rise above 1 percent of the total population. To maintain firm control, under such tenuous circumstances, proved a most daunting assignment—to say the least. The global economic depression of the 1930s, which hit primary producing areas such as Southeast Asia particularly hard, and which generated considerable restiveness among indigenous peoples, made the task ever more vexing.

The colonial order depended on more than just repressing, or gaining the passive acquiescence of, local populations; it also required that the colonial powers maintain sufficient military strength to deter any outside power, or powers, from challenging the status quo. Yet the military vitality of the European imperial states was fast declining relative to that of their chief competitors. By the mid-1930s, France, the Netherlands, and Britain were, moreover, increasingly preoccupied with the threat posed to their security at home by a rapidly remilitarizing Germany. Ensuring the security of distant colonial possessions ranked as a distinctly secondary priority.

By the early twentieth century, vigorous nationalist movements had blossomed across the breadth of Southeast Asia. Those movements, committed to the replacement of alien rulers with indigenous ones, posed a formidable internal challenge to the colonial order. The emergence, by the 1930s, of an assertive and militant Japan, determined to forge an Asian empire of its own and covetous of Southeast Asia's valuable raw materials, posed an even more immediate external challenge. Together, those forces were destined to topple the colonial order.

Modern nationalist movements in Southeast Asia arose as a direct consequence of Western imperial rule, defining themselves largely in terms of their unyielding opposition to alien authority. The most complex of phenomena, nationalism defies easy categorization or generalization. That is especially so in modern Southeast Asia, where the prototypical nationalist movement agitated for the establishment of an indigenous state that would inherit the precise boundaries that had been so arbitrarily drawn by the very imperialists it sought to replace. Yet those boundary lines had often cut right through the traditional homelands of relatively homogeneous ethnic groups and had joined together peoples who had few, if any, common bonds.

In this sense, Indonesian nationalism, to take an obvious example, did not—and could not—exist before the establishment of Dutch suzerainty over the East Indian archipelago. The ethnically, religiously, and culturally diverse populations of those far-flung islands possessed no prior sense of belonging to a common nation. "Unity out of diversity" thus became the political rallying cry adopted by those who sought to create a unified Indonesian national state in territory that the Dutch had merged together as an administrative convenience—even though no previous national "state" had ever existed within those boundaries. Similar patterns, if less extreme in the case of Burma and Vietnam, each of which had a stronger sense of national consciousness, obtained among the region's other anticolonial, nationalist movements. Some indigenous groups, to be sure, clung (and some cling to this day) to a different nationalist vision. But those who sought to replace European rule with smaller and more homogeneous polities—the Shan and Karens in Burma, the Baba in Malaya, various Muslim groups throughout insular Southeast Asia—found themselves shunted aside as the unity-in-diversity approach came to dominate indigenous nationalist movements.

The inherently oppressive nature of the colonial systems imposed by the West, even taking important individual variations into account, served as the indispensable incubator for Southeast Asia's indigenous nationalist movements. The arrogance and haughtiness of so many colonial administrators, coupled with their frequently contemptuous, race-conscious attitudes, bred strong native resentment. The decline in the material well-being of most colonial subjects, the wholesale degradation of indigenous institutions, the undercutting of traditional elites, the economic distress occasioned by fluctuations in commodity prices—those negative consequences of imperial rule each contributed, as well, to the periodic bursts of anticolonial activity in which both peasants and elites engaged. Peasant rebellions, though often unfocused and poorly organized, served as a constant reminder to Western rulers that their subjects were anything but quiescent. In 1930, for example, a peaceful protest against tax and land policies in Nghe An province in central Vietnam led to a march of more than six thousand peasants on the provincial capital. The French, quick to meet any challenges to their rule with brutal force, responded with an air strike that killed 174 of the protesters; they took another fifteen lives when a second air strike hit those who had come to claim the bodies of the initial victims.

If the destabilizing changes wrought by colonialism proved an essential precondition for the emergence of a nationalist resistance, it was the Western-style education provided to select native elites that shaped the ideas and strategies of those who would actually lead that resistance. Each colonial power encouraged the education of a small number of local elites in order to fill the middle tiers of the colonial bureaucracy. The United States was the one exception in this regard in that it made public education widely available in the Philippines, a policy shaped by the American commitment to egalitarian education and the concomitant determination to prepare Filipinos for eventual self-rule. Elsewhere, expediency governed native education policy. A bitter Malay nationalist hardly exaggerated when, in 1927, he exclaimed that "the knowledge that is given to people under foreign influence has no purpose other than to impoverish the intellect and teach them to lick the soles of their masters' boots."[5] Yet the educational opportunities that colonial authorities offered to the chosen few in order to help fill manpower needs throughout the civil service had the ironic effect of stirring nationalist consciousness among colonial subjects. Western schooling in the colonies and, for a very tiny group, in Europe also exposed impressionable young people, well aware of their second-class status in their own lands, to Western ideas about freedom, democracy, and self-determination—even to revolutionary thought and Marxist ideology. The leadership of every major anticolonial nationalist movement in Southeast Asia during the first half of the twentieth century was dominated by men who had attained the benefit of a Western education, and who managed to turn the ideas of the rulers against them.

Events elsewhere in Asia also spurred the development and proliferation of Southeast Asian nationalist movements. The extended resistance of Filipino guerrillas to American rule, the emergence of a modernizing nationalist movement in China under Sun Yat-sen, the nationalist struggle of the Congress Party in India, the rapid economic and military development of Japan, Russia's stunning defeat at the hands of the Japanese in 1904–1905—all gave heart to nationalist leaders determined to bring down the colonial order. The Japanese example proved especially inspiring. "A shock went through the edifice of Western imperialism when the Land of the Rising Sun defeated the Russian colossus in 1905," recalled Indonesian nationalist Mohammed Hatta. "This brought about a revision of ideas both in the white as well as the coloured world. The herald of a new day had come!"[6] As nationalist movements grew larger and bolder in the 1920s and 1930s, especially in Vietnam, Burma, and the East Indies, colonial authorities met the threat with stepped-up repression.[7]

Events on the larger world stage brought a dramatic boost to the fortunes of Southeast Asia's nationalists. The outbreak of war in Europe in September 1939, and the subsequent German conquest and occupation of the

Netherlands and France, severely weakened the power and authority of the colonial regimes in the East Indies and Indochina. Britain's preoccupation with the European conflict correspondingly weakened its hold on Burma and Malaya. Sensing a historic opportunity to create a greater East Asian empire, the Japanese moved quickly to capitalize on the unique opportunities afforded them by the European conflict, forcing French officials in Indochina to grant them a series of military rights. Unable to reach an acceptable settlement with the United States, Japanese leaders gambled that they could buy critical time for their ambitious regional plans by striking simultaneously at the U.S. Pacific Fleet in Hawaii and the American and European colonial possessions in Southeast Asia. Following the Pearl Harbor attack of December 7, 1941, the Japanese swiftly overcame surprisingly weak Western resistance across the breadth of Southeast Asia.

By March 1942, Japan stood in occupation of the Philippines, Indochina, Burma, Malaya, and the East Indies. For their part, nationalist statesmen in the newly occupied territories glimpsed fresh opportunities to advance their own long-term goals. Although dramatic comebacks in world politics, as in sports, can never be ruled out, it certainly appeared by the early months of 1942 that the Western colonial order in Southeast Asia had come to a rather ignominious end.

The United States, the Colonial Question, and World War II

Of the myriad diplomatic problems facing President Franklin D. Roosevelt during the Second World War, few were more complex, contentious, or plagued by a tangle of conflicting interests than the future of the colonial empires. This issue was most immediately posed, of course, by the Southeast Asian colonies overrun by the Japanese. Nationalists in those areas and their former European imperial overlords alike looked to Washington with a curious mixture of hope and apprehension. Would Roosevelt press for colonial liberation as a measure consistent with traditional American anticolonial sentiments? Or would he instead favor the reestablishment of the colonial order in line with the wishes of his European allies and the principle of territorial sovereignty so grievously violated by the Japanese? As it appeared likely that U.S. troops would eventually liberate those territories from the Japanese, such questions were of more than academic interest. Precedents established in Southeast Asia would, furthermore, exert a significant impact on the future course of colonial rule throughout the rest of the world.

Much to the delight of native nationalists in Southeast Asia and elsewhere, FDR gave several strong indications during the early war years that he would place the power and prestige of the United States unequivocally behind the principle of self-determination for all peoples. At the president's insistence, the Atlantic Charter, signed by Roosevelt and British Prime Minister Winston S. Churchill in August 1941, included a commitment to the "right of all people to choose the form of government under which they will live." In a radio address to the nation on February 23, 1942, the president specified that "the Atlantic Charter not only applies to the parts of the world that border on the Atlantic, but to the whole world." His undersecretary of state, Sumner Welles, echoed this theme in a Memorial Day address that same year, declaring that the war should ensure "the liberation of all people." He continued: "The age of imperialism is ended. The right of people to their freedom must be recognized, as the civilized world long since recognized the rights of an individual to his personal freedom."[8]

U.S. spokesmen often pointed to the American commitment to postwar independence for the Philippines as an appropriate model for the European imperial powers to emulate. "The President and I and the entire Government," declared Secretary of State Cordell Hull in November 1942, "earnestly favor freedom for all dependent peoples at the earliest date practicable. Our course in dealing with the Philippines situation in this respect, as in all other important respects, offers, I think, a perfect example of how a nation should treat a colony or a dependency in cooperating with it in all essential respects calculated to assist it in making all necessary preparation for freedom."[9]

Nor were American anticolonial pronouncements restricted merely to pious public statements. Rather, Roosevelt and senior administration spokesmen espoused the same ideas in numerous private conversations both among themselves and with various foreign leaders, especially during the first few years of the war. The president himself often took the lead on this issue, alternately chiding British, French, and Dutch officials on past colonial practices while urging more enlightened postwar policies. His seemingly offhanded suggestion to the British that they return Hong Kong to the Chinese as a gesture of good will typified his approach, as did his repeated efforts to prod the British on the emotional issue of Indian independence.

At various times Roosevelt urged European officials to commit themselves to a timetable for eventual colonial independence. Much to the discomfiture of French, Dutch, and British diplomats, FDR and Secretary of State Hull proposed that a trusteeship system be established in the postwar period through which different developed nations, acting as overseers or trustees, would prepare native elites to assume the responsibilities of self-government.

Trusteeship represented a compromise solution to Roosevelt; he believed it would guarantee future independence while avoiding the pitfalls inherent in a premature transfer of power to inexperienced local elites.

Roosevelt's plans for the colonial world represented a nearly indistinguishable blend of American ideals with American interests. The president found the conditions under which so many subject peoples lived appallingly primitive. After passing through the British colony of Gambia in early 1942, for example, he railed against the poverty and disease he had witnessed everywhere, referring to the dependency as a "hellhole" and calling native living conditions "the most horrible thing I have ever seen in my life."[10] Although he never visited Indochina, the lack of personal contact did not prevent the president from berating the colony's French overlords in equally harsh terms. In fact, FDR considered the French the least enlightened of all the colonizers; he often singled out for particular censure their sorry record in Indochina. Despite "nearly one hundred years" of French colonial rule there, he complained on one occasion, "the people are worse off than they were at the beginning."[11]

Roosevelt's genuine humanitarian impulses coexisted with a more practical strain. The preservation of the colonial system stood as an impediment to the kind of world most conducive to American interests. Roosevelt was convinced that the imperial order, with its restrictive trading practices, economic exploitation, and political repression, simply sowed the seeds for future instability within the colonies and for conflicts among the great powers. "The colonial system means war," FDR exclaimed at one point. "Exploit the resources of an India, a Burma, a Java; take all the wealth out of those countries, but never put anything back into them, things like education, decent standards of living, minimum health requirements—all you're doing is storing up the kind of trouble that leads to war."[12]

The United States sought a more open world, one characterized by free trade, self-determination, basic human freedoms, and respect for democratic principles. Only such a world, FDR and his chief advisers were convinced, would ensure the peace, prosperity, stability, and security that the United States sought. Hull spoke for many of his governmental colleagues when he recalled in his memoirs that as early as World War I he had recognized that "unhampered trade dovetailed with peace; high tariffs, trade barriers, and unfair economic competition with war."[13] The existence of colonial trading blocs represented one of the most glaring affronts to the American vision of an open world. Before World War II the colonial economies of Southeast Asia had been geared almost exclusively to the needs of the mother country, serving as protected sources of raw materials and labor and as privileged markets for the manufactured goods of the metropole. If the colonial system were reestablished in Southeast Asia without fundamental change after the war, Roosevelt and Hull realized that American exporters and importers could once again expect the kind of discriminatory treatment that had proven so frustrating in the past. The administration's proselytizing on behalf of a more liberal approach to dependent areas thus bespoke an unsentimental calculation of national interests as much as it did a revulsion against the immorality of colonialism.

For a range of reinforcing reasons, then, the Roosevelt administration sought to prevent a return to the pre-World War II status quo in the colonial areas of South and Southeast Asia. The president's repeated efforts to push the British toward a commitment to Indian independence, his gentler but equally determined entreaties to Queen Wilhelmina on the future of Dutch rule in the East Indies, his various trusteeship schemes for French Indochina and other areas, and his own commitment to postwar independence for the Philippines all reflected this important policy objective.

Well before his death, however, Roosevelt modified significantly his approach to the colonial question. Late in 1944 he jettisoned trusteeship planning for Indochina, the East Indies, and other dependencies, promising instead not to interfere with the reimposition of colonial rule in Southeast Asia. This policy shift reflected the president's essential pragmatism in the face of a complex amalgam of crosscutting interests. From its inception, his trusteeship formula generated heated rebukes from the colonial powers. British Prime Minister Churchill, Roosevelt's most important ally, made clear on numerous occasions his unbending opposition to U.S. tampering with European colonies. Free French leader General Charles De Gaulle was an equally vehement critic of the trusteeship idea, as were representatives of the Dutch government-in-exile. Alexander Loudon, the Dutch ambassador to the United States, bluntly informed Hull that his countrymen resented the constant "propaganda" barrage in the United States regarding self-determination and racial equality. It was both irresponsible and unfair, he complained, "that the Dutch East Indies are being held up as a horrible example of imperialism and other aggravated violations of all the liberal policies that should govern international relations and peoples in every part of the world."[14]

Roosevelt feared that an aggressive advocacy of trusteeship, in the face of such angry and unified opposition, might create intolerable strains within the wartime alliance and might jeopardize postwar cooperation in Western Europe, the most vital region of all to the United States. "We had frequent conversations with these parent countries," Hull subsequently related, "but we could not press them too far with regard to the Southwest Pacific in view of the fact that we were seeking the closest possible cooperation with them in Europe." He cut right to the heart of the matter, observing that "we could not alienate them in the Orient and expect to work with them in Europe."[15]

Defense needs also militated against persisting in a quixotic anticolonial campaign. Planners in the War and Navy departments insisted that U.S. national security required exclusive control over the Japanese-mandated islands in the Pacific. With the president's concurrence, they intended to make permanent America's military presence throughout the Pacific in order to add depth and flexibility to the nation's air and naval strength. That high-priority goal, military experts argued, could not be compromised by trustee-ship principles that could be applied to strategic U.S.-occupied territory just as easily as they could be applied to European colonies.

Broader political, strategic, and military concerns, in short, necessitated a tactical retreat from earlier anticolonial pronouncements and plans. To for-malize the shift in policy, State Department representatives quietly reassured their British, French, and Dutch counterparts late in 1944 that the United States would not contest their reassertion of sovereignty in Southeast Asia. The Roosevelt administration never abandoned completely its interest in effecting a liberalization of colonial rule, to be sure. Precisely how it would advance such a goal, however, remained exceedingly vague. With FDR's sud-den death in April 1945, Harry S. Truman fell heir not only to the myriad details connected with wartime operations and postwar planning but also to the complex and ambiguous legacy surrounding his predecessor's record on the colonial question.[16]

World War II virtually ensured that the United States would become a major Southeast Asian power. The Roosevelt administration's efforts to help build a new world order out of the ashes of history's most horrendous conflict naturally extended to a region whose resources had factored so prominently in Japan's path to Pearl Harbor. More specifically, the desire of Washington decision-makers to maintain a permanent U.S. military presence in the postwar Pacific, their interest in effecting the orderly devolution of political power from European colonizers to local nationalists, and their commitment to the revival of regional productivity and trade all presupposed a far more active and involved United States. What almost no one could have foreseen, from the perspective of 1945, was the extent and the degree to which the United States would become enmeshed in the affairs of postwar Southeast Asia. And what would have startled even the sagest observer of international affairs at war's end was the extent and the degree to which U.S. leaders would within just a few years come to equate the security and stability of this turbulent area with the preservation of America's own national security.

America's Postwar Ambitions—and Fears

As World War II hurtled toward its fiery close, the leaders of the United States prepared to assume what they, almost to a person, took to be their nation's historic responsibility: the construction of a new, more stable, more prosperous, and more equitable world order. They never doubted that the country which had saved the world from the scourge of German and Japanese barbarity could effect so momentous a transformation. Nor did U.S. leaders see any potential conflict between the global order they sought to impose and the needs and interests of the rest of the world's people. If challenged, they would likely have wondered how anyone could doubt the nobility and selflessness of the United States.

Since the foundation of the republic, Americans had drawn attention to what they considered the uniqueness of their civilization, their history, their character, their motives. Many even found divine sanction for the conceit that America had a global mission to share its superior values, institutions, and culture with others. The United States was "the world's best hope," Thomas Jefferson proclaimed in his 1801 inaugural address.[1] A century later, Woodrow Wilson articulated that missionary imperative with even greater fervor. "We created this nation not just to serve ourselves," he declared, "but to serve mankind." In a similar vein, Harry S. Truman, at the height of the Cold War, professed his belief "that God has created us and brought us to our present position of great power and strength for some great purpose."[2]

To Jefferson, to Wilson, to Truman, as to most American leaders, foreign policy encompassed more than the mere pursuit of national interest. U.S. statesmen convinced themselves that their country's engagement with the world also advanced such universalistic goals as democracy, economic development, individual liberty, and social justice. That U.S. national interests happened to coincide with those exalted goals simply served for them as confirmation of their nation's special purpose. Ever since the era of the founding fathers, most American decision-makers had simply taken for granted that what was best for the United States was best for the world as a whole. "The United States was the locomotive at the head of mankind," as Secretary of State Dean Acheson liked to say, "and the rest of the world was the caboose."[3]

The world order that U.S. planners strove to build from the wreckage of World War II owed much to the assumptions, hopes, dreams—and setbacks—of the past. With the self-confident arrogance of a people who had known few failures, Americans thought that they could, in Acheson's choice words, "grab hold of history and make it conform."[4] They were sure that under benevolent American leadership peace could be restored, potential enemies defanged and co-opted, war-torn economies reconstructed, and future stability and prosperity guaranteed. Many of the specific details essential for the realization of that grandiose vision remained to be worked out, to be sure. Long before the shooting stopped, however, American strategists had effectively sketched the broad outlines of the postwar order they desired. The economic, political, and security dimensions of that order, not surprisingly, were tightly interwoven, each representing in turn a nearly indistinguishable blend of American ideals and American interests.

Essential to U.S. plans was the establishment of a new economic regime based on the principles of free trade, equal investment opportunities, and full

currency convertibility. Those long-standing American precepts were successfully enshrined in the Bretton Woods agreements, negotiated in rural New
Hampshire late in 1944. Determined to rid the world of the economic nationalism and restrictive trading practices that had plagued the depression decade,
U.S. representatives at the Bretton Woods conference gained support for the
creation of several new international financial institutions designed to help
stabilize the global economy. In accordance with U.S. plans, the International
Monetary Fund and the International Bank for Reconstruction and Development (World Bank) came into being; capitalized largely with U.S. funds, those
institutions were to be dominated by the United States. In addition, the Roosevelt administration gained tentative support from Great Britain and other
nations for the establishment of stable exchange rates, a key mechanism for
promoting the expansion of world trade. The administration also began to
move forward with its even more ambitious plans for eliminating restrictive
trade practices. Experience had taught Americans, according to Secretary of
State Hull, that free trade was an essential prerequisite for peace.[5]

Predicated on the notion that expanding trade and productivity
redounded to the benefit of all nations, the new, American-inspired economic regime sought to impart structural stability to the international economic system by eliminating the trade barriers, exchange controls, and discriminatory practices that gave rise to interstate tensions and conflict. That
such a multilateral commercial order well served the material interests of the
United States was a given. The more open and liberal the prevailing trading
system, the more the planet's most prosperous and productive capitalist state
naturally stood to gain. Other nations also saw advantages in this system,
though. Most were eager to see order replace disorder, economic interdependence supplant unrestrained commercial competition. If American financial hegemony was the price that had to be paid for global stability, many
nations were more than willing to accept that cost in the aftermath of a conflict that had claimed more than 55 million lives.[6]

The would-be architects of the new Pax Americana faced even greater
challenges in the political and strategic realms. How could the United States
best use the unparalleled power, influence, and prestige it possessed at the
end of the war to promote a durable peace? That question haunted U.S. planners throughout the war years. Ultimately, it was Roosevelt's vision of a traditional great power peace that prevailed. FDR believed, as had Wilson, that
active American participation in a global political forum would be of cardinal importance. The United Nations organization that he advocated could
promulgate general "rules" for orderly political change, offer all nations an
opportunity to debate and vote on issues affecting both them individually

and the world community as a whole, and develop mechanisms for preventing and, once started, helping to resolve interstate conflicts. The principles that American leaders had traditionally championed—democracy, self-determination, freedom of expression, individual rights—were upheld in the UN charter as universal ideals to which all peoples should aspire. Unlike Wilson, however, Roosevelt had no interest in surrendering even a portion of America's sovereignty to an international body that it might not always be able to control. The Security Council, which gave veto power to the United States and a handful of other major powers, served as the key assurance that America's historic unilateral inclinations would be safeguarded. Maintaining global peace and stability, Roosevelt was convinced, depended ultimately neither on the UN nor on the important principles that that organization embodied but on cooperation among the wartime "Big Three."

For all their fundamental differences, the United States, Britain, and the Soviet Union wanted to ensure the maintenance of a peaceful, stable, and predictable world. The Soviet Union, which the United States had viewed so warily ever since the Bolshevik revolution of 1917, remained the greatest riddle. Would its postwar security needs and its competing ideological commitments clash with the vital interests of the United States? Roosevelt thought not. He was confident that his personal rapport with wartime ally Joseph Stalin could facilitate a smooth transition to the postwar era. For FDR, a kind of cooperative great power condominium among the Americans, Soviets, and British offered the best recipe for international peace and order. At the same time, he was insistent upon maintaining naval and air forces second to none, a worldwide string of U.S.-controlled military bases, extensive air transit rights, a strong military presence in the Pacific, a dominant U.S. role in the occupations of Italy, Germany, Austria, and Japan, and a continued monopoly on the atomic bomb. Roosevelt's plans for the postwar world, in sum, left ample room for the military muscle and power projection of the United States. If push ever did come to shove again, he was determined that the United States would have recourse to more than moral suasion and appeals to reason. One of the lessons he read from the turbulent interwar period was that financial hegemony alone would never be sufficient to maintain international peace and order.[7]

Southeast Asia in American Planning and Strategy

Southeast Asia certainly never loomed as an overriding concern for Roosevelt and his coplanners. Long a preserve of the colonial powers, the region seemed destined to remain indefinitely on the margins of world politics. Southeast Asia boasted important natural resources, to be sure; the Japanese attacks of 1941–42 made that much clear. But with the defeat of Japan imminent, Southeast Asia appeared ready once more to move to the outer reaches of American consciousness. Despite its rich reserves of rubber, tin, petroleum, timber, and rice, the region lacked the other ingredients—to be specific, industrial infrastructure, technological prowess, and skilled workforces—that made Western Europe and Japan areas of such vital importance in the overall balance of world power.

The Roosevelt administration's wartime planners certainly did not ignore Southeast Asia. Rather, as noted earlier, Roosevelt, Hull, Welles, and other top policymakers made a number of stirring public pronouncements throughout the war years in which they called for the liberation of all colonial peoples. They even initiated a series of general plans for the future status of Southeast Asian colonies conquered by the Japanese, including most importantly the trusteeship concept. FDR and most of his chief foreign policy advisers were agreed that the broader U.S. goals of world peace, stability, and prosperity would best be served by the gradual dismantling of the European colonial empires. They did not desire the precipitous removal of Western power and influence from those areas. Instead, they hoped that the Europeans would be savvy enough to seek the same basic goal that the Americans were pursuing in the Philippines—namely, the gradual transfer of political authority to moderate, Western-leaning, local elites. That transfer could occur over a period of decades, FDR envisioned, and would not require the British, French, or Dutch to relinquish entirely their sizable commercial, military, and political footholds.

The orderly devolution of political authority within the colonial territories of Southeast Asia made sense given the broader framework of the world order Roosevelt and his leading strategists hoped to construct. Gradual decolonization would presumably open markets to American businessmen on a more equitable basis, spur regional productivity, remove a potential source of future interstate conflict, defuse revolutionary ferment, and provide a healthy outlet for the legitimate nationalist aspirations of native peoples. To further such important objectives, Roosevelt hatched the trusteeship scheme, and he never wavered in his commitment to the overall goals signified by that initiative. The complex balancing act that his plans for the postwar world required, however, forced the president to choose for the time being between conflicting policy goals. Once FDR had gauged the depth of British, French, and Dutch resistance to his trusteeship proposals, consequently, he beat a hasty tactical retreat. That he opted to accommodate his

European allies in Southeast Asia instead of opposing them further should hardly be surprising in view of the much higher priority that all leading U.S. strategists placed on European issues and concerns.

With Roosevelt's sudden death in April 1945, Harry S. Truman simply ratified and continued what he understood to be his predecessor's Southeast Asian policy. During his early months in office, the new chief executive quickly pledged support for the sovereign authority of the European colonial powers. In the event, some of the nuance, complexity, and conditionality of Roosevelt's approach to the colonial problem was lost. Apparently unaware of the bureaucratic battles that had been raging within the government over the future of the colonial empires, Truman in effect sided openly with his European-minded subordinates who favored the earliest possible restoration of the status quo ante bellum in Southeast Asia. What the untested and inexperienced new president could not possibly have envisioned—and what virtually none of even his administration's most seasoned Asian experts did envision—was how wide the gap would be between U.S. expectations for postwar Southeast Asia and the rapidly changing situation on the ground.[8]

Colonialism Under Siege

World War II brought profound changes to Southeast Asia, changes that caught most American planners unaware and that would wreak havoc with the vague policy goals they had formulated for the region. The surprisingly easy Japanese defeat of American, British, and Dutch forces in the opening weeks of the war decisively shattered both the aura of Western invincibility and the myth of racial superiority upon which it rested. In the Netherlands East Indies, observed the American Office of Strategic Services, "the subsequent retreat and internment of the Dutch and their Allies altered radically the position of the white man in the estimation of the Indonesians."[9] The attitudes of Filipinos, Vietnamese, Burmese, and Malayans toward their former rulers followed a similar pattern. Indeed, so great was the pent-up fury with Western rule that indigenous peoples throughout Southeast Asia initially greeted the invading Japanese as liberators.

The ensuing honeymoon proved remarkably short-lived, of course, the arrogance and brutality of local Japanese commanders insuring that. But for all its excesses, and for all the important local variations in its direction and duration, the Japanese occupation left a powerful imprint. Both wittingly and unwittingly, the Japanese conquerors facilitated an explosive growth in nationalist sentiment across the entire region. In all the territories they occupied, the detested soldiers of the rising sun provided a convenient rallying point for restive nationalists and would-be revolutionaries. In Indochina and Burma, active anti-Japanese guerrilla movements gained control of their respective national independence movements. At war's end, they stood poised to seize power. In the East Indies and the Philippines, many elites chose instead to cooperate with Japanese authorities, calculating that that path offered a more promising route toward future independence. By so doing, they also opened themselves up to subsequent accusations of collaborationism, hurled not only by returning imperialists but just as frequently by political opponents at home. In many cases, including those of Burma and Indonesia, ardent nationalists actually saw accommodation and resistance as complementary strategies, each advancing in a different way the ultimate goal of national independence. Whether choosing accommodation, resistance, or some combination of the two, local elites capitalized masterfully on the forces set in motion by Japanese policies to catapult movements aimed at self-rule toward a prominence and strength that scarcely seemed conceivable just a few years earlier.

Wartime exigencies had impelled Tokyo's military leaders to provide political, administrative, and martial experience to tens of thousands who had previously been denied such opportunities under the strictures of colonialism, further boosting the nationalist cause. Those who enjoyed an elevation in social and economic status under the Japanese occupation gained a strong personal stake in resisting any return to the status quo ante bellum. Tokyo's nominal bestowal of independence on Burma and the Philippines in 1943 and its cynical grant of independence to Indonesia during the war's waning months suggest policies born of political and military desperation. Dictated by the imperatives of war, those policies nonetheless bequeathed a powerful legacy.[10]

The suffering, death, destruction, economic dislocation, and social turmoil that proved the Pacific War's most grisly by-product left no less powerful a legacy, bolstering the appeal of those who would offer an alternative to Japanese—and Western—rule. As many as four million Indonesians may have perished as a direct or indirect result of the conflict. Nearly 300,000 were dispersed throughout the Japanese empire as forced laborers, many of whom never returned. Tens of thousands of women from Indonesia, the Philippines, and elsewhere in Southeast Asia, though a final accounting may never be possible, were forced to service the Japanese military as prostitutes—the infamous "comfort girls" whose plight postwar Japanese governments failed for so long even to acknowledge. Wartime fighting claimed about 120,000 Filipino lives; and in Indochina, over one million died during the great famine of 1945, caused when Japan callously diverted rice stocks from starving peasants to feed its own armed forces.[11]

Areas in the direct line of fire experienced a special brand of horror and devastation. In the spring of 1945, British forces drove the Japanese from Burma after a bloody struggle, only to discover far greater destruction, dislocation, and human misery than they had anticipated. The fighting, lamented Burma's wartime leader Ba Maw, "had reduced an enormous part of the country to ruins."[12] Key harbors, bridges, and military installations had been destroyed, the country's internal communications system badly disrupted. Many urban dwellers had been forced to flee to the countryside, significant portions of which remained isolated from the rest of the nation. In the Philippines, the returning American liberators were shocked by the devastation they saw. Manila, the venerable Spanish colonial capital, lay in ruins, four-fifths of its buildings razed during the savage, house-to-house fighting of February and March 1945 that preceded the American reoccupation. In the words of one resident, the city "presented the appearance of some hellish fair or carnival against a background of ravage and ruin." With much of their livestock slaughtered, their farm tools gone, and their irrigation systems and rice mills destroyed, rural Filipinos stood on the verge of massive starvation.[13]

The sudden surrender of Japan on August 14, 1945, in the wake of the atomic blasts over Hiroshima and Nagasaki, gave Southeast Asia's aspiring nationalists a precious gift: time. When Japan sued for peace, U.S. troops were already occupying the Philippines, and British forces were trying to reestablish order in Burma. Much of the rest of Southeast Asia remained under Japanese control, however, including Thailand, Indochina, Malaya, and most of Indonesia. The Southeast Asia Command (SEAC) of British Admiral Lord Louis Mountbatten faced a monumental task. Instead of the prolonged struggle against Japanese troops for which it had been preparing, SEAC overnight inherited responsibility for occupying and restoring civil authority over 1.5 million square miles of land area, containing a population in excess of 128 million, while simultaneously disarming and repatriating 750,000 Japanese troops. Since Mountbatten's forces were not yet positioned or prepared to begin assuming those responsibilities, who would exercise civil authority in the crucial interim period? The defeated Japanese? The surviving remnants of the old colonial power structures, many of whom had been interned or jailed during the war? Or indigenous nationalists?[14]

In the East Indies and in Indochina, it was the latter contestants for power who stepped into the breach. In Jakarta, only three days after the Japanese capitulation, Sukarno proclaimed an independent Republic of Indonesia. In

Hanoi, just a few weeks later, Ho Chi Minh announced the formation of an independent Democratic Republic of Vietnam. Although the two men provided the starkest of contrasts, the robust, mercurial, sybaritic "Bung" Sukarno bearing little resemblance to the frail, self-sacrificing, ascetic "Uncle" Ho, both were charismatic leaders with impeccable nationalist credentials. Both, moreover, commanded wide and deep support within their respective countries; both were canny politicians, deeply—even fanatically—committed to national independence; and both were willing to solicit support for that cause from virtually any quarter.

In the six weeks that elapsed between Sukarno's proclamation of an independent republic and the arrival of the first contingent of Allied occupying forces at the end of September, Indonesian nationalists moved quickly to solidify their bid for power. During that hectic period, Sukarno and Mohammed Hatta were unanimously named the new republic's president and vice president, respectively, a constitution was drafted and promulgated throughout the far-flung archipelago, a cabinet form of government was established, police forces and an embryonic army formed, and a structure of civil authority put in place. Nearly all the Indonesian civil servants who had worked for the Japanese swore allegiance to the new national regime. Those dizzying changes at the top of the Indonesian political and social pyramid were mirrored at the mass level. A socioeconomic upheaval with far-reaching implications for the future swept through the cities and the countryside in the aftermath of Japan's defeat. Spearheaded by peasants and workers who were driven not just by patriotic fervor but by a desire for land, material advancement, personal freedom, and social status—commodities in short supply under Holland's harsh colonial yoke—the upheaval soon reached revolutionary proportions.[15]

Upon their arrival in late September, British and Indian occupying forces confronted a dynamic Indonesian political landscape that quickly gave a lie to the complacent, uninformed intelligence reports they had been receiving. Those reports, which Mountbatten later characterized angrily as "patently inadequate and erroneous," had led SEAC planners to expect a quiescent populace prepared to welcome, or at least acquiesce in, the restoration of Dutch rule.[16] British Lt. Gen. Sir Philip Christison, the commander of the Allied occupation, found instead a functioning native government, actively supported by the great majority of politically conscious Indonesians and operating at a high degree of efficiency. Under the circumstances, he saw no choice but to adjust pragmatically to existing realities. Consequently, he declared that British and Indian forces would not interfere in local political affairs; they would confine themselves to their primary function of disarming the Japanese and releasing prisoners of war and internees. Christison also said that he welcomed Indonesian nationalist forces to play a role in the maintenance of law and order. Much to the horror of the Dutch, the blunt general offered them some gratuitous political advice as well. "What form of government the Dutch are going to give [the Indonesians]," he remarked at his first press conference, "I don't know. They'll certainly have to give them something."[17]

Developments in nearby Vietnam were no less tumultuous in the immediate aftermath of Japan's surrender. Ho Chi Minh's formal declaration of independence on September 2 came as the fitting climax to a period of intense revolutionary activity. The so-called "August revolution" was the handiwork of Viet Minh fighters and political cadres who, during the waning days of Japanese rule, spread out from their northern base to lead a truly national, and immensely popular, movement. Capitalizing on widespread discontent fueled by a horrendous famine and the callous response of occupation authorities to the untold human suffering that accompanied it, Viet Minh guerrillas took the offensive. They launched a brutal but effective political assassination campaign against both Japanese officials and the equally detested local landholding elite, attacked government offices and military installations with impunity, liberated rice stocks being held for export to Japanese forces overseas, redistributed land to landless and land-poor peasants, and restored to long-silenced villagers a political voice at the local level. Led ably by Ho and a handful of equally determined communist compatriots, the Viet Minh drew support from all groups and classes within Vietnamese society. To those who would march under its banner, the movement offered land, food, justice, and national independence; to those who would not, it threatened violent reprisals.

In the chaotic days that followed Japan's surrender, the Viet Minh assumed the mantle of civil authority, brilliantly filling the existing power vacuum. With virtually no opposition—indeed, with hardly any shots being fired—Ho's insurrectionary movement gained control of all major cities and provincial capitals by the end of August. On August 30, Emperor Bao Dai abdicated, symbolically handing over the imperial seals and swords to the Viet Minh. He possessed no real power, having served as titular sovereign only because first French and then Japanese interests benefited from the sham. Still, the formal abdication to Ho's insurgents of the heir to the century-and-a-half-old Nguyen dynasty conferred even more legitimacy on Vietnam's new, de facto rulers.[18]

In his speech proclaiming Vietnamese independence, Ho quoted liberally—and quite deliberately—from the American declaration of independence. Later that day, a Vietnamese band joined the independence-day festivities in Hanoi with a rendition of the "Star-Spangled Banner." U.S. Army officers listened from the reviewing stand as one after another Vietnamese nationalist echoed Ho with glowing paeans to America's anticolonial heritage. The previous evening Ho had invited two OSS officers to dinner. After thanking them for the valuable material assistance rendered by the United States to his guerrilla movement during the war, he appealed for "fraternal collaboration" in the future.

Those calculated gestures bespoke the Vietnamese leader's hopes as well as his realism. During the struggle against Japan, U.S. military and intelligence officials had struck up a mutually beneficial relationship with Viet Minh fighters in the rugged jungles of northern Tonkin. Coupled with America's anticolonial traditions and wartime proclamations, of which he was keenly aware, Ho thought that a promising foundation for Vietnamese-American friendship was being laid. He would do what he could to build upon it. Fully aware that France would not passively acquiesce to an independent Vietnam, Ho reasoned that the United States could prove an invaluable ally in the struggle that lay ahead.[19]

He was right on one count: France would not relinquish its empire without a fight. An Allied compromise at the Potsdam Conference of July 1945 had provided for Chinese troops to occupy the northern part of Vietnam while British troops assumed that responsibility in the country's southern half. As in the East Indies, the occupying forces found their prime goal of disarming and repatriating Japanese troops enormously complicated due to the unanticipated existence of a native government demanding recognition and the uncompromising determination of colonial authorities to reassert imperial control. In contrast to the East Indies, where they played a more neutral role, British occupying forces in southern Indochina facilitated the reestablishment of French power. Meanwhile, in the north, the 150,000-man Chinese army initially provided desperately needed arms and supplies to the Viet Minh. By the end of 1945, however, the Chiang Kai-shek regime agreed to recognize French sovereignty throughout Indochina in return for future economic concessions. Neither the British nor the Chinese extended any form of recognition to the Democratic Republic of Vietnam.

Ever the pragmatist, Ho sought to buy time for his beleaguered, isolated republic. Fearing that as French troop strength swelled his own ill-equipped army could be easily overwhelmed, the Vietnamese leader welcomed negotiation and compromise. On March 6, 1946, he signed a preliminary political accord and truce with Jean Sainteny, the chief French official in northern

Vietnam. The agreement suffered from excessive vagueness, however. It left unresolved the basic issue of sovereignty, thus postponing rather than averting the inevitable clash of wills—and arms.[20]

The peoples of Indonesia and Indochina spearheaded the political, economic, and social transformations that were taking place throughout Southeast Asia in the shadow of World War II. Nationalist groups in both those areas proved stronger, bolder, better prepared, and better led than their counterparts elsewhere in the region. They benefited as well from more favorable political, military, and psychological circumstances. France and the Netherlands had, after all, been defeated, occupied, and humiliated during the war. Heavily dependent on Allied support, matériel, and armed forces, neither was capable alone of reasserting control over their rebellious colonies following V-J Day. The British and the Americans, on the other hand, were the Pacific War's victors. They were already on the ground in Burma and the Philippines when Japan sued for peace, having helped liberate their former subjects from Tokyo's heavy-handed suzerainty. Unlike their colleagues in Paris and The Hague, moreover, who saw native self-government as a distant prospect, if that, authorities in Washington and London had already promised to grant independence to their Philippine and Burmese dependencies.

It is especially striking, in view of those fundamental differences, that the region's ferment was not confined to Indonesia and Indochina. In Burma, the popular Anti-Fascist People's Freedom League (AFPFL) of Aung San demanded immediate independence following the war, showing little patience with Britain's cautious approach. As London continued to procrastinate throughout 1945 and 1946 in its response to the AFPFL's demands, discontent and anti-Western sentiment spread, capped by the debilitating general strike of September 1946. In Malaya, historic animosity between the dominant Malay and Chinese ethnic groups militated against the emergence of a unified nationalist movement in that colony. Still, strong opposition to continued British rule surfaced. The Malayan Communist Party took the lead, agitating openly for immediate independence, inspiring a wave of angry protests and violent strikes. Emboldened by its role in the anti-Japanese resistance and its growing popularity, the party proved itself a potent political and social force. In the Philippines, another anti-Japanese resistance force, the Hukbalahaps, or Huks, also challenged the prewar status quo, refusing to relinquish their arms until fundamental reforms of the grossly inequitable land tenancy system had been effected. In short, across the region powerful revolutionary nationalist currents surged, posing an unprecedented challenge to the old colonial order.[21]

America's Dilemma

U.S. policymakers were almost completely unprepared for the depth and intensity of the nationalist rebellions that erupted in Southeast Asia at war's end. Some of the more astute Asian experts in the State Department had warned that the conflict would lead to intensified nationalist sentiment throughout the Pacific. No one, however, either inside or outside the government, predicted the rapid establishment of popular, broad-based native governments in Vietnam and Indonesia and the concomitant Burmese challenge to British power. Most top U.S. policymakers, preoccupied with more pressing matters, expected the reassertion of European authority to be relatively smooth and orderly. Poor intelligence on actual conditions in the region reinforced that complacency. At least one official report had confidently speculated, for example, that the Indonesians would greet their returning Dutch rulers as liberators.[22]

It quickly became apparent during the fall of 1945 that the reimposition of colonial rule would be neither smooth nor orderly. The Truman administration, as a consequence, found itself impaled on the horns of a cruel dilemma. America's history, traditions, and interests seemed to point toward a policy of enthusiastic support for colonial self-determination. The Roosevelt administration's anticolonial proclamations throughout the war years had certainly nurtured the hope among leaders such as Sukarno, Ho Chi Minh, and Aung San that they could look to Washington for moral, political, and material succor. Although FDR had halted, even begun to reverse, America's aggressive anticolonial advocacy well before his death, he left his successor a legacy no less powerful for all the ambiguity surrounding it. Truman instinctively appreciated and supported America's historic identification with the principles of self-determination. He had no desire to repudiate his nation's traditionally liberal stance on so fundamental an issue. Nor did the president and his top advisers want to risk taking steps that might alienate expectant nationalists throughout the colonial world. They feared that, in purely practical terms, an American policy designed to bolster discredited European imperialists could radicalize nationalist movements, turn them against the United States, even push them into the arms of the Soviet Union.

The Truman administration worried, at the same time, that it might open an irreparable breach with its European allies if it failed to give them the diplomatic and material backing they sought in Southeast Asia. Washington could hardly afford to run that risk. It needed to maintain warm relations with France, the Netherlands, and Great Britain; senior administration planners considered the support of those nations for U.S. policy initiatives in Europe, and around the globe, to be nothing short of indispensable.[23]

The State Department, consequently, groped for a middle ground in its response to the explosive colonial question. The admittedly imperfect solution that it adopted was an official policy of nonintervention and neutrality toward the colonial upheavals wracking Southeast Asia. That equivocal stance conditioned all U.S. statements about the region until about 1947. Thus while conceding the legal right of France, the Netherlands, and Great Britain as "territorial sovereigns" to restore their prewar rule over territories seized as an act of war, the United States periodically indicated that it would favor any progressive steps toward eventual self-government in Southeast Asia. That position remained consistent with overall U.S. policy goals in Asia which, according to the administration's first formal paper on the subject, would best be served by "a Far East progressively developing into a group of self-governing states—independent or with Dominion status—which would cooperate with each other and with the Western powers on a basis of mutual self-respect and friendship."[24]

In reality, however, U.S. "neutrality" was never truly impartial. Stanley K. Hornbeck, the Asian expert who served as U.S. ambassador to the Netherlands during the early postwar years, later recalled correctly that the United States "in effect attempted to support neither side and yet favored one and hoped not unduly to offend the other."[25] When Sukarno asked Truman to serve as a mediator between the Dutch and the Indonesians, the president summarily dismissed the offer, explaining that such a request could come only from the "territorial sovereign." Ho Chi Minh also appealed to Truman, imploring the American leader in a series of personal letters to extend American recognition to his fledgling regime. "The carrying out of the Atlantic Charter and San Francisco Charter implies the eradication of imperialism and all forms of colonial oppression," the veteran nationalist pleaded in one message. Truman never bothered to respond to any of Ho's appeals. Even more revealing of U.S. sympathies, Truman ordered that the "Made in the U.S.A." labels be removed from Lend-Lease equipment that, Indonesians and Vietnamese complained, were being used by European troops to suppress them; but the president did not interrupt the transfer of that equipment to Dutch and French authorities bent on restoring the prewar order.[26]

That manifest tilt toward the colonial powers stands as the logical outgrowth of a foreign policy centered on European concerns and interests. Neither the president nor any of his top advisers ever seriously contemplated direct support for or diplomatic recognition of either the Republic of Indonesia or the Democratic Republic of Vietnam. For an inexperienced, insecure chief executive to have pursued so radical a departure from previous commitments would have been astonishingly rash—especially since any positive gestures toward colonial independence movements would surely have incurred the wrath of valuable European allies. The steady deterioration of U.S.-Soviet relations during the early postwar period underscored the critical importance of cultivating reliable partners in Western Europe. In comparison, Southeast Asia seemed to Truman and his senior aides an annoying, and potentially divisive, sideshow.

Besides, U.S. policymakers remained hopeful that the problems of Southeast Asia could be ameliorated. Enlightened self-interest, they believed, would eventually compel British, French, and Dutch authorities to grant meaningful concessions to native nationalists, leading eventually to some form of local self-rule. Such an approach would likely defuse current tensions, bolster moderate forces within the various national independence movements, strengthen the region's pro-Western orientation, and spur regional economic recovery. Most knowledgeable American analysts were convinced, in sum, that a historic compromise with the irresistible force of nationalism would serve the interests of colonizers and colonized alike. If the British, French, and Dutch acted with forbearance and sensitivity, bowing to the inevitable rather than seeking to resist it, they could serve as proud midwives at the birth of responsible new nation-states—without jeopardizing the sizable economic and strategic interests that they sought to retain in those states. According to this rosy scenario, friendly American pressure would nudge the imperial powers toward devolution while American behavior in the Philippines would establish the appropriate model for them to follow.[27]

True to its earlier pledges and numerous wartime promises, on July 4, 1946, the United States conferred independence on its former Asian colony. During a solemn, rain-drenched ceremony at Manila, the United States became the first imperial power in history to voluntarily relinquish political power to former subjects. Its representatives made the most of the occasion's weighty symbolism. The birth of an independent Philippine republic, pontificated Gen. Douglas MacArthur, foretold "the end of mastery over peoples by force alone—the end of empire as the political chain that binds the unwilling weak to the unyielding strong." He exclaimed to a friend after the formal proceedings ended: "America buried imperialism here today."[28]

Behind those smug, self-congratulatory words lay a more complex reality. True, the United States had kept its promise. It had both encouraged and facilitated the creation of an independent Philippine republic. Some degree of pride in so substantial an achievement was certainly warranted. Yet, at the same time, the new republic that the Truman administration praised so extravagantly, and that it served up as the model for other imperial states to emulate, fell well short of American democratic traditions and ideals. Power in the postcolonial Philippines continued to be monopolized, as it had been throughout the half century of American rule, by a tiny elite that controlled most of the islands' economic resources and wielded a commensurate degree of influence over both political processes and governmental authority. The smoldering rebellion in the countryside, emblemized most visibly by the Huks' peasant armies, bore eloquent testimony to the continuing maldistribution of wealth and power throughout Philippine society.

Nor did the United States actually effect the wholesale withdrawal from the Philippines that its boastful rhetoric implied. With independence came the restrictive Bell Trade Act, which bound Filipino producers to the American market for the indefinite future. The product of a vicious bureaucratic and congressional battle between liberal free traders and ultimately victorious protectionists, the act fostered so dependent a relationship between the Philippines and the United States that the new nation's economic freedom was severely curtailed from the very moment of birth. Equally ominous to the new nation's independence, American defense planners were determined to retain base sites in the Philippines—presumably on a permanent basis—in order to enhance America's defense posture in the postwar Pacific.[29]

The enormous economic, strategic, and political influence that it maintained in the Philippines after independence clearly suggests that the United States neither expected nor desired a precipitous removal of European influence from Southeast Asia. Rather, U.S. policymakers sought the gradual transfer of political authority to responsible, moderate, West-leaning native elites. In the view of U.S. planners, such elites would best ensure long-term political stability while protecting Western strategic and material interests and safeguarding the region from communist penetration.

British policy in Burma came closest to the American ideal. Much to the delight of U.S. officials, the Labour government of Clement Attlee announced in December 1946 its intention to grant Burma independence, two months before making a similar pledge to Indian nationalists. Fearing that a failure to accommodate the moderate nationalism represented by the AFPFL might increase the appeal of Burmese communists, the United States had exerted friendly pressure on the British to pursue precisely such a course. The Truman administration, accordingly, praised the statesmanlike stance that led to the formal transfer of power on January 4, 1948. The tragic assassination six months earlier of Aung San, Burma's ablest and most popular figure, and six of his cabinet members, clouded the new regime's prospects, however. U Nu, Burma's new president, lacked his predecessor's political skills and popular appeal. State Department experts worried that pervasive economic problems and mounting ethnic unrest, joined in March 1948 by a communist revolt against the Rangoon government, would lead—at best—to chronic instability. They could at least draw a modicum of comfort from the fact that Britain had demonstrated, as the United States had earlier in the Philippines, that decolonization could proceed in a peaceful and orderly manner.[30]

They could draw no such comfort from developments in either Indochina or Indonesia. Following a series of abortive negotiations between French and Vietnamese representatives in Paris during the summer of 1946, the imperative of diplomacy yielded inevitably to preparations for war. The fundamental question of political sovereignty simply could not be compromised, as both sides ultimately recognized. In November of that year hostilities erupted with shattering suddenness. Following a brutal French naval bombardment of Haiphong that claimed more than six thousand Vietnamese lives, Ho Chi Minh and his supporters fled Hanoi, the French moved quickly to establish their administrative control in the north, and the Viet Minh mobilized for another guerrilla struggle. Conflict soon engulfed much of Vietnam.[31]

In Indonesia, Dutch authorities and Indonesian nationalists also entered into a series of fitful negotiations. At first, those efforts seemed sufficient to avert open warfare. The Linggadjati agreement of November 1946 delighted American observers since it appeared to smooth the way for eventual Indonesian self-rule while maintaining intact Dutch political, military, and economic influence in the islands. The agreement collapsed soon after both parties ratified it in March 1947, however. Unwilling to acquiesce to nationalist demands for true independence, the Dutch, like the French, inexorably gravitated toward a military solution. Ignoring U.S. entreaties, on July 20, 1947, they suddenly launched a full-scale offensive against the Republic of Indonesia, quickly capturing substantial portions of the republic's territory and presenting the United States—and the world—with a fait accompli.[32]

The United States viewed Southeast Asia's colonial conflicts with alarm. To be sure, neither the French-Vietnamese nor the Dutch-Indonesian struggle for power preoccupied Truman and his senior advisers during the early Cold War years. With tension mounting between Washington and the Kremlin over a host of divisive issues, top U.S. policymakers could hardly be expected to devote much attention to hostilities in far-off Southeast Asia. But the unrest in Indochina and Indonesia was inseparably linked to other, more central, concerns. War in Southeast Asia undermined Western Europe's political stabilization and its economic recovery, two of America's commanding postwar priorities. A report prepared for the president in 1947 by the newly created Central Intelligence Agency (CIA) emphasized this link.

"Of important concern in relation to Western European recovery," it noted, "is the existing instability in colonial (or former colonial) areas upon the resources of which several European powers (the United Kingdom, France, and the Netherlands) have hitherto been customed to depend." Cutting to the heart of the problem, the report stressed that "the continuance of unsettled conditions hinders economic recovery and causes a diversion of European strength into efforts to maintain or reimpose control by force."[33]

Toward Indonesian Independence

Given those interlocking concerns, it should not be surprising that, in the wake of the Dutch military action, the United States abandoned its hands-off policy and offered its services as a mediator to the two parties. After failing to prevent the Dutch "police action" with its last-minute remonstrations, the Truman administration reasoned that U.S. mediation might at least limit the damage of that ill-conceived assault and perhaps bring both sides back to the negotiating table. Still, the United States proffered its good offices with some reluctance, acting only after the governments of India and Australia had called formally for action by the United Nations Security Council. Fearing that international debate on the Dutch offensive would prove contentious, and might compromise as well its cherished neutrality stance, the United States sought to preempt UN intervention with its unilateral mediation offer. But Indonesian leaders, wary of Washington's decidedly pro-Dutch orientation, preferred UN consideration, in effect rejecting the U.S. overture. Its initiative rebuffed, the Truman administration quickly shifted gears; if international involvement was unavoidable, then it would try both to limit and control the nature of that involvement. The subsequent action of the Security Council in forming a Good Offices Committee whose counsel would be strictly noncompulsory, with the United States in the strategic middle position on the three-nation grouping, well accommodated that new strategy.[34]

From the formation of the Good Offices Committee in October 1947 to the establishment of a sovereign nationalist government on December 27, 1949, the United States played a major, and ultimately decisive, role in the resolution of the Dutch-Indonesian conflict. The U.S.-sponsored Renville settlement of January 1948, signed on board a U.S. naval vessel after perceptible U.S. pressure was brought to bear on both parties, established a framework for a settlement. Much to the dismay of U.S. diplomats, the unilateral Dutch abrogation of that internationally sanctioned agreement in late 1948 culminated in their preemptive military offensive in December of that year.

In response, the United States threatened to withhold its substantial economic and military assistance to the Netherlands unless the Dutch committed themselves clearly and irrevocably to Indonesian independence. Recognizing the necessity of U.S. support, the Dutch relented. In April 1949 they agreed to transfer sovereignty within months to an independent nationalist government. Before the close of the year they proved true to their word, although persistent U.S. pressure during the final negotiating stages was necessary to remove some lingering obstacles. That U.S. policy smoothed the path toward Indonesian independence is indisputable. Probably more than any other factor, the application of direct U.S. economic pressure early in 1949 compelled the Dutch to relinquish their prized colony.[35]

It must be emphasized, however, that U.S. support for the Indonesian Republic came only very slowly and with the greatest reluctance. Before the second Dutch military offensive, the actions of the Truman administration consistently bolstered the position of the Netherlands. The statements of U.S. spokesmen at the UN as well as the actions of U.S. representatives on the Good Offices Committee reflected that bias. Marshall Plan aid to the Netherlands, which began to flow in the spring of 1948, hopelessly compromised any remaining pretense to neutrality. "The practical effect of ECA [Economic Cooperation Administration] aid on the political conflict," noted a State Department intelligence report in April 1948, "is to strengthen the economic, political, and military position of the Netherlands in Indonesia. . . . Reactions to ECA grants by the Dutch and by the Indonesians show that this effect is clearly understood by both sides."[36]

The reason for this marked U.S. tilt toward the Netherlands lies in the heavy European orientation of Truman's foreign policy during this period. No initiatives during the early Cold War years were more important to the administration's overall foreign policy objectives than the Marshall Plan and the North Atlantic Treaty Organization (NATO). Those programs, designed to rehabilitate and strengthen Western Europe in the face of a perceived global Soviet threat, were indispensable to the administration's developing strategy of containment. As Dutch support was important, if not crucial, to the success of both programs, the Truman administration carefully avoided any rupture with its ally over the sensitive issue of colonial relations. The United States was not uncritical of Dutch policy, of course; it repeatedly urged the negotiation of an equitable settlement with the republic, pressured the Dutch to sign the Renville agreement, and warned against resorting to force before both police actions. Still, the administration operated within certain clearly defined parameters. As the State Department instructed its representatives in Indonesia before the signing of the Renville agreement: the

"Netherlands is [a] strong proponent [of] US policy in Europe. Dep[artmen]t believes that [the] stability [of the] present Dutch government would be seriously undermined if Netherlands fails to retain very considerable stake in NEI and the political consequences of failure [of] present Dutch Gov[ernmen]t would in all likelihood be prejudicial to US position in Western Europe."[37]

The sharp reversal in U.S. policy following the second Dutch police action occurred when it became clear to the administration that the new offensive jeopardized those European priorities. Appalled by the unilateral Dutch violation of an agreement backed by the United States, a vocal minority in Congress threatened to cut off funds to the European Recovery Program and block passage of the Atlantic pact in retaliation. The very cornerstone of the administration's foreign policy thus appeared likely to unravel as a result of what many U.S. policymakers considered a foolishly anachronistic resort to military muscle. Consequently, Secretary of State Dean Acheson bluntly informed Dutch Foreign Minister Dirk Stikker in a climactic meeting that an immediate change of policy would be essential for a continuance of U.S. economic support. "Money talked," as one U.S. diplomat later recalled wryly.[38]

Asian considerations joined with those European ones to hasten the abrupt change in U.S. policy. Most important in this regard was the abject failure of the Dutch to accomplish their military objectives. Months after the offensive began, guerrilla warfare in Java and Sumatra was intensifying, with Dutch forces actually on the retreat in some areas. A report by the National Security Council (NSC) predicted that the Dutch would prove unable to pacify the archipelago and in the process would likely strengthen the appeal of radical elements within the nationalist movement. Given the demonstrably moderate character of the Indonesian Republic, which had suppressed an internal communist revolt at Madiun in September 1948, the NSC paper recommended that the administration support independence as "the only channel lying between polarization and Stalinization." Recognizing that support for native self-rule would be a "difficult course," the NSC nonetheless judged it necessary in order to develop "an effective counterforce to communism in the Far East leading eventually to the emergence of SEA [Southeast Asia] as an integral part of the free world."[39]

The Indochina Quagmire

Ironically, a similar blend of European and Asian concerns, shaped, as in Indonesia, by the administration's global strategy for containing the Soviet Union, prompted a sharply differentiated response to the Vietnamese struggle for independence. Until mid-1947, U.S. officials tended to view the two colonial conflicts in broadly comparable terms. With the advent of the first Dutch police action, however, U.S. policy toward the two struggles began to diverge markedly. The Truman administration inserted itself actively into the Indonesian imbroglio at that juncture while clinging to its hands-off posture in Indochina. Cautious optimism toward the prospects for a settlement in the Indies helps explain the adoption of an active U.S. policy toward that dispute; senior officials were far less sanguine about the possibility of a breakthrough in the French–Viet Minh war. UN consideration of the Indonesian question added a significant new coloration to that conflict as well. With the issue suddenly thrust before the world community, continuing American noninvolvement became increasingly untenable. By exercising its veto in the Security Council, France could of course easily circumvent any proposed international mediation of its colonial difficulties.[40]

At the same time, Washington displayed no desire to intervene directly in yet another nettlesome regional conflict and even less interest in exerting unwanted pressure on an important ally. "We have only [the] very friendliest feelings toward France," noted Secretary of State George C. Marshall in a February 1947 cable to the U.S. Embassy in Paris, "and we are anxious in every way we can to support France in her fight to regain her economic, political and military strength and to restore herself as in fact one of [the] major powers of [the] world."[41] The enunciation in mid-1947 of the containment strategy and the Marshall Plan just underscored the indispensability of France to the broader foreign policy aims of the Truman administration. Both initiatives were conceived as part of the administration's overall strategy for containing Soviet influence and power by fostering the economic recovery and political stability of Western Europe. In the intensifying Cold War struggle between the United States and the Soviet Union, no area loomed more vital than Western Europe and no country loomed more crucial than France.

In view of its transcendent importance to the United States, France's persistence in a colonial conflict that most U.S. experts believed would leave it drained and weakened posed a fundamental dilemma to the Truman administration, one that it never adequately resolved. Precisely how could the United States help France recognize that its own self-interest required a nonmilitary solution in Indochina? And what specific course of action should the United States urge France to pursue? The dilemma was posed far more easily than it could be resolved. "Frankly we have no solution of [the] problem to suggest," Marshall conceded. "It is basically [a] matter for [the] two parties to work out [for] themselves."[42]

The communist character of the Vietnamese independence movement and the absence of viable noncommunist alternatives further clouded an already murky picture. U.S. officials were keenly aware that the movement's outstanding figure had a long record as a loyal communist. Not only had Ho Chi Minh received political training in Moscow, but he served for decades as a dedicated agent of the Communist International (Comintern) outside Indochina. Most U.S. diplomatic and defense officials worried that if Ho prevailed over the French it would lead to "an independent Vietnam State which would be run by orders from Moscow."[43] A handful of junior State Department officials dissented from that analysis, advancing the argument that Ho's ardent nationalism superseded his fraternal links to the Kremlin's rulers; they speculated that he might even emerge as an independent communist leader, much as Josef Broz Tito had in Yugoslavia. However prescient such unorthodox views might seem in retrospect, they never permeated the upper reaches of the Truman administration. Regardless of Ho's undeniably strong credentials as a Vietnamese patriot, most senior policymakers calculated that the establishment of a Viet Minh-dominated regime would redound to the benefit of the Soviet Union. Moreover, other nations would almost certainly view the emergence of such a regime as a defeat for the West.[44]

Yet, as the State Department acknowledged in September 1948, "we are all too well aware of the unpleasant fact that Communist Ho Chi Minh is the strongest and perhaps the ablest figure in Indochina and that any suggested solution which excludes him is an expedient of uncertain outcome."[45] Much to Washington's consternation, the French search for an alternative figure with whom to negotiate produced only the weak and vacillating former emperor Bao Dai. Charles Reed, the U.S. consul in Saigon, reminded Washington that "the reputed playboy of Hong Kong" commanded little support. Bao Dai counted among his followers only "those whose pockets will be benefited if he should return."[46] Notwithstanding American reservations and objections, the French promoted the pliant Bao Dai as their answer to Ho Chi Minh. Most U.S. analysts viewed France's "Bao Dai solution" as a transparent effort to retain colonial control; they saw it as confirmation of the bankruptcy of French policy. The restoration of the former emperor as titular head of an "impotent puppet Gov[ernmen]t," worried the State Department as early as May 1947, may prompt charges that the democracies are forced to "resort [to] monarchy as [a] weapon against Communism."[47]

In September 1948 the State Department offered an internal assessment of U.S. policy in the Indochina dispute that was remarkable both for its candor and for its self-critical tone. "The objectives of U.S. policy towards

Indochina have not been realized," it admitted flatly. "Three years after the termination of war a friendly ally, France, is fighting a desperate and apparently losing struggle in Indochina. The economic drain of this warfare on French recovery, while difficult to estimate, is unquestionably large. The Communist control in the nationalist movement has been increased during this period. US influence in Indochina and Asia has suffered as a result." American objectives could only be attained if France satisfied "the nationalist aspirations of the peoples of Indochina." Yet a series of fundamental impediments bedeviled all U.S. efforts to nudge the French in that direction: the communist coloration of the nationalist movement; the seeming dearth of popular noncommunist alternatives; the reluctance of the Truman administration to offer unsolicited advice to an ally on such an emotional issue; Washington's "immediate interest in maintaining in power a friendly French government, to assist in the furtherance of our aims in Europe"; and, perhaps most basic of all, the administration's "inability to suggest any practicable solution of the Indochina problem."[48]

Redefining American Policy

Over the next year and a half, the Truman administration engaged in a wide-ranging reexamination of American policy toward Southeast Asia. A series of unsettling global and regional developments deepened the administration's appreciation for Southeast Asia's strategic and economic salience, lending urgency to the internal debate. As a result of its reassessment, the administration made a series of new commitments throughout the region. Most significantly, it abandoned its quasi-neutral approach to the Indochina dispute in favor of a policy of open support for the French. On February 7, 1950, Secretary of State Acheson formally announced U.S. recognition of the Bao Dai regime, the nominally independent entity established by France the previous year, and its sister regimes in Cambodia and Laos. Emphasizing U.S. concern that neither security, democracy, nor independence could exist "in any area dominated by Soviet imperialism," he promised economic aid and military equipment for France and the Associated States of Vietnam, Cambodia, and Laos.[49] At about the same time, Washington increased its support for British forces in Malaya that, since early 1948, had been engaged in a full-scale effort to suppress another communist insurrection. It also extended, or promised to extend, economic and technical aid to the governments of Burma, Thailand, Indonesia, and the Philippines.

Those commitments sprang from a common root: the growing U.S. fixation with the communist threat to Southeast Asia. Although specific problems differed widely from country to country, American analysts detected alarming amounts of economic disorder, political unrest, and social turmoil in each one of the region's states. If allowed to fester, those internal difficulties could lead to chronic instability from which communists—local, Russian, and Chinese—would eventually benefit. The proximity of Burma and Thailand to the recently triumphant Chinese Communist regime added an acute external dimension to the dangers faced by those struggling nations. Administration planners believed that a more active U.S. role in Southeast Asia could help reverse those disturbing trends. American material and moral support could invigorate the hard-pressed regimes in Burma, Thailand, and the Philippines, bolster the newly independent government in Indonesia, and at the same time contribute to the suppression of the region's two major communist insurgencies in Indochina and Malaya.[50]

The Truman administration's deepening commitments in Southeast Asia cannot be understood without reference to the wider forces shaping U.S. foreign policy at this time. Those forces impelled both a searching reevaluation of the world situation and a fundamental redefinition of the goals and tactics of U.S. diplomacy. Between mid-1949 and early 1950, American policymakers faced what may have been the gravest global crisis of the entire postwar era. In the summer of 1949 the Soviet Union exploded its first atomic device, putting an end to America's brief atomic monopoly and posing a host of unprecedented challenges to U.S. national security. American leaders feared that possession of the bomb might incline the Kremlin to take greater risks in an effort to extend its global reach and power. The collapse of the U.S.-backed Kuomintang regime in China and the establishment of a communist government in its stead provoked additional fears in U.S. policy circles. Events in China begot as well a round of nasty finger-pointing at home; a swelling chorus of Republican critics blamed Truman personally for China's fate. Events outside the communist bloc appeared even more ominous to America's Cold Warriors. By the end of the year it was increasingly evident that the economic recoveries of Western Europe and Japan had stalled badly. U.S. decision-makers feared that continued economic stagnation in those lands would generate social unrest and political instability, conditions that might prove a fertile breeding ground for communism.[51]

Taken together, those developments portended a potentially catastrophic threat to U.S. national security. As the communist world gained strength and self-confidence, America and its allies seemed poised to lose theirs. To U.S. policymakers the stakes in this global struggle for power were extraordinarily high, involving nothing less than the physical safety and economic health of the United States. "The loss of Western Europe or of important parts of Asia or the Middle East," warned Acheson, "would be a transfer of potential from West to East, which, depending on the area, might have the gravest consequences in the long run."[52] By early 1950, senior U.S. diplomatic and defense officials concentrated much of their energy on defusing this hydra-headed crisis by resuscitating the economies of Western Europe and Japan and regaining for the West political and psychological momentum in the Cold War.

Truman administration strategists recognized that a multiplicity of links bound Southeast Asian developments to this daunting string of global crises. In Asia the administration's overriding objective was to orient a politically stable and economically prosperous Japan to the West. "Were Japan added to the Communist bloc," Acheson warned, "the Soviets would acquire skilled manpower and industrial potential capable of significantly altering the balance of world power."[53] The secretary of state and other leading officials were convinced that Japan needed the markets and raw materials of Southeast Asia in order to spark its industrial recovery. The revitalization of Asia's powerhouse economy would create the conditions necessary for stability and prosperity within both Japan and Southeast Asia. American geopolitical and economic interests in this regard were woven into a seamless web. Truman administration planners envisioned a revitalized Japan emerging once again as the dynamic hub of commercial activity throughout Asia, in the process giving a much-needed boost to the regional and global economic systems, thwarting communism's military threat and ideological appeal, and insuring Tokyo's loyalty to the West. According to the logic subscribed to by nearly all top American strategists, Japan's economic health demanded that peace and stability prevail throughout Southeast Asia. The Viet Minh insurgency in Indochina, which posed the most serious threat to regional peace and stability, thus had to be vanquished with the greatest possible dispatch, as did the communist rebellion in Malaya.[54]

For a somewhat different set of reasons, American strategic and economic interests in Europe pointed in the same direction. By the end of 1949 the optimism that the Marshall Plan's inception generated on both sides of the Atlantic had long since dissipated. The unprecedented commitment of U.S. resources to the economic rehabilitation of Western Europe had yet to engineer the dramatic transformation that the Truman administration so desperately sought. Instead, America's most important allies found themselves facing a frightening panoply of economic and political difficulties. The increasingly costly war in Indochina stretched France's resources to the breaking point, severely hampering its contribution to the European Recovery Program. Although West Germany's economic performance remained a bright spot in an otherwise dismal picture, U.S. officials continued to fret about the fragility of Bonn's commitment to the West. Certain that the ultimate success of the Marshall Plan required the reintegration of Germany into Europe, U.S. planners agonized about how to ease France's understandable fears about a resurgent Germany.[55]

The enormous dollar gap between the United States and its European trading partners posed an even more immediate threat to American interests. It continued to grow, reaching over $3.5 billion by the middle of 1949 and posing a particularly painful dilemma for Great Britain.[56] "Unless firm action is taken," British Foreign Secretary Ernest Bevin implored Acheson in July 1949, "I fear much of our work on Western Union and the Atlantic pact will be undermined and our progress in the Cold War will be halted."[57] Policymakers in Washington shared Bevin's fears. William Clayton, the assistant secretary of state for economic affairs, spoke for many when he conjured up the image of "the patient little man in the Kremlin [who] sits rubbing his hands and waiting for the free world to collapse in a sea of economic chaos."[58]

By early 1950, the Truman administration's senior planners were convinced that Western Europe's troubles, like Japan's, could be aided by the stabilization and pacification of Southeast Asia. France, Great Britain, and Holland had avoided a dollar gap problem during the prewar years through the establishment of triangular trading patterns in which their colonial dependencies in Southeast Asia earned dollars through the sale of raw materials to the United States. The health of the British sterling bloc area had grown unusually dependent on American purchases of rubber and tin in Malaya. The disruption of traditional trading patterns as a result of raging colonial conflicts in Malaya, Indochina, and (until mid-1949) Indonesia thus compounded the already desperate economic conditions plaguing Western Europe. The Truman administration's initial commitments to Southeast Asia, then, must also be placed within this context. American officials believed that financial and material assistance to the French in Indochina and British in Malaya would abet military pacification, economic recovery, and political stabilization in Southeast Asia while simultaneously narrowing the dollar gap and permitting a more active French contribution to European recovery. U.S. aid to Southeast Asia's independent states would advance those broader goals as well, facilitating the restoration of prewar levels of commercial activity in important primary producing areas.[59]

Political pressures reinforced the Truman administration's inclination to link Southeast Asian developments to larger issues. The ferocity of the partisan assaults on Truman in the wake of Chiang Kai-shek's collapse increased the political pressure on the president to show greater resolution vis-à-vis the communist challenge in Asia. Aid to the French in Indochina enabled the beleaguered Truman to answer his critics' charges by demonstrating a determination to hold the line against further communist advances *somewhere*. It is of no small significance that the initial U.S. dollar commitment to the French in Indochina was drawn from funds earmarked by the president's congressional critics for the containment of communism within "the general area of China."[60]

More diffuse psychological considerations also shaped the U.S. commitment to Southeast Asia. Administration analysts were convinced that in many corners of the world the belief that historical momentum lay with the communist powers and not with the West had taken hold. U.S. strategists feared that such a perception, whether rooted in fact or fantasy, might take on a life of its own, producing a bandwagon effect that would have an extremely pernicious impact on America's interests. In the words of NSC 68, the comprehensive reappraisal of U.S. national security policy completed in April 1950, the Soviet Union sought "to demonstrate that force and the will to use it are on the side of the Kremlin [and] that those who lack it are decadent and doomed."[61] Because the fighting in Indochina was widely viewed as a contest between East and West, however erroneous that view might have been in fact, the challenge it posed to Washington was almost as much psychological as it was geostrategic. State Department and Pentagon officials agreed that the U.S. commitment to Indochina and other parts of the region helped meet that psychological challenge by demonstrating to adversaries and allies alike Washington's strength, resolution, and determination. The Truman administration's concern with such intangible matters as America's prestige, image, and reputation—in a word, its credibility—thus also entered into the complex policy calculus that made U.S. intervention in Southeast Asia seem as logical as it was unavoidable.[62]

U.S. fears about Soviet and Chinese ambitions in Indochina, it bears noting, were by no means illusory. Strong fraternal bonds, and common interests, definitely existed between Ho's movement and the regimes of Mao Zedong and Joseph Stalin. In January 1950 the Vietnamese leader made a secret trip to Beijing in search of Chinese diplomatic support and material aid. Mao, at that very same time, was holding a series of face-to-face meetings with Stalin in Moscow. Following extensive negotiations, the two dictators concluded, in February, a thirty-year treaty of mutual assistance between their two countries. That treaty greatly alarmed the Truman administration as it appeared to portend a commingling of the economic assets, military prowess, and ideological appeal of the two communist giants. Ho himself arrived in Moscow early in February, just before the Sino-Soviet alliance was formalized, and personally beseeched Stalin and Mao for assistance. Stalin had already agreed to extend formal recognition to Ho's Democratic Republic of Vietnam, a decision announced on January 31, just two weeks after Beijing recognized the nationalist regime. The Soviet leader offered no material aid, however. Unwilling to commit scarce resources to so unfamiliar—and remote—a theater, he instead urged Mao to take the lead in providing the Viet Minh with military equipment and training.

The Chinese revolutionary agreed to do so for a blend of strategic and ideological reasons. By strengthening the Vietnamese communists, Mao believed he could safeguard China's southern frontier, diminish the threat posed to his regime by the United States and its allies, contribute positively to what he viewed as the broader anti-imperialist struggle in Asia, and solidify Beijing's position as the ideological center of that struggle. In April 1950, Mao created a Chinese Military Advisory Group which he dispatched to northern Vietnam to help organize Vietnamese forces and lend expertise to the planning of the Viet Minh's overall military strategy. From the first, the Chinese ruler took a strong personal interest in the Vietnamese war against the French. That interest, and Chinese assistance, intensified with the outbreak of war on the Korean peninsula in June 1950. On June 27, just two days after the North Korean invasion, Mao told a contingent of Chinese military advisers en route to Vietnam that "since our revolution has achieved victory, we have an obligation to help others. This is called internationalism." Zhu De, commander of the Peoples' Liberation Army, added that "we should spare no effort to help the Vietnamese achieve victory."[63]

With the onset of the Korean fighting, the strategic, economic, political, and psychological fears undergirding America's initial commitment to the French also intensified. Convinced that Moscow and Beijing had become even more dangerously opportunistic foes, the Truman administration redoubled its efforts to contain the communist threat on every front. At the same time, it pursued with ever greater vigor initiatives designed to strengthen America's own sphere of influence in Western Europe. Those vital global priorities demanded nothing less than an all-out effort to contain the communist threat to Southeast Asia, a threat manifested most immediately and most seriously by the Viet Minh insurgency. Virtually all national security planners in the Truman administration were agreed that Indochina was the key to Southeast Asia. If the Viet Minh succeeded in routing the French, according to an analysis prepared by the Joint Strategic Survey Committee in November 1950, "this would bring about almost immediately a dangerous condition with respect to the internal security of all of the other countries of Southeast Asia, as well as the Philippines and Indonesia, and would contribute to their probable eventual fall to communism."[64]

With uncommon unanimity, U.S. civilian and military policymakers concurred that a communist triumph in Indochina would be a strategic nightmare for the United States. It would likely destabilize the entire region, disrupt important trading ties to Japan and Western Europe, deny to the West and make available to the communist powers important raw materials, endanger vital transportation and communication routes between the Pacific Ocean and the Middle East, render vulnerable America's chain of offshore military bases in the Pacific, and enhance the power and prestige of both the Soviet Union and China. "In addition, this loss would have widespread political and psychological repercussions upon other non-communist states throughout the world."[65] Under such dire circumstances, an ever-deepening U.S. commitment to the region appeared unavoidable.

The Korean War, coming so close on the heels of the Chinese Communist triumph, the Soviet atomic bomb blast, NSC-68's gloomy admonitions, and the unusually brittle foreign policy debate at home, steeled the resolve of an embattled president and his equally embattled inner circle. Truman believed that he—and the nation he led—could ill afford another humiliation. Certain that a communist breakthrough anywhere in Southeast Asia would constitute such a humiliation, he authorized in mid-1950 stepped-up U.S. military support, economic aid, and political intervention throughout the region.

Those measures aimed to stabilize Southeast Asia, arrest communist advances, and preserve Western strategic and economic interests—all, presumably, at a cost that could be borne without too much pain by a nation with a rapidly expanding set of international commitments. Only time could tell, of course, whether such measures would prove sufficient to achieve the results desired. If they proved insufficient, crucial questions loomed: Precisely how important to the United States was the emergence of a stable, noncommunist Southeast Asia relative to other pressing policy goals? And exactly how great a cost was the United States prepared to accept in order to achieve that objective? More economic aid? Additional military assistance? Deeper political involvement? Explicit bilateral or multilateral security commitments? A regional defense pact? The dispatch of military advisers? The dispatch of combat troops? American leaders would be forced to consider each of those unwelcome options far sooner than they could ever have imagined.

With the outbreak of the Korean conflict in June 1950, the Cold War in Asia entered a far more dangerous and uncertain phase. Acutely concerned about what seemed a concerted effort by Moscow and Beijing to extend their sway across the Asian continent, the Truman administration quickly drew a series of lines in the sand. Southeast Asia appeared especially unstable, and hence especially susceptible to communist blandishments. The administration, accordingly, concentrated its line-drawing efforts there, bringing substantial increases in U.S. political, economic, and military involvement throughout the region.

As communist-led insurgencies continued to rage in Indochina and Malaya, Huk rebels boldly defied the legitimacy of the newly established Philippine government, and inexperienced, financially pressed regimes in Burma, Indonesia, and Thailand struggled to overcome daunting internal problems, the Western position throughout the area appeared on the verge of collapse. Absent a vigorous American effort to shore up the region's noncommunist forces, Truman administration strategists feared that all of Southeast Asia would soon drift into the communist camp, dealing a catastrophic blow to the economic and security interests of the United States. The question that preoccupied U.S. planners was not whether such an outcome could be prevented—but how.

Southeast Asia and the United States: How High the Stakes?

In the view of nearly all senior U.S. policymakers, Southeast Asia ranked by the early 1950s as a region of vital importance to the United States. Every major policy paper, strategic assessment, and intelligence estimate drove home that point. Paul Nitze, head of the State Department's Policy Planning Staff, observed in early 1952 that the "loss of Southeast Asia would present an unacceptable threat to [the] position of [the] U.S., both in [the] Far East and world-wide."[1] Soviet expert Charles Bohlen put the implications of "the loss of Southeast Asia" in even starker terms. A communist victory there would exert so profound an impact on the overall balance of power, he insisted, that if it occurred "we would have lost the Cold War."[2]

Since Southeast Asia at first glance appears so far removed from the fundamental strategic and economic interests of postwar America, such apocalyptic reasoning demands careful scrutiny. The United States certainly harbored no territorial ambitions in the region. Nor was its direct economic stake in the area substantial. Americans depended less on Southeast Asian rubber and tin than they had during the prewar years; as a surplus rice producer, the United States had no need for the region's most important export crop; and American purchasers could easily find alternative sources for the oil, timber, and copra that Indonesia and the Philippines provided. Neither did any of Southeast Asia's newly emerging nations possess significant international prestige or carry meaningful clout in world councils.

Why, then, would foreign policy experts as savvy as Nitze and Bohlen attach such enormous weight to Southeast Asian developments? Why would they insist that events unfolding in that region carried far-reaching consequences for the United States? The answers to those questions are complex. They derive, essentially, from the perceived links—geostrategic, economic, political, and psychological—between the fate of Southeast Asia and the realization of overall U.S. foreign policy objectives. In purely economic terms, Southeast Asia's importance to the United States was based far less on America's own needs than on those of its key allies in Western Europe and Japan. The economic recoveries of those core states, U.S. analysts were convinced, required the rapid reestablishment of commercial ties with the primary producing areas of Southeast Asia. A severance of those links, on the other hand, could gravely set back the economic recoveries of Western Europe and Japan, harming in the process not just the economic health of America's most valued allies but the national security of the United States as well.[3]

Southeast Asia's value to the United States was also based on the Pentagon's military plans and priorities. U.S. defense planners believed they had no choice but to prepare for the prospect, however remote, of a future hot war with the Soviet Union and/or China. To that end, the United States erected a worldwide network of military bases during the early postwar years to provide both defense in depth and the tactical flexibility needed to project offensive air and naval power from multiple points across the globe. U.S. bases in the Philippines played an important role in that global defense strategy, anchoring the offshore defense chain that ran from Alaska down through the Ryukyu Islands. If Southeast Asia were lost to the communists, American strategists worried that the transportation routes linking the Pacific to the Persian Gulf and the Middle East would be broken; the island defense chain would become increasingly vulnerable; important U.S. bases would grow isolated from each other; and American defense capabilities throughout the Western Pacific would be gravely diminished.[4]

Southeast Asia's importance derived as well from a more generalized set of security fears, fears reflected in the pervasive "bandwagon" and "domino" metaphors employed by American strategists when assessing the communist threat. The basic ideas underlying those metaphors were really quite simple. If any one country succumbed to communist pressure, either internal or external, so the common thinking went, the likelihood of an adjacent area succumbing to that pressure rose—the domino effect. Even nonadjacent areas would feel the resultant pressure since communist victories anywhere would probably bolster communist appeals everywhere, leading more and more nations to see communism as an irresistible force—the bandwagon effect. Regardless of whether those ideas were based on reasonable fears or irrational ones, they exerted a great pull on American policymakers concerned with the fate of Southeast Asia. The conjunction in that region of several powerful historical streams—the dislocation induced by the Pacific War, decolonization, revolutionary nationalism, the communist victory in China—made that area seem unusually susceptible to communist blandishments. Hence Southeast Asia factored more prominently than any other part of the planet in the grim domino and bandwagon scenarios sketched so routinely by U.S. decision-makers.[5]

The Truman administration's mounting apprehension about Southeast Asia during the late 1940s and early 1950s was primarily a function, then, of threat perceptions. U.S. officials were much too sophisticated to *blame* Moscow, or Beijing, for the distressing conditions prevailing in Southeast Asia. They were certain, however, that Stalin and his associates in the Kremlin were shrewdly capitalizing on those conditions to the detriment of the West. Their fears increased substantially with the communist victory in China. Although some U.S. officials, including Acheson, believed that an ultimate rift between the Soviet Union and China was likely, they needed to deal with present realities rather than future prospects. The conclusion in February 1950 of a thirty-year treaty of mutual assistance between Moscow and Beijing confirmed some of their worst fears since it raised the specter of a two-headed communist adversary. As early as May 1950, Acheson confided to European representatives that "from our viewpoint, the Soviet Union possesses [a] position of domination in China which it is using to threaten Indochina, push in Malaya, stir up trouble in the Philippines, and now to start trouble in Indonesia."[6] U.S. leaders particularly worried that China could use its superior military might to overrun mainland Southeast Asia, or, if it chose less heavy-handed means, could communize Southeast Asia through covert means, utilizing the huge overseas Chinese minorities scattered throughout the region as agents of internal subversion.

American fears about Sino-Soviet expansionist proclivities in Southeast Asia appear, in light of existing evidence, to be greatly overdrawn. Both communist powers, to be sure, believed that their national interests would be enhanced if communist insurgents gained power in Indochina, Malaya, or anywhere else in the region. Stalin was convinced that fellow communists in all locales would gratefully defer to Moscow, harnessing their policies to the needs of international communism as determined by the Soviet fatherland—much as the Russian autocrat tried to force such deference upon his new Chinese ally. The ever-opportunistic Stalin almost certainly calculated, moreover, that breakthroughs in the former colonial areas would have a positive demonstration effect throughout the Third World by confirming for other would-be revolutionaries the applicability and appeal of the communist model. Such breakthroughs would be widely interpreted as political-ideological victories for the Soviet Union, a point Soviets appreciated every bit as much as Americans. They would also rob the West of some of the economic and military strength it derived from control over a resource-rich area.

Yet, it must be emphasized, Southeast Asia was never of commanding significance to a Soviet ruler whose gaze remained fixated on Europe throughout this early Cold War period. Stalin could not imagine any developments in Southeast Asia exerting an immediate or fundamental impact on the overall balance of global power. Hence, he proved unwilling to invest substantial resources in so peripheral a theater. Following a division-of-responsibility model, he pressed Mao to take the lead in supplying guidance and matériel to Southeast Asian insurgents.[7]

As already noted, Mao willingly complied with his senior partner's directive. Beginning in the spring of 1950, he authorized the immediate provision of logistical support, military equipment, and tactical advice for the Viet Minh. That support proved crucial to the Vietnamese guerrillas' ability to survive French offensives in 1950–51 and to the military gains they began scoring soon after. Throughout the course of the French-Vietnamese struggle, according to one authority, the Chinese supplied the Vietnamese insurgents with 116,000 guns and 4,630 cannons while equipping approximately five infantry divisions, one engineering and artillery division, one antiaircraft regiment, and one guard regiment. Mao also sent some of his top generals to coordinate military strategy; they played an instrumental role in helping to plan the military campaigns that eventually broke the back of the French defenders.[8]

But Indochina, in many respects, was a special case. Mao's support for the Vietnamese insurgents was probably based as much on the traditional Chinese penchant for seeking friendly, subservient governments along the Indochina borderland as it was on the ideological affinity existing between Chinese and Vietnamese communists—or the wishes of Stalin. Existing evidence suggests that Chinese support for antigovernment rebels in Malaya never moved much beyond the rhetorical stage, even though indigenous, ethnically Chinese Communists led that revolt. Chinese support for Burmese and Filipino insurgents remained exceedingly modest as well. Beijing, not surprisingly, did seek to develop close ties with the leadership of the Indonesian Communist Party at this time, as it did with other Asian communist parties.[9] Taken together, though, those actions hardly equate to the kind of expansionist military threat conjured up by American planners. The massive intervention of Chinese troops in the Korean War, coupled with the important aid Mao lent to Ho's insurgency, led American analysts—understandably perhaps—to distort both the extent and the nature of the threat China posed to Western interests in Southeast Asia.

Meeting the (Perceived) Threat

During its final year in office, the Truman administration engaged in a systematic reexamination of U.S. policy toward Southeast Asia. Its efforts were carried out against the backdrop of a deteriorating French military position in Indochina, growing concern that domestic political pressures might lead to a total French withdrawal from that battle-scarred land, and renewed fears about the possibility of direct Chinese Communist intervention in Indochina or elsewhere in the region. The numerous reappraisals prepared by the State Department, the Defense Department, and the National Security Council emphasized once again the critical importance of Southeast Asia to the United States. During a meeting of the NSC in March 1952, Secretary of Defense Robert A. Lovett referred to "the grave danger to U.S. security interests" that would materialize "should Southeast Asia pass into the Communist orbit."[10] Likewise, Acheson candidly informed British Foreign Secretary Anthony Eden several months later that "we are lost if we lose Southeast Asia without a fight" and thus "we must do what we can to save Southeast Asia."[11]

According to NSC 124/2, a new statement of policy approved by Truman on June 25, 1952: "Communist domination, by whatever means, of all Southeast Asia would seriously endanger in the short term, and critically endanger in the longer term, United States security interests." The possibility of "overt or covert" aggression by Beijing posed the most immediate threat. If a single Southeast Asian nation succumbed as a result of Chinese intervention, it "would have critical psychological, political and economic consequences. In the absence of effective and timely counteraction, the loss of any single country would probably lead to relatively swift submission to or an alignment with communism by the remaining countries of the group." The long-term alignment of India and the nations of the Middle East with the communist bloc, the report noted, would almost certainly follow. "Such widespread alignment would endanger the stability of Europe." Further, a communist Southeast Asia would deprive the West of a range of strategic commodities, thus exerting even greater economic and political pressure on nations allied to the United States and likely impelling "Japan's eventual accommodation to communism."[12]

Dwight D. Eisenhower's ascension to the presidency in January 1953 did nothing to alter those judgments. Indeed, the Eisenhower administration's first policy paper on Southeast Asia, completed in April 1953, just reaffirmed the conclusions of NSC 124/2.[13] Regardless of individual political persuasion or party affiliation, America's Cold Warriors were agreed that the communist threat to Southeast Asia had to be contained. Differences of opinion between and within the Truman and Eisenhower administrations concerned not the ends of policy, but its means. A joint State-Defense mission to Southeast Asia had earlier cut to the essence of the problem. "What," it asked, "is the United States able and willing within the confines of its over-all commitments and its over-all resources to pay for Southeast Asia?" Until that question could be answered satisfactorily, it warned, "we can only expect that American activities will be aimless, conflicting, and self-defeating."[14]

Convinced that Southeast Asia had become a major Cold War battleground, the Truman administration had intensified America's engagement with all of the region's countries in the months preceding, and those immediately following, the outbreak of the Korean War in June 1950. President Truman launched at that time a series of initiatives designed both to help France and Britain quell the communist-led insurgencies in Indochina and Malaya and to help ensure the stability and pro-Western orientation of Southeast Asia's postcolonial regimes. If combating insurgencies required tough, military measures, the second challenge clearly demanded more subtle and imaginative approaches. Economic and defense assistance, technical support, political advice, diplomatic backing, even such intangibles as understanding, patience, and sympathy—those gestures seemed likely to win more friends among the proud yet uncertain nationalist leaders of Indonesia, Burma, the Philippines, and Thailand than the flexing of military muscle. With widely varying rates of success, U.S. policymakers explored each of those approaches during the early 1950s as they strove with increasing urgency to convert the region's independent nation-states into stable, reliable partners in the anticommunist cause.

Adjusting to Independence: Indonesia

Indonesia initially struck U.S. observers as the most promising prospect within the region for the emergence of a truly stable, pro-American regime. The United States had of course played an instrumental role in pressing a reluctant Holland to accept the inevitability of Indonesian independence. For that, the new nation's leaders were grateful, a gratitude tempered only slightly by the grudging and belated nature of U.S. support. Truman administration planners were accordingly hopeful that a warm, mutually beneficial relationship could be forged between the United States and Southeast Asia's most populous and resource-rich nation. Not only were President Sukarno, Vice President Hatta, and other Indonesian luminaries distrustful of communism, but they were sufficiently pragmatic to recognize their war-ravaged nation's need for external military and economic aid.

U.S. officials, consequently, sought to exploit those favorable circumstances by encouraging the solidification of Indonesia's ties to the United States. Its alignment with the West, they were convinced, would exert a salutary impact on other noncommunist states throughout Asia. "With the Communist threat to the Asian mainland increasing," Acheson cautioned Truman in January 1950, "the importance of keeping Indonesia in the anti-Communist camp is of greater and greater importance. The loss of Indonesia to the Communists would deprive the United States of an area of the highest political, economic and strategic importance."[15] Following his secretary of state's strong recommendation, Truman authorized the dispatch of modest amounts of economic, technical, and military assistance to Jakarta during the first half of 1950. The president also supported a $100 million loan from the Export-Import Bank that enabled Indonesia to purchase capital goods from the United States, and he dispatched separate study missions to Indonesia to survey the nation's developmental and military needs.[16]

The outbreak of the Korean War brought to the surface some of the underlying barriers to the kind of relationship U.S. diplomats sought with postindependence Indonesia. As the Cold War in Asia moved into a more dangerous and unpredictable phase, the Truman administration grew ever more testy with Indonesia's neutralist inclinations. Much to the exasperation of the State Department, Indonesia clung to its self-styled "active and independent" foreign policy even after North Korea's act of naked aggression. In view of the ongoing struggle they saw themselves waging against a brutal, totalitarian Soviet state, armed with its godless, freedom-denying ideology, U.S. diplomats could brook no such temporizing. The State Department reminded Ambassador H. Merle Cochran in July 1950 that Indonesia simply had to choose between the Soviet Union and the "free world," a theme that U.S. representatives sounded repeatedly in discussions with Indonesian authorities.[17]

But all U.S. attempts to force such a choice on Indonesia just proved counterproductive. The leaders of the young republic, much like their counterparts in India and Burma, adamantly refused to make any moves that might compromise the hard-won independence of their people. In October 1950, Indonesia informed the United States that it could not accept any military assistance under America's mutual security program since the acceptance of such aid brought unwanted strings and would inevitably be interpreted by the communist countries as "having taken sides." The Truman administration found that rebuff hard to accept. Between December 1951 and February 1952, as the Korean conflict raged on, U.S. representatives tried again to anchor Indonesia to the West with a defense pact. Washington's timing could not have been more ill-considered. Many of Indonesia's major political figures, already uncomfortable with Prime Minister Sukiman's policies, condemned the pro-American leader's willingness to sign a mutual security agreement with Washington as a betrayal of Indonesian independence. The ensuing uproar led both to the scuttling of the proposed agreement and to the collapse of the Sukiman cabinet. It also taught ambitious nationalist politicians an instructive lesson about the risks of too open an identification with the United States.[18]

The inability of American officials to appreciate Indonesia's virtual obsession with West Irian (called West New Guinea by the Dutch) proved to be an even more serious impediment to the development of closer ties between Washington and Jakarta during the early postindependence period. According to the terms hammered out by Dutch and Indonesian representatives during the tortured negotiations preceding independence, the future disposition of that disputed territory was to be determined at a later date by direct negotiations between the Netherlands and Indonesia. Subsequent discussions quickly bogged down, however, as the Netherlands showed no inclination to relinquish control over West Irian. Sukarno saw the continuing Dutch presence there as an insult to his nation, insisting in fiery public speeches that the nationalist revolution would not be complete until West Irian became part of the Indonesian state. That uncompromising stance was endorsed by virtually all political factions within Indonesia. The Dutch were equally obstinate; they continued to cling to this one remaining vestige of their colonial empire in Southeast Asia, more for psychological reasons than for economic or strategic ones. The United States found itself caught in the middle, with both sides actively courting its support. Eager to establish a friendly relationship with Jakarta and yet unwilling to offend a loyal NATO ally on such an emotionally charged issue, Washington opted for a position of strict neutrality. President Sukarno's promise of warmer Indonesian-American relations in return for a more accommodating U.S. stand on West Irian failed to budge the Americans from their neutral stance.[19]

Overall, developments in Indonesia during the first several years following independence generated mixed reviews among U.S. observers. In a national intelligence estimate of June 11, 1953, the CIA noted that Indonesia's foreign policy was determined chiefly by its leaders' desire to maintain national independence and to avoid taking sides in the East-West conflict. "However," it added, "so long as Indonesia's major trade relations remain with the West, Indonesia will probably continue to be closer to the West than to the Soviet Bloc."[20] Internal political trends induced more concern. Sukarno's appointment of Ali Sastroamidjojo as the nation's fifth prime minister on August 1, 1953, disquieted the Eisenhower administration's Indonesia-watchers since it brought a significant increase in communist influence at the upper levels of the government. According to U.S. analysts, eight of the twenty ministers in the Ali cabinet were either communists themselves or highly sympathetic to the aims of the Indonesian Communist Party (PKI). Coupled with the PKI's growing influence within labor and peasant organizations, the advent of the Ali cabinet rang some early alarm bells in an official Washington that continued to equate communist gains anywhere with blows against the "free world."[21]

Adjusting to Independence: Burma and Thailand

Burma posed no less complex a set of challenges to the United States during this period. Following its independence from Great Britain in January 1948, the young nation found itself lurching from crisis to crisis. The government of Prime Minister U Nu faced several major internal rebellions, led respectively by adherents of the leftist Peoples' Volunteer Organization, by two different communist factions, by Burmese army mutineers, and by the Karens. The latter, a disaffected ethnic group that sought an independent Karen state, proved the Rangoon government's most formidable foe. Although Prime Minister Nu surprised British and American experts with his vigorous leadership and his partial success in curbing the appeal of the communist rebels, insurgent forces still controlled more than half of Burma's territory. The arrival of Chinese Communist troops at Burma's northern border by the end of 1949 further clouded the Nu regime's prospects for achieving genuine sovereignty. Its economic problems were equally worrisome. Three years after independence, economic activity within Burma had virtually come to a standstill; normally Southeast Asia's largest exporter of rice, Burma's rice production hovered at a mere fraction of prewar totals.[22]

Burma's decision to emulate neighboring India's nonaligned foreign policy derived as much from practical as from ideological considerations. As wartime leader Ba Maw recalled bitterly about the Pacific War: "A power conflict with which we had nothing to do soon claimed us and all our resources." With such vivid memories of the devastation so recently visited on their homeland, Burma's rulers were exceedingly wary of any commitments that might suck their fragile nation once again into the vortex of great power rivalry. They searched, consequently, for a middle ground in the Cold War. In December 1949, Burma became the first noncommunist government to extend formal recognition to the new communist regime in Beijing. At the same time, the Nu cabinet accepted a $70 million loan from the British Commonwealth, relaxed its previous restrictions on foreign investment, and avidly pursued closer ties with both London and Washington. By the early months of 1950, Burmese leaders displayed growing apprehension about their country's vulnerability to Chinese Communist penetration, a problem exacerbated by the presence of a sizable Chinese minority within Burma. That apprehension did not impel Burma to tilt openly toward the West, however. After accepting the grant of ten U.S. Coast Guard cutters for use as river patrol craft in May 1950, Rangoon informed Washington that it could accept economic, but no further military, aid.[23]

The Burmese, like the Indonesians, feared that acceptance of mutual defense aid from the United States would compromise their nonaligned foreign policy, inciting domestic opinion and provoking their powerful neighbor to the north. Henry B. Day, the U.S. chargé d'affaires in Rangoon, well summarized Burmese thinking in a cable of February 15, 1952. Burma "believes its best hope of being spared disaster lies in maintaining the friendliest possible relations with Communist China," he noted. "This is not a sentiment based on ideological sympathies but a conviction founded on instinct to survive." Day advised his State Department superiors that they should abandon any lingering hopes of aligning Burma with the West and instead "see if we cannot actually derive advantage from Burma's position of neutrality, even if it is only the negative one of keeping Burma out of the Communist camp."[24]

The Truman and Eisenhower administrations essentially followed that sage, if frustrating, advice throughout the early 1950s. Activist-inclined officials accepted with reluctance the limits imposed by Burmese realities; they simply had no other choice. The presence in northern Burma of approximately twelve thousand Nationalist Chinese troops further diminished American influence with the Nu government. The Burmese correctly viewed the influx of those ragged, marauding forces as an unfortunate by-product of America's misguided effort to keep up the pressure on China's new communist rulers. Ambassador David M. Key angrily informed the State Department that U.S. support for those Chinese Nationalist troops, "conducted in flagrant disregard [of] Burmese sovereignty, cannot but make a mockery in Burmese eyes of our officially expressed desire to aid in the restoration of internal stability and to strengthen Burmese independence." It was, moreover, "prejudicing everything which we are striving to accomplish here and threatens all our future prospects."[25] In late 1953, Prime Minister Nu appealed personally to President Eisenhower to help secure the removal of the unwanted foreign presence from Burmese soil.[26] This nettlesome issue, which would not be resolved for years to come, served as a major roadblock to the development of warmer Burmese-American relations.

As in so many other parts of the world, U.S. policymakers found too great a gap between their objectives in Burma and their actual achievements there, between the ends they sought and the means available to them. A State Department memorandum of December 1951 succinctly captured the basic dilemma. "British and American officials generally agree," it noted, "that the situation in Burma is deteriorating at an alarming rate, that Burma is the 'soft spot' of Southeast Asia[,] and that because the Government and people of Burma are apathetic to the Communist threat and highly suspicious of British and American motives, it is difficult to find any way in which we can render assistance."[27] Yet the stakes remained extremely high from the standpoint of the overall U.S. position in Asia. "Communist control of Burma would be a great strategic advantage to both the Chinese Communists and the USSR," warned a CIA analysis. "It would drive a wedge between India-Pakistan and Southeast Asia, facilitate Communist penetration into

Indochina and the other countries of South and Southeast Asia, and in a psychological sense give impetus to the claim that Communism in Asia is an irresistible force." Communist control of Burma would also give the Sino-Soviet bloc control over what ranked as potentially the richest rice surplus area in Asia, much to Japan's detriment.[28]

To the dismay of U.S. officials, continuing internal strife and economic weakness made such dire scenarios seem increasingly plausible, even as the imperatives of Burmese nationalism militated against any direct U.S. initiatives to help stabilize the situation. U.S. experts took some comfort from growing signs throughout 1953 and 1954 that Burma was beginning to tackle a few of its most pressing internal problems. They took less comfort from the fact that U.S. influence with Burma's governing elites remained on the margins.

Thailand presented a dramatically different story. Unlike Indonesia and Burma, it openly invited American support. In the wake of the Chinese Communist triumph, the government of Prime Minister Phibun Songgram declared its firm opposition to communism and expressed its need for military assistance to make that opposition more effective. Thailand, in effect, offered to align itself with the United States in return for U.S. military and economic aid and promises of U.S. defense protection. The Truman administration, anxious for any Asian allies it could attract, responded exactly as the Thais hoped that it would. Despite some concerns about the reliability of Phibun, an inveterate opportunist who had collaborated with the Japanese during the war and returned to power via a military coup in 1947, the United States warmly welcomed Thailand into the anticommunist camp.

In March 1950, Truman approved a recommendation from the departments of State and Defense that Thailand be provided with $10 million in military assistance in order to help it resist "communist aggression from without and subversive activities from within." The State Department laid out the case for aid in the strongest possible terms. Thailand found itself under increasing internal and external stress as a result of communist successes in both China and Vietnam. Its Chinese minority, three million strong, posed a special danger since it might over time evolve into a subversive fifth column within the country. Without military assistance, the State Department declared emphatically, Thailand "cannot hold out against communist pressure." Yet if it succumbed to that pressure the results would be disastrous for the American position in Asia. "If Thailand should be lost to the communists," the assessment concluded, "then it would be unlikely that Malaya could be held. This would mean that from Korea to India, there would be no place on the Asian mainland where the United States would have an open friend and ally."[29]

Under Phibun's leadership, Thai actions conformed perfectly with the Asian policy goals of the Truman administration. Thailand became the first Asian state to recognize the Bao Dai regime, refused to recognize Mao Zedong's government, sent a contingent of troops to Korea to fight alongside American and UN units, and voted in the UN to condemn Communist China for aggression in Korea. On October 17, 1950, Washington rewarded Bangkok with a military assistance agreement that soon opened up a pipeline of arms and supplies to the Thai armed forces—the same armed forces, not coincidentally, that maintained a hammerlock on political power within the country. "Thailand has irrevocably severed its ties with the communist countries," glowed a State Department policy assessment, "and committed itself positively to the cause of the free nations."[30]

The U.S. ambassador in Thailand, Edwin F. Stanton, saw less exalted motives behind the Thai commitment to the West. Characterizing Phibun as "a gambler," Stanton identified two self-interested assumptions behind the former military officer's decision to align Thailand with the United States: "1. That the democratic powers ultimately will win the struggle with the Communist powers. 2. That by committing his Government to the cause of the West, he is actually buying an insurance policy which will guarantee that in the event of aggression the United Nations and the United States will step in—in force—to help defend Thailand against the Communists." The realistic Stanton guessed that, gambler that he was, "Phibun has probably decided that having made his choice, the only sensible thing to do is to put everything behind it." Extending his Las Vegas metaphor, the ambassador speculated that with each pro-Western gesture Phibun "successively adds chips to a stack which he has placed on the United States."[31]

Stanton's analysis hit close to the mark. Phibun's decision to align Thailand with the United States was more the product of Phibun's self-interested calculation that alignment with the United States could ease Thailand's historic sense of vulnerability than it was of Thai anticommunist convictions. The decision was heavily reinforced, though, by the interplay between Thai political factionalism and Phibun's personal ambitions. The Thai prime minister sought arms and aid from the United States primarily to enhance the power of the military at the expense of its civilian competitors and to increase his own stature within Thailand's military establishment. To achieve those goals, he was willing to make the foreign policy commitments demanded by the United States, no matter how unpopular at home. Before 1950, substantial opposition existed within Thai society toward any policy that would either limit Bangkok's diplomatic options or, even worse, antagonize so powerful a neighboring state as China. Once U.S. aid began to flow, a politically strengthened Phibun moved quickly to silence dissident voices, solidifying in the process his own faction's hold on power and Washington's support for it. As a direct consequence of U.S. military aid, the Thai government thus became increasingly repressive and authoritarian.[32]

Delighted to find so compliant an Asian ally, the United States hardly concerned itself with the self-interested motives behind Bangkok's staunch anticommunist professions or the antidemocratic consequences of this new relationship. Secretary of State John Foster Dulles expressed the dominant American view when he called Thailand "an essential element in the front against the advance of communism in southeast Asia."[33] The relationship was not without problems, to be sure. Political instability remained rife within Thailand. The more astute U.S. observers recognized that Washington was supporting less a nation than a political clique—an unrepresentative and antidemocratic clique at that, comprised almost entirely of military officers who stood to benefit personally from the American connection. A few U.S. observers worried about how long that group could maintain its grip on power and what the future might hold in store. They also fretted about Thai sensitivity to the charge, frequently leveled by fellow Asians, that Bangkok had become Washington's puppet. "Thailand," admitted Stanton, "has in effect assumed some of the characteristics of a protege."[34] But even the skeptical Stanton held such misgivings in check when assessing the overall value of the Thai-American alliance. "It is really remarkable," he rhapsodized in one message to the State Department, "that this small country surrounded by turmoil and exposed to communist aggression should so openly side with us."[35] His successor at the embassy in Bangkok, legendary World War II spymaster William "Wild Bill" Donovan, possessed fewer doubts about and even greater ambitions for one of America's most reliable Asian allies.

Adjusting to Independence: The Philippines

Given a half century of American tutelage, the Philippines might have been expected to emerge as the most reliable and stable of Southeast Asia's newly independent states. Reliable, maybe—at least if judged by the consistently pro-American tenor of its foreign policy. But far from stable. Indeed, the government of Elpidio Quirino was by mid-1949 drowning under so colossal a wave of economic and security problems as to give pause even to the most seasoned Burma-watcher. And Quirino, the plump, lackluster lawyer who had ascended to the presidency after the death of Manuel Roxas in April 1948, appeared oblivious to it all.

The Truman administration was not. Acheson and other senior officials found disturbing parallels between recent developments in China and current trends in the Philippines. During a face-to-face meeting in Washington in the summer of 1949, Acheson tried, without notable success, to impress upon Quirino the precariousness of his nation's plight. He shared with the Philippine leader a recent World Bank report that called attention to the slow capital accumulation, inadequate tax base, growing capital flight, rising inflation, and swelling budget deficits that could soon spell disaster for his country. But Quirino showed no inclination to institute the necessary reforms. Nor did he seem to grasp the connection between his country's dismal economic performance and the resurgent Huk rebellion in central Luzon. The Philippine president, lamented John F. Melby, the State Department officer in charge of Philippine affairs, was "ineffectual, dilatory, and disturbingly corrupt. He does not seem to understand most of the problems he is facing, nor does he appear to have much intention of doing anything about those he does understand." Instead, Quirino seemed concerned primarily with his chances for reelection. His government must operate, Melby thought, "on the happy postulate that when conditions get bad the United States will bail it out."[36]

In fact, Quirino and his associates did operate on such a postulate—and it proved not so ill-founded. No matter how corrupt, procrastinating, and ineffective the Manila government might be, the United States could not afford to see it sink under the weight of its own incompetence. "The unique American record and position in the Philippines creates a special problem," Melby worried. To Asians, "the Philippines is the American show window on Asia and the tangible evidence of American intentions and performance."[37] Given the increasing urgency with which the Truman administration was seeking to shore up the U.S. position throughout the continent, America's response to the deepening internal crisis in the Philippines thus assumed great symbolic significance. What messages would it send to Burma, Indonesia, and other reluctant allies if the United States proved unwilling to come to the rescue of a former dependency? Another factor pushed the administration toward intervention. With the fall of China, U.S. bases in the Philippines became more important to America's perimeter defense strategy in East Asia. As early as May 1949, defense officials told Truman that U.S. military capabilities in the region depended on the air and sea power that could be projected from the Philippines. Secretary of Defense Louis Johnson stated flatly that the United States could not hold either Japan or Southeast Asia without the military installations it maintained in the Philippine islands.[38]

For those reasons, the Truman administration committed itself by early 1950 to a full-fledged effort aimed at defusing the Philippine time bomb. Following meetings in Washington in February of that year, Truman and Acheson forced Quirino to accept an official U.S. economic survey mission. Banker Daniel Bell, a former Treasury Department official, headed the mission which arrived in the islands in August. The outbreak of war in Korea just two months earlier lent added urgency to the team's task. In the final report, sent to Truman on September 2, Bell stressed that the calamitous financial state of affairs he encountered raised the specter of a wholesale collapse of the Manila government. He recommended that to avert such a disaster the United States should provide the Philippines with $250 million in loans and grants in return for a commitment by the Quirino administration to raise taxes and submit to U.S. fiscal supervision and control.[39] The report closely mirrored an earlier recommendation from Melby that had insisted upon the need to impose "direct, if camouflaged" U.S. supervision over Philippine finances. In a comment that spoke volumes about underlying American attitudes toward the Filipinos, Melby quipped that such supervision was necessary with a people who "are only one generation out of the tree tops."[40] Truman promptly approved the recommendations of the Bell mission. Let us "see if we can't arrange to save the Philippine Republic," he said to Acheson.[41]

Whether the United States saved the Philippine Republic or not is open to question. Certainly U.S. aid helped alleviate desperate economic conditions. By the early 1950s, buoyed by the Korean War, the Philippine economy was experiencing real growth. Public confidence in the economy was also rising, in good measure because of the U.S.-imposed controls. At the same time, U.S. defense and intelligence officials helped the Philippine armed forces suppress the Huk rebellion. After cresting in mid-1950, the insurgency steadily lost ground to resupplied government forces under the capable leadership, after August 1950, of Defense Minister Ramon Magsaysay. Magsaysay recognized correctly, as did his American advisers, that the insurgency fed on social and economic discontent and hence would wither as the government addressed peasant grievances. When compared to the limited policy achievements elsewhere in Asia during these years (Japan excepted), U.S. intervention in the Philippines appears a stunning success.[42]

At a deeper level, however, U.S. support, advice, and dollars offered only a partial solution to the core problems facing the Philippine state. It may even have exacerbated some of them. The *caciques*, that tiny elite of planters and industrialists who traced their dominant position back to the period of Spanish and American colonial rule, maintained a stranglehold on all the levers of economic and political power within the country. The U.S. decision to bolster Quirino, who like Roxas served as their handmaiden, simply strengthened cacique dominance. It also mitigated the need for far-reaching reforms in the Philippine political economy. The more the United States attached its prestige to the Philippine government, the less leverage it had with that government; Manila's very weakness thus became a strength, as so many of America's other Cold War allies would come to recognize.

The election of Ramon Magsaysay—"America's boy"—as president in November 1953 blinded most U.S. observers to the continuing structural imbalances undergirding the Philippine state. Magsaysay's ritualistic professions of pro-Americanism delighted the Eisenhower administration, as did his steady support for U.S. policy initiatives throughout Asia. But their efforts to coax him into adopting a meaningful land reform campaign largely fell on deaf ears. Like his predecessors, the vigorous, ingratiating Magsaysay had no inclination to act against the interests of the entrenched elites who had nurtured and financed his candidacy. His four years in office, not surprisingly, brought little more than cosmetic reforms to a society that continued to be plagued by the grossest maldistribution of wealth and power.[43]

Indochina—Still the Quagmire

If the intersection of geostrategic, economic, political, and psychological imperatives helped crystallize U.S. policy objectives throughout Southeast Asia, they did little to clarify the means necessary for the attainment of those objectives in the region's most turbulent area. By the autumn of 1950 the Viet Minh had achieved a string of stunning military successes; the French, increasingly demoralized and immobilized, appeared on the verge of defeat in Indochina. U.S. intelligence experts feared that open intervention by Chinese Communist units, which were providing valuable matériel as well as technical and training assistance to the Viet Minh, might precipitate a complete French collapse. State Department Consultant John Foster Dulles called attention in November 1950 to "what might be a hopeless military situation."[44] A month later an interagency intelligence assessment, coordinated by the CIA, offered an equally grim prognosis. "If this [Chinese Communist] aid continues and French strength and military resources are not substantially increased above those presently programmed," it forecast, "the Viet Minh probably can drive the French out of North Viet Nam (Tonkin) within six to nine months." The French position in the rest of Indochina would soon become untenable, leading eventually to "the transformation of Indochina into a Communist satellite."[45]

Determined to help prevent such a calamitous occurrence, the Truman administration steadily accelerated its military and economic aid commitments to the French. By the end of 1950, Washington had committed more than $133 million in aid to Indochina. By fiscal year 1951 the total value of U.S. military supplies earmarked for the Indochina war had swelled to approximately $316.5 million. Indochina ranked second by then, behind only Korea, as a worldwide recipient of U.S. military aid. That aid helped reinvigorate a faltering French military effort. Together with the appointment of the flamboyant and self-assured Gen. Jean de Lattre de Tassigny as the commander of French forces in Indochina, it led to a substantial—albeit short-lived—improvement in French military fortunes throughout 1951. American observers exulted, hoping that the most acute phase of the crisis might be behind them.[46]

Still, realism tempered the Truman administration's appreciation of the de Lattre-inspired turnaround. Too much hinged on one man, an individual "not always concerned about how many eggs he breaks for his omelette."[47] Furthermore, no matter how vigorous a military campaign the French waged, and no matter how much aid the United States pumped into Indochina, American analysts understood that those factors could not by themselves resolve the Indochina crisis and secure Southeast Asia for the West. Reflecting a view widely shared within the Truman administration, the Joint Chiefs of Staff noted that "without popular support of the Indochinese people, the French will never achieve a favorable long-range military settlement of the security problem of Indochina."[48]

American officials in Washington, Saigon, and Paris were keenly aware that the political and military challenges of Indochina were inseparable. The more astute among them recognized as well that U.S. support for the French pacification effort might work at cross-purposes with American encouragement of Vietnam's noncommunist elites. As early as May 1950, U.S. ambassador to France David K. E. Bruce shrewdly put his finger on the core problem. The ultimate success of U.S policy, he observed, "depends upon encouragement and support of both local nationalism and [the] French effort in Indochina. . . . Yet these two forces, brought together only by common danger of Communist imperialism, are inherently antagonistic and gains of one will be to some extent at expense of other."[49] Much to the dismay of U.S. officials, the military dynamism of de Lattre found no political counterpart. The French, who remained extremely unpopular among the Indochinese, simply refused to transfer any genuine power to Bao Dai and his associates in Vietnam or to the similarly handcuffed native rulers in Laos and Cambodia. The independence of the Associated States remained a sham; the peoples of Indochina accordingly viewed with disdain the coterie of local leaders serving as little more than French puppets. Lamented U.S. Minister in Saigon Donald R. Heath, the "fact is that Ho Chi Minh is [the] only Viet[namese] who enjoys any measure of national prestige."[50]

Notwithstanding its deep and well-founded misgivings about the direction of French policy, the United States carefully avoided open criticism of its European partner. Washington was footing a substantial portion of the bill for the Indochina war; so indispensable a financial commitment would ordinarily bring a commensurate degree of leverage. The Indochina conflict, however, was anything but ordinary. The French military effort in Southeast Asia served American interests at least as much as it served French interests, a point understood equally well in Paris and Washington. For all its dependence on the United States, France retained the ultimate leverage in the relationship. If American advice became too meddlesome, or if the United States sought to tie strings to its aid, the French could simply withdraw from Indochina entirely. The threat, repeatedly made by French leaders, frightened U.S. decision-makers who feared that they might by default inherit direct responsibility for the Indochina morass.[51]

From the outset of U.S. involvement in Indochina, the Joint Chiefs of Staff had insisted upon, and the Truman administration had accepted, a critical limitation on available U.S. options—namely, that under no circumstances could American troops be deployed in Southeast Asia. With American resources already stretched to the breaking point by the nation's ever-expanding global commitments, the military establishment worried constantly about an increasingly dangerous overextension of American power.[52] Threats to American interests may have been multiplying, but American resources remained finite. John Ohly, deputy director of the Mutual Defense Assistance Program in the State Department, articulated the fundamental dilemma faced by U.S. planners as well as anyone. As he reminded Secretary of State Acheson: "We have reached a point where the United States, because of limitations in resources, can no longer simultaneously pursue all its objectives in all parts of the world and must realistically face the fact that certain objectives, even though they may be extremely valuable and important ones, may have to be abandoned if others of even greater value and importance are to be attained."[53] Ohly's argument applied with especial force to Indochina, an area where American interests had escalated far more rapidly than had the resources available to military planners. State Department and White House officials were convinced, every bit as much as their counterparts in the Pentagon, that the United States must contain the communist threat in Southeast Asia without utilizing American ground forces. That consensus also pointed to an unresolved—and unresolvable—contradiction at the root of American policy in Indochina. If Southeast Asia was so vital that its loss to communism would severely compromise American national security, how could the United States accept *any* limits on its actions?

The Truman administration struggled in vain to resolve that contradiction. The president and his civilian and military advisers were agreed that a set of interdependent global interests made the defeat of the Vietnamese insurgency and the preservation of a noncommunist Southeast Asia vital to U.S. security. Developing a consensus within the administration on the steps essential to secure those critical objectives, however, proved more elusive. Certain the French resistance would crumble rapidly if Communist Chinese divisions entered the fray, military and civilian analysts agonized over how the United States might respond to such a move. Some Pentagon officials believed that only military action against China itself, or the threat of such action, could deter Beijing, raising the frightening question of whether preserving a noncommunist Indochina might necessitate another Sino-American conflict. The pragmatic Defense Secretary Robert A. Lovett suggested that the United States should be prepared instead to spend more money—"perhaps at the rate of a billion or a billion and a half dollars a year"—to support the French; "this would be very much cheaper," he argued, "than an all-out war against Communist China, which would certainly cost us fifty billion dollars."[54]

Neither Truman, Acheson, Lovett, the service chiefs, nor any other senior administration official developed a satisfactory response to the multiple challenges posed by the Indochina conflict. In the end, the Truman administration had to content itself with an ever-deepening monetary commitment to the French. By the end of 1952 the United States was underwriting approximately 40 percent of the cost of the Indochina war. Obviously, as the formulators of U.S. policy themselves would have been quick to admit, it was an imperfect solution. At best, that commitment simply postponed the inevitable reckoning. Even if the much-discussed Chinese intervention never materialized, the United States could expect little more than a continuation of the present stalemate; and in the absence of meaningful French political concessions to noncommunist Vietnamese leaders, such a stalemate would simply play into the hands of the Viet Minh. The blunt Army Chief of Staff Gen. J. Lawton Collins doubtless spoke for many when he predicted in March 1952 that "the French will be driven out—it is just a question of time."[55]

The advent of the Eisenhower administration in January 1953 brought no substantive change to America's Indochina policy. U.S. leaders continued to express unease with France's misguided efforts at recolonization. They continued to bankroll those efforts, nonetheless, since, like their predecessors, the new administration's planners found no viable alternative to such an approach. U.S. policy remained driven by pervasive fears about the crushing impact that a communist victory in Indochina might have on American regional and global interests. Eisenhower embellished on his personal assessment of the Indochina situation only slightly when he declared publicly in February 1953 that France's struggle there was helping "hold the line of freedom" against "Communist aggression throughout the world."[56] By early 1954 his administration was bearing approximately 80 percent of the cost of the Indochina war.

The president and his senior advisers would certainly have preferred a more imaginative—and more effective—French response to the Viet Minh insurgency. The need to maintain solidarity with a NATO ally and the fear that France might lay down its arms altogether if American pressure became too intrusive combined, however, to mute any dissident voices. Potential critics within the administration were particularly apprehensive about the growing war-weariness of the French body politic. They worried that widespread public disaffection might lead eventually to a French withdrawal, which would just lay the Indochina problem at Washington's doorstep.[57]

Toward a New Security Structure? Dienbienphu, Geneva, and SEATO

Much to the anguish of American decision-makers, the French appeared headed in exactly that direction by early 1954. The government of Prime Minister Joseph Laniel at that time accepted a Soviet proposal that a multinational conference be convened at Geneva, beginning in April 1954, in order to find a diplomatic solution to the conflict in Indochina. The bold Viet Minh assault in March 1954 against a surrounded French garrison at an isolated outpost called Dienbienphu greatly complicated the upcoming diplomatic showdown. U.S. officials feared that a military defeat at Dienbienphu might hasten a French diplomatic surrender, jeopardizing in the process the entire Western position in Southeast Asia.[58]

Given those stakes, what steps would the United States be willing to take to block a Viet Minh breakthrough at Dienbienphu? Was Indochina of sufficient import to justify direct U.S. military intervention if other options seemed unlikely to work? Eisenhower and his top military and civilian advisers agonized over those questions throughout the spring of 1954, as the French garrison's plight daily grew more desperate. In the end, the former general decided against any last-minute heroics, despite the staunch pro-interventionist arguments of Joint Chiefs of Staff Chairman Adm. Arthur W. Radford and several other prominent officials. At least three key considerations inclined Eisenhower against a U.S. air or atomic strike to rescue the French: the lack of support for such an effort from Britain or any other Western ally; the unsympathetic attitude of congressional leaders from both parties; and the dubious prospects for military success. Without U.S. intervention, the French position was hopeless. On May 7, just one day before the opening of the Indochina phase of the Geneva Convention, Dienbienphu's last ragged defenders capitulated to the triumphant forces of Viet Minh Gen. Vo Nguyen Giap.[59]

Although they attributed the debacle to French incompetence and loss of nerve, Eisenhower administration officials were convinced that Dienbienphu dealt as bruising a blow to the security interests of the United States as it did to those of France. Even before the French surrender, they had begun casting about for ways to lessen the impact of that blow. On March 29, 1954, in a celebrated public speech, Dulles warned with characteristic solemnity that "the imposition on Southeast Asia of the political system of Communist Russia and its Chinese Communist ally, by whatever means, would be a grave threat to the whole free community." Such a threat "should not be passively accepted," he exclaimed, "but should be met by united action," even if united action brought "serious risks."[60]

Over the next several months, the peripatetic secretary of state tried to translate his vague call for united action into something substantive. To prevent further communist gains in Southeast Asia, Dulles believed the United States needed to salvage what it could from the military defeat at Dienbienphu and what looked like a certain diplomatic setback at Geneva. Consequently, with Eisenhower's blessing, he directed that the United States distance itself from the negotiations taking place at Geneva. At the same time, Dulles hatched plans for a new regional defense initiative. Some form of collective security arrangement for Southeast Asia would, he reasoned, signal America's continuing commitment to the region, reassure Southeast Asia's noncommunist states, and serve as a deterrent to Chinese aggression.[61]

American policymakers identified the Chinese, not the Soviets, as their principal foe in Southeast Asia at this time. On that point, diplomatic and defense officials were in virtually total accord. "The aggressive attitude and the growing military power of Communist China," concluded the Joint Chiefs of Staff, "represent the primary and immediate threat to the non-Communist countries of the Far East." Threat assessment requires careful analysis of a potential adversary's intentions as well as its capabilities. U.S.

analysts found ample reason for worry on both scores. According to the Joint Chiefs, the Chinese "have demonstrated that with Soviet logistical assistance, and by virtue of sheer numbers alone, they constitute a formidable force and one which, if unopposed by United States power, is considered to be capable of overrunning all of Southeast Asia." Their intentions, moreover, appeared aggressively expansionist, aimed at nothing less than control over the strategic resources and rice surpluses of the region.

If China achieved that goal—and indigenous forces were judged woefully inadequate as a deterrent—it could then "force Japan to terms, due to her dependence upon the resources of this area for her livelihood." The result would be disastrous for the security interests of the United States since Japan, "the keystone of United States policy in the Far East," would then have no choice but to reach an "accommodation with the Communist bloc."[62]

Although American analysts offered scant evidence to support so alarmist a hypothesis about China's proclivities for southward territorial conquest, such generalized fears proved determinative in the making of American policy. The Southeast Asia Treaty Organization (SEATO) emerged as the Eisenhower administration's principal, if self-admittedly imperfect, response to the set of imponderable challenges it identified. Dulles's brainchild, it occasioned lively debate and substantial division within the American government—and between Washington and its allies—throughout the spring and summer of 1954. The debate was carried out simultaneously with the Geneva proceedings that would decide Indochina's fate. Radford and the Joint Chiefs of Staff were cool at first to the SEATO concept. They disliked the idea of so vague a security arrangement, saw little value in a pact that would probably be scorned by most of Asia's noncommunist states, and preferred to plan for direct retaliation against China if it precipitated aggression in Southeast Asia.[63]

Dulles was keenly aware of the manifold shortcomings of the collective security arrangement he was proposing. With unusual candor, he confided to Eisenhower at one point that it was simply "the lesser of two evils."[64] But the secretary of state also saw important political and psychological benefits in the SEATO concept. There was much to the British point of view, he told Radford in early May, "that if you draw a line in advance then you serve notice on the enemy. At the same time you give him an opportunity to retreat or stay his hand which is not open to the enemy if you intervene in a war already under way."[65] The potential deterrent value of a formal U.S. commitment to the region could not be underestimated, Dulles insisted, no matter how deficient local forces might be. Nor, he argued, could the importance of a U.S. commitment to Southeast Asia's noncommunist states be trivialized. As Dulles emphasized during a later meeting with Eisenhower, the United States needed "to take account of political factors, to give the Thai people, the Burmese, and the Malayans some hope that their area would not simply be overrun and occupied until China was destroyed, in order to keep them on our side."[66] He summarized his thinking at a June 3 meeting of the NSC: "At some point in time or space, some nation has got to be strong enough to stand up against further Communist aggression. . . . If the United States is really prepared to resist overt Chinese Communist aggression, it was very unlikely that the Chinese Communists would risk committing such aggression."[67]

The results of the Geneva Convention, announced on July 21, 1954, just strengthened Dulles's conviction that the immediate negotiation of a Southeast Asia defense pact stood as one of America's most urgent diplomatic priorities. The Geneva Accords provided for the cessation of hostilities in Indochina, established independent states in Laos and Cambodia, demarcated a temporary division of Vietnam at the seventeenth parallel, and stipulated procedures that would lead to the eventual unification of Vietnam. The "great problem from now on out," Dulles observed the next day, "was whether we could salvage what the Communists had ostensibly left out of their grasp in Indochina."[68]

From the American perspective, the Geneva verdict could easily have been much worse. Ho Chi Minh's Democratic Republic of Vietnam conceded more at the conference table than its commanding position on the battlefield would seem to have warranted. Pressure from his erstwhile allies in Moscow and Beijing forced Ho to settle for half a loaf. Neither communist power wanted to press the Viet Minh's advantage in such a way as to compel a strong counteraction from Washington. The Chinese, whose military support had been so critical to the decisive victory at Dienbienphu, retained considerable leverage with their Vietnamese partners. They used that leverage to advance their own foreign policy agenda, discouraging Ho from insisting upon a unified Vietnam under his control. Beijing saw wisdom, at this juncture, in a compromise settlement; it would likely nullify the frightening possibility of open American intervention, earn the Chinese a much-needed respite after five years of bitter confrontation with the West, and enhance their regime's prospects for gaining acceptance as a responsible player on the world stage. Not for the last time, the interests of the Democratic Republic of Vietnam diverged sharply from those of its senior partners in Beijing and Moscow.[69]

Soviet and Chinese moderation did little, though, to soothe American fears. Indeed, the Eisenhower administration drew deeply pessimistic conclusions from the Geneva results. The "Communists have secured possession of an advance salient in Vietnam," concluded an NSC appraisal, "from which military and non-military pressures can be mounted against adjacent and more remote non-Communist areas." Furthermore, the Chinese and Soviets increased their military and political prestige in Asia while the United States suffered a "loss of prestige" that "will raise further doubts in Asia concerning U.S. leadership and the ability of the U.S. to check the further expansion of Communism in Asia."[70] At a meeting of the NSC on August 12, Harold Stassen spoke for the whole U.S. foreign policy establishment when he said that the French defeat in Indochina demonstrated once again that "a gain by the Communists was a loss to us, no matter where it occurred." Eisenhower recorded his agreement with his foreign aid chief, adding that "some time we must face up to it: We can't go on losing areas of the free world forever."[71]

Those concerns led directly to the founding of SEATO in September 1954, following an organizational meeting at Manila. Composed of the United States, Great Britain, France, Australia, New Zealand, the Philippines, Thailand, and Pakistan, the treaty organization was, at best, an exceedingly fragile instrument. It contained only two nations within the treaty area, the Philippines and Thailand, both of which were already firmly tied to the West. More significant than their presence—and that of out-of-region Pakistan—was the absence of Indonesia and Burma and the open hostility of India. SEATO quite obviously failed to increase the number of noncommunist states in the area willing, in one of Dulles's favorite phrases, "to stand up and be counted." It also exposed sharp differences between the Southeast Asian policies and priorities of Washington and London. The conservative government of Prime Minister Winston S. Churchill did not share the Eisenhower administration's fixation with the Chinese threat to the region, nor did it view the French defeat in Indochina as an unmitigated disaster for the West. In the end, SEATO emerged as little more than a paper alliance, its capacity for dealing with either overt aggression or internal subversion surprisingly limited. Vice Adm. A. C. Davis of the U.S. delegation to the Manila conference probably hit the nail on the head when he suggested that SEATO served "more a psychological than a military purpose. The area is no better prepared than before to cope with Communist aggression."[72] On the other hand, SEATO did achieve something. As Dulles intended, the alliance demonstrated the continuing U.S. interest in a noncommunist Southeast Asia, drawing a clear line in the sand for China or any potential aggressor. In accordance with the budgetary constraints that shaped nearly all of Eisenhower's foreign policy decisions, moreover, it also limited the direct military costs to be borne by an already overtaxed United States.

By 1954, then, the United States had significantly deepened its commitments in Southeast Asia. The determination of the Truman and Eisenhower administrations to block further communist advances in the region had led not only to substantial U.S. exertions and expenditures but had brought the country to the very brink of military intervention at the time of the Dienbienphu siege. Exercising the prudence that proved one of the hallmarks of his presidency, Eisenhower pulled back from the abyss at the last moment, rejecting the pleas of more hawkish advisers. Following the French defeat, however, a less cautious Eisenhower made two commitments that carried wide-ranging future implications for U.S. policy in Southeast Asia. First, he authorized a formal commitment to regional security with the U.S.-initiated SEATO grouping. Next, he inaugurated an all-out U.S. effort to help establish a viable, noncommunist regime in the southern half of Vietnam. South Vietnam was to be, in the argot of that anxiety-filled yet confident age, a showcase for democracy: a conclusive demonstration of the superiority of American values and institutions.

The manifold problems that Southeast Asia posed for the United States deepened appreciably during the mid- and late-1950s. Determined to "hold" as much of the region as possible within the Western sphere, the Eisenhower administration redoubled its efforts in the wake of the Geneva Conference to nudge regional developments in a pro-Western direction. It fought tenaciously throughout this period to deter potential aggression from the outside, to gain friends and allies among the area's postcolonial states, to convince the leaders of those states that America could play a responsible, active, and constructive role as a regional power, and to defuse the ideological appeal of communism, neutralism, and radical nationalism. Yet, to the great frustration of Eisenhower, Dulles, and their top lieutenants, far too many developments in Southeast Asia ran disturbingly counter to U.S. interests—and just reminded them of the limits of American power in that corner of the globe.

Virtually everywhere, it seemed, the United States was reduced to plugging holes in a soon-to-be-flooded dike. Burma, Cambodia, and Indonesia insisted on pursuing nonaligned foreign policies and proved resistant to all American efforts aimed at lining them up on the side of the "Free World." In Indonesia the impulsive Sukarno was not only given to periodic anti-American outbursts but presided over and actively encouraged the growth of a huge communist party. At mid-decade that party, much to the dismay of observers in Washington, actually seemed on the verge of achieving power via the ballot box. In South Vietnam and Laos, communist revolutionaries appeared poised to gain power the old-fashioned way: through the barrel of a gun. Nor could the Eisenhower administration afford complacency in its dealings with Thailand and the Philippines. Although those SEATO allies remained exuberantly anticommunist and heavily dependent on U.S. aid, they proved themselves ambivalent allies, buffeted by the same nationalist and neutralist currents flowing throughout the region.

Given the zero-sum world of the Cold War, the Eisenhower administration continued to believe that communist victories anywhere would constitute major foreign policy defeats for the United States. Such defeats, it was convinced, would strengthen, and embolden, the Soviet Union, China, and the revolutionaries that looked to them for support. Such defeats would simultaneously corrode the global power, prestige, and credibility of the United States. With Ho Chi Minh's victory over the French, a communist state blossomed in North Vietnam, one that was closely allied with China and the Soviet Union. Its emergence was affront enough for Washington; American decision-makers were agreed that the United States could afford no additional setbacks in Southeast Asia. To ensure that one did not occur, the Eisenhower administration used nearly every weapon in its superpower arsenal: military and economic aid, technical assistance, diplomatic backing, bilateral and multilateral security pacts, defense advisory teams, even, in the case of Indonesia and Laos, covert paramilitary intervention. Eisenhower balked only at the use of American combat troops.

For Eisenhower administration strategists, an abiding concern about the economic health and political orientation of Japan—Asia's "super domino"—provided another basis for active involvement in Southeast Asia. Eisenhower, Dulles, and other top U.S. officials were convinced that Japan needed to expand its trade with Southeast Asia, not only for the potential commercial benefits the region promised to a recovering Japan but to preclude the reestablishment of its prewar trade connections with mainland China as well. American diplomats worked hard throughout the 1950s to dissuade the Japanese from reopening trade links with their communist neighbor—for fear that such links might over time weaken Tokyo's pro-Western orientation. Southeast Asian resources were thus essential, in Eisenhower's words, to keep Japan "in our orbit."[1] It bears emphasizing that U.S. planners no longer viewed Southeast Asian resources and markets as crucial to the economic recovery of Western Europe. That economic connection, which had factored so prominently in America's gravitation toward an activist policy in 1949–50, faded in importance as European revitalization moved from hope to reality by the early and mid-1950s.

The other economic, psychological, political, and geostrategic considerations underpinning earlier commitments remained firmly entrenched in the thinking of the U.S. policy-making establishment, however. Added to those, by the middle of the decade, was a fresh worry: it concerned evidence that a major alteration in the Cold War strategy of the Soviet Union was under way.

A New Kind of Threat?

The death of Joseph Stalin on March 5, 1953, did not usher in any immediate changes in the tenor or direction of Soviet foreign policy. Nor did Stalin's demise lead to any fundamental transformation in a Cold War that had dominated and polarized international affairs ever since the late 1940s. Soviet Premier Georgi Malenkov, soon to be ousted in an internal Kremlin power struggle, did set off a temporary flurry of concern among U.S. policy analysts by stressing, in the spring of 1953, the need for an amicable resolution of outstanding East-West issues. Eisenhower administration planners worried that the Malenkov "peace offensive," as they dubbed it, might signify the emergence of a more adroit and flexible adversary than that of the past. They breathed a collective sigh of relief, consequently, when the arrow of conciliation quickly disappeared from the Soviet quiver. By early 1955 it suddenly reappeared, this time as part of a fresh Cold War strategic departure engineered by the new Soviet strongman, Communist Party Secretary Nikita S. Khrushchev. Pledging a commitment to peace, diplomacy, negotiation, and accommodation, Moscow appeared to be metamorphosing into a very different kind of enemy.[2]

American analysts remained as suspicious as ever about Soviet motives. They were convinced that their principal rival was simply altering tactics, not changing fundamental goals. According to a reappraisal of overall U.S. national security policy, prepared by Eisenhower's National Security Council and approved by the president on January 7, 1955, the Soviet Union "has not modified its basic hostility toward the non-Communist world, and especially toward the U.S. as the power center of that world, or its belief in the ultimate triumph of Communism." It was turning from confrontation to conciliation, instead, out of a cynical conviction that conciliation offered the "most effective present tactic for dividing the free world and isolating the U.S. from its allies." Among other initiatives, the Soviets, during the first half of 1955 alone, signed an Austrian peace treaty that provided for the withdrawal of their troops from that country, sought a rapprochement with Yugoslavia, offered a disarmament proposal to the West that represented a significant modification of earlier positions, and accepted a Western offer to hold a summit meeting with leaders of the United States, Britain, and France.[3]

Although policymakers in Washington concentrated initially on the threat that the Soviet diplomatic offensive posed to the cohesiveness of the Western alliance, by the fall of 1955 they were focusing on what appeared an equally ominous trend: friendly Soviet overtures toward the uncommitted nations of the Third World. Those overtures included, most notably, generous aid and trade offers that Moscow was beginning to dangle before many of the non-aligned countries of Asia, Africa, and the Middle East. On November 1, 1955, the CIA circulated an intelligence assessment that identified Moscow's more conciliatory global foreign policy, and particularly its newfound interest in the Third World, as the most salient new factor in East-West relations. A "grave danger" existed, the report warned, that the new policy being pursued by Moscow and, to a much lesser extent, Beijing, "will create an even more serious threat to the Free World than did Stalin's aggressive postwar policies."[4]

Intelligence analysts in the United States were certainly correct in ascertaining that significant changes were taking place in Soviet foreign policy. The post-Stalinist leadership's emphasis on pursuing peaceful coexistence with the West, adjudicating outstanding diplomatic disputes, repairing bridges to Eastern European allies, and forging closer ties to Third World states did, in fact, represent a fundamental departure from past policies. Nowhere was this more striking than in Moscow's approach to the Third World. Under Stalin the Kremlin had adopted a rigid "two camps" theory which left no more room for neutrality in the Cold War than did the "you-are-with-us-or-you-are-against-us" mentality of the United States. Stalin and his fellow ideologues had regularly denounced nonaligned states such as India, Egypt, and Indonesia as bourgeois puppets of the West; rather than seeking mutually beneficial connections with such contemptible regimes, the Stalinist approach to the Third World inclined instead toward building up local communist parties as the most reliable instruments of Soviet influence. Now, under the leadership of Khrushchev and Premier Nikolai Bulganin, the Soviets were pursuing a more flexible, more active, and far more adroit approach.

The bold and flamboyant Khrushchev, the principal architect of this new strategy, was convinced that the careful cultivation of close ties with the Third World's nonaligned regimes, and a corresponding de-emphasis on Moscow's links to opposition communist parties, could enhance the global position of the Soviet Union. An inveterate opportunist and risk-taker, Khrushchev saw multiple advantages in so brazen a departure from Stalinist orthodoxy. The ideological rigidity of the past had, after all, allowed the West to seize the initiative in much of the developing world, leading to the encirclement of the Soviet Union with such U.S.-initiated alliance systems as SEATO and the Baghdad Pact. Khrushchev believed that the active pursuit of Third World friends through liberal aid and trade offers could bolster the neutralist inclinations of many of the newly emerging states, thereby diluting the military and economic strength that the West derived from its ties to the developing nations. The Soviet Union, in addition, could accumulate a string of potential strategic and economic assets for itself while ending its international isolation and demonstrating to the rest of the world that it had become a truly global power.[5]

As a doctrinal rationalization for this new policy, Khrushchev posited a world separated into two zones: a zone of peace and a zone of war. The capaciousness of the "peace zone" category enabled the Soviets to embrace even capitalist-leaning Third World states as worthy partners—so long as their policies and interests dovetailed with those of the Soviet Union. By that logic, the Soviets could—and did—offer warm support for the embryonic nonaligned movement. "The peoples of the Soviet Union understand fully the struggle of the nations of Asia and Africa against any form of colonial domination and economic dependence," announced Deputy Foreign Minister Vasily V. Kuznetsov on the eve of the historic Bandung Conference of April 1955, the first major gathering of the newly emergent nations of Asia and Africa.[6] During a closed plenum of the Communist Party's Central Committee, Khrushchev maintained that the developing world now represented the main arena of East-West competition.[7]

What made this opening to the Third World so attractive to Khrushchev, and what so worried U.S. analysts about it, was that the Soviet Union seemed to possess a number of distinct advantages over the West in any competition for the loyalties of the emerging postcolonial societies of Asia and Africa. Lingering anticolonial sentiments, deep-seated resentments toward the West, a series of emotionally charged regional disputes, an abiding desire for rapid economic development—all made Third World areas highly susceptible to Soviet overtures. Many Third World leaders and intellectuals both admired and sought to emulate the Soviet developmental model. In little more than a generation, Lenin, Stalin, and their compatriots had transformed a backward, underdeveloped country into a military-industrial powerhouse. How could the architects of Third World development help but take notice? The Soviet Union, moreover, remained unsullied on the all-important colonial question—an Achilles' heal of crippling proportions for the Western powers. Nor did the persistent efforts of the United States to highlight the tyranny and brutality of Soviet communism meet with much success amongst peoples who considered the exercise of European imperial and neocolonial authority to be far more tyrannical and brutal. The Soviets, furthermore, could help new, financially strapped regimes satisfy a desperate need for external assistance, a need that the United States seemed either unable or unwilling fully to meet.

By the end of 1955, senior officials in Washington consequently displayed heightened concern about the widening circle of Soviet diplomatic and economic activities in the Third World. On November 15, Director of Central Intelligence Allen Dulles brought the problem before the National Security Council. The CIA, he reported, had recently pieced together all available information concerning Soviet offers of economic assistance in South Asia, Southeast Asia, and the Middle East. Analyzed collectively, these various moves revealed what Dulles called "a pattern of coordinated long-term and high-level operations designed to advance Communist influence in all these areas." The agency found evidence that in recent months "the Soviet bloc" had extended offers of economic support to India, Afghanistan, Indonesia, Burma, Syria, Lebanon, Iran, and Turkey.[8]

What especially discomfited the intelligence chief was that many Third World nations seemed inclined to accept not only rubles from Moscow but the efficacy of the Soviet development model as well. Impressed with the Soviet Union's economic progress under a statist, command-style economy, they had come to believe that the Soviet system "might have more to offer in the way of quick results than the US system." Although Dulles noted that in their totality the Soviet promises of aid remained quite modest, he feared that they might nonetheless undermine U.S. influence throughout the developing world. Calling the report an "eye-opener," Vice President Richard M. Nixon remarked that the Soviet economic offensive raised "very painful alternatives" for the United States.[9]

On November 21, the NSC considered some of those alternatives in an unfocused, yet revealing, discussion. After listening to Allen Dulles's attempt to explain once again why the Soviet development model appealed to so many Third World states, Eisenhower suggested that an increase in the foreign aid budget might help check the inroads that the Soviets appeared to be making in the Third World. Eisenhower called foreign assistance programs "the cheapest insurance in the world" and recommended that the United States keep extra contingency funds on hand so that it could respond rapidly to Soviet initiatives. John Foster Dulles heartily concurred. Placing the problem in its broadest context, the secretary of state declared that "the scene of the battle between the free world and the Communist world was shifting." Therefore, the United States and its allies "must be prepared henceforth to meet much more serious Soviet economic competition."[10]

One of the areas where they faced particularly stiff competition, plainly, was Southeast Asia. The United States, as a consequence, made the promotion of Southeast Asia's economic growth one of its top regional priorities. Rapid capitalist economic development, U.S. planners were convinced, would innoculate Southeast Asian societies against the communist virus in two ways: by alleviating the hunger, poverty, and despair that typically served as the strongest allies of communist recruiters; and by proving the superiority of the capitalist path to development over the communist/socialist route. Such growth would also provide Japan with the markets and raw materials upon which its economic recovery seemed to hinge. In each of these respects, Vietnam posed the most immediate, and most urgent, regional challenge for U.S. policymakers during the mid-1950s.

The South Vietnamese Experiment

With the collapse in 1954 of the French military effort in Indochina, the Eisenhower administration increasingly fixated on that part of Vietnam lying south of the seventeenth parallel. Labeled a "regroupment zone" in the prosaic terminology of the Geneva agreement, South Vietnam appeared to U.S. officials as the indispensable key to the entire Southeast Asian region. Other areas, to be sure—certainly Indonesia with its wealth of natural resources and the Philippines with its crucial base sites—possessed greater intrinsic value. But in no other part of Southeast Asia did the threat of a communist breakthrough appear so imminent. Unless a viable noncommunist regime could be established quickly in the south, Vietnam would almost certainly soon be unified—either through violent or nonviolent means—under Ho Chi Minh's leadership.

Ho's broad popularity among the Vietnamese people, north and south, his impeccable credentials as a patriot, and his stature as the heroic conqueror of the detested French made him the prohibitive favorite to win the free, nationwide election scheduled by the Geneva Accords for 1956. U.S. officials were keenly aware of that reality, as they were of the fact that a Vietnam reunified under Ho would mean a communist Vietnam. The regional and global implications of such an occurrence were what most troubled them. American strategists were convinced that Vietnam's unification under a communist regime would deal a severe geopolitical and psychological blow to the prestige and credibility of the United States, embolden China and the Soviet Union, undermine the independence of other states in the region, rock Japan, and ravage SEATO.[11]

The Eisenhower administration determined that, in view of such dire possibilities, the establishment of a viable noncommunist regime in South Vietnam must be its highest regional priority. Yet, as Eisenhower, Dulles, and their chief foreign policy advisers freely acknowledged, the prospects for success there were hardly promising. The Saigon regime that emerged, by mid-1954, from the smoldering ashes of French colonialism possessed none of the standard prerequisites for statehood. It lacked a distinctive national identity, had no meaningful military or coercive power, held the slimmest imaginable claim to popular legitimacy, and suffered from a dearth of leadership.

Into this quicksand stepped Ngo Dinh Diem, appointed prime minister by a desperate Emperor Bao Dai in June 1954, just as the Geneva negotiations were entering their final phase. The son of a court official at the imperial city of Hue, the Catholic Diem was a Vietnamese rarity: a French-speaking aristocrat with strong credentials as both a nationalist and an anticolonialist. Even Ho recognized the strength of his nationalist credentials, offering Diem a cabinet post within his fledgling Democratic Republic of Vietnam in 1945 only to have the adamantly anticommunist Diem reject the position out of hand. Diem subsequently fled Vietnam, spending the final years of the French-Vietnamese conflict abroad, including a sojourn at a Maryknoll seminary in New Jersey.

With mixed emotions, the Eisenhower administration rallied to Diem's side. U.S. experts were aware from the beginning of the new prime minister's weaknesses; his aloofness, rigidity, and authoritarian tendencies were well known and much discussed. Worse, Diem aroused substantial opposition from within the military and bureaucracy while attracting minimal support from the people he aspired to rule. General "indifference and skepticism" greeted his accession, the ranking U.S. diplomat in Saigon recorded at the time. The prime minister's strong anticommunist views, his personal integrity and honesty, and the powerful political friends he had cultivated during his years in the United States partially counterbalanced his manifold shortcomings. More to the point, though, as one U.S. official put it, Washington had to back Diem because there was "no one else."[12] Quipped another: "We are prepared to accept the seemingly ridiculous prospect that this yogi-like mystic could assume the charge he is apparently about to undertake only because the standard set by his predecessors is so low."[13]

The Eisenhower administration's support for Diem, tentative at first, hardened after the watershed sect crisis of April 1955. Eisenhower sent wartime colleague Gen. J. Lawton "Lightning Joe" Collins to Saigon in November 1954 as his personal representative. Collins's principal responsibilities included establishing a decent working relationship with the soon-to-depart French authorities, overseeing the development of South Vietnam's military and bureaucratic institutions, and, not least, assessing Diem's strengths, weaknesses, and future potential. The imperious prime minister struck the notoriously blunt and tough-minded Collins as a poor bet. Convinced that he lacked the dynamic leadership qualities essential to South Vietnam's nation-building struggle, Collins urged Eisenhower in the spring of 1955 to withdraw U.S. backing from Diem in favor of one of several alternative South Vietnamese political figures. Persuaded by Collins's withering criticisms of Diem that the prospects for South Vietnam's survival would actually improve if he were removed from the scene, Secretary of State Dulles agreed to instruct the American Embassy in Saigon to cooperate with a group of South Vietnamese coup plotters. At the very moment that those instructions were being transmitted from Washington to Saigon, Diem launched with unprecedented speed, resolution, and force a military campaign against the religious sects and criminal syndicates that stood as his main rivals for power. The prime minister's surprising success in crushing the sects, with an able assist from CIA agent and confidante Col. Edward G. Lansdale, overnight transformed Diem in American eyes from an incompetent autocrat to the "miracle man" and "savior" of Southeast Asia.[14]

Following the sect crisis, the Eisenhower administration's embrace of Diem grew unreserved. With the final withdrawal of the French by the close of 1955, the United States had become his regime's indispensable patron. By the end of the decade, South Vietnam ranked as the fifth leading recipient of U.S. aid worldwide, receiving approximately $250 million in U.S. support annually. There were by then more than 1,500 Americans in South Vietnam advising the government in one capacity or another; fittingly, the American Embassy in Saigon stood as the largest U.S. diplomatic mission in the world. Political leaders of both parties rallied to the South Vietnamese cause, which began assuming the trappings of an ideological crusade. South Vietnam, declared Sen. John F. Kennedy in 1956, "represents the cornerstone of the Free World in Southeast Asia, the keystone in the arch, the finger in the dike." Without a strong anticommunist ally there, the "red tide of communism" would spread inexorably throughout the region. "It is our offspring," the Massachusetts Democrat proclaimed, "we cannot abandon it, we cannot ignore its needs."[15]

South Vietnam had, indeed, become America's "offspring" in countless respects. Yet therein lay a basic problem for both nations. American aid dollars, technical know-how, consumer products, and military advisers flowed into the struggling young nation throughout the second half of the 1950s, helping keep the Diem regime afloat. But those props, however necessary, also fostered an inevitably dependent relationship between Washington and Saigon. Between 1955 and 1961 the United States contributed on average 58 percent of South Vietnam's overall budget. The Saigon regime, lamented one of Diem's former tax advisers at the end of the decade, was fast becoming a permanent mendicant.

The South Vietnamese government's dependence on its Western patron undercut the regime's legitimacy while circumscribing its bid for popular support. Diem's personality and policies compounded the problem. Although he accepted the outer trappings of democratic governance, Diem actually ruled as an old-fashioned despot, relying for support on a small, unrepresentative clique of Catholics, wealthy merchants, and large landowners, along with select members of his own family. The economic interests of those key backers militated against any program of substantive socioeconomic reforms, as did the conservative prime minister's own inclinations. Diem provided next to nothing to the millions of his landless and land-poor countrymen, many of whose material aspirations had been stirred by the land reform agenda of the Viet Minh. To those peasants, intellectuals, and others who opposed his regime, and their numbers grew as its repressive, undemocratic character increasingly became evident, Diem promised swift and often brutal retribution.[16]

Beginning slowly in 1957, and growing steadily throughout the next several years, a guerrilla insurgency arose to challenge the Diem government. Some of the fighters were dedicated communist cadres, Viet Minh veterans who had stayed south after the 1954 cease-fire; others were new recruits to the cause, embittered by one or more of Diem's actions. Throughout 1957 and 1958 the North Vietnamese Politboro engaged in a series of wrenching debates about whether to support this new insurgency. The debates pitted those who considered the construction of a socialist state in the north an overriding priority against those who insisted that the North Vietnamese must come to the assistance of, and assert control over, their revolutionary brethren in the south. With the prospects for peaceful unification foreclosed by Diem's unilateral abrogation of the scheduled 1956 elections, the latter group ultimately prevailed. President Ho Chi Minh had, after all, never wavered from his goal of reunifying the country under his leadership. Northern support and guidance gave the southern revolutionaries a much-needed boost. The "Viet Cong," as Diem derisively tagged them, killed more than 2,500 government officials in 1960 and began shifting from hit-and-run operations to full-scale military assaults on government installations.[17]

Those ominous developments deeply alarmed U.S. observers. The United States had invested considerable money and prestige in the experiment of nation-building in South Vietnam. It had done so because of the acute concern that virtually all U.S. policymakers shared about the dangerous regional and global consequences that would likely follow a communist victory in

Vietnam. Despite all the administration's efforts, communist guerrillas had now plainly seized the initiative, in the process baldly exposing the fragility of America's "offspring." At an NSC meeting of May 1960, Eisenhower remarked that "the U.S. ought to do everything possible to prevent the deterioration of the situation in South Vietnam. We had rescued this country from a fate worse than death and it would be bad to lose it at this stage."[18] But he was not prepared to sever the U.S. connection to Diem, despite the pleas of some State Department experts, nor was he willing even to contemplate the dispatch of U.S. combat forces to help check the insurgency. Eisenhower's days in office were numbered by then, of course. Worse, he confronted a mounting insurgency by the communist Pathet Lao in bordering Laos that seemed of even greater moment than the Viet Cong threat. Neither the South Vietnamese nor the Laotian crises could be resolved on his watch. Each would have to await decisions by his successor, as he confided to John F. Kennedy during his briefing of the president-elect after the November 1960 elections.

Combating Communism in Laos, Neutralism in Cambodia

It is one of the great ironies of postwar American foreign policy that tiny, landlocked Laos vaulted to the very top of U.S. national security concerns in the late 1950s and early 1960s. A country of barely three million people, Laos has been aptly characterized by journalist Bernard Fall as "neither a geographical, nor an ethnic, nor social entity, but merely a political convenience."[19] Vientiane, the capital and largest city, numbered a mere 35,000 residents; yet it boasted the only paved roads in the entire country. With few schools, Laos had an illiteracy rate of approximately 90 percent. The mountainous kingdom, traditionally a buffer zone and frequent source of contention between the more powerful and aggressive Vietnamese and Thais, possessed few of the basic prerequisites for statehood. Among other problems, the poor, overwhelmingly agricultural land encompassed so diverse a collection of ethnic and linguistic groupings that "a multicolored ethnographic map of Laos," one observer quipped, "resembles a Jackson Pollock painting."[20]

Laos emerged as an independent nation-state, along with Cambodia, as a result of the Geneva Accords of 1954. Although Laotians played but a minor role in the nationalist struggle against French colonial rule in Indochina, they inevitably were drawn into the bloody eight-year conflict that erupted in 1946. The French and the Viet Minh came to prize the rugged Laotian hill country as a useful part of what each treated as a single, integrated theater of war. It is of no small significance that the French fortress at Dienbienphu, whose destruction at the hands of the Viet Minh became the war's climactic battle, was emplaced to help cut the strategic supply routes between Laos and Vietnam.

In 1950 the Pathet Lao were formed as the Laotian counterpart to the Viet Minh. Led by former members of Ho Chi Minh's Indochina Communist Party, the Pathet Lao forged a loose alliance with the Viet Minh, an alliance cemented by personal ties, common detestation of French colonialism, and a parallel commitment to socioeconomic transformation. At war's end, the continuing presence of an armed, committed, guerrilla force of approximately 25,000 troops stood as a major obstacle to the political cohesion sought by traditional Laotian elites.

The great powers who convened at Geneva in 1954 treated Laos and Cambodia largely as afterthoughts. The settlement reached there, nonetheless, significantly shaped the future of both former French colonies. Laos, like Cambodia, was recognized by the Geneva signatories as a unified, independent state that was to remain free from undue foreign influence. Under the terms of the settlement, the Pathet Lao guerrilla forces were required to regroup to the two northern provinces of Sam Neua and Phong Saly pending either their demobilization or their integration into the Royal Lao Army.[21]

The newly constituted government in Vientiane, searching for the surest path to an independent and secure existence, initially opted to pursue a neutralist course externally and an accommodative course internally. The key architect of those policies was Prince Souvanna Phouma, prime minister in 1954 and on several subsequent occasions. Souvanna wanted Laos to avoid foreign entanglements while moving to integrate fully the Pathet Lao, headed by his half-brother Prince Souphanouvong, into the new state's administrative and defense apparatus. His approach pointed logically to a coalition government that would include some communist Pathet Lao elements, in at least a minority status.[22]

That approach, coupled with Souvanna's friendly visits to Moscow and Beijing in 1956, sparked strong opposition from the Eisenhower administration. What made eminent sense from the perspective of an underdeveloped, weak, and insecure state whose politics had long been dominated by a few dozen families, looked very different from the perspective of a superpower committed to the containment of communism on every front. American involvement in Laos grew steadily throughout the mid- and late-1950s, coincident with the deepening commitment to the Diem regime in South Vietnam. U.S. aid became the principal prop behind the Royal Lao Army, a force whose anticommunist inclinations can be considered both cause and effect of the rapid inflow of U.S. dollars. When the Pathet Lao won thirteen of fifty-nine legislative seats in the national elections of May 1958, the Eisenhower administration grew alarmed. "It would be a serious matter," the president remarked at a subsequent meeting of the NSC, "if any country such as Laos went Communist by the legal vote of its people." To prevent such an outcome, U.S. representatives encouraged right-wing Laotian military officers to enter the political fray more directly.[23]

With covert U.S. encouragement, the pliant, pro-American Gen. Phoui Sananikone challenged Souvanna, successfully ousting the latter as prime minister in August 1958. Over the next twelve months, Prime Minister Phoui reversed Souvanna's neutralist course; most significantly, he repudiated the prince's opening to the Pathet Lao. In May 1959, Phoui ordered that all Pathet Lao units must be integrated forthwith into the Royal Lao Army. Fearing destruction, the Pathet Lao leaders refused to comply; two months later they launched a military counteroffensive against government troops and installations. Civil war quickly ensued, an unintended by-product of the U.S.-inspired rightward movement of the Phoui regime.[24]

Lao politics quickly grew so complex and convoluted that few outsiders, American or otherwise, could keep straight the different contenders for power or the rapid shifts in the local political landscape. Suffice it to say that a series of coups, countercoups, arrests, escapes, personal rivalries, internal intrigues, and external interventions left the country hopelessly divided. By the end of 1960 a new, U.S.-supported leader had fought his way to power in Vientiane, thanks in good part to American advisers, Thai technicians, and CIA air support. After toppling the phoenix-like Souvanna Phouma, Gen. Phoumi Nosovan prepared to do battle with his communist-neutralist adversaries, now concentrated in the Plain of Jars area to the north of the capital. Those forces, led still by the Pathet Lao, had begun to receive weapons and ammunition courtesy of Moscow, airlifted in Soviet planes.[25]

The Laotian civil war thus increasingly assumed global Cold War significance. That beleaguered nation, the State Department claimed in a published white paper, constituted "a front line of the free world."[26] In December 1960, Washington and Moscow publicly accused each other of interfering in the affairs of Laos. Those accusations were, of course, correct. Both superpowers *were* interfering in the affairs of Laos: the United States because it could not reconcile itself to a communist or neutralist government there, the Soviet Union because it could not abide the loss of influence and prestige that would accompany the U.S.-sponsored suppression of a friendly, peoples' liberation movement. The danger of a direct Soviet-American confrontation in the jungles and mountains of Laos grew with each day. Yet neither patron would countenance a halt to this proxy war. "We cannot let Laos fall to the communists," Eisenhower told his National Security Council on December 31, "even if we have to fight . . . with our allies or without them."[27] Several weeks later, he advised president-elect Kennedy that Laos was the "key to Indochina" and that the United States should "intervene unilaterally," if necessary, to prevent a communist takeover.[28]

Developments in Cambodia at this time, if not placid, were considerably less chaotic than in neighboring Laos. That part of Indochina, as a result, attracted substantially less U.S. concern and involvement. The pragmatic Prince Norodom Sihanouk dominated political life within Cambodia throughout the 1950s as no single figure in Laos ever could, and the common language, history, Buddhist faith, and respect for the monarchy that united the Khmer peoples made for a far more cohesive polity there. The hereditary ruler of the kingdom, Sihanouk assumed the trappings of power while still a high school student; real power, of course, continued to be held by the French. Early in 1953, however, Sihanouk began pressing the French aggressively for a genuine grant of independence, a move that enhanced the prince's nationalist credentials while earning him the respect and gratitude of his long-suppressed countrymen. The French reluctantly complied by the end of the year, largely because the politically astute Sihanouk managed to present himself as the only viable alternative to a communist-dominated Cambodia. The presence of at least 10,000 Viet Minh infiltrators in Cambodia by 1953, coupled with Sihanouk's threat to join forces with them if France remained recalcitrant on Cambodian self-rule, forced the issue. The Geneva Accords, concluded half a year later, provided formal, great-power recognition of Sihanouk's regime.[29]

U.S. policy toward the newly independent regime in Phnom Penh was complicated from the outset by the ambivalent and conflicted attitudes that Americans harbored toward Sihanouk. The mercurial, tough-minded Cambodian monarch refused to fit into the pliant, anticommunist mold that Eisenhower and his top advisers so clearly preferred in Third World leaders. Sihanouk's regular and insistent proclamations about Cambodian neutrality, his friendly visits to the Soviet Union and China in 1956, his decision to recognize Beijing in 1958, and his too-frequent public criticisms of the United States all rankled administration officials. They had hoped, of course, to foster as unequivocally pro-American a government in Phnom Penh as that in Bangkok. But Cambodia, plainly, was no Thailand. Sihanouk, like Souvanna Phouma in Laos, was convinced that national—and personal—self-preservation required a stance of at least nominal neutrality. He was more than willing to accept American aid (and he gratefully received $160 million in U.S. military assistance between 1955 and 1959)—but only on his own terms.[30]

The Eisenhower administration ultimately came to accept the unalterable character of Cambodia's fiercely independent, nonaligned foreign policy. At least Sihanouk was a staunch anticommunist who not only brought much-needed stability to his corner of Indochina but actually welcomed a direct U.S. military presence. Those, from the American perspective, were major assets. Ambassador Robert McClintock effectively summed up the case for a flexible and tolerant U.S. approach to Sihanouk. "It seems to us," he argued in March 1956, "that [the] basic issue is not whether Cambodia is neutralist or more positively in [the] Western bloc, but whether Cambodia can be denied to Communism. I am less concerned about Cambodia joining SEATO than that it maintain armed neutrality against Communist aggression with American aid." It should not be forgotten, McClintock noted, that Cambodia was "the only neutralist nation on earth" which had accepted a U.S. Military Assistance Advisory Group and was tied to the United States by a mutual defense assistance agreement.[31] "Let us walk quietly and turn the inert force of Asiatic neutralism against its ultimate enemy which is communism," he advised in a subsequent cable. "This may be making a virtue of necessity but there is no harm in using the shield before we use the sword."[32]

The road to acceptance of McClintock's logic proved anything but smooth, to be sure. The United States cautioned Sihanouk repeatedly about what it considered an insufficiently vigilant attitude toward communism, actively considered cutting off aid to Cambodia as punishment for his presumed transgressions, and angrily recalled its ambassador after Phnom Penh's recognition of Beijing. Most grievously, Washington failed to distance itself from a series of attempted coups hatched against Sihanouk in 1958 and 1959 by the Thais and the South Vietnamese, one of which nearly killed Sihanouk and his mother when a bomb exploded inside the royal palace at Phnom Penh. Eisenhower sought to assuage Sihanouk's suspicions by assuring him that the United States would do everything within its power to restrain its Thai and South Vietnamese allies.[33] Those assurances came rather late in the game, however. For his part, Sihanouk remained decidedly wary of a superpower whose aid he needed but whose words of support he could never take at face value. That Cambodia's and America's interests did not always run along parallel tracks had long been obvious to this prudent leader of a country surrounded by enemies. Which international direction he would tack Cambodia's sails toward in the future would depend less on his personal ideological convictions than on the course of developments elsewhere in the region.[34]

Indonesia and the Limits of Intervention

Throughout the mid-1950s the Eisenhower administration viewed Indonesian political trends with a curious combination of guarded hope and fear of impending disaster. On the one hand, U.S. policymakers decried the intensely nationalistic, anti-Western attitudes that were so prevalent throughout the country. The much-ballyhooed gathering of the nonaligned nations at the central Java city of Bandung in April 1955 well symbolized Indonesia's continuing search for a leadership role within the emerging neutralist bloc. U.S. analysts worried even more about the growing internal strength and legitimacy of the Indonesian Communist Party (PKI). On the other hand, they recognized that powerful anticommunist forces served as a check on PKI influence, especially within the army, the national police, the bureaucracy, and the two major Muslim political parties—the Masjumi and the Nahdatul Ulama.[35]

American predictions about Indonesia's future during these years of political crisis and change tended to veer from one pole to another. The fall of the Ali Sastroamidjojo cabinet in August 1955 led to a temporary burst of false optimism. U.S. observers were elated at the departure of a ministry whose leftist policies and toleration of the PKI had driven a wedge between Washington and Jakarta. The "alterations of the last forty-eight hours in the political climate," exulted Ambassador Hugh Cumming, "are little short of breathtaking."[36] He and other Indonesia specialists in the State Department and the CIA believed the important parliamentary elections of October 1955 would further that positive trend. They expected the conservative, Western-leaning Masjumi party to triumph at the polls and to form a cabinet favorably disposed toward U.S. economic aid and toward American Cold War foreign policies.[37]

Those confident projections missed the mark. The Indonesian electorate instead fractured, giving a slim plurality to the conservative, religious parties but also rewarding the PKI with 16 percent of the vote (20.8 percent on the main island of Java). "There is no question," conceded a dejected Cumming, "that [the] results are somewhat disappointing from our viewpoint and that of our most reliable friends here."[38] Most problematic, from the American point of view, was that the election gave the unpredictable Sukarno increased stature, power, and influence. CIA director Allen Dulles forecast that the Indonesian president would use his enhanced political position to "play along with the Indonesian Communists."[39]

In large part because of that fear, Eisenhower approved Dulles's recommendation that Sukarno be invited to visit the United States. A formal state visit offered a number of potential benefits—and few risks. The Indonesian leader, Dulles pointed out, will likely "continue to exercise an important, if not decisive, role in determining the internal structure and political orientation of the developing Indonesian state." Since he appeared not to be irrevocably committed to a leftist course, moreover, a series of face-to-face meetings in Washington and a subsequent tour of the country might "broaden his outlook and increase his understanding."[40]

From Sukarno's initial arrival in Washington on May 16, 1956, to his departure from Hawaii seventeen days later, everything went according to plan. American officials experienced firsthand the charming Sukarno's cooperative, ingratiating side. For his part, he got to meet a number of female film stars during his stay in Hollywood (though his favorite, Ava Gardner, was out of the country) and was treated to a personal tour of California's Disneyland by none other than Walt Disney himself. The Indonesian's evident fascination with America delighted his hosts almost as much as did his private denunciations of communism. So impressed were U.S. officials with the results of the Sukarno trip that in the summer of 1956 the Eisenhower administration quietly approved $25 million in developmental assistance for Indonesia's struggling economy. "The picture in Indonesia is more favorable in terms of U.S.-Indonesia relations than it has been for some time," applauded Assistant Secretary of State Walter Robertson.[41] Although Ali Sastroamidjojo had regained the prime ministership in early 1956, this time the Nationalist Party leader pointedly excluded PKI members and their sympathizers from key posts. Both Prime Minister Ali and President Sukarno seemed more inclined than before to rely upon the anticommunist and noncommunist parties as their principal base of support. U.S. policymakers thought they were witnessing the dawning of a new era in Indonesian-American relations.[42]

Their reading of Indonesia's opaque political scene once again missed the mark, however. On September 15, 1956, the Soviet Union reached a tentative agreement with Indonesia to provide a $100 million credit for unspecified aid projects, part of Communist Party Chairman Nikita Khrushchev's broader campaign for gaining influence among the Third World's nonaligned states. News of the Soviet loan reached Washington simultaneously with bulletins concerning Sukarno's critical comments about capitalism and the West during state visits to the Soviet Union and China. Those developments deeply unsettled the same Eisenhower administration officials who had so recently been trumpeting what they identified as an evolving pro-Western trend within Indonesia. Their dismay increased when the ever-unpredictable Sukarno delivered a fiery address on October 30 that called for the dissolution of Indonesia's political parties as a first step toward rebuilding national unity and strength. On February 22, 1957, Sukarno followed up that speech with an even stronger denunciation of parliamentary democracy, calling for its replacement with what he vaguely termed a system of "guided democracy."[43]

Even worse, from the American perspective, those developments were being played out against the backdrop of a wave of regional revolts that had plunged Indonesia into its most serious internal crisis since independence. Between December 1956 and March 1957, Army commanders in North, Central, and South Sumatra and in Eastern Indonesia formed local "councils" that in turn issued proclamations defying the authority of the central government. The bloodless coups were led by army officers dissatisfied with poor living conditions, inadequate pay, outmoded equipment, and the cumbersome organizational structure of the nation's military hierarchy. They were supported by substantial portions of the civilian populace in those outer islands who resented Javanese domination of the central government and who wanted greater local control of government and finances. Economic problems, rife throughout the far-flung archipelago, were particularly acute in the outer islands. Residents of resource-rich Sumatra, where the rebellions originated, were especially frustrated by their island's failure to receive economic benefits commensurate to its contribution to overall national revenues.

Sukarno's guided democracy concept was designed in large measure to defuse the simmering regional crisis. He proposed the formation of a national council to be composed of representatives of all the political parties within parliament, augmented by representatives from the country's various "functional groups," such as labor, the military, veterans' organizations, and youth groups. The council, according to the president's ill-defined plan, would offer advice—presumably mandatory—to the cabinet and parliament. Sukarno was wagering that the inclusiveness of such a supra-governing body might not only short-circuit the divided and fractious legislature but also restore some of the spirit of national unity that had dissipated following independence. To that end, he also deliberately stoked the embers of popular patriotic and anticolonial feelings by refocusing attention on Indonesia's claims to Dutch-ruled West Irian and formally repudiating Indonesia's debt to the Netherlands.[44]

Allen Dulles informed the National Security Council on February 28, 1957, that Indonesian developments "had taken a dramatic turn," creating a "critical situation" for the United States. The CIA chief, hitting upon the cardinal concern of U.S. officials, emphasized that the PKI would be represented on the all-powerful advisory council Sukarno was forming, enabling the party to ensconce itself formally within the state's administrative and legislative apparatus.[45] Five days later, the Intelligence Advisory Committee chaired by Dulles offered an even more alarming appraisal of the budding Indonesian crisis. It predicted that the regional insurgencies, "in conjunction with Sukarno's willingness to accept Communist support, will continue to offer excellent opportunities for the Communists to improve their position and have the potential of leading to major civil disturbances, an attempted coup d'etat, or political fragmentation of the Indonesian Republic."[46]

U.S. analysts worried increasingly about Indonesia's ability to hold itself together as a unitary state. In a meeting with Australian Foreign Minister Richard G. Casey, John Foster Dulles said he actually expected Indonesia to break apart, with "some form of loose-jointed federation" eventually emerging. The West, he quickly added, should be ready to help shape Indonesia's future political structure since the communists, who were "past masters" at such matters, would surely be competitors.[47]

Their apprehension about the future shape and orientation of the Indonesian state preoccupied senior Eisenhower administration strategists throughout the remainder of 1957 and into 1958. They engaged in regular and intensive discussions throughout that period about how best to further U.S. interests in a confusing and rapidly changing political environment. Unable to curb the tide of regional dissidence, on March 13 the Ali Sastroamidjojo cabinet resigned. The very next day, Sukarno declared martial law throughout the entire archipelago. In the immediate wake of those momentous developments, Allen Dulles framed for the NSC the key policy question the United States now faced. What, he asked, should it do "in the event that Sukarno proves unable to pull the situation together and all the outlying islands break away from Java and become independent entities?" U.S. policymakers "would be up against a very tough problem," observed Eisenhower, "if we ever had to face the contingency of recognizing several governments in the Indonesia area."[48] At a subsequent meeting of the NSC, on August 1, the president returned to that crucial issue. Boiling the problem down to what he considered its essence, Eisenhower declared: "The best course would be to hold all Indonesia in the Free World. The next best course would be to hold Sumatra if Java goes Communist."[49]

U.S. experts increasingly doubted their ability to "hold all Indonesia in the Free World." Quite to the contrary, the CIA predicted that Indonesia's communist party would continue to expand its power and influence. If relations between the central government and the provinces worsened, moreover, "the Communists as the best organized group have a good opportunity to seize control of Java."[50] To a generation of policy planners haunted by the prospect of communist gains anywhere across the globe, that was a terrifying possibility indeed. They were agreed that the emergence of a communist Indonesia, or even a communist Java, would carry grave implications for U.S. security. "In the short run," observed an interagency committee formed to assess the crisis, "the most important implications of a Communist takeover on Java would be psychological and political. The general position of non-Communists in Asia would be weakened as the non-Communist states of Southeast Asia would feel themselves squeezed between Communist China and Communist Viet-Nam on the north, and Communist Java on the south." It added that the longer term impact would be equally serious since "from bases on Java, [Soviet] bloc military forces could threaten directly Malaya, Singapore, British Borneo, the Philippines, New Guinea, and Australia." If the communists gained eventual control of the entire Indonesian archipelago, the report continued, "the U.S. strategic posture in Southeast Asia and the Southwest Pacific would be jeopardized." To avert those strategic catastrophes, the committee recommended that the United States covertly support anticommunist elements on the outer islands, in particular the rebellious military commanders from Sumatra and Sulawesi (Celebes) who were currently defying the central government.[51]

Eisenhower approved that recommendation at an NSC meeting of September 23, setting the stage for one of the most misguided, ill-conceived, and ultimately counterproductive covert operations of the entire Cold War era. The operation was based on a series of dubious assumptions about the Indonesian situation. One held, as Assistant Secretary Robertson phrased it, that "time is running in favor of the Communists and against us." Another posited that Sukarno had reached "the point of no return," and hence efforts to moderate his behavior by any means short of force were doomed to fail. Still another identified the rebellious military chieftains in Sumatra and Sulawesi as strong, popular figures capable of resisting central authority indefinitely and, if need dictated, leading their fellow outer-islanders to establish sovereign states independent of the Jakarta regime.[52]

The American effort to remake Indonesia for its own purposes failed on a grand scale. The details of the covert operation, as is true of so many Cold War cloak-and-dagger affairs, remain shrouded in mystery. The basic outlines of U.S. policy are, nonetheless, quite clear. A State Department memorandum of January 2, 1958, described that policy succinctly as follows: "The U.S. should employ all feasible covert means to strengthen the anti-Communist forces in the outer islands in order through their strength to affect favorably the situation in Java and to provide a rallying point if the Communists should take over Java." The memorandum also referred obliquely to "more forthright means" that would have to be employed "if the situation in Java continues to deteriorate." Those "more forthright means" included clandestine U.S. financial and military support for the regional dissidents, one group of whom proclaimed on February 15 an independent Revolutionary Government of the Republic of Indonesia (PRRI).[53] U.S. officials had exaggerated the political appeal and martial prowess of the rebels, however, much as they had underestimated the unifying power of Indonesian nationalism. The armed forces, under the able leadership of Army Gen. Abdul Haris Nasution, backed the central government fully. In a matter of months, those forces had routed the U.S.-backed dissidents on Sumatra and Sulawesi. In the process, they exposed the American role, seizing not only large caches of U.S. weapons in rebel territory but capturing pilot Allen Pope, a CIA agent shot down while flying a bombing mission for the dissidents.

Washington had supported the losing side in a civil war and, Eisenhower's disingenuous denials to the contrary, been caught red-handed doing so. What was widely condemned throughout Indonesia as neocolonialist intervention aroused the ire of nationalists of all political hues. Recalled former Indonesian Foreign Minister Anak Agung: "The general opinion in Indonesia was unanimous that the CIA had a hand in the rebellion"; this suspicion "was to linger on for a long time and was the main cause of further deterioration in Indonesia-US relations, despite the effort of the US government to bring some improvement."[54]

In the aftermath of its disastrous intervention in Indonesia's civil war, the Eisenhower administration tried desperately, and with some limited success, to repair its relations with Jakarta. Following the advice of newly appointed Ambassador Howard P. Jones, Washington initiated a program of military assistance to the Indonesian armed forces in mid-1958. The rationale for the program was that the Indonesian military was strongly anticommunist and, partly as a result of its impressive performance during the rebellion, had emerged as a rival center of power. The Eisenhower administration hoped that it could bolster the position of the military as a counterforce to Sukarno and the PKI; the orientation of the all-important Indonesian Army, headed by the influential and vigorously anticommunist Nasution, was a key to this strategy. Jones predicted that an eventual clash between the army and the PKI was virtually inevitable.

The new policy direction, while infinitely more farsighted than the previous one, met with little immediate success. West Irian remained a major stumbling block, as the United States refused to depart from its neutral position, which amounted to nothing less than support for the status quo—that is, continued Dutch control. American aid to the Indonesian military, moreover, was cautiously limited. When Nasution visited Washington in October 1960, American officials informed him that they simply could not meet his substantial arms requests. The Soviets were more generous. In January 1961 he traveled to Moscow and signed a major arms agreement with the Soviet Union, a development that once again aroused American fears. Washington worried, in particular, that the Indonesians might use this new Soviet equipment, as Sukarno had repeatedly warned, in an effort to liberate West Irian from Dutch rule.[55]

A Different Kind of Threat in the Philippines

The Philippines posed a challenge of a radically different sort to the Eisenhower administration. The specter of the Chinese and Soviets gaining influence through the vehicle of a powerful indigenous communist party never materialized there. Nor did a flamboyant nationalist crusader of Sukarno's ilk emerge to mobilize the masses against the depredations of Western imperialism. Quite to the contrary, America's former colony remained anchored in the Western camp throughout the 1950s. A charter member of SEATO, formed not coincidentally during a conference at Manila, the Philippines supported American Cold War policies down the line. Ramon Magsaysay, the Philippine president from 1953 until his untimely death in an airplane crash in 1957, ranked among the staunchest anticommunists anywhere in the Third World.

The Philippines appeared, in short, to be a model ally. The image it evoked most typically in the American mind was that of the grateful, loyal, reliable partner. Washington policymakers even hoped that other Asian states might learn about the manifold benefits of formal ties with the United States from the Philippine case. From Washington's perspective, those benefits appeared ample: U.S. military bases in the islands provided Filipinos with money, jobs, and security; American aid dollars underwrote important development projects; and favored access to American markets stimulated the Philippine economy, enriching in the process well-placed local exporters and entrepreneurs.

Beneath the surface harmony in Filipino-American relations, however, roiled undercurrents of profound discontent. Filipino elites resented their dependence on Washington, bristled at the hauteur and arrogance of their former colonial overlords, and defined material, political, and security interests in ways that ofttimes conflicted with those of their American counterparts. As a result, an increasingly assertive nationalism emerged during the 1950s, centered especially among prominent Filipino politicians, landowners, and businessmen. That nationalism challenged the complacent American assumption that the Philippines would long remain content in its role of client state to the benevolent superpower patron.[56]

The U.S. desire to expand and improve its military base system in the Philippines provided the spark that ignited the subsequent nationalist firestorm. Throughout 1953 and early 1954 its sprawling complex of bases in the Philippines assumed ever greater military and strategic salience to the United States. Clark Air Force Base had emerged by that time not only as an important transshipment point for U.S. military equipment being sent to bolster the French war effort in Indochina, but also as the most likely staging ground for any U.S. aerial assault on Viet Minh or Chinese Communist positions. Similarly, U.S. naval bases in the Philippines were by then providing crucial logistical support to the Seventh Fleet's operations throughout the South China Sea. Mindful of the growing importance of Philippine bases to the projection of American power in the Pacific, the Pentagon determined in early 1954 that additional land and facilities needed to be acquired to make those bases more efficient and secure. Uncertain how best to approach the Philippine government with such a request, and fearful of a budget-minded Congress' likely opposition to new land purchases, the Eisenhower administration made a major tactical blunder. On February 11, 1954, just before the opening of formal negotiations on the proposed expansion of U.S. bases, Ambassador Raymond Spruance presented Philippine officials with a legal opinion, written by Attorney General Herbert Brownell, which asserted the U.S. claim to hold legal title over existing bases in the Philippines. It fell like a bombshell across the political landscape of the Philippines.[57]

The Brownell memorandum incited a wave of nationalistic vitriol against the presumptiveness and arrogance of the Americans. The ensuing outcry "bordered on the hysterical," according to a U.S. Embassy report. One Filipino political leader warned that the United States intended "to gobble us completely"; another said that the Americans might force Filipinos "to become strangers in their own land"; still another charged that the United States aimed to create "little Hong Kongs" in its former colony. The influential Philippine senator Claro Recto, author of the national constitution and a renowned legal scholar, drafted a formal rebuttal to the Brownell memorandum in which he accused the United States of seeking "an obnoxious extraterritoriality" that would impair "the status of the Republic." The Magsaysay administration abruptly canceled the scheduled base negotiations.[58]

The fury unleashed by the Brownell memorandum caught the Eisenhower administration off guard. Secretary of State Dulles at first dismissed the nationalist upsurge as a mere tactical maneuver by "cheap politicians" scheming either to bait Magsaysay before the 1955 election or to maximize the Filipino bargaining position vis-à-vis the United States. He predicted that the tempest would soon blow over.[59] Dulles was sorely mistaken. In fact, the broad-gauged Filipino condemnation of the Brownell memorandum represented something far deeper than a mere political ploy. It combined elite ambitions and fears, especially in the economic realm, with a burgeoning sense of national pride and long-simmering resentments toward and suspicions about the United States.

Taken together those forces have provided the principal wellspring for modern Filipino nationalism, a phenomenon that some scholars trace directly to the initial furor surrounding issuance of the controversial Brownell opinion. As in so many other postcolonial societies, Philippine nationalism derived in large measure from the ambiguous and conflicted relationship between a newly emerging nation-state and its former colonial sovereign. That relationship was unusually complex in the case of the United States and the Philippines. Manila looked to Washington as the chief guarantor of its security against external and internal threats, as an indispensable trading partner, and as a source of jobs, economic aid, and technical assistance. Yet the more the Philippines needed the United States, and the larger the American presence loomed in the islands, the more Philippine resentment at their still-dependent status grew; collaboration and resistance, attraction and repulsion—those contradictory impulses existed in uneasy harmony.[60]

The American bases certainly contributed to Philippine security while stimulating the local economy, as U.S. officials so frequently reminded their Filipino hosts, but not without a significant price. The "baselands," as they were called by the local population, encompassed tracts of territory so vast that Filipinos inevitably questioned the degree to which they compromised national sovereignty. Clark Air Force Base, for example, occupied 250 square miles, an area equivalent to Manhattan, Brooklyn, the Bronx, and Staten Island combined. Subic Bay Naval Station included within its boundaries an entire city, Olongapo, which contained sixty thousand Filipino citizens. Navy and Marine officers administered the municipality as if they were small-town mayors in the American heartland. In addition, the United States held claim to thirteen undeveloped and unused bases that comprised another five hundred square miles of Philippine land. Much of the land held by the United States was commercially valuable; some of it contained unexploited natural resources and mineral wealth. In the baselands, gambling and prostitution were rife and black marketeering in supplies from American PX's flourished.

In the wake of the Brownell memorandum, agitated Filipinos railed against the extent of U.S. base holdings and the privileged legal stature of U.S. military and civilian representatives within the country. Their intent was not solely to call attention to an affront to Philippine sovereignty. The wealthy landowners and industrialists who led the charge, along with their political allies, also feared that the U.S. base properties could undermine their own private commercial interests. Thus Recto emphasized economic concerns even more than those connected to national sovereignty in his broadside against the Brownell memorandum. Worried that the United States might use its military power to open Philippine markets to U.S. goods, in the process crippling infant Philippine manufacturing enterprises, he listed among the nationalist movement's main goals the "exploitation of our natural resources by Filipino capital" and the "development and strengthening of Filipino capitalism, not foreign capitalism."[61]

Other recent U.S. actions also contributed to Manila's unease about the intentions and reliability of its ally. Preoccupied with more critical Cold War hot spots, Congress cut U.S. aid to the Philippines in 1953 and 1954. Reduced levels of U.S. support ironically undercut the staunchly pro-American Magsaysay since he owed much of his elite-based support to the common assumption that he would attract more aid dollars from the United States than had his predecessors. Further, as the Cold War in Asia heated up, Filipino leaders grew more apprehensive about the possibility of American abandonment. The memories of the humiliating defeat of American forces at the hands of the Japanese invaders a decade earlier, after all, remained vivid. During the Manila conference of September 1954 that hatched SEATO, Magsaysay pressed Dulles hard for a firm U.S. pledge to retaliate swiftly against any aggressor. He gained the pledge he sought in the course of the treaty negotiations. Magsaysay and other Filipino leaders, nevertheless, fretted about what they considered needlessly provocative U.S. actions toward China; U.S. brinkmanship, they worried, might increase the risk of a Chinese-American military confrontation that would inevitably envelop the Philippines.[62]

Those various tributaries together helped form a nationalist stream that grew increasingly turbulent and powerful throughout the mid- and late-1950s, posing a major obstacle to the achievement of U.S. objectives in the Philippines. Given the importance of the Philippines to the overall U.S. defense posture in the Pacific, the Eisenhower administration recognized it had no choice but to adjust to changing political circumstances. That meant seeking to co-opt rather than trying to resist Philippine nationalist demands. In 1955 the United States renegotiated the Bell Trade Act of 1946, offering extremely generous trade concessions that managed to satisfy the diverse interests represented by Filipino industrialists, landowners, and exporters. The following year, Vice President Richard Nixon traveled to Manila to withdraw formally the controversial title claim contained in the Brownell memorandum. In the summer of 1956, a new U.S. negotiator arrived in the Philippines to reopen the long-stalled base negotiations, armed with instructions from Eisenhower to "bend over backwards" to accommodate Philippine demands.[63]

Those measures, while extraordinarily conciliatory from the perspective of decision-makers in Washington, failed to sufficiently placate political authorities in Manila. In 1957, Filipino-American base talks broke down once again. U.S. negotiators, wary about establishing too liberal a precedent for other host nations, staunchly resisted Philippine demands for control over criminal jurisdiction within the base areas. That emotional issue defied easy resolution. Violent clashes between Philippine citizens and American servicemen had long been common on the islands. The adamant U.S. refusal to permit its nationals to be tried in Philippine courts, no matter how serious the offense, deeply offended local sensibilities. The American position at best suggested a mistrust of the Philippine system of justice; at worst, it betrayed a lack of respect for Filipinos that verged on racism. The further reduction of U.S. economic aid to the Philippines during the late 1950s also strained relations between Washington and Manila. Carlos Garcia, the traditional-style Philippine politician who was elected in 1957 as Magsaysay's successor, pressed the Eisenhower administration continually for additional aid dollars—but to no avail. U.S. economic and military aid by the late 1950s was by then being funneled mostly into countries that Eisenhower administration strategists considered to be far more pressing priorities than the relatively quiescent Philippines.[64]

Filipino-American relations did not, to be sure, enter into a dangerous downward spiral at this time. Each side depended too much on the other for matters of tangible value to permit an open breach. Indeed, the two nations temporarily put aside their irreconcilable differences on the criminal jurisdiction issue and, in October 1959, reached an interim agreement on some of the other nettlesome base issues. Manila agreed to a U.S. enlargement of the Subic Bay and Sangley Point facilities, for example, while Washington agreed to shorten its ninety-nine-year leases to twenty-five-year leases, return sovereignty over Olongapo to the Philippine government, hand back unused bases, and prohibit the emplacement of ballistic missiles on any of its base sites. The pact did much to ease tensions between the two allies. The huge crowds that turned out to greet Eisenhower during his June 1960 visit to Manila testified eloquently to the respect and good will millions of ordinary Filipinos still had for the United States. Yet it is equally plain that a far more conflictual relationship between the United States and the Philippines was being forged during the second half of the 1950s as American strategic imperatives increasingly clashed with the imperatives of a newly aroused and assertive Filipino nationalism.[65]

Thailand: The "Hub" of U.S. Regional Policy

Thailand proved a somewhat less troublesome ally than the Philippines during this period, though U.S. observers still fretted periodically about the depth of Thailand's commitment to the West. Like the Filipinos, the Thais believed that their open alignment with the United States entitled them to more aid dollars than they were receiving; and like the Filipinos, the Thais thought their unequivocal embrace of the anticommunist cause entitled them to greater security assurances than they were obtaining. By the middle of 1955 the United States had provided Thailand with $140.9 million in military matériel, with another $64.8 million already programmed but not yet shipped. Those amounts not only fell well short of Thai expectations, but yearly allotments of military assistance seemed almost certain to be reduced in the future by congressional budget-cutters. The justifiable Thai complaint that nonaligned nations such as India often garnered more economic aid than did allied nations compounded the problem.

An equally sensitive security problem also strained Thai-American relations. Thailand had enthusiastically responded to Secretary of State Dulles's original call for "united action" in Southeast Asia, subsequently joining SEATO as a charter member. The Thais even managed to agitate successfully for the alliance to be officially headquartered at Bangkok. But the vagueness of SEATO's protective clauses failed to satisfy Thailand's need for a firm guarantee that the United States would defend its borders against China or other potential aggressors.[66]

Allen Dulles voiced the strongest U.S. concern when he noted in November 1955 that the diminution of U.S. aid, "coupled with [the] Thai realization that the Manila Pact provides them little real security, may well move Thailand in the direction of neutralism." He and other leading officials worried that the Thai leadership might temper its adamant anticommunism, adopt a more independent foreign policy, and move eventually toward a normalization of relations with Beijing and Moscow. Such moves could signify a reversion toward Thailand's "historical practice of 'bending with the wind.'"[67]

Much to the exasperation of the Eisenhower administration, the Phibun regime appeared heading in exactly that direction. In June 1956 Thailand announced that it would be resuming trade with China in nonstrategic commodities such as rice and timber. American protests fell on deaf ears; after all, other American allies, including Britain, had already taken such steps. In addition to the trade initiative, the Thai government lifted its prohibition on travel to China, arranged for a labor delegation, a basketball team, and a group of entertainers to tour the Chinese mainland, and permitted the commercial screening of Chinese films in Thailand. Although those moves were small, representing little more than a modest effort at rapprochement with Asia's military powerhouse, they unsettled U.S. officials who worried increasingly about their ability to hold any Asian nation within the anticommunist fold. "Thailand will probably continue a generally anti-Communist foreign policy, including association with the US in collective defense measures," concluded a CIA analysis of June 1957. "However, we believe Thailand's leaders will continue to modify their past policy of unequivocal alignment with the US and will probably seek to develop a more flexible foreign policy, particularly in respect to relations with Communist China."[68] Beginning in 1955, Prime Minister Phibun had allowed a degree of democratization and freedom of the press in an effort to undercut his two chief factional rivals: Sarit Thanarat, the army commander, and Phao Siyanon, the CIA-backed national police chief. The growing neutralist sentiment that resulted from that calculated political move demonstrated to American observers that democratic freedoms in Thailand were not compatible with the unequivocal political, military, and diplomatic support that Washington wanted from Bangkok.[69]

On September 16, 1957, Field Marshal Sarit engineered a bloodless coup that toppled Phibun's decade-old regime. Four days later Sarit assured U.S. Ambassador Max Bishop that Thailand would "strictly observe" its "old foreign policy" of "adherence to [the] UN and SEATO."[70] The political turmoil and uncertainty surrounding the coup nevertheless alarmed U.S. observers. Secretary of State Dulles emphasized that it raised doubts about the "continuing feasibility [of] our primary objective [of] maintain[ing] Thailand as [the] hub [of the] US security effort [in] Southeast Asia."[71] Those fears soon receded as Sarit, who remained Thailand's strongman over the next several years, made clear his government's unwavering commitment to the West. The colorful Sarit certainly had his share of personal peccadilloes. Those included an apparently insatiable sexual appetite, which he flaunted in an effort to impress countrymen with his presumed virility, and a penchant for consuming four or five "fifths" of scotch daily. Despite a "very disordered personal life," in the choice phrase of U.S. Ambassador U. Alexis Johnson, the authoritarian Sarit proved a reliably pro-American leader who maintained order at home while setting his nation's diplomatic compass in a decidedly Western direction.[72]

The emergence of a politically stable Thailand by the late 1950s, its latent neutralist tendencies held firmly in check, comported perfectly with American policy goals for the region. Ever since the initiation of U.S. military assistance programs in October 1950, strategists in Washington projected Thailand as the indispensable "hub" or "prop" for U.S. security efforts across Southeast Asia. That projected role remained a constant throughout the decade, which helps explain the trepidation with which U.S. analysts greeted any hint of a shift in Thailand's loyalties. The only SEATO ally on mainland Southeast Asia, Thailand gave the United States a staging ground for various region-wide military, intelligence, political, and psychological operations. Thai support was essential, for example, to Operation Paper of the early 1950s, the CIA-run plan for infiltrating Chinese Nationalist troops into southern China from their bases in Burma. The CIA also created at that same time an elite paramilitary force of Thai hilltribesmen for subsequent use in guerrilla-style operations in Indochina, and especially Laos.[73]

Other operations remain shrouded in mystery, though more than passing significance surely attaches to the fact that legendary World War II spymaster William "Wild Bill" Donovan and John F. Peurifoy, architect of the notorious CIA-sponsored coup of 1954 in Guatemala, followed each other as U.S. ambassadors to Thailand in the mid-1950s. We do know that Donovan pressed aggressively—if unsuccessfully—for the establishment of a permanent U.S. air base in Thailand and, with the Laos insurgency heating up in the late 1950s, one of his successors oversaw the construction of four airstrips in northern Thailand as emergency fields for U.S. medium-range strategic bombers. That successor, U. Alexis Johnson, recalled in his memoirs that Thailand's value to the United States derived especially from its geopolitical location. "Thailand was," he reflected, "the key member of SEATO on the Southeast Asian mainland, for if China or North Vietnam penetrated fragile Laos, Thailand was next on the road south to Malaya, Singapore, and the Straits of Malacca, to say nothing of Indonesia, the biggest and richest country of the area."[74]

On Christmas Eve 1960, Johnson struck a highly positive note in a year-end summary of the main trends in Thai-American relations. Sarit and his associates, the American envoy noted approvingly, had maintained a "more forthright free world posture" than their predecessors. Developments in

Thailand over the past five years, Johnson enthused, have "definitely been favorable to US interests." Although the Thais were "increasingly self-conscious" of the accusation that they were "too closely tied to [the] US and isolated from [their] neighbors" and hence might become more "self-assertive" in the future, that was not yet a major worry. "Thailand," he concluded with a characteristic rhetorical flourish, "represents an especially healthy and vigorous plant in the free world garden, but like all such plants its future growth will depend upon it receiving a sufficient amount [of] care, nourishment and attention. US policy must assure it receives such treatment. The cost is not high and the rewards can continue to be substantial."[75]

Burma and the Dilemmas of Aid

Burma's rulers, in sharp contrast to their counterparts in neighboring Thailand, continued to swear allegiance to the precepts of nonalignment and anticolonialism throughout the 1950s. Forged during the struggle for independence, those bedrock principles guided all of Burma's foreign policy decisions. They commanded such widespread popular support that any Burmese leader who might advocate a different diplomatic course ran the risk of public condemnation. That essential fact of Burmese political life, recognized in Washington as well as Rangoon, rendered a U.S.-Burmese alliance a virtual impossibility. It also made the acceptance of any military or economic assistance from the United States exceedingly problematic for Burma's ruling elite, especially if such aid even hinted at direct supervision or political strings of any kind. In January 1952, Burma briefly suspended all U.S. economic and military aid programs on precisely those grounds, only to terminate them completely a year later in the midst of the controversy surrounding the continued presence of U.S.-supported Chinese Nationalist troops within its borders.[76]

With Chinese troop evacuations well under way by the middle of 1954, the government of U Nu once again sought to open an arms supply relationship with the United States—albeit on its own terms. The Burmese made their overtures toward the United States in part to reduce their dependence on British sources of supply, in part to strengthen the ability of their armed forces to resist external aggression, and in part to obviate the need for Soviet matériel. U Nu and his associates made it clear, however, that Burma did not want grant assistance but rather the right to purchase arms from the United States on a (nominally) reimbursable basis. The Burmese, as one U.S. report put it, "must pay for what they get, for political reasons, and cannot pay more than a nominal price, for budgetary reasons."[77]

Burma's desire to secure U.S. weapons gave the Eisenhower administration what appeared to be a most welcome opportunity for regaining lost footing in that strategically located country. U.S. planners regarded Burma, which shared borders with both China and India, as a potentially valuable link in the containment shield. They were impressed with the strength and popularity of the U Nu regime, the vigor with which it was addressing internal problems, and not least with its staunch professions of anticommunism. A formally neutral Burma that leaned toward the West might even strengthen America's position with Asia's other uncommitted states, or so U.S. analysts speculated. By the same token, American diplomats believed that Burma had become a major target of Sino-Soviet diplomatic pressures and feared that, without external help from the United States, it might succumb to those pressures and draw away from the West altogether. In October 1954 the Eisenhower administration endorsed a plan to provide Burma with up to $20 million in reimbursable military hardware only to have the deal founder on Burmese skittishness. Burma's leaders worried that legislative mandates governing U.S. foreign assistance programs might compromise their precious freedom of action in international affairs.[78]

There matters stood until Moscow made an unexpectedly bold bid for closer ties with Rangoon. In early December 1955, Soviet Communist Party Chairman Khrushchev and Premier Bulganin traveled to Burma, part of a broader Asian diplomatic jaunt that also took them to India and Afghanistan. "For many decades alien colonialists oppressed you and robbed your country," proclaimed Khrushchev in Rangoon. "We are ready to assist your development so that the colonialists may never climb on your back again." The two Russian visitors, still uneasily sharing power in this early post-Stalinist period, proposed a solution to Burma's most pressing economic problem: they offered to purchase 400,000 tons of Burmese rice annually over the next four years on a barter basis. Since rice represented fully 80 percent of Burma's export trade, and the financially strapped young state was experiencing great difficulty finding markets for its surplus rice, the deal proved unusually alluring.[79]

U.S. observers were greatly alarmed at this Soviet economic offensive, as they quickly tagged it. Focused primarily on prominent nonaligned states such as Egypt, India, Indonesia, Afghanistan, and Burma, the generous aid and trade offers emanating from Moscow appeared to signal a major tactical shift in Soviet foreign policy; economic weapons might now be joining military ones in the Kremlin arsenal. Burma's economic vulnerability made it especially susceptible to the more flexible Khrushchev-Bulganin approach to the Third World. Warned Assistant Secretary of State Robertson: "The grave danger is arising that Burma may fall under Communist domination because of the success of Communist economic warfare tactics." He saw those tactics "steadily enveloping Burma in the Communist vise, despite Burmese intentions."[80] On April 1, 1956, Burma and the Soviet Union formalized the proposed trade agreement. Along with the rice barter provisions first discussed during the Khrushchev-Bulganin visit, the agreement promised Burma capital equipment, consumer goods, and technical assistance. Most worrisome from the American perspective, the deal lent a degree of credence to Robertson's fears, guaranteeing the Soviets "a very substantial long-run economic and commercial foothold in Burma."[81]

Burmese officials beseeched their American counterparts for U.S. economic and military assistance to offset and counterbalance the new Soviet connection. They insisted that Burma remained committed to freedom, independence, and nonalignment, feared Soviet and Chinese intentions, and would avoid joining the communist bloc at all costs. U.S. experts recognized the sincerity of those protestations and, over the next two years, the Eisenhower administration struggled to forge a bureaucratic consensus behind a concrete Burma aid program. In the economic realm, Washington offered modest developmental loans as well as technical advice and surplus agricultural commodities under the Public Law 480 program.[82] Military aid was far more complex and controversial on both sides. State Department Counselor Douglas MacArthur II stood on one extreme in the ensuing intra-administration debates about arms sales. Burma, he exclaimed, "has turned toward us for assistance to prevent it from becoming dependent on the Communist bloc. If we can *rapidly* exploit this situation, the effect on all the uncommitted and neutralist Arab-Asian States will be tremendous." Calling Burma's request for U.S. aid a "God-given opportunity" to reverse currently unfavorable international trends, MacArthur argued that Burma was "the key to the prevention of Communist domination of Southeast Asia."[83]

His State Department superiors accepted the essential logic of MacArthur's position, if in less hyperbolic terms. But Defense Department representatives proved considerably less enthusiastic. They pointed out that military aid to Burma, or any other neutralist nation, could sow dissension among America's allies. Why should neutrals be rewarded for their unwillingness to commit themselves to the West? JCS Chairman Arthur Radford framed the issue with characteristic bluntness. "We would never be able to retain our allies in Southeast Asia," he thundered, "if our allies felt that other countries were in a position to obtain U.S. assistance without ever joining any kind of an alliance with the United States."[84] Secretary of State Dulles countered that if the United States chose not to aid neutrals they would surely acquire such aid from the Soviets. At an NSC meeting of August 30, 1956, Eisenhower resolved that philosophical dispute in favor of the more pragmatic State Department position, authorizing the provision of military equipment to Burma at highly subsidized prices.[85]

Even so, nearly two more years elapsed before the United States and Burma could decide upon specific terms. Disputes arose over whether the arms to be provided would be "substantial," as Burma sought, or "modest," as the Eisenhower administration preferred, over the degree to which the receipt of U.S. weapons might compromise Burma's policy of nonalignment, over the precise terms of repayment, and over several other contentious matters. Finally, in June 1958 the two nations signed separate agreements that provided for a $10 million U.S. loan for the purchase of defense and police equipment and the provision of U.S. technical assistance in exchange for deferred payment in Burmese currency.[86]

For all the debate and anguish that preceded that commitment, it brought no essential change to the Burmese-American relationship. Burma did not tilt openly—or covertly—toward the West following the reestablishment of an aid relationship with the United States. Nor did it tilt openly in the direction of the communist powers. Burma, instead, continued to walk an international tightrope, clinging to neutralism as much for practical security reasons as for ideological ones. A small, embattled country, rent by internal divisions, surrounded by more powerful neighbors, and keenly aware from its World War II experience that ants can be crushed when elephants fight, Burma grasped nonalignment as a diplomatic liferaft in the uncertain waters of the Cold War. A military coup toppled U Nu from power in 1958, elevating Gen. Ne Win to the position of paramountcy that he would maintain for the next quarter century. The coup set in motion profound internal changes, but brought no alteration in Burma's external orientation. To the perpetual frustration of American observers, the Ne Win government simply followed established precedent by avoiding scrupulously any entanglement with the major power blocs. As one U.S. assessment accurately pointed out, its unwavering commitment to nonalignment "limits both the scope and mode of U.S. assistance to and influence in Burma."[87]

Malaya and Singapore

The United States exerted somewhat more influence with Malaya at this time, especially after the federation achieved full-fledged independence on August 31, 1957. The decidedly pro-Western orientation of Malaya's leaders, both before and after statehood, certainly generated much less anxiety among American decision-makers than did Burma's neutralism. Even so, U.S. observers cast a wary eye throughout the mid-1950s at what a senior CIA officer called the "rising tide of Communist subversive activity" there. Such activity was, in his judgment, "a direct reflection of developments elsewhere in Southeast Asia."[88]

On the positive side of the ledger, British and local forces had by 1955 almost completely suppressed the communist insurrection that had been raging throughout Malaya's jungles since 1948. On the negative side, communists remained active within the trade unions, schools, press, and political parties of both Malaya and Singapore. Their evident strength within the strategically located city of Singapore, whose majority ethnic Chinese population appeared very favorably disposed to the Chinese Communist regime, particularly distressed American observers. Britain's announcement on February 8, 1956, of its intention to grant Malaya independence at the end of August 1957 did not allay American concerns. "My personal opinion," Kenneth T. Young wrote Assistant Secretary Robertson, "is that Singapore is probably already lost and little can be done to save it from Communist domination in the near future. If this should occur the effect will, of course, be explosive in Malaya and all over Southeast Asia."[89]

Young's heightened sense of alarm derived from his conviction that the Malayan peninsula ranked as an area of substantial strategic and economic value to the West. He and most other top administration strategists viewed it as essential to the control of Southeast Asia's sea lanes. "The Japanese used Malaya as a steppingstone when they invaded the East Indies," noted an interdepartmental committee charged with assessing the potential threat there. "It could be used so again by an aggressor should its defense be neglected by the Free World." For U.S. analysts, strategic and economic concerns were tightly interwoven in Malaya, as they were throughout Southeast Asia. In their view, holding Malaya within the "Free World" meant retaining Western access to vitally important reserves of tin and rubber; in 1954, Malaya produced 32.4 percent of the world's natural rubber and 35 percent of its tin. It also meant ensuring Western control over the Indian Ocean and South China Sea, without which the resources of Southeast Asia could easily fall prey to Chinese or Soviet aggression. "The accretion to the communist bloc of the rubber, tin, and oil of this area would," moreover, "enormously increase [Chinese and Soviet] war potential."[90]

U.S. strategic thinkers worried as well about the politico-psychological effects of a Western failure to prevent communist gains in Malaya and Singapore. Such a failure could not only render SEATO impotent but could lessen appreciably the power of the West to influence events in Burma, Thailand, Indonesia, Laos, Cambodia, and Vietnam. "Indeed," the interdepartmental team concluded in December 1955, "the U.S. position throughout the Far East would be profoundly altered to the detriment of our interests."[91]

Those fears were abetted by political developments within Singapore. The electoral appeal of the leftist-oriented People's Action Party (PAP), ably led by general secretary Lee Kuan Yew, prompted grave, if misplaced, apprehension on the part of U.S. observers. In fact, the Americans completely misread Lee, seeing the intensely nationalistic leader as a radical demagogue who would facilitate communist penetration of the soon-to-be-independent city-state. "We are especially worried over the prospects of Lee coming to power," explained a U.S. diplomat in February 1959, "because we not only do not trust him but have great doubts that he could control the Left-wingers on whom his strength depends." When Lee's PAP achieved a landslide victory in the May 1959 general election, and he emerged soon thereafter as prime minister of the city-state's first independent government, the Eisenhower administration registered alarm about a turn of events that seemed seriously "adverse to US and free world interest." The administration soon softened those views, however, as the politically deft Lee moved to secure firm control over communist and other radical elements within the PAP coalition while managing to reassure U.S. officials that he was neither a wild-eyed radical nor a stalking horse for Beijing.[92]

By the end of the decade, then, U.S. fears about the communist threat to the Malayan peninsula had proven to be vastly exaggerated. The dangers that so exercised U.S. observers in the mid- and late-1950s simply never materialized. Instead, the emergence of Malaya as an independent nation-state in 1957, with Singapore following suit two years later, brought more rather than less stability to the region. The vigorously pro-Western foreign policy of Malaya's first prime minister, Tungku Abdul Rahman, especially pleased the Eisenhower administration, while the relative moderation displayed by Lee Kuan Yew removed a major source of American anxiety. The administration's earlier concerns about dangerous political trends and the potential for communist subversion throughout the peninsula gradually receded.[93]

Those concerns are suggestive, nonetheless, of the overall sense of impending regional crisis that pervaded U.S. policy circles throughout the 1954–1960 period. The exaggerated American alarm about the presumed communist threat to the Malayan peninsula stemmed from the abiding sense of insecurity and vulnerability shared by virtually all U.S. national security planners at this time. However misplaced that sense of insecurity and vulnerability might seem in retrospect, it exerted an irresistible influence on American perceptions and actions in Southeast Asia. The possibility of communist inroads in any one of the region's newly emerging states could, in the view of U.S. strategists, spread dangerous ripples throughout the region—and beyond. Indeed, few areas of the globe troubled Eisenhower, Dulles, and their chief advisers as much as Southeast Asia, and few areas brought such frenzied episodes of U.S. intervention. Ranging, at the extremes, from attempts to overthrow governments in Indonesia and Laos to efforts at nation-building in South Vietnam, the Eisenhower administration sought repeatedly to recast the face of Southeast Asia in an American image. Unfortunately, for both Americans and Southeast Asians, those efforts had just begun.

Like Truman and Eisenhower before him, President John F. Kennedy perceived critical U.S. interests at stake in Southeast Asia. Like his predecessors, the new chief executive believed that America's credibility as a global power lay on the line in that part of the world. He worried especially about Laos and Vietnam, where communist-led guerrilla movements were threatening to overthrow U.S.-backed regimes, and Indonesia, where the world's largest nonruling communist party seemed poised to effect a legal seizure of power. The growth of neutralist sentiment throughout the area and the growing misgivings about U.S. reliability on the part of allies such as Thailand and the Philippines further contributed to this image of Southeast Asia as an all-important Cold War testing ground.

The young Democratic president identified opportunities as well as problems in the region. Vesting Laos and Vietnam with great symbolic importance, he was determined that the United States demonstrate in both lands its unwavering commitment to contain communist advances along the Third World periphery. Activist by nature, he was equally determined to chart new policies toward the nonaligned states. The inflexible stance of Eisenhower and Dulles had needlessly alienated Indonesia and other key nonaligned states, Kennedy and his leading advisers reasoned; they were confident that a more tolerant and innovative approach could reverse that trend.

To fail in Indochina, on the other hand, would almost certainly lead adversaries and allies alike to doubt the power and question the resolve of the United States. To fail in Indochina, moreover, would almost certainly harm him politically. JFK was sure that outright victories on the part of either the Pathet Lao or the Viet Cong would be widely interpreted as defeats for the United States, diminishing his own stature as a world leader and inflicting considerable political damage on his presidency. Referring specifically to Vietnam, Kennedy confessed to a friend at one point: "I can't give up a piece of territory like that to the Communists and get the American people to reelect me."[1]

The Kennedy administration's sense of Southeast Asia's vital importance to the United States thus grew from many of the same calculations that had shaped policy during the Truman and Eisenhower years. Top administration planners, in fact, appear not to have critically reevaluated any of the basic premises upon which U.S. policy toward the area had been based since the late 1940s. Yet fundamental changes had taken place in the overall international picture in the intervening years. One of the earliest arguments for Southeast Asia's relevance to American national security, it will be recalled, stemmed from the important contribution that this primary producing region could make to the economic recoveries of Western Europe and Japan. Those commanding economic-strategic priorities, largely achieved by the time Kennedy entered office, factored far less prominently in U.S. thinking about Southeast Asia during the 1960s. In fact, Japan had, by the late 1950s, followed the Western European example and entered into a period of high-level sustained growth. Tokyo achieved more than a 12 per cent increase in its Gross National Product during each of the three years preceding Kennedy's entry into the White House. That phenomenal performance was fueled by a doubling in U.S.-Japanese trade between 1955 and 1960, demonstrating to U.S. planners that Japan's economic success was actually much less dependent on Southeast Asian markets and resources than they had previously believed.[2]

Another of the earliest arguments for Southeast Asia's relevance to American national security revolved around the presumed monolithic nature of the communist threat. That argument, too, had lost much of its potency with the increasingly acrimonious Sino-Soviet split, well evident by Kennedy's election.

Notwithstanding those fundamental changes, Kennedy and later Lyndon B. Johnson operated from the same core assumptions as had their predecessors. Although they placed greater weight on symbolic, psychological, and political factors in their decision-making than had either Truman or Eisenhower, both Democratic presidents continued to believe that adverse developments in Southeast Asia could harm vital U.S. national security objectives. All their subsequent actions flowed from that central premise.

Kennedy Draws the Line in Vietnam

During his less than one thousand days in office, John F. Kennedy nudged the United States ever closer to open warfare in Indochina. First, the new president carefully deliberated about, and nearly sanctioned, the use of U.S. ground troops in Laos, only to draw back from the precipice at the last moment and offer support for a Laotian neutralization scheme. Then, in the immediate aftermath of that decision, and partly to compensate for it, Kennedy substantially deepened the American commitment to neighboring South Vietnam. It was there, rather than in Laos, that JFK chose to draw the line in Southeast Asia.

Kennedy's commitments to the Saigon regime carried momentous consequences for the U.S. position in Southeast Asia—and well beyond. In order to help South Vietnam quell an increasingly effective communist insurgency, he increased the number of U.S. advisers from just under six hundred at the time that he assumed office to over sixteen thousand by the end of 1963. In addition, JFK permitted those advisers to participate in combat operations; authorized the profligate use of helicopters, napalm, and defoliants in fighting the Viet Cong insurgency; launched covert operations against North Vietnam; pronounced publicly America's unequivocal commitment to the preservation of a noncommunist South Vietnam; warned the Soviet Union to curtail its support for the guerrillas; and, after he grew disillusioned with Prime Minister Diem, encouraged the South Vietnamese military to assume power through extralegal means. Kennedy's assassination on November 22, 1963, and Lyndon B. Johnson's subsequent decision to escalate even more dramatically the national commitment in Vietnam have combined to raise intriguing but ultimately unresolvable questions about what path JFK would have followed had he lived.

The question of why Kennedy saw vital U.S. interests at risk in Indochina has sparked less controversy. As early as 1956, then-Senator Kennedy called South Vietnam "the cornerstone of the Free World in Southeast Asia," characterizing that struggling young nation as "a test of American responsibility and determination."[3] Even though he recognized that Vietnam's intrinsic economic and strategic value to the United States remained minimal, Kennedy and his top foreign policy advisers believed that it possessed incalculable symbolic value. The president and his senior aides feared that a communist victory in Vietnam would further embolden aggressive adversaries in Moscow and Beijing while leading its allies to doubt U.S. power and resolve. Further, Kennedy worried that a communist victory in Vietnam would spark an intensely divisive political debate at home, comparable to the "who lost China" inquisition that so damaged Truman a decade earlier. Thus international and domestic factors impelled Kennedy toward ever-greater involvement in Southeast Asia during his three years in the White House.[4]

Vietnam did not immediately emerge as a critical foreign policy concern for the new president. Cuba, the Congo, Berlin—all occupied far more of Kennedy's attention during his early months in office. So did another corner of Indochina. As Kennedy entered office, a dangerous civil war raged in Laos. With the United States and the Soviet Union each backing a different Lao political faction, the chances of a superpower confrontation there could not be discounted. Eisenhower warned Kennedy as much during several of the transition briefings he held for the president-elect in January 1961. Laos, he stressed, was "the present key to the entire area of South East Asia." Despite the obvious risk, observed the former general, U.S. combat troops might eventually be required to block a Pathet Lao triumph. Laos was "the cork in the bottle," added Secretary of State Christian Herter; if it fell, Thailand, the Philippines, and Taiwan would surely follow.[5]

Kennedy, like Eisenhower and Herter, saw tiny Laos as a central Cold War battleground, a test of wills between Washington and Moscow from which other powers, large and small, would draw lessons about the strength and staying power of each. Though it possessed no tangible strategic or economic significance, Laos had *become* critical through this curious logic of Cold War geopolitics. Just before Kennedy's inauguration, Khrushchev had provocatively declared the Kremlin's intention to support wars of national liberation in the Third World. The young American leader saw Laos, where the Soviet-backed Pathet Lao had gained the upper hand over the U.S.-backed Boun Oum regime, as an early test case of the Khrushchev doctrine. He vowed not to give ground or even appear vacillating in the face of so audacious a challenge. As the intelligence community reminded the new president, the stakes were high. The governments of Southeast Asia "tend to regard the Laotian crisis as a symbolic test of intentions, wills and strengths between the major powers of the West and the Communist Bloc," read one high-level assessment; a Pathet Lao triumph "would severely damage the US position and its influence in Thailand and South Vietnam."[6]

Fearing those domino-like consequences, JFK signaled to Moscow in March and April 1961, both through public and private channels, that he would stand behind the Boun Oum government—whatever the cost. "My fellow Americans, Laos is far away from America, but the world is small," he declared in a televised address to the American people of March 23. "Its 2 million peaceful people live in a country three times the size of Austria. The security of all of Southeast Asia will be endangered if Laos loses its neutral independence. Its own safety runs with the safety of us all—in real neutrality observed by all."[7] That alarmist rhetoric aimed to prepare the public for the possible dispatch of U.S. combat forces to Laos, an option Kennedy was seriously entertaining at the time. He was simultaneously weighing the potential benefits, and risks, of a negotiated settlement. The Joint Chiefs of Staff, who judged Laos a poor location from which to take a stand, advised Kennedy that to insure success of any military operation he needed to commit "120,000–140,000 men, with authority to use nuclear weapons if necessary."[8]

Distrustful of his uniformed Pentagon advisers in the wake of the Bay of Pigs fiasco, uncomfortable with the risks inherent in so large an operation, and convinced that South Vietnam would be a more effective place to draw the line against communist expansion in Southeast Asia, Kennedy pushed hard for a diplomatic settlement. That effort bore fruit with the convening of an international conference at Geneva in May 1961. The Geneva negotiations led eventually to a cease-fire, communist participation in a coalition government, and a nominal agreement between the United States and the Soviet Union to respect a neutralized Laos. Although the shortcomings of the Geneva agreement would soon become clear, Kennedy had at least averted full-scale military intervention—an eminently sensible move under the circumstances.

State Department expert William H. Sullivan, later appointed ambassador to Laos, has perhaps best summarized the tactical considerations that led the Kennedy White House in the end to choose conciliation over confrontation. "The attitude was that Laos was a secondary problem," Sullivan recalled.

> Laos was a poor place to get bogged down in because it was inland, had no access to the sea and no proper logistics lines . . . that it was rather inchoate as a nation; that the Lao were not fighters et cetera. While on the other hand if you were going to have a confrontation, the place to have it was in Vietnam because it did have logistical access to the sea and therefore, we had military advantages. It was an articulated, functioning nation. Its troops were tigers and real fighters. And, therefore, the advantages would be on our side to have a confrontation and showdown in Vietnam and not get sucked into this Laos operation.[9]

In a curious way, the Laotian neutralization initiative actually undermined the prospects for a similar compromise in Vietnam. Acutely conscious of images, Kennedy was fearful that political foes at home would attack him unmercifully if he pursued conciliation once again in Vietnam. Already under withering criticism for the earlier debacle at the Bay of Pigs and what many considered a political setback in Laos, JFK determined to avoid any additional Cold War defeats or retreats. Consequently, in May 1961, coincident with the opening of the Geneva sessions on Laos, he authorized a modest increase in the number of advisers attached to the U.S. Military Assistance Advisory Group in Vietnam. He also dispatched four hundred Special Forces units, or Green Berets, to help train the South Vietnamese military in counterinsurgency techniques.

That modest increase in U.S. support did little, however, to ease the panoply of problems facing the Diem regime. In September 1961, Diem urgently requested a significant increase in U.S. economic assistance. The growing strength and boldness of the Viet Cong guerrillas, who already controlled more than 50 percent of the South Vietnamese countryside, prompted Diem's request. It forced a painful set of decisions on the ever-cautious Kennedy. Fearing that an allied government's very survival might be hanging in the balance, yet instinctively reluctant to permit an open-ended expansion in the American commitment, Kennedy dispatched trusted military adviser Gen. Maxwell D. Taylor and National Security Council aide Walt W. Rostow to Saigon to provide him with a firsthand report.

The Taylor-Rostow assessment proved sobering. The two analysts recommended the immediate dispatch of an 8,000-man logistical task force as a minimal step in order to prevent the collapse of the Saigon regime, with the caveat that more drastic measures might be required in the near future. During the administration's extended deliberations about the Taylor-Rostow report, several advisers, including the Joint Chiefs of Staff, urged the dispatch of regular combat troops. Others urged the president to seek a negotiated settlement similar to that pursued in Laos. Kennedy rejected the combat force option as "a last resort." He also opposed staunchly any neutralization scheme as a potentially dangerous sign of American weakness. Instead, the president chose a middle course, opting to increase the number of American advisers and the volume of American aid in the hopes that those steps would bolster the South Vietnamese government sufficiently to preclude the need for regular U.S. combat units.[10]

Kennedy's limited commitment of November 1961 postponed, but did not resolve, the core problems facing America's ally in South Vietnam. Over the next year, his middle course brought greater American influence to bear on the conduct of military operations in Vietnam. U.S. equipment and expertise lent valuable assistance to the counterinsurgency campaign of the South Vietnamese Army, enabling it to gain the initiative for the first time. Upon the urging of U.S. advisers, Saigon also inaugurated a strategic hamlet program to separate and protect the peasantry from the Viet Cong and their North Vietnamese allies, a program that served as a political adjunct to the military effort. In tandem, the new American-aided initiatives appeared to yield at least modest progress throughout 1962, generating optimistic forecasts about the Diem government's prospects among many top U.S. experts. Yet that military-political progress soon proved illusory; by early 1963 the insurgents had once again seized the initiative. Moreover, the growing dependence of the Diem government on the United States led to increased tension, resentment, and bitterness between Washington and Saigon.

Early in 1963, Kennedy sent Assistant Secretary of State Roger Hilsman and National Security Council staffer Michael Forrestal to South Vietnam to gauge the efficacy of the U.S. program. Upon their return, they sent Kennedy an appraisal that mixed frank criticism of the current situation with cautious optimism about the future. The Hilsman-Forrestal report questioned the effectiveness of the South Vietnamese Army, the degree to which the strategic hamlet program was being successfully implemented, and the level of popular support for Diem. Although Hilsman and Forrestal concluded that the United States and South Vietnam were "probably winning" the conflict, they cautioned that the war would "probably last longer than we would like" and "cost more in terms of both lives and money than we had anticipated." Still, for all its harsh criticisms about the leadership and efficiency of the Diem regime, the Hilsman-Forrestal report gave Kennedy no hint of impending crisis. The president consequently saw no need to redirect or even reassess U.S. policy; at that juncture, he viewed the conflict in Southeast Asia as primarily an operational problem.[11]

The complacent assumptions undergirding Kennedy's approach to Vietnam were decisively shattered in the spring and summer of 1963. A series of demonstrations against Diem's dictatorial rule, led by Buddhists, students, and other disaffected groups within South Vietnam, crystallized for Kennedy and his foreign policy experts the depth of the internal opposition to Diem. The prime minister's heavy-handed response to those protests, capped in August by brutal government-sanctioned raids on Buddhist pagodas, plunged South Vietnamese society into chaos. Even more alarming, from Kennedy's perspective, were the indications that Diem was seriously considering negotiations with the National Liberation Front, the political arm of the Viet Cong insurgency.

A consensus soon developed among the president, most of his top national security aides in Washington, and Ambassador Henry Cabot Lodge in Saigon that Diem posed a fundamental obstacle to the achievement of U.S. objectives in Vietnam. Diem's removal was necessary, pontificated Lodge, to bring "this medieval country into the 20th century."[12] Kennedy accordingly authorized Lodge to cooperate in August with a group of South Vietnamese officers who were plotting a coup against the prime minister.

That plot proved abortive, but in November another group of coup planners asked for U.S. backing. His advisers divided on the question of how the United States should respond, Kennedy struck a characteristic middle course, ordering that American representatives neither directly encourage nor discourage the plotters. The anti-Diem generals almost certainly interpreted that ambiguous signal as a green light for their plans. On November 1, 1963, the military intriguers seized power, in the process murdering Diem and his brother, Ngo Dinh Nhu. The brutal double slaying greatly disturbed Kennedy, who doubtless accepted a degree of personal responsibility for the deaths. Ironically, only three weeks later the president himself was murdered in Dallas.[13]

The question of how Kennedy would have responded to the mounting political turmoil that gripped postcoup South Vietnam has divided analysts of the Vietnam War ever since. Just before his fateful trip to Dallas, the president made a few statements that betrayed a growing skepticism about U.S. involvement in Vietnam; he even ordered a modest reduction in the number of U.S. advisers stationed there. On the other hand, there is no evidence that JFK had ever reexamined the cardinal assumption on which U.S. involvement had been based—namely, that the preservation of a noncommunist South Vietnam was vital to American global interests. Indeed, Lyndon Johnson rightly noted that Kennedy, during his final months in office, "had not revised his assessment of our role there or of the importance of South Vietnam to Southeast Asia and our own security. He continued to believe that the conquest of Southeast Asia would have the most serious impact on Asia and us."[14]

LBJ's Decisions for War

It was not Kennedy, of course, who brought the United States into a major land war in Asia. JFK may have taken the nation to the very threshold of war, but it was LBJ who crossed that threshold. When Johnson assumed the reins of power, approximately 16,000 U.S. military personnel were stationed in South Vietnam, none in a direct combat role. The U.S. mission up to then remained strictly an advisory one. By the end of 1965 the number of U.S. military personnel had mushroomed to over 180,000, soon to top the half-million mark. In the intervening months, LBJ had ordered a sustained bombing campaign against North Vietnam, authorized aggressive U.S. land and air operations against Viet Cong and North Vietnamese units in the south, and reduced South Vietnamese generals and politicians to the role of bit players in the struggle engulfing their homeland. The Vietnam conflict cannot fairly be termed LBJ's war, as the president's critics sometimes labeled it; within a year and a half of Kennedy's assassination, though, the Johnson administration had most definitely transformed it into America's war.

In light of the profound consequences that flowed from LBJ's decisions to escalate and Americanize the war in Vietnam, it is hardly surprising that those decisions have been subjected to seemingly endless critical scrutiny. Why did Johnson and his principal advisers choose to make so open-ended a commitment to the preservation of a noncommunist government in South Vietnam? How did they come to equate the survival of a corrupt, unpopular, unstable, and faction-ridden regime with the protection of America's own national security? What fears lay behind Johnson's actions? And why was his administration not more prudent in view of the long odds against outright politico-military success in Vietnam and the obvious risks—at home and abroad—of failure? For all the differences in emphasis and nuance that mark individual scholarly explorations of those fundamental questions, the now voluminous historical literature on LBJ's decisions for war paints a fairly clear and consistent portrait of a president haunted by fears about the nightmarish consequences of a communist victory.

For Johnson, as for Kennedy before him, an interconnected set of international and domestic concerns made the very thought of defeat in Vietnam unacceptable. Like Kennedy, Johnson subscribed to a worldview that equated communist success in any corner of the globe with a significant diminution in U.S. credibility. Widespread domino effects, according to this mindset, would surely follow a communist breakthrough in South Vietnam. They would reverberate across the entire Asia-Pacific region; and they would in turn drastically undermine America's global position. Virtually all of Johnson's principal national security advisers accepted those premises. As early as May 1961, following a vice-presidential tour of Vietnam, Johnson himself had urged JFK in a private memorandum that "the battle against communism must be joined in Southeast Asia with strength and determination to achieve success there—or the United States, inevitably, must surrender the Pacific and take up our defenses on our own shores."[15]

Nothing had occurred in the interim to force a reconsideration of the assumptions undergirding that apocalyptic scenario. Indeed, in March 1964, less than four months after entering the White House, Johnson approved a new policy position on Vietnam rooted in the same logic as his 1961 reflections. It identified the results certain to flow from an American failure to maintain an independent noncommunist South Vietnam as follows:

Unless we can achieve this objective in South Vietnam, almost all of Southeast Asia will probably fall under Communist dominance (all of Vietnam, Laos, and Cambodia), accommodate to Communism so as to remove effective U.S. and anti-Communist influence (Burma), or fall under the domination of forces not now explicitly Communist but likely then to become so (Indonesia taking over Malaysia). Thailand might hold for a period without help, but would be under grave pressure. Even the Philippines would become shaky, and the threat to India on the West, Australia and New Zealand to the South, and Taiwan, Korea, and Japan to the North and East would be greatly increased.[16]

Johnson's fears about the international consequences of defeat in Vietnam merged with a parallel set of fears concerning the impact such a setback would have at home—to be specific, on his presidency, on his political party, on his ability to govern, and on his prospects for achieving the ambitious legislative program he sought to enact. LBJ was convinced that he would be pilloried by the political right if the South Vietnamese regime collapsed, rendering his administration ineffectual and killing the domestic reform agenda, the so-called Great Society, that constituted his overarching goal as president. Johnson worried, according to political adviser Jack Valenti, that Republicans and conservative Democrats together would have "torn him in pieces" had he failed to hold the line against communism in Vietnam.[17] "I knew Harry Truman and Dean Acheson had lost their effectiveness from the day that the Communists took over in China," he confided to biographer Doris Kearns. "I believed that the loss of China had played a large role in the rise of Joe McCarthy. And I knew that all these problems, taken together, were chickenshit compared with what might happen if we lost Vietnam."[18]

Much has been made by biographers of the stark contrasts between the elegant, patrician, self-assured Kennedy and the rough-hewn, earthy, insecure Johnson. For all their differences in background, style, and temperament, however, the two men held remarkably similar views about the stakes at risk in Vietnam—for themselves personally and for the country at large. The intensely political Johnson, to be sure, may have placed somewhat greater weight than did Kennedy on the domestic side of the equation. Even so, their assessments of Vietnam's importance as a foreign policy-cum-political issue bear a striking resemblance. Moreover, the foreign policy advisers whose judgment the two chief executives most valued were one and same. Included among the trusted inner circle of each were Secretary of Defense Robert S. McNamara, National Security Adviser McGeorge Bundy, Secretary of State Dean Rusk, and Gen. Maxwell Taylor. Throughout the critical period from 1964 to early 1965, every one of those men counseled Johnson on the need for U.S. escalation.

Johnson, unburdening himself to a friend, described the dilemma he confronted in characteristically colorful language. "I knew from the start that I was bound to be crucified either way I moved," he said. "If I left the woman I really loved—the Great Society—in order to get involved with that bitch of a war on the other side of the world, then I would lose everything at home. All my programs. . . . But if I left that war and let the Communists take over South Vietnam, then I would be seen as a coward and my nation would be seen as an appeaser, and we would both find it impossible to accomplish anything for anybody anywhere on the entire globe."[19]

LBJ spoke in a similar vein to McGeorge Bundy, early in his presidency. In an unguarded exchange, captured verbatim by his secret White House tape recorder, a frustrated Johnson spelled out the no-win situation he faced. "I don't see what we can ever hope to get out of there with, once we're committed," he confided. "I don't think it's worth fighting for and I don't think we can get out. It's the biggest damn mess I ever saw." Gazing with uncanny accuracy into the future, LBJ added: "It's damn easy to get in a war but it's gonna be awfully hard to ever extricate ourself if you get in."[20]

It was the steady deterioration of the situation on the ground in South Vietnam, politically and militarily, that forced that painful dilemma on Johnson. The less drastic options open to Kennedy—moderate expansion of the U.S. advisory role, increased aid dollars, and the like—were simply no longer feasible. They had been tried and had proven insufficient. Those officials who had predicted that a change at the top would stabilize the Saigon regime and reenergize its military efforts against the Viet Cong were quickly disabused of such notions as well. South Vietnam suffered from a spate of palace intrigues and coups in the post-Diem period. No fewer than nine different governments emerged during the chaotic year that followed the toppling of Diem. None of them claimed appreciable popular support, and none proved able to check an insurgency that boasted control over fully one half of the territory and population of the south. "And so it really boils down to one or two decisions," lamented Johnson in February 1964, "—getting out or getting in."[21]

By early 1964, Johnson's leading military and civilian advisers had concluded that only two measures could conceivably prevent the imminence of a communist victory: increased pressure against the north, including full-scale aerial bombardment; or the deployment of U.S. combat troops in the south. Yet the president initially refused to approve either escalatory option. Instead, following a full-scale policy review in March 1964, he ordered little more than a beefed-up version of the Kennedy program, dispatching more U.S. military advisers (bringing the total up to 23,000 by the end of the year) and additional aid dollars. With an election pending, the politically astute Johnson was determined to postpone any painful decisions likely to cost him votes; expanded military involvement in Southeast Asia clearly fell into that category. To cover his flank, Johnson did direct his military planners to ready, for possible future use, a series of specific and detailed actions designed to turn the tide in South Vietnam—but those plans were to be kept under wraps until after the election.[22]

The campaign unfolded largely according to Johnson's script. His opponent, Arizona's Republican Sen. Barry Goldwater, a loose-tongued hawk, proved a perfect foil for Johnson's centrist, peace-focused candidacy. Then, in August 1964, just three months before the election, an episode occurred in the murky waters of the Tonkin Gulf that wound up further strengthening Johnson's hand.

On August 2, two U.S. naval vessels operating in the Tonkin Gulf encountered hostile fire from the North Vietnamese. Two days later they again fell under what seemed to be enemy shelling. The second attacks may never actually have taken place; most experts now believe that they did not. U.S. naval units, moreover, were not simply involved in routine patrols in international waters, as Pentagon spokesmen insisted; rather, they were providing intelligence to South Vietnamese commandos engaged in raids against North Vietnamese coastal installations. The operations formed part of a covert program approved by Johnson in February 1964, code-named OPLAN 34A. Despite ample ambiguities and significant mitigating circumstances, the president nonetheless used the alleged attacks as a pretext for sending Congress what became the Gulf of Tonkin Resolution.

After little debate and even less analysis, the Senate and House of Representatives passed, with only two dissenting votes, Johnson's sweeping resolution—a resolution already drafted *before* the incident occurred. As a Capitol Hill veteran, Johnson was adamant in the belief that it would be political suicide to move forward in Vietnam without first securing congressional support. "It was my impression," recalled McGeorge Bundy, "that President Johnson had been looking for some time for the proper peg to hang this resolution on, and what he was looking for was something that was overt, some hostile attack on American forces which would give an excuse to the Congress to pass the resolution that he wanted." He got precisely what he wanted. Congress authorized the president "to take all necessary measures to repel any armed attack against the forces of the United States and to prevent further aggression." In addition to that virtual blank check for future action, the legislative branch heartily approved the administration's decision to respond to what LBJ characterized as a blatant act of unprovoked, North Vietnamese aggression with a one-time, retaliatory bombing raid.[23]

After demonstrating his bonafides as a no-nonsense commander-in-chief who would brook no affront to the national honor, a pose that led to a significant jump in his public approval ratings, Johnson moved back to the political center. We "seek no larger war," he declared repeatedly on the campaign stump, further burnishing his credentials as the candidate of peace and moderation.[24] His campaign operatives, meanwhile, were busy painting Goldwater as a dangerous, trigger-happy, extremist. It proved a masterful strategy. On November 3, 1964, the American people gave Lyndon Johnson the landslide victory he craved. The Washington veteran now presumably had the mandate he needed to turn his Great Society dreams into legislative reality. The election provided no such easy mandate with regard to Vietnam, however. LBJ, after all, had reassured voters that he did not "want our American boys to do the fighting for Asian boys" and that he did not want to "get tied down in a land war in Asia."[25] Yet at the very same time he was making those pledges, his closest advisers were telling him that American boys were exactly what was needed in Vietnam—along with American bombs.

Events in South Vietnam soon forced Johnson's hand. The growing aggressiveness of the Viet Cong, coupled with Hanoi's escalating infiltration of supplies and troops into the south, had created an increasingly desperate situation. On January 5, 1965, Robert McNamara and McGeorge Bundy bluntly informed the president that "our current policy can lead only to disastrous defeat." They implored Johnson to authorize sustained U.S. bombing of North Vietnam, arguing that aerial warfare constituted the only possible means for staving off defeat in the south.[26] Following a bold Viet Cong attack on a U.S. military advisers' camp outside Pleiku on February 7, an attack that took seven American lives and wounded one hundred, LBJ found himself left with few choices. "To take no action now," argued Gen. Maxwell Taylor, the newly appointed ambassador in Saigon, "is to accept defeat in the fairly near future."[27] Gen. William Westmoreland, head of U.S. forces in Vietnam, echoed that assessment. In mid-February, after a few retaliatory air strikes above the seventeenth parallel, Johnson approved a program of sustained aerial bombardment of North Vietnam. He had now taken U.S. involvement in the Vietnam conflict to an entirely new level. Within two months, U.S. and South Vietnamese pilots were flying more than one hundred sorties per day over North Vietnam.[28]

The dispatch of U.S. ground forces quickly—and almost inevitably—followed the onset of the air war. Westmoreland worried that, without combat troops to provide security, American air bases in South Vietnam would remain highly vulnerable to enemy attacks. Consequently, he asked for two battalions of Marines to help defend the key air base at Da Nang. On February 26, Johnson approved that request and, on March 8, 3,500 U.S. troops waded ashore at the beaches of Da Nang.

Having crossed that threshold, the next steps along the escalatory ladder proved somewhat easier for Johnson to take. The ever-cautious Texan agonized about each one of those steps, to be sure. But he could not resist the logic of escalation given the core assumptions he and nearly all his advisers shared about the cataclysmic consequences of defeat in Vietnam. "If we ran out on Southeast Asia, I could see trouble ahead in every part of the globe—not just in Asia but in the Middle East and in Europe, in Africa and in Latin America," Johnson subsequently exclaimed. "I was convinced that our retreat from this challenge would open the path to World War III."[29]

He did hear a few contrary voices. The most eloquent by far proved that of Under Secretary of State George Ball. The savvy Ball, who played the role of in-house skeptic to the hilt, argued eloquently against escalation. In July 1965, during a series of intensive, high-level deliberations about Vietnam policy, Ball made a powerful case for cutting America's losses and seeking a negotiated, compromise settlement with Hanoi. "The alternative—no matter what we may wish it to be—is almost certainly a protracted war involving an open-ended commitment of U.S. forces," he observed, "mounting U.S. casualties, no assurance of a satisfactory solution, and a serious danger of escalation at the end of the road."[30]

But Johnson turned a deaf ear to Ball's prudent counsel. Virtually all of LBJ's other advisers were urging escalation. Virtually all saw catastrophe at home and abroad if Johnson acquiesced to a communist Vietnam. Nor could the skeptical under secretary, who essentially constituted a minority of one, prove his guiding premise that defeat in Vietnam would have but minimal effects on the global position of the United States. "Wouldn't we lose credibility by breaking the word of three presidents?" rejoined Johnson. The president concluded the July deliberations by remarking that he saw "very little alternative to what we are doing." It would be "more dangerous" to lose the war, he declared, "than [to] endanger a greater number of troops."[31]

At the end of the month, Johnson announced his decisions. He was immediately dispatching an additional 50,000 U.S. troops to Vietnam, bringing the total number of U.S. forces stationed there to 125,000. He was also doubling the number of draft calls to 35,000 per month. Privately, LBJ directed that an additional 50,000 men be sent by the end of the year. For all Johnson's efforts to play down the significance of those decisions, there was no mistaking their import: his administration was embarking on an open-ended commitment to forestall a Viet Cong/North Vietnamese victory in the south. Twenty years after the end of the Pacific War and twelve years after the end of the Korean conflict, the United States was once again going to war in Asia.

Reversal of Fortunes in Indonesia

At almost the exact same time that Johnson was approving those major escalatory steps in Vietnam, U.S. goals in the region were given a sudden, unanticipated boost by developments to the south. Indonesia, home of the largest and most powerful nonruling communist party in the world, and a nation whose neutralist, anti-Western inclinations and volatile leader had made it an enormous headache for U.S. policymakers for the past decade, underwent a political transformation of seismic proportions. That transformation was precipitated by the shadowy events that occurred on September 30, 1965. On that date, a group of junior army officers, likely acting at the behest of elements within the Indonesian Communist Party (PKI), assassinated six of the seven top Indonesian military commanders. The so-called "Gestapu," though its precise origins and intent remain a subject of considerable controversy to this day, may have represented the prelude to an all-out bid for power on the part of certain PKI leaders.

One thing is certain: the action brought a dramatically different result from that intended by the conspirators. General Suharto, a second-echelon army commander largely unknown to top U.S. officials, responded with brutal efficiency in crushing the incipient revolt. He then ordered a ruthless purge of the party and presided over the subsequent slaughter of hundreds of thousands of presumed communists and communist-sympathizers. The resulting bloodbath ultimately claimed as many as half a million lives. The conservative, pro-Western Suharto also started easing Sukarno out of power while simultaneously courting Western support and encouraging the influx of Western capital.[32]

The Johnson administration could not contain its glee at this stunning turn of events in Indonesia. "It is hard to overestimate the potential significance of the army's apparent victory over Sukarno," senior NSC staffer Robert Komer wrote Johnson in early 1966. "Indonesia has more people—and probably more resources—than all of mainland Southeast Asia. It was well on the way to becoming another expansionist Communist state, which would have critically menaced the rear of the whole Western position in mainland Southeast

Asia," he emphasized. "Now, though the unforeseen can always happen, this trend has been sharply reversed."[33] Reflecting decades later on the significance of Indonesia's political earthquake, Robert McNamara mused that it "significantly altered the regional balance of power and substantially reduced America's real stake in Vietnam"—though the defense secretary conceded that he and most other senior officials did not at first appreciate fully the latter connection. "The largest and most populous nation in Southeast Asia had reversed course and now lay in the hands of independent nationalists led by Suharto," McNamara observed. "China, which had expected a tremendous victory, instead suffered a permanent setback."[34]

Indonesian-American relations had reached a historic low just prior to the fateful Gestapu. Indeed, by mid-1965 pessimism about the course of developments in the archipelago had become so pervasive in official circles that some U.S. experts expected Sukarno to announce a break in diplomatic relations at any moment. Others feared that the Sukarno regime would soon align itself openly with the communist powers, rendering a body blow to U.S. interests in the region. The United States faced the "cold possibility," Secretary of State Dean Rusk lamented, "that before long this key strategic nation may be for all practical purposes a Communist dictatorship and that when events have progressed that far they will be irreversible."[35]

It was Indonesia's great strategic significance, of course, that made that prospect so frightening to the United States—and the reversal of fortunes set in motion on September 30, 1965, so gratifying. The sixth most populous nation in the world at that time, Indonesia possessed a wealth of natural resources, including vast oil reserves in which U.S. firms had invested a half-billion dollars. The sprawling island chain also sat astride vital sea lanes connecting the Indian and Pacific oceans. A communist Indonesia would not only threaten to outflank the struggling noncommunist states of mainland Southeast Asia; it would isolate Australia and New Zealand, deny to the West Indonesia's tremendous oil, tin, and rubber resources, and challenge the U.S. base complex in the Philippines. "The loss of Indonesia to the communists would gravely undermine the Free World military position in the Western Pacific," declared the Joint Chiefs of Staff in a graphic strategic appraisal prepared early in the Kennedy administration. In addition, the chiefs warned that "the loss of Indonesia to the communists might well start a chain reaction that would culminate in the eventual relinquishment of the principal US military bases in the Far East, with consequent serious implications for the over-all US military posture in the Western Pacific."[36] Asked Komer pointedly: "What price holding on to mainland Southeast Asia if we have a hostile Indonesia at its back?"[37]

Not surprisingly, in the face of such lofty stakes, both the Kennedy and Johnson administrations had tried to channel the Sukarno regime's energies in a more Western-leaning direction. Their efforts had done little, however, to staunch Indonesia's seemingly inexorable drift to the left. Throughout the first half of the 1960s, that trend was made manifest by the growing power and influence of the PKI, the country's increased reliance on Soviet economic and military assistance, and the impetuous Sukarno's rhetorical excesses, anti-Western foreign policy stances, and regional provocations.

Kennedy had of course inherited from Eisenhower a relationship already beset with suspicions and mistrust. The wounds opened by the CIA's intervention in Indonesia's civil war a few years earlier had not yet healed. Modest U.S. military aid to Indonesia's largely anticommunist armed forces, begun in mid-1958, had helped the Americans gain favor with one critical segment of the Indonesian power structure. Even so, Soviet aid dwarfed that provided by the United States, and General Nasution had come to rely more and more on Moscow for the hardware he considered essential for his armed forces. In fact, by the end of 1962 Soviet aid to Indonesia amounted to approximately $1 billion in military and $650 million in economic assistance, a total greater than that invested by the Kremlin in any other Third World state up to that time.[38] The continuing controversy over the disposition of the disputed territory of West Irian (West New Guinea to the Dutch) further muddied the waters, adding an emotional colonial issue to the other matters souring relations between Washington and Jakarta.

To counter those negative trends, the Kennedy administration had launched a series of initiatives designed to improve relations, the most significant of which concerned West Irian. Early in 1962, JFK decided to support Indonesia's claims to the territory, knowing full well that by doing so he would infuriate the Dutch. The American leader was gambling that a U.S. tilt toward Indonesia would not only forestall open warfare between Indonesia and the Netherlands over a territory that possessed far more symbolic than substantive importance, but could open a new, more cooperative phase in Indonesian-American relations as well. The new policy orientation achieved the first goal; the second proved far more elusive.

In February 1962, Attorney General Robert F. Kennedy, the president's brother and closest confidante, met with Sukarno in Jakarta in an effort to help defuse the ticking time bomb. As a result of that meeting, the Indonesian president agreed to enter into negotiations with the Dutch once again, provided that the United States serve as a mediator. The Kennedy administration jumped at the bait and pressed the Netherlands to fall in line. Although "hopping mad," in one official's apt words, the Dutch bowed to

American pressure. With veteran diplomat Ellsworth Bunker at the helm, talks opened the next month at a secluded estate in Middleburg, Virginia. In the end, only unrelenting American pressure on the Dutch made possible a settlement acceptable to the Indonesians. The final agreement, reached on August 15, 1962, specified that Indonesia would acquire administrative control of West Irian by May 1, 1963, with a plebiscite to be conducted no later than 1969, under UN supervision, to let the 700,000 native Papuans choose between continued Indonesian rule and independence.[39]

Flushed with hope for warmer ties in the wake of the West Irian breakthrough, Kennedy authorized stepped-up U.S. economic assistance and financial stabilization programs for the Sukarno regime. Aware that the tempestuous Indonesian ruler placed great stock in personal relationships, he also tentatively accepted Sukarno's personal invitation to visit Indonesia. This conciliatory diplomatic strategy toward Indonesia formed an important part of the Kennedy administration's broader effort to regain lost ground with the Third World's leading neutralists. "The best way to keep Nasser or Sukarno from becoming prisoners of the USSR," advised Komer, a key architect of this policy, "is to compete for them, not threaten them into Soviet hands."[40]

But Sukarno once again deflated American expectations. Not only did he prove unwilling to turn his attention to the internal economic problems that U.S. experts considered so pressing, but by mid-1963 he had latched on to another external issue: the creation of Malaysia. The Indonesian president's irredentist ambitions in the region and his deep antipathy toward what he considered Western neocolonial schemes led him to oppose vigorously the British-sponsored Federation of Malaysia, which consisted of Malaya, Singapore, and the British crown colonies of North Borneo. The ensuing "crush Malaysia" campaign, which also served internal political needs, drove a new wedge between Washington and Jakarta. Congressional antipathy to foreign aid for so meddlesome and uncooperative a regime as Sukarno's effectively tied Kennedy's hands, prompting his announcement on November 14, 1963, that the United States was suspending part of its financial aid program to Indonesia.[41]

Following Kennedy's assassination, relations further deteriorated. Sukarno was convinced that the CIA was again scheming to topple him, a suspicion that he shared freely with Ambassador Jones. The United States of course denied such allegations as preposterous. What it could not deny was the obvious failure of the Kennedy administration's accommodationist strategy either to rein in the aging revolutionary's excesses or to nudge Jakarta any closer to the West. President Johnson sought initially to maintain some

U.S. influence via a modest aid program, despite the steady drumbeat of anti-Sukarno invective emanating from Capitol Hill. The Indonesian leader made even that limited effort untenable, however, when he told the United States publicly in early 1964 to "Go to hell with your aid!" In response, Democratic Sen. Birch Bayh expressed his strong opposition to "throwing good money after bad" for a regime headed by a man "who is arrogant, insulting, incompetent and unstable." Republican Rep. William Broomfield agreed, scoring the Johnson administration for "mollycoddling this minor-league Hitler." LBJ could do little more than beat back a congressional move to suspend all U.S. aid programs to Indonesia.[42]

Henceforth, the Johnson administration aimed chiefly to weather the storm. It sought to avoid a full-scale rupture in relations while maintaining friendly links to the Indonesian military and waiting for the eventual dawning of a post-Sukarno era. Even those limited goals were severely tested, though, by Sukarno's continued provocations vis-à-vis Malaysia and the numerous anti-American demonstrations he encouraged at home. Johnson and his top aides found it extraordinarily difficult to maintain equanimity as the fever pitch of anti-Americanism continued to spread across Indonesia and the fever pitch of anti-Sukarnoism continued to rise over Capitol Hill. Under Secretary of State Ball lamented in February 1965 that Indonesia was "falling apart." Close to despair, the administration put U.S.-Indonesian relations into a "deep freeze."[43]

That, at the very moment when Indonesian-American relations appeared to be spinning dangerously out of control, they would suddenly reverse course almost 180 degrees forms one of the great ironies of America's Southeast Asian policy over the past half century. The ill-considered actions of Lieutenant Colonel Untung and his fellow conspirators wound up ushering in a new epoch in U.S.-Indonesian relations, providing the Johnson administration with a wholly unexpected diplomatic windfall. However favorable to Washington that outcome proved, neither the coup attempt itself nor the army's prompt response to it were influenced to any significant degree by the United States. Rather, those events were determined, as one U.S. diplomat had observed earlier, "by basic forces far beyond our ability to control."[44] Recalled Hugh Tovar, the CIA station chief in Jakarta during the Gestapu: "I was stunned. At the time we did not know what had happened."[45]

The Johnson administration searched in vain for evidence that the Indonesian army might have been fortified by the burgeoning U.S. troop commitments in Vietnam. CIA director Richard Helms reported that his experts found no such link. To the contrary, the agency concluded that the rise of Suharto and the subsequent destruction of the PKI "evolved purely from a complex and long-standing domestic political situation."[46] The abrupt change in Indonesia's internal and external direction, occurring at the close of Sukarno's aptly named "Year of Living Dangerously," might have illuminated for Johnson and his national security advisers the very real limits on American power in Southeast Asia. That it did not soon became painfully apparent in Vietnam.

Harnessing Regional Allies

The deepening American involvement in Indochina during the early and mid-1960s bore more direct and immediate consequences for Thailand and the Philippines than it did for Indonesia. The importance of both of those nations to the United States grew substantially during this period for two basic reasons. First, Thailand and the Philippines each provided the United States with vital military facilities, facilities whose value increased in direct proportion to the intensification of the U.S. combat role in the region. Second, Johnson considered it politically imperative to demonstrate that strong allied support existed for America's Vietnam commitments, especially among SEATO member states. To that end, LBJ pressured the governments in Manila and Bangkok to contribute not only unqualified public support for U.S. actions in Vietnam but also token numbers of troops to what he invariably depicted as a collective struggle against external aggression. For their part, Thai and Filipino leaders learned quickly that America's need for military installations and diplomatic backing brought a commensurate gain in their bargaining leverage. U.S. escalation in Vietnam reversed the traditional relationship between patron and client. The United States wound up needing Thailand and the Philippines every bit as much as those countries needed the United States, a state of affairs that political authorities in Bangkok and Manila would do everything within their power to capitalize upon.

When Kennedy entered office in January 1961, that sense of mutual dependence was not yet much in evidence. Burgeoning differences over bilateral and regional security issues proved far more prominent. The new administration's much ballyhooed opening toward the nonaligned nations did not play well in Bangkok or Manila, any more than that policy shift won acclaim in Taipei, Seoul, or Karachi. What advantages were they gaining from open alignment with the United States, Asian allies grumbled, when Washington was preparing to reward Indonesia, India, Egypt, and other fence-straddlers with economic and military largesse? Throughout the early months of the Kennedy administration, disgruntled politicians and diplomats in Thailand

and the Philippines hurled charges of inconstancy and unreliability at their erstwhile ally with disturbing regularity. Officials of both nations complained openly that SEATO was affording them precious little real protection. They also blamed SEATO—and the Kennedy administration—for pursuing a policy of vacillation and retreat in Laos that jeopardized their own security interests.[47]

Speaking to an American reporter in May 1961, Philippine president Carlos Garcia declared that the United States had to stand firm against communist expansion in Asia "before it's too late." He urged the United States to "put out the fires" in Laos and Vietnam "now before they get too large." Earlier, Foreign Minister Felixberto Serrano voiced concern about the ineffectiveness of SEATO and the evident inability, or unwillingness, of the United States to block communist advances in Laos.[48] Nagging bilateral disputes concerning the Philippine sugar quota and long-standing Filipino war damage claims stemming from World War II served to further unsettle relations between Manila and Washington.

American observers were temporarily relieved with the election in November 1961 of Diosdado Macapagal as Garcia's successor, expecting that the new president would move quickly to close the breach. They were taken aback when he opened it still further. Described by one U.S. expert on the eve of the election as "pro-American to the point where it is a source of some embarrassment to us," Macapagal showed his nationalist colors immediately upon assuming the presidency.[49] He bristled when the Kennedy administration brushed aside Philippine requests for additional economic assistance. Then, when the House of Representatives defeated a bill that would have paid $73 million to some 88,000 Filipino war damage claimants, his fury boiled over. Macapagal shocked the Kennedy administration by canceling a scheduled visit to Washington. "It seems the United States treats her friends more shabbily that those who are not with her," the Philippine president charged in a statement issued to the press. "The feeling of resentment among our people and the attitude of the U.S. Congress," he subsequently wrote Kennedy, "negate the atmosphere of good will upon which my state visit to your country was predicated."[50]

As always when problems muddied relations with its former colony, the United States focused first and foremost on the security of its invaluable base sites. Macapagal brought that issue to the surface when he told a reporter that the continued deterioration of U.S.-Philippine relations could endanger American base rights in his country.[51] However empty that threat might have been, it certainly caught the attention of U.S. diplomatic and defense officials. They moved quickly to heal the wound. Philippine bases were far too critical to the overall U.S. defense posture in the Pacific to allow them to be jeopardized by minor irritants. The Kennedy administration, consequently, made a concerted effort to reassure the Filipinos about its intentions and its commitment. JFK even twisted some arms in Congress to gain passage of a generous Philippine war damage bill that he signed in August 1962. Those efforts, though they helped alleviate some of the more pronounced strains in U.S.-Philippine relations, did little to erase the underlying—and largely accurate—suspicion from which they sprang, namely, that the United States took the Philippines for granted and paid little heed to Philippine interests and concerns.[52]

Thailand's complaints about U.S. policy at the start of the Kennedy administration proved even harsher and more frequent than those being issued from the Philippines. The success of communist insurgencies in neighboring Laos and nearby South Vietnam just heightened the historic Thai sense of vulnerability. It was that sense of vulnerability, of course, that had impelled the Bangkok government to cast its fate with the United States a decade earlier. As the Pathet Lao insurgency to the north gained strength, the faith of Thai leaders in the ability of the United States to guarantee their security correspondingly weakened. In a series of personal letters to JFK and in several face-to-face meetings with U.S. representatives, Prime Minister Sarit Thanarat and Foreign Minister Thanat Khoman laid bare their concerns. The deterioration of the situation in Laos directly threatened Thailand's security, they stressed. Yet SEATO, saddled not only with unwieldy procedural mechanisms but, in Britain and France, with two members adamantly opposed to military intervention in Laos, afforded little hope of positive action. Sarit, in exasperation, told the CIA representative in Bangkok, "We are not threatening to get out of SEATO, we *are* getting out."[53] Underlying that persistent focus on SEATO's inadequacies lay a far broader concern: in a real crisis, could Thailand trust the United States? That question became increasingly urgent with the Kennedy administration's push for the neutralization of Laos, a policy choice anathema to the ardently anticommunist Thais and one they equated with appeasement.

From the first, the Kennedy administration recognized that Thai dissatisfaction posed a potentially grave threat to the U.S. position throughout the region. Ambassador Kenneth T. Young hardly exaggerated when he called Thailand "an unofficial and disguised base of operations for the United States in Southeast Asia." The government of Thailand, Young added, "is allowing us to carry on an increasing number of operations in and out of Thailand which we could not conduct from any other piece of real estate in Asia. If we lose this base of operations we will have to retreat to the island chain and depend solely on sea and air power."[54] Beginning in 1960, more-over, the United States had been using an elite, CIA-trained group of Thai paramilitary operatives as an instrumental part of its secret war against communist forces in the mountains of northeastern Laos. All contingency planning for direct U.S. military intervention in either Laos or South Vietnam was predicated on a friendly Thailand providing liberal access to military bases and intelligence facilities on its soil. Thailand, in short, was America's indispensable ally on mainland Southeast Asia.

The Kennedy administration labored to reassure Thai leaders about the depth and reliability of the U.S. commitment, much as it had been doing with their Filipino counterparts. In March 1961, JFK instructed the U.S. ambassador to tell Prime Minister Sarit that Washington continued to place a very high value on its ties with Bangkok. Any Pathet Lao or North Vietnamese air strikes against Thai territory, Kennedy's message made clear, would bring forth a direct and immediate U.S. military response. Moreover, if American forces needed to be deployed to Thailand, the United States was prepared to provide directly for the air defense of Thailand by positioning U.S. fighter planes on Thai soil. In March 1962, following a meeting between Secretary of State Dean Rusk and Foreign Minister Thanat, a joint public statement stipulated that the United States "regards the preservation of the independence and integrity of Thailand as vital to the national interests of the United States." In other words, the United States fully accepted its obligation to protect Thailand from a communist attack—whether such an attack emanated from Laos, North Vietnam, or China.[55]

Those efforts did not fully succeed, however, in curbing what one U.S. observer described as the "morbid fears gripping the Thais."[56] Throughout 1961 and early 1962, U.S. officials explored another tack as well. They debated the feasibility of deploying a small contingent of U.S. combat troops to Thailand as a tripwire, or "plate glass window," that might serve to deter hostile action against Thailand—much, presumably, as the presence of U.S. troops in Germany helped deter Soviet aggression. At a minimum, the emplacement of ground forces would signal to the Thais the seriousness of the U.S. commitment.[57]

The sudden unraveling of the Laotian cease-fire in the spring of 1962 provided the United States with both the opportunity and the perceived need to implement such a plan. Pathet Lao seizure of the town of Nam Tha in northwestern Laos precipitated the crisis. Developments in that area actually resembled an opera bouffe more than they did an actual military engagement. Some five thousand Royal Lao troops, evidently seeking to provoke a Pathet Lao attack and hence create the pretext for U.S. intervention, responded to enemy maneuvers by fleeing across the Mekong River into Thailand. Thailand responded with alarm to this curious set of events, as did the Kennedy administration, which worried that its credibility once again lay on the line. JFK rushed Secretary of Defense McNamara and Joint Chiefs of Staff Chairman Lyman Lemnitzer to Thailand to inspect conditions and consult with Sarit on possible U.S. and Thai countermoves. In Washington, Kennedy held a series of intensive meetings with his top national security advisers. As a result of those deliberations, the president authorized the immediate dispatch of 1,800 U.S. ground forces, together with an Air Force fighter squadron and a Marine air squadron. On May 14, Sarit approved the deployment and U.S. troops began arriving several days later.[58]

The dispatch of U.S. troops at the height of the Nam Tha crisis opened a new chapter in Thai-American relations. However trivial the precipitating episode might seem in retrospect, the Kennedy administration's swift and decisive response earned it considerable respect among Thai elites, easing doubts about the credibility of American promises. "This action," remarked one high-ranking Thai official approvingly, "shows that SEATO is no 'paper tiger.' "[59] Increased economic and military assistance to Thailand, which rose to $73 million in military and $32 million in economic aid for fiscal year 1963, also helped strengthen the Thai-American connection. Tensions still existed, to be sure. Sarit continued to harbor doubts about U.S. resolve vis-à-vis the communist challenges in Laos and Vietnam. Moreover, he was convinced—as were most U.S. allies—that his government was entitled to greater assistance from Washington than it was receiving; and he deeply resented the U.S. decision to renew aid to the neutralist Cambodian regime headed by his bête noire, Sihanouk. For its part, the United States watched closely for signs that discontent throughout Thailand's northeastern provinces might trigger yet another communist insurgency. It also worried that Sarit's periodic threats to reorient Thai foreign policy along more neutralist lines might someday go beyond mere posturing. The history of Thai foreign policy, as U.S experts well understood, was that of a weak nation accommodating itself to shifting power realities. Cognizant of past Thai behavior, Ambassador Young voiced the deepest fear of U.S. planners when he observed in October 1962 that "the real danger is Thailand's wavering confidence in US determination to beat the communists in S[outh] E[ast] A[sia]."[60]

With his dramatic escalation of the U.S. military commitment to the Saigon regime in 1964 and 1965, Lyndon Johnson certainly went a long way toward easing such lingering doubts about U.S. resolve—in both Thailand and the Philippines. LBJ's decision to embroil the United States in a major land war on the Southeast Asian mainland enhanced, in turn, the value of each of those SEATO allies to the United States. Thailand and the Philippines, each of which provided military facilities essential for the swift movement of troops and the necessary projection of U.S. air and naval power throughout the region, became irreplaceable props behind the U.S. war effort. In July 1965, the State Department alerted U.S. diplomats in Manila that they should prepare President Macapagal for the "greatly increased use" of U.S. bases; shortly thereafter, the Pentagon pushed for a blanket approval of U.S. overflights of Philippine territory.[61] Also in the summer of 1965, coincident with the arrival of large numbers of U.S. combat units in South Vietnam, the Joint Chiefs of Staff called attention to the necessity for "a suitable build-up in Thailand to enable the expeditious deployment there of major US forces." Specifically, the chiefs recommended the immediate development of additional logistic support bases, the construction of new airfields, the improvement of existing air bases so as to increase their capacity, and "measures to increase the readiness of Thai armed forces."[62]

In addition, Johnson personally pressed first the Filipinos and later the Thais to contribute troops to the struggle in Vietnam. At a White House meeting at the end of 1964, McNamara observed candidly that a few thousand troops from such countries as the Philippines, Australia, and Britain did "not make much diff[erence] militarily, but much politically."[63] If the Philippines committed a contingent of troops to Vietnam, American representatives made clear, the United States was "prepared to pick up the tab."[64] No one could anticipate, at this early stage, how many other payments would be needed to ensure continued Filipino and Thai support.

Fighting an Unwinnable War

In the two and a half years bracketed by the major troop buildup of mid-1965 and the climactic Tet offensive of early 1968, the Johnson administration committed massive amounts of firepower, manpower, and dollars to the war in Vietnam in a fatally flawed attempt to achieve military victory. American bombs pulverized North Vietnam throughout this period; the total tonnage of bombs dropped on that poor, predominantly agricultural land by the end of 1967 substantially exceeded the total dropped on Japan throughout the entire course of World War II. And even more bombs were dropped on South Vietnam during those same years, with devastating effects on the countryside and the local population. The United States also brought its most sophisticated technology to bear in the struggle against the North Vietnamese and Viet Cong. It used defoliants, such as Agent Orange, to destroy an estimated one half of South Vietnam's forests so as to deny the enemy cover; it utilized portable radar units, capable of detecting human urine, to sniff out the enemy; and it relied on advanced computer programs to predict the likely time and place of enemy attacks.[65]

The ground war also proceeded with unmatched ferocity. Commanding Gen. William Westmoreland devised aggressive "search and destroy" tactics to bring enemy forces out into the open where superior American firepower could cut them down. His war of attrition aimed to deplete enemy ranks so severely that the will and capability of North Vietnamese and Viet Cong forces would be sapped. "The solution in Vietnam is more bombs, more shells, more napalm," argued Gen. William Depuy, a key army strategist, "till the other side cracks and gives up."[66] To accomplish that feat, Westmoreland demanded ever-higher troop levels—and Johnson nearly always met his commander's requests. By July 1967 the United States had approximately 450,000 troops in Vietnam, and Westmoreland was clamoring for 200,000 more. Yet, the general conceded, even with the additional 200,000 men he sought, the war would probably continue for another two years; without them, victory was not likely in less than five years.[67]

The failure of American military strategy to produce anything more than a stalemate after two and a half years of furious fighting against a clearly outmatched opponent provoked intense debate—along with rumbles of dissent—within the Pentagon and the Johnson White House, as it did well beyond Washington's corridors of power. That debate continues to this day among historians, politicians, and military analysts. Why was the United States unable to translate its obvious advantages in military strength, mobility, resource base, and technological prowess into outright battlefield triumph? In the most fundamental sense, America's failures stemmed from its gross violation of nearly all the classic rules of warfare. Those precepts, set forth in the writings of nineteenth-century Prussian strategist Karl von Clausewitz and virtually every other serious military thinker throughout the ages, boil down to the following: first, you must know your enemy—who he is, what his intentions are, what his capabilities and will are; second, you must define clear, achievable goals; third, you must devise tactical means appropriate to the realization of those goals; and, fourth, you must maintain domestic support for your efforts. Military action, in the final analysis, must serve political goals; it can never be an end in itself.[68]

Partly out of ignorance, and partly due to arrogance, American planners from the first grievously misjudged the resiliency and determination of their foe. It is difficult to argue with McNamara's retrospective admission that

American policymakers "underestimated the power of nationalism to moti-vate a people (in this case, the North Vietnamese and Vietcong) to fight and die for their beliefs and values."[69] Most top U.S. officials at the time, includ-ing McNamara, simply assumed that the North Vietnamese and Viet Cong could not long withstand the full military might of the United States. The sus-tained aerial bombardment of the north and Westmoreland's ground war of attrition in the south were each predicated on the belief that Hanoi had a breaking point. Once the United States inflicted enough pain on North Viet-namese industry and society, Ho Chi Minh would not only curtail drastically the infiltration of northern troops and cadres into the south but would sue for peace. "We'll just go on bleeding them," observed Westmoreland with characteristic overconfidence, "until Hanoi wakes up to the fact that they have bled their country to the point of national disaster for generations."[70] The general's optimism about the final outcome of the conflict also stemmed from his conviction that before long the United States would be killing more North Vietnamese soldiers than could be replaced, thus arriving at what came to be called the "crossover point."

Those complacent assumptions about the likely behavior of a people few Americans truly understood made the development of a realistic war-fight-ing strategy virtually impossible. In view of the approximately 200,000 North Vietnamese reaching draft age each year, not to mention the nearly equal number of potential recruits to the insurgency coming of age annually south of the seventeenth parallel, it would have been extraordinarily difficult for the United States to ever reach the elusive crossover point on which the attrition strategy pivoted. The grossly inflated "body counts" produced by U.S. and South Vietnamese forces as the principal index of military progress never even approximated the needed figure. Nor could any mere statistical measure capture the indomitable will and determination of the other side, a side conditioned by historical experiences and cultural values that few Amer-icans knew and fewer still appreciated. Americans soldiers and commanders alike often expressed befuddlement at the high degree of commitment, resiliency, and willingness to sacrifice displayed by their opponents in the field. Similarly, CIA experts marveled at the ability of North Vietnamese society to withstand, adapt to, and even gain strength and cohesion from the unrelenting U.S. bombing campaign.[71]

In fact, Hanoi was pursuing a far simpler and far more realistic strategy for the conflict than was Washington. Ho, General Giap, and other top North Vietnamese planners knew that their forces could not defeat the bet-ter-equipped Americans in open combat. They knew that their troops were likely to suffer huge losses relative to those of the United States, even if they restricted their military activities to defensive, guerrilla-type actions. Realists to the core, they were prepared to accept a ratio of ten or even fifteen Viet Cong and North Vietnamese casualties for every one American. Hanoi's goal from the beginning of the U.S. troop buildup in mid-1965 was not to defeat the foreigners but to wait them out. "Don't worry," Ho told his associates. "I've been to America. I know Americans. They are an impatient people. They will leave."[72] If the North Vietnamese and Viet Cong stayed in the contest, the United States would grow weary of a protracted conflict; by inflicting significant casualties on the Americans, they could hasten that process— no matter how great their own losses. "American boys being sent home in body bags will steadily increase," Giap prophesied. "Their mothers will want to know why. The war will not long survive their questions."[73] Once the Americans left, and Ho, Giap, and the north's other revolutionary leaders were convinced that in time they would, then the nationalist revolution begun against the French could be completed. Without U.S. troops to prop it up, they were certain that the Saigon regime could easily be toppled, leading to the patriotic reunification of the fatherland.

America's goals were as foggy as North Vietnam's were clearcut, as unrealistic in light of prevailing military, political, and socioeconomic conditions as Hanoi's proved largely compatible with those very same conditions. U.S. intervention in Vietnam's revolutionary civil war was prompted of course by a set of broad, global calculations that transcended the specific circumstances obtaining within Vietnam. The United States sought not merely to block a communist victory in the south but to prevent further communist advances in and beyond Southeast Asia, to reassure allies worldwide about U.S. resolve, and to deter both Moscow and Beijing from supporting wars of national liberation. The Johnson administration was convinced that those broader goals required that the United States defeat the insurgency and its northern backers, not just hold off a communist victory. Yet, wary of any actions that might provoke direct Chinese or Soviet intervention, the Johnson administration believed it had to pursue that objective by means of a limited, rather than a total, war. Therein lay a major inconsistency in American strategy. Simply put, how could the United States, with anything less than a total commitment, defeat so determined a foe as North Vietnam, a nation willing to make unimaginable sacrifices to advance its cause? And how could the United States force Hanoi to cease its support for the insurgency in the south without resorting to more extreme measures, such as the bombing of population centers, the invasion of the north, even the use of nuclear weapons? Yet to resort to extreme measures of that sort would have represented a wholesale repudiation of American values; it would also have been so wildly disproportionate a response to the Vietnam problem that the very allies the United States was seeking to reassure would more likely have been revulsed. Finally, such extreme measures likely *would* have invited the very countermoves from Beijing that Johnson most feared.

Beginning in 1964, both China and the Soviet Union provided substantial support to the North Vietnamese, support that enhanced Hanoi's war-fighting ability while simultaneously constricting American military options. In 1965 the two communist powers combined to supply North Vietnam with military and economic aid valued at $250–$400 million. The volume of that outside assistance increased steadily over the next several years. Although, by 1968, Soviet aid to North Vietnam outstripped the Chinese contribution, China consistently maintained the warmer relationship with North Vietnam. In January 1964, in fact, the Soviets had resisted North Vietnam's initial appeals for support of their escalating offensive actions in the south; Russian leaders valued the budding detente between Moscow and Washington and had not wanted to jeopardize it. The Soviets relented later in the year, largely because they calculated that continued resistance to Hanoi's appeals would just hurt their standing within the socialist camp and redound to the benefit of arch-rival China. The intensity of the Sino-Soviet rivalry thus gave the North Vietnamese far greater leverage with the two communist giants than they otherwise would have possessed. For its part, China from the first provided North Vietnam with the assistance it requested. "Our two parties and two peoples must cooperate and fight the enemy together," Mao told North Vietnamese Gen. Van Tien Dung in June 1964. "Your business is my business and my business is your business." China's active support for North Vietnam was a product of Mao's revolutionary fervor, his bitter struggle with the Soviet Union for leadership of the communist bloc, Chinese apprehension about possible American military actions along their southern border, and the long-standing ties of intimacy between Beijing and Hanoi. The resulting policy brought approximately 320,000 Chinese troops to North Vietnam between 1965 and 1969, in addition to the sizable military and economic aid Beijing supplied. The troops performed a variety of important functions, including building and maintaining roads, factories, bridges, and rail lines, manning antiaircraft batteries, and, not least, serving by their very presence as a deterrent to U.S. ground operations north of the seventeenth parallel.[74]

To complicate matters further for the Johnson administration, its murky military goals in Vietnam could not be separated from an equally murky political objective. Success in Vietnam necessitated the establishment of a viable, noncommunist regime in the south. Yet it was the Saigon regime's abiding structural weaknesses that had fed the insurgency in the first place and that in 1964–65 had brought it to the very brink of extinction. The United States had intervened with troops and bombs only because it was sure that any less forceful a response to the republic's plight would not have saved it. The Viet Cong's ability to maintain control over at least half the territory and population of South Vietnam, even after the introduction of U.S. combat forces, did not rest on coercive power alone; it also rested on the communists' positive appeals to a peasantry deeply alienated by an unresponsive, repressive regime.[75]

At times, Johnson administration strategists deluded themselves into believing that the mere presence of several hundred thousand American fighting men would transform the Saigon regime into something that it had never been. More typically, they paid lip service to the critical importance of nation-building while conceding that the immensity of the task lay beyond their capabilities. Although the South Vietnamese government achieved a modicum of political stability following the 1965 coup that brought Air Marshall Nguyen Cao Ky and Gen. Nguyen Van Thieu to power, the core problems remained. The Ky-Thieu government, admitted McNamara in June 1967, "is still largely corrupt, incompetent and unresponsive to the needs and wishes of the people."[76]

To gain success, then, the United States had to defeat the insurgency *and* help build a strong, self-sustaining South Vietnamese government. Those were quite distinct, at times even contradictory, goals. With their characteristic can-do spirit and proud military tradition, the Americans naturally focused most of their energies on the first goal. Lt. Philip Caputo, who arrived at Danang with the earliest U.S. combat unit, recalled that "America seemed omnipotent then" and that he and his fellow soldiers "carried, along with our packs and rifles, the implicit convictions that the Viet Cong would be quickly beaten and that we were doing something altogether noble and good."[77] For all the troops, equipment, and technology it poured into the effort, however, and for all the individual battles it won, the United States could not defeat the Viet Cong. The American way of war, moreover, frequently alienated the very people whose hearts and minds the United States was seeking to win. With its indiscriminate use of bombs, napalm, defoliants, and free-fire zones, the U.S. military machine wreaked havoc throughout the countryside, disrupting traditional patterns of rural life and driving four million South Vietnamese from their ancestral homes. Most of the refugees streamed into the swollen cities, where homelessness, corruption, and prostitution were rife—and Viet Cong recruitment efforts active.[78]

Despite official protestations about steady progress and lights glimpsed at the end of distant tunnels, the United States was, in truth, locked in an inconclusive war of attrition throughout 1966 and 1967, its military objectives frequently working at cross-purposes with its political objectives. American military might had prevented a North Vietnamese–Viet Cong victory, to be sure, and probably could continue to do so indefinitely. But at how high a cost in American lives and treasure? Johnson, McNamara, Westmoreland, and other top U.S. decision-makers could not answer that essential question. They could not answer it because they had flunked the most basic tests of sound military leadership: they had grossly misjudged the strength and determination of their adversary; failed to articulate the precise goals for which their nation was fighting; and proved unable to devise military or political tactics consistent with the fundamental purpose of U.S. intervention.

By failing, at the same time, to build a strong domestic consensus behind the U.S. effort in Vietnam, the architects of U.S. strategy violated still another fundamental maxim of warfare. The American people and their congressional representatives at first overwhelmingly supported the Johnson administration's Vietnam commitments, much as they had other Cold War foreign policy initiatives. That support remained solid even after the major troop buildup of mid-1965, though a few isolated student and intellectual groups did begin to raise their voices in protest. As the war dragged on inconclusively throughout 1966 and 1967, the ranks of the dissenters swelled. Demonstrations, marches, sit-ins, and peace vigils proliferated during those years, fed by mounting U.S. casualties and the inability of Johnson administration spokesmen either to demonstrate real progress or to articulate a clear and consistent rationale for the sacrifices they were asking Americans to make.

"You cannot at the present time sell the killing of American boys in South Vietnam to the American people," Oregon Sen. Wayne Morse had prophesied with uncanny accuracy back in February 1964. "They won't buy it and I don't think they should buy it."[79] On Capitol Hill, Senators Morse, J. William Fulbright, Mike Mansfield, Frank Church, and other so-called "doves" helped legitimate dissent. As chair of the powerful Senate Foreign Relations Committee, Fulbright held widely publicized hearings on America's Vietnam policy in mid-1966 that featured stinging criticisms from former diplomat George Kennan, retired general James Gavin, and other establishment figures. In the fall of 1967 a symbolic march on the Pentagon by antiwar activists drew tens of thousands of protesters. An American general, witnessing the spectacle, expressed fear that "the empire was coming apart at the seams."[80]

A few months earlier, a popular periodical had brilliantly captured the nation's growing divisions over the war in an editorial appropriately entitled, "A Nation at Odds." "Cleft by doubts and tormented by frustration," observed *Newsweek*,

> the nation this Independence Day [1967] is haunted by its most corrosively ambiguous foreign adventure—a bloody, costly jungle war half a world away that has etched the tragedy of Vietnam into the American soul. . . . Few scars show on the surface. . . . No war fever grips the countryside, no gasoline ration stamps dot the car windshields, no Gold Stars decorate picture windows. The casualty lists run inconspicuously on the inside pages of the newspapers; wounded veterans are kept mostly out of sight, remain mostly out of mind. Save on the otherwordly mosaic of the TV screen, the war is almost invisible on the home-front. But, like a slow-spreading blight, it is inexorably making its mark on nearly every facet of American life.[81]

In Vietnam's Shadow

The Americans and the Vietnamese were not the only peoples on whom the war was casting a long, ominous shadow. By the mid- and late-1960s, the conflict in Vietnam had left a deep imprint throughout all of Southeast Asia. In view of their proximity to the heart of the struggle, Laos and Cambodia, try as they might, could not avoid being sucked into the vortex. North Vietnamese and Viet Cong forces found those neighboring states marvelously convenient as transit points, sanctuaries, and base camps, much as had their Viet Minh forerunners during the war against the French. Just as its communist adversaries violated with impunity the nominal neutrality of Phnom Penh and Vientiane, so too did the United States. Both sides, in fact, treated the neutrality they were pledged to uphold in those countries as little more than a legal fiction.

Thailand and the Philippines became directly embroiled in the Vietnam conflict as well, even if actual fighting did not take place within their borders. Essential props of the American war effort, those countries provided the United States with crucial air, naval, and logistics bases, unswerving political support, and token contingents of troops. The war in Vietnam also brought to Thailand and the Philippines enhanced stature and influence, increased aid dollars, and a boom in GI-related local businesses. Indonesia, Malaysia, and Singapore, although they stood at greater remove from the fighting on the Indochina peninsula, were inevitably affected by the conflict as well. The presence in their immediate neighborhood of a half-million American troops seeking to contain a Soviet- and Chinese-backed war of national liberation inspired a complex mix of fear, relief, ambivalence, and soul-searching. Out of those conflicted feelings emerged the Association of Southeast Asian Nations (ASEAN) in August 1967, the first major indigenous effort to grapple with the economic, political, and security needs of postcolonial Southeast Asia. Only Burma managed largely to insulate itself from the war—and from most other outside influences as well—as the Rangoon regime increasingly turned in on itself in a strange experiment with self-imposed isolation.

Laos had no hope of insulating itself from the war raging next door. Following the Geneva agreements of 1962, Washington and Moscow solemnly agreed to respect the neutrality of that fragile, embattled nation. It was not to be. North Vietnam never removed its troops from Laotian soil, as U.S. officials had, perhaps naively, expected; Hanoi, instead, continued to use sizable portions of eastern Laos for the infiltration of troops and supplies into the South Vietnamese battlefield. The so-called Ho Chi Minh Trail, the principal overland route for troops and supplies moving south, passed right through Laos. The United States brazenly contravened the Geneva agreements as well, orchestrating a "nonattributable" covert war against all communist forces within Laos. That war moved from a small-scale, guerrilla-based affair during the early 1960s to a high-tech aerial war after 1965. Laos, viewed by the North Vietnamese and Americans alike as an adjunct to the larger conflict in South Vietnam, soon earned the dubious distinction of becoming history's most bombed nation. Close cooperation with Thai authorities and the liberal use of U.S.-constructed air bases within Thailand permitted the United States to run regular bombing missions throughout this technically neutral country. Legendary CIA operative James W. "Bill" Lair personally directed many of those guerrilla and aerial operations from his headquarters at the Udorn Thani air base in northern Thailand.

The purpose of America's covert war in Laos was twofold: first, it aimed to prevent a Pathet Lao triumph by providing military support for the rightist and neutralist forces that constituted the governing coalition in Vientiane; and, second, it sought to monitor and, if possible, debilitate the North Vietnamese forces transiting Laos en route to South Vietnam. The United States preferred, in the words of William H. Sullivan, the U.S. ambassador in Laos from 1964 to 1969, to "act through a clandestine, deniable system of paramilitary assistance, with any actual fighting being done by indigenous forces." The CIA, which coordinated America's extensive Laotian operations with representatives of the State Department and the Agency for International Development, enlisted the Hmong and other Laotian hill tribes as surrogates in this campaign. A minority ethnic group whose traditional mountain homeland had been encroached upon by communist forces, the Hmong willingly joined the U.S.-led crusade—with ultimately tragic consequences.[82]

Cambodia's wily Prince Sihanouk, for all his vaunted maneuvering, also found it impossible to resist the war's spillover effects. Late in 1963, angered by American political meddling in Cambodia, Sihanouk refused to accept any more U.S. economic or military aid. The vitriolic anti-American statements that accompanied his termination of all U.S. aid programs were intended to gain sympathy from the communist powers while also stealing the thunder from leftist opponents at home. In April 1965 the Cambodian monarch officially severed relations with Washington. Those bold moves were designed to help protect Cambodia from what Sihanouk considered the most immediate threats to its sovereignty. "When we become pro-American," he explained, "the Chinese and Vietnamese immediately become our enemies and bring us insecurity. It is for this reason I think we have greater advantages in continuing to quarrel with the Americans."[83] Following that logic, Sihanouk secretly agreed at the end of 1963 to allow North Vietnamese and Viet Cong fighters to establish protected sanctuaries in the border areas of eastern Cambodia. Then, early in 1964, the Cambodian ruler worked out another secret modus vivendi with the North Vietnamese, allowing them to utilize the port of Sihanoukville to receive arms and ammunition from China.

The Johnson administration detested the duplicitous game Sihanouk was playing. While publicly characterizing his country as a neutral "island of peace" in warring Indochina, the prince was actually facilitating Hanoi's military efforts in South Vietnam. Westmoreland and the Joint Chiefs regularly requested that U.S. forces be allowed to destroy the enemy's sanctuaries in Cambodia. Although he did occasionally permit U.S. forces to pursue enemy units across the border and continued to approve clandestine interdiction operations within Cambodia, Johnson prohibited attacks on the sanctuaries. LBJ recognized that Sihanouk's secret dealings with the North Vietnamese were driven not by pro-communist sympathies but by a desperate determination to preserve Cambodian sovereignty. Moreover, Johnson was convinced that, for all his foibles and inconsistencies, Sihanouk played a constructive, stabilizing role; he ensured that North Vietnamese activities within the kingdom were carefully circumscribed, kept a check on Cambodia's own communist insurgents, the Khmer Rouge, and prevented a more staunchly anti-American ruler from seizing the reins of power. The United States, it appeared, could live indefinitely with a nominally neutralist Cambodia.[84]

Thailand, of course, was never neutral. Throughout the course of the war, it served as a crucial forward base for U.S. military and intelligence operations across Indochina. As already noted, Thailand made its air bases available for U.S. bombing missions against Pathet Lao and North Vietnamese targets within Laos, starting in the early 1960s and continuing with increasing intensity through the late 1960s and after. Without Thai support, the United States simply could not have carried on its covert war in Laos. In addition, the Bangkok regime actively supported the U.S. bombing of North Vietnam. Nearly half of all American bombing missions flown over North Vietnam from the initial sorties of February 1965 through the middle of 1966 took off from Thai airfields.[85]

Not surprisingly, the Chinese and North Vietnamese, from the first, decried Thailand as an American surrogate and accomplice. On April 25, 1965, an official statement issued by the North Vietnamese Foreign Ministry denounced the Thais for "their complicity in the United States aggressive war in South Vietnam and for having let the United States use bases on Thailand territory to attack the Democratic Republic of Vietnam."[86] Despite Chinese and North Vietnamese protests, Thailand refused to shift course. Prime Minister Thanom Kittikachorn, Foreign Minister Thanat Khoman, and their chief associates in the military-dominated regime were convinced that Thai security demanded nothing less than an all-out commitment to what they saw as a common struggle against communist expansion. Chinese and North Vietnamese support for a burgeoning communist insurgency within northeastern Thailand just buttressed that conviction.

Initially, the Bangkok government sought to shroud its role in secrecy. Thai officials scrupulously avoided any public mention of the growing American military presence within their country. But as *New York Times* columnist C. L. Sulzberger commented in April 1966, it was "one of Asia's worst kept secrets." Assistant Secretary of State William Bundy acknowledged as much during an executive session of the Senate Foreign Relations Committee. "It is a matter of common knowledge," he conceded, "known to any reporter who visits Thailand." The Thais preferred, nonetheless, to avoid public revelation of their role in the bombing of North Vietnam and Laos because they did not want to expose "themselves to unnecessary abuse and exacerbation of the situation from Radio Peiping and Radio Hanoi." The United States, Bundy explained, has "had to go along with their basic desire not to publicize those operations."[87] After several U.S. newspaper articles called attention to the growing ties of intimacy between Washington and Bangkok, Prime Minister Thanom broke his government's official silence.[88] On August 10, 1966, the field marshal opened the newly constructed, $140 million air base at Sattahip with formal ceremonies. In the heat of the midday sun, Thai and American generals mixed with chanting, saffron-robed Buddhist monks and parading soldiers from both countries along the impressive, 11,500-foot concrete runway. The lengthy runway had been built to accommodate B-52 bombers, the largest in the American fleet. Previously, B-52s operated from Guam, some 2,550 air miles from Saigon, where they were restricted to a single sortie per day, and from Okinawa. The advantages of the new Thai base, from which the huge bombers began operating against guerrilla strongholds within South Vietnam in March 1967, were manifold; just 125 air miles from Saigon, the Sattahip facility allowed the B-52s to fly several sorties per day, carry larger bomb loads, and save on fuel and maintenance costs.[89]

The opening of the sprawling Sattahip–U Thapao base complex, which included, along with the fully equipped airfield, a new, deep harbor port and a large ammunition depot, testified powerfully to America's growing reliance on Thailand. By the end of 1967, 37,000 U.S. troops were serving there, most of them stationed at one of the eight air bases constructed from scratch or expanded by the United States within the past several years. That was more than twice as many soldiers as had been present in South Vietnam when Johnson assumed office. The hundreds of millions of dollars that the Johnson administration had poured into Thailand during that time certainly seemed a sound investment. When LBJ saw political advantages to be reaped from the presence of "many flags" in South Vietnam, he naturally turned again to his Thai friends. And they came through once again, dispatching a 2,300-man combat force in January 1967 and supplementing that force with another ten thousand men at the end of the year.[90] Thai and American interests, cemented by common security concerns and lubricated by Washington's willingness to pay liberally for what it needed, appeared to be running along parallel tracks. "The people of America," declared a grateful U.S. Ambassador Graham Martin immediately after the Sattahip festivities, "do not fully understand the extent of the cooperation between the two countries."[91]

The same observation could doubtless have been made about Filipino-American cooperation during the war. The mammoth air and naval installations at Clark Field and Subic Bay had, by the mid-1960s, become indispensable to U.S. military operations and troop movements throughout the region. "The bases," observed National Security Council staffer Marshall Wright, "are central to our operations in Viet Nam and our longer range military effectiveness in Southeast Asia."[92] The United States had always insisted upon its right to use those facilities as it saw fit. Political leaders in Manila, consequently, could not capitalize on the sudden increase in the bases' value as easily as had their counterparts in Bangkok. Johnson's interest in foreign troop commitments to Vietnam proved another matter. President Macapagal pledged late in 1965 to send a 2,000-man engineer battalion to Vietnam, only to have nationalist opposition in the Philippine senate block the legislation needed to authorize the commitment. With the election of the ambitious Ferdinand Marcos to the presidency in November 1965, the very man who as leader of the senate had led the opposition to the Macapagal troop proposal, the Johnson administration had to start from ground zero.

U.S. officials discovered that in Marcos they were dealing with a tough, relentlessly self-interested bargainer. After intense pressure from the Johnson White House, punctuated by special appeals from such high-level visitors as Vice President Hubert Humphrey and Ambassador-at-Large Averell Harriman, Marcos finally relented. But he extracted a substantial quid pro quo for the troop commitment, gaining an additional $80 million in U.S. economic aid in return for the long-promised battalion of combat engineers as well as a U.S. subsidy for the cost of the troops. Jack Valenti, one of Johnson's top political advisers, asked with resignation: "What is too high a cost for the presence of 2,500 Philippine fighting men in Viet Nam?"[93]

In September 1966, at almost the exact same time that the Philippine engineers were disembarking for Vietnam, Marcos was departing Manila for his first state visit to the United States. The Filipino leader's knack for telling his listeners what they wanted to hear was fully in display throughout the two-week trip. During a formal reception at the White House, Marcos lavishly praised Johnson for his wisdom, courage, and leadership. "The compulsion of the timorous you have discarded," proclaimed the Philippine visitor; "the importunings of friends you have rejected. But staying close to the image that you knew of America and your vision of what is America, you have insured the security of my part of the world." In a seventy-minute speech before Congress the next day, Marcos saluted the United States for its decision to stand tall against communist aggression in Southeast Asia and urged Americans to remain intensively involved in the defense and economic affairs of Asia.[94] It was music to the notoriously vain Johnson's ears, even if Marcos's fawning rhetoric could not entirely disguise the blatantly self-interested agenda that lay behind it.

Indonesia, Malaysia, and Singapore were much less directly affected by the war in Vietnam. Neither frontline states nor regional allies, they did not experience the pressures so prevalent in Laos, Cambodia, Thailand, and the Philippines. The leaders of those states shared a concern about communist expansion, but at the same time were wary of a permanent American presence. They were, first and foremost, nationalists. Suharto of Indonesia, Abdul Rahman of Malaysia, and Lee Kuan Yew of Singapore consciously walked a narrow line. They spoke out about the war rarely, that silence chiefly a consequence of their desire neither to alienate an American leadership that they looked to for trade and economic assistance nor to upset domestic audiences for whom the war symbolized Western interventionism. In one of his rare public comments, Suharto declared in October 1966 that the Vietnam problem "should be solved by Asia, in an Asian way and by Asian people."[95] What that meant precisely, he did not specify. Prime Minister Lee Kuan Yew of Singapore offered, on a few occasions, strong support for the U.S. war effort in Vietnam. "The stakes are very large," he stated in a March 1967 interview. "We cannot allow the same forces that have emasculated South Vietnam to emasculate the whole region." In order to contain the communist threat to their independence, Lee continued, the countries of the region "may very well prefer a permanent American military presence."[96] If they did, though, few were saying so publicly, and Lee himself was usually much more circumspect on the issue.

Although little recognized at the time, America's Vietnam-related spending carried economic consequences for the entire East Asian region that were nearly as significant as the war's political consequences. Japan proved the chief economic beneficiary of the conflict, as it capitalized upon U.S. procurement orders, directly and indirectly, to push its already soaring economic growth rate ever higher. According to data compiled by its Ministry of International Trade and Industry (MITI), Japan earned at least an additional $1 billion per year from Vietnam war-related export growth. Many of the additional dollars harvested by Japan were poured back into the Southeast Asian region in the form of investments, grants, and loans. At the same time, U.S. procurement orders within Southeast Asia, especially in Thailand, the Philippines, and Singapore, sparked a modest consumer boom that also benefited Japan—and for which the ubiquitous Honda motorbike served as the most conspicuous symbol. Thailand, for example, experienced an average growth rate of 7 percent per annum throughout the 1960s, sparked in significant measure by war-induced U.S. aid, construction costs, procurement orders, and GI spending. An indirect, and unintended, result of America's military exertions in Indochina, then, was the stimulation of the kind of regional economic growth and trade that the Americans, and Japanese, had sought since the inception of the postwar era.[97]

From the beginning, one of the stated goals of American intervention in Vietnam was to bolster the noncommunist states of the region by reassuring them about the power, resolve, and high-mindedness of the United States. That goal appeared little closer to realization toward the end of 1967 than did the goal of military victory in Vietnam. Even those states formally allied to the United States expressed resentment at the arrogance and self-interestedness of their superpower patron and felt profound unease with the presence of a half-million foreign troops in Vietnam. Nationalism remained a potent force in an area just emerging from centuries of colonial oppression; and regionalism—the search for Asian solutions to Asian problems—remained a powerful dream.

Even the Thai elite, who had embraced the anticommunist cause—and the United States—as unequivocally as any other ruling faction within Southeast Asia, dreamed of a future free of external interference. Thai Foreign Minister Thanat, though a rabid backer of the U.S. war effort in Vietnam, told the foreign ministers of Malaysia and the Philippines in August 1966 that it was time "to take our destiny into our hands instead of letting others from far away mold it at their whim."[98] In April 1967, Thanat confidently predicted that the nations of Southeast Asia would move "fairly rapidly" toward regional cooperation in the economic, cultural, and political spheres, free from the "dictation" of the great powers. He continued to emphasize the need for victory in Vietnam, a struggle whose outcome the Thai diplomat considered essential to his nation's security. Yet peace, when it came, Thanat insisted, must be "an Asian peace"—a peace that would spur regional progress, bring an end to Western interference, and lead to the removal of all foreign troops.[99]

On August 7, 1967, Thailand, the Philippines, Malaysia, Indonesia, and Singapore formed a new regional grouping, the Association of Southeast Asian Nations, in an effort to bring that dream closer to reality. The primary purposes of ASEAN, according to its founding charter, were nothing less than the "promotion of regional peace and stability," the avoidance of "self-defeating and wasteful" interstate conflicts in the area, the promotion of regional economic, social, and cultural cooperation, and the establishment of a framework for regional order.[100] With the Vietnam War then at its height, few observers paid much attention to the ASEAN initiative or to the lofty goals articulated by its founders. Those who did tended to dismiss the salience of the new grouping. It was, to be sure, a most unlikely and brittle alliance, containing a strange mix of aligned and nonaligned nations. To add to the strange mix, Indonesia and Malaysia had just ended a bitter three-year-long confrontation, and Singapore had just become independent two years earlier, after being expelled from the Malaysian federation. Yet this halting step toward regional cooperation tapped a deep root. In the long run, ASEAN would prove far more dynamic and durable than any observers at the time could have imagined. It would also, ironically, prove far more critical to Southeast Asia's future than the savage conflict currently raging across the jungles, hills, rice paddies, and urban centers of Indochina.

As 1968 opened, President Johnson detected few signs of impending disaster in Southeast Asia. Problems abounded, to be sure.
The Vietnam War's mounting costs, its maddening inconclusive-
ness, the rippling opposition it had spawned on Capitol Hill and
throughout the broader society—those easily ranked among the
greatest frustrations of LBJ's entire public career. Doubts about
the war's course had even begun seeping into his own inner circle, best symbolized by McNamara's private dissent of late 1967
and the Pentagon chief's subsequent decision to resign. But Johnson himself, along with most of his top military and civilian
advisers, possessed great faith in the ability of U.S. forces to attain
ultimate military victory. All his public pronouncements about
the course of the fighting in Vietnam heavily accentuated the positive. In November 1967, as part of a concerted public relations
campaign to reassure the American people that the United States
was truly winning the war, the president summoned General
Westmoreland and Ambassador Ellsworth Bunker to return
briefly to Washington. "I am very, very encouraged," Westmoreland told the Washington press corps upon his arrival. "We are
making real progress." He reiterated that message in a major
address to the National Press Club. "We have reached an important point," the general proclaimed, "where the end begins to
come into view."[1]

Johnson, too, appears to have believed that victory was finally
moving within sight. He was hopeful that 1968, as Westmoreland had been assuring him, would bring a decisive turning of the
tide on the battlefield. LBJ remained confident, moreover, that
the year would end with the crowning personal triumph of his
own reelection. Throughout January 1968, Johnson displayed
nervousness about the North Vietnamese siege of an isolated
Marine garrison at Khe Sanh, just south of the demilitarized
zone, and with intelligence reports warning that some kind of
enemy offensive was brewing. He retained supreme confidence,
nonetheless, in his commanders' ability to thwart any enemy

operations, just as he retained supreme confidence in his own reelection prospects. That confidence, and much else, was soon to be put to the test.

The Tet Offensive

In the early morning hours of January 30, 1968, Viet Cong and North Vietnamese forces launched a series of well-coordinated attacks throughout South Vietnam, extending from the demilitarized zone to the country's southern tip. The offensive, involving approximately 84,000 troops, targeted five of the six major cities of South Vietnam, thirty-six of the forty-four provincial capitals, and sixty-four district seats. Particularly audacious was the Viet Cong assault on the American Embassy in Saigon, the nerve center of the U.S. war effort. On January 31, at 2:45 A.M., a Viet Cong sapper team blew a large hole in the wall surrounding the embassy, entered the compound's courtyard, and over the next six hours exchanged heavy rocket and small arms fire with U.S. military police and marines. All nineteen of the insurgents were ultimately killed or severely wounded in a battle whose weighty symbolism was captured by live television cameras and broadcast to astonished viewers across the United States.

Elsewhere in Saigon, Viet Cong units penetrated such strategic sites as the presidential palace, the South Vietnamese army headquarters, several government ministries, Tan Son Nhut airport, and the Bien Hoa air base. In each of those attacks, the Viet Cong capitalized upon the element of surprise to achieve early success only to be quickly routed by superior U.S. and South Vietnamese forces. In less than a week, order had largely been restored throughout the capital.

A similar pattern obtained in the other cities and towns that came under Viet Cong fire. The invaders, operating under the cover of the Tet lunar New Year's celebrations and the accompanying cease-fire, achieved almost total strategic surprise. But they failed to establish strong defensive positions, received little support from the local population, and soon succumbed to the greater mobility and overwhelming firepower of the American and South Vietnamese defenders. Only in Hue, the former imperial capital, was the fighting prolonged. There, a combined force of North Vietnamese regulars and Viet Cong overran the old part of the city, hoisted the Viet Cong flag over the Palace of Peace, and dug in. Fierce house-to-house fighting ensued, punctuated by extensive American artillery shelling and aerial bombardment. On February 24, with two-thirds of their original number killed in action, the remaining communist forces surrendered. Hue lay in ruins. More than half the city's homes had been destroyed, leaving 100,000 residents homeless. The "beautiful city of twenty-five days ago," recalled Gen. Dave Richard Palmer, "was a shattered, stinking hulk, its streets choked with rubble and rotting bodies."[2]

The Tet campaign clearly exacted a heavy toll—on all sides. According to the most reliable estimates, more than 30,000 of the attacking communist forces were killed, wounded, or captured during the fighting. Those losses were devastating to the southern communist infrastructure at the local level, built up so painstakingly over the past decade. In fact, the Viet Cong would never again be the fighting force that it had been prior to Tet. The North Vietnamese army, for its part, would need several years to regain its former strength. U.S. and South Vietnamese losses, although much lighter, were still substantial: about 1,100 American and 2,300 South Vietnamese servicemen were killed in action during the initial wave of the Tet fighting. In addition, at least 14,000 civilians lost their lives and nearly one million more, many of them in the Saigon area, were turned into refugees.[3]

But perhaps the most telling blow dealt by the Tet offensive was to the credibility of the United States. Hanoi and its southern-based allies had plainly failed to achieve their more ambitious goals: they proved unable to rally significant popular support for the uprising; could not hold any of the cities and towns they had targeted; and failed of course to topple the Saigon regime. Gen. Tran Van Tra, one of the architects of the offensive, later admitted ruefully that "we suffered heavy losses of manpower and material, especially of cadres at various echelons, which caused a distinct decline in our strength."[4] Hanoi's bold gamble did succeed, nonetheless—and spectacularly so—in puncturing the illusion of progress that the Johnson administration had been holding before the American public. Support for the administration's policies began to erode steadily in the wake of Tet. In that crucial sense, the offensive can rightly be seen as the war's critical turning point.

Confidential assessments of the offensive's impact by senior U.S. military officials, in contrast to their public claims of outright military victory, ranged from sober to somber. "From a realistic point of view," Westmoreland reported to Gen. Earl Wheeler, chairman of the Joint Chiefs, "we must accept the fact that the enemy has dealt the GVN [Government of Vietnam] a severe blow. He has brought the war to the towns and cities and has inflicted damage and casualties on the population. . . . Distribution of the necessities has been interrupted . . . and the economy has been disrupted. . . . The people have felt directly the impact of the war."[5] Wheeler himself called it "a very near thing." Without prompt action by U.S. forces, he calculated that the communists could have gained control in a dozen or more places.[6]

Gen. Harold K. Johnson was more blunt. "We suffered a loss," he told Wheeler, "there can be no doubt about it."[7]

Shocked by the sweep and boldness of the enemy assault, many ordinary Americans were prompted to ask the same fundamental questions being posed by officials in Washington and Saigon: How, after two and a half years of intensive American air and ground operations, and after countless optimistic reports claiming steady military progress, could enemy forces have managed to launch so extensive and so carefully planned an offensive? What, in the final analysis, would it take to defeat this foe? The oft-cited reaction of respected CBS television anchorman Walter Cronkite reflected the widespread public bewilderment. "What the hell is going on?" he reputedly exclaimed. "I thought we were winning the war!"[8]

On February 8, New York Sen. Robert F. Kennedy, a sworn political enemy of LBJ and an increasingly outspoken dove, offered a withering critique of administration policy that resonated with the growing ranks of skeptics. "Our enemy, savagely striking at will across all of South Vietnam, has finally shattered the mask of official illusion with which we have concealed our true circumstances, even from ourselves," declared the late president's brother in a major public address. They "have demonstrated that no part or person of South Vietnam is secure from their attacks. . . . They have demonstrated despite all our reports of progress, of government strength and enemy weakness, that half a million American soldiers with 700,000 Vietnamese allies, with total command of the air, total command of the sea, backed by huge resources and the most modern weapons are unable to secure even a single city from the attacks of an enemy whose total strength is about 250,000." Kennedy called for immediate negotiations aimed at a peaceful settlement, emphasizing that the United States appeared "unable to defeat our enemy or break his will—at least without a huge, long and ever more costly effort."[9]

Disillusionment with administration policy proliferated in the aftermath of Tet. Former National Security Adviser McGeorge Bundy, now head of the Ford Foundation, told Johnson that "sentiment in the country on the war has shifted very heavily since the Tet offensive" because "a great many people— even very determined and loyal people—have begun to think that Vietnam really is a bottomless pit."[10] Even the conservative and until-then consistently pro-war *Wall Street Journal* acknowledged that "the American people should be getting ready to accept . . . the prospect that the whole Vietnam effort may be doomed."[11] In late February, Walter Cronkite, that reliable bellwether of mainstream opinion, tellingly concluded a prime-time documentary about Tet's impact with the personal observation that the United

States appeared "mired in stalemate" in Vietnam. "To say that we are closer to victory today," the veteran newscaster declared, "is to believe, in the face of the evidence, the optimists who have been wrong in the past."[12] Public opinion polls indicated that such skepticism was widely shared. Before Tet, 50 percent of those polled thought that the United States was making progress in bringing the war to a successful conclusion; after Tet, only 33 percent held that view. A remarkable 49 percent expressed the opinion that the United States should never have intervened there in the first place.[13]

Westmoreland added fuel to the rising flames of public doubt when he asked Johnson to authorize another 206,000 troops for combat duty in Vietnam. When news of the Westmoreland troop request was leaked to the press in early March, it ignited a political firestorm at home—both inside and outside the Johnson administration. The beleaguered commander's appeal was rooted in what seemed to him irrefutable military logic: an infusion of fresh troops would hasten the defeat of an enemy now reeling from the substantial losses it had incurred during the recent fighting. Critics almost immediately seized upon the illogic of that assertion by arguing, as Robert Kennedy and others had earlier, that additional troops and resources could not bring victory—at least not without imposing enormous, and completely unacceptable, costs on the United States.[14]

Setting Limits

Westmoreland's appeal for more troops thus unwittingly brought to a head the key question overhanging the whole U.S. war effort—namely, how high a price was the country prepared to pay in order to achieve military success in Southeast Asia? That question inevitably begot some equally basic queries: How important, in the end, was Vietnam to the security of the United States? And how, precisely, did it stack up relative to other priorities and needs? Finding answers to those questions had become increasingly urgent in the wake of Tet because the offensive exacerbated a set of ongoing economic, political, and foreign policy crises, crises that were themselves largely by-products of U.S. intervention in Indochina.

The Tet attacks broke at the very same time that the United States was facing a ballooning trade deficit and a record run on its gold reserves. Investors at home and abroad were rapidly losing confidence in the overvalued dollar, the pillar of the international economic system since the end of World War II. Europeans, who complained that they were being forced to subsidize a Vietnam-induced inflationary spiral, were protecting themselves by exchanging dollars for gold at unprecedented levels throughout late 1967 and early 1968. That speculative activity led to the temporary closure of the world's gold markets early in March. Suddenly the Johnson administration found itself struggling to cope with the most serious challenge to the international monetary system of the entire postwar era. On March 15, President Johnson privately warned the European prime ministers that "these financial disorders—if not promptly and firmly overcome—can profoundly damage the political relations between Europe and America and set in motion forces like those which disintegrated the Western world between 1929 and 1933."[15] The complex gold-dollar crisis, as LBJ and his leading economic advisers well understood, was indissoluably linked to the war in Vietnam.

As if the war and its accompanying financial tangles were not enough for one president to handle, LBJ also faced a domestic political revolt of epic proportions. That revolt was manifested in several ways. First, mainstream public opinion, as noted earlier, had grown increasingly disaffected with the Vietnam stalemate; cracks in a Cold War consensus that had buoyed the foreign policy commitments of every president since Truman were now glaringly evident. Second, the antiwar movement, little more than a fringe phenomenon just a few years earlier, had blossomed by the time of the Tet offensive into one of the largest, most vocal, and most disruptive opposition movements in American history. It brought in its train not only hundreds of thousands of protesters onto the streets of America's cities and periodic disruptions to many of the nation's most prestigious colleges and universities, but overt challenges to virtually all forms of authority and received wisdom throughout American society.

Third, Johnson's own political party, dominant since the New Deal of the 1930s, was now profoundly split over the war. Minnesota's antiwar Sen. Eugene McCarthy announced, in November 1967, what seemed a curiously quixotic challenge to the president's renomination, only to confound the experts by scoring a near victory in the first presidential primary in New Hampshire. Then, on March 16, 1968, only four days after McCarthy's stunning performance in New Hampshire, Robert Kennedy announced his candidacy for the Democratic presidential nomination, confronting Johnson with a much more formidable political challenge. Meanwhile, from the other end of the political spectrum, Republican contender Richard Nixon and third-party aspirant George Wallace, the former Alabama governor, ardent segregationist, and Vietnam hawk, were readying their challenges to the globalism and liberalism of an increasingly fractured Democratic party.

The embattled Johnson responded to those mounting political, economic, and diplomatic pressures by announcing, on March 31, a major shift in U.S.

policy. In an address to a nationwide television audience, LBJ said that he was ceasing nearly all bombing raids against North Vietnam and calling upon Hanoi to enter into formal negotiations with the United States looking toward a peace settlement. At the close of his address, Johnson shocked his listeners by declaring that he would neither seek nor accept his party's presidential nomination.[16]

After extensive discussions with his closest advisers and much anguished soul-searching, Johnson had rejected both Westmoreland's appeal for additional troops and the thinking that lay behind it. He had, instead, reluctantly accepted Bundy's characterization of the war as a "bottomless pit." The American commitment in Vietnam was sucking up an alarming portion of the nation's resources, LBJ now recognized; more, it was undermining America's global leadership, undercutting the international economic system on which that leadership rested, and encouraging dissension and discord at home. Faced with a clear choice between ordering further escalation, a course of action almost certain to accentuate each of those critical problems, and limiting U.S. troop deployments while simultaneously seeking a negotiated settlement, Johnson in effect opted for the less risky path.

Newly appointed Secretary of Defense Clark Clifford proved instrumental in forcing the president to face those hard realities. A politically experienced and extremely well-connected Washington attorney, close personally and politically to LBJ, Clifford had replaced McNamara after the latter's growing doubts about the war had made it impossible for him to remain in office. The new defense secretary retained close ties to the upper tier of the business and financial communities across the country and was keenly aware of spreading doubts about the war within elite circles. "Until a few months ago," Clifford recalled in March 1968, business leaders and top corporate lawyers with whom he maintained intimate contact "were generally supportive of the war. They were a little disturbed about the overheating of the economy and the flight of gold, but they assumed that these things would be brought under control; and in any event, they thought it was important to stop the Communists in Vietnam. Now all that had changed." He continued: "These men now feel we are in a hopeless bog. The idea of going deeper into the bog strikes them as mad. . . . It would be very difficult—I believe it would be impossible—for the President to maintain public support for the war without the support of these men."[17]

Clifford's perceptions were right on the mark. The war's crippling costs had compelled nongovernmental elites, government officials, and ordinary citizens alike to take a hard look at the overall Vietnam balance sheet, and especially at the risks inherent in further escalation. Was a continuance of the war worth the loss of America's economic supremacy? Was it worth the diminution of America's military strength? Was it worth the alienation of some of America's most important allies? Was it worth spreading social disorder, political turmoil, and cultural fragmentation at home? Few thoughtful individuals could respond in the affirmative to any of those questions. Indeed, any reasonable risk-benefit assessment of the U.S. commitment in Vietnam at this juncture made the need for disengagement painfully obvious. A continuation of the struggle in Vietnam could, arguably, have shown the perseverance of the United States in the face of the most trying of circumstances; it might even have demonstrated—to allies and to adversaries—the absolute sanctity with which Americans viewed all their commitments. Those potential benefits had to be weighed, however, against the almost certain damage that a policy of stubborn perseverance would render to America's military strength, its economic health, its alliance relationships, and its domestic tranquillity. Lyndon Johnson's watershed speech of March 31 is best understood as a capitulation to those broader forces. It heralded the president's belated recognition that the United States simply could not achieve victory in Vietnam—*at least not at an acceptable cost*. It also heralded America's shift to a policy of de-escalation and disengagement.[18]

This policy shift carried momentous consequences for the noncommunist nations of Southeast Asia. Many of them shared with the United States a genuine fear of the threat posed by China to the region's security and, more broadly, by communist expansion and locally based insurgent movements. Yet now the United States was beginning to extricate itself from Vietnam while moving to limit its commitments throughout the region—or so it seemed. Leading officials in the Philippines, Thailand, and Singapore, not to mention their counterparts in South Vietnam and Laos, found this new policy direction highly worrisome. Presented to them as a fait accompli, Johnson's announcement of a partial bombing halt and his call for a negotiated settlement with Hanoi seemed to presage American withdrawal from the region and abandonment of its friends.

Within a week of Johnson's March 31 speech, Philippine President Marcos expressed concern publicly that the United States was beginning to pull out of Asia. If that occurred, he warned solemnly, Manila might need to reach an accommodation with Beijing. Earlier, Marcos had warned that the loss of South Vietnam to the communists would push the nonaligned countries of the region into China's arms. "Probably all the countries in Asia and the leaders of Asia would start reassessing their positions," he said.[19]

Thai Foreign Minister Thanat voiced similar fears following Johnson's surprise announcement of the U.S. bombing halt and renewed commitment to negotiations with North Vietnam. Thais, he exclaimed, suddenly found themselves "in much greater danger." They needed, consequently, to bring pressure on Washington to prevent it from "compromising with the Communists in any way that would be tantamount to capitulation." Complained Thanat on another occasion: "How can you expect others to have faith in you, if you have no faith in yourselves?"[20] The Thais, who had chosen to trust their fate to the United States as much as any other Southeast Asian people, felt the ground shifting ominously beneath them. "The impact of the Vietnam war is total," observed a Thai political science professor in April 1968. "It relates directly to our own security, it has altered our way of life and swollen our economy. It should not surprise anyone that we are vitally concerned about what happens there." In early May, Premier Thanom traveled to Washington in a frustrating attempt to find out exactly what the new U.S. position portended for his country.[21] His visit, the State Department rightly observed, "comes at a time when the Thai are very uneasy about the constancy of the U.S. commitment to the defense of Thailand in particular and Southeast Asia in general."[22]

Although it had not participated actively in the war effort, as had the Philippines and Thailand, Singapore too found Johnson's policy shift alarming. In late April 1968, President Lee Kuan Yew told the *New York Times* that "if, having put the stakes up so high, [South Vietnam] is abandoned, then I think the neighboring countries, the countries adjacent to Vietnam, will find American will to stay and hold the line not credible, and everybody will shift in posture." Echoing the earlier rhetoric of Johnson's own advisers, Lee remarked that Vietnam had acquired great symbolic importance because the United States had chosen to draw the line there against further communist expansion. To abandon that commitment now, he declared, would have "a tremendous psychological impact on the Thais, the Cambodians, the Laotians, the Australians, the New Zealanders, the Filipinos and everybody else."[23]

Those critical reactions to the American policy shift did not exactly catch the Johnson administration by surprise. The United States had, after all, consistently justified its military intervention in Vietnam by emphasizing the need to bolster Southeast Asia's noncommunist states, demonstrate to them America's credibility and dependability, and prevent any potential regional dominoes from toppling. It was easily predictable, if no less problematic for being so, that the nations in whose names the United States was making its stand in Indochina would protest at the first hint of a diminished American commitment. Top administration officials responded by denying that any fundamental change in U.S. policy was taking place, a ploy whose utter transparency was as evident in Asian capitals as it was in Washington.

The South Vietnamese, as expected, howled the loudest. Thieu, president since September 1967, Ky, now vice president, and their associates muttered openly about an American sellout. Their greatest worry was that the peace negotiations between American and North Vietnamese representatives, which formally opened in Paris on May 13, would lead to communist participation in a coalition government—and guarantee their own demise. To reassure Thieu, LBJ flew to meet him in Honolulu in July. The lame-duck American president told the skeptical South Vietnamese premier that the United States would not permit the establishment of a coalition government and that it would insist upon Saigon's participation in the peace talks. Thieu was not assuaged.

That anguished, if anticipated, reaction from South Vietnam and other key regional allies helps explain why Johnson never completed the policy reorientation he set in motion. Acute financial and diplomatic pressures, rippling domestic unrest, and the doubts of some of his closest advisers had turned LBJ around, impelling him to limit U.S. troop commitments while pressing for a peace settlement. But this proud, strong-willed politician, nearing the end of over three stormy decades in public life, refused to tolerate even the thought of defeat in Vietnam. Nor would he countenance any action that might erode the very international credibility that he had sought from the first to preserve by his Vietnam decisions. North Vietnam's recalcitrance at the Paris peace talks just fortified those inclinations.

LBJ's final months in office were thus characterized by a bloody stalemate on the ground in Vietnam and a frustrating impasse around the conference table in Paris. In a last-minute effort to break the diplomatic deadlock and boost in the process the waning presidential hopes of Democratic nominee Hubert H. Humphrey, Johnson approved a complex compromise with North Vietnam that allowed Viet Cong and South Vietnamese participation in the Paris peace talks. Neither side, according to the formula worked out by chief American negotiator Averell Harriman, would need formally to recognize the other. The South Vietnamese balked, nonetheless, Thieu charging that the compromise amounted to a "clear admission of defeat" by the United States.[24] At this juncture, the South Vietnamese leader was doubtless awaiting the outcome of the American election, calculating that he could cut a better deal with Republican nominee Richard Nixon than with the White House's current occupant.

In a final attempt to end the deadlock, Johnson on October 31 announced a complete halt of all U.S. bombing operations against North Vietnam. It proved too little, too late. Once again, Thieu balked. Only after another two weeks had elapsed did the South Vietnamese leader reluctantly agree to send a delegation to Paris. And by that time Nixon was the president-elect, having defeated Humphrey by a razor-thin margin. Whatever modest hopes Johnson might have nourished for a diplomatic breakthrough on his watch now vanished. Broken in spirit by a war that had wrecked his presidency, his reputation, and his health, LBJ prepared to depart Washington for the solace of his beloved Texas ranch. A resolution of the Vietnam morass would depend henceforth on the actions of a man whose fierce anticommunism had earned him a reputation for ideological rigidity, yet who approached foreign policy with consummate flexibility and pragmatism. "I'm not going to end up like LBJ, holed up in the White House afraid to show my face on the street," Nixon vowed early in 1969. "I'm going to stop that war. Fast."[25]

A New Grand Design

Richard Nixon prided himself on his foreign policy acumen and strategic vision. He believed that the time had come for the United States to forge a new grand strategy for a new world. Nixon was determined to craft and implement such a strategy, one more consistent with current international realities than the knee-jerk anticommunism and dangerous overinvolvement of the past. Central to his vision were America's relations with its two principal communist adversaries. He desperately wanted to end the two-decade-long hostility between Washington and Beijing while simultaneously encouraging a more businesslike and less ideologically driven relationship with Moscow. For all the differences that separated the great powers, the new chief executive was convinced that they shared a common interest in the promotion of global peace, order, and stability. He saw the increasingly bitter enmity between the Soviet Union and China, moreover, as a great opportunity for the United States to play one communist adversary off against the other. "International Communist unity has been shattered," declared Nixon's first annual foreign policy report.[26] He was determined to capitalize on that fortuitous development.

An early supporter of U.S. military intervention in Vietnam, Nixon, ever the realist, had by early 1968 soured on the war. It represented to him a grievous overcommitment of American resources and prestige in an area marginal to the core interests of the United States. The continuing conflict in Indochina also stood as an irritating obstacle to the broader foreign policy goals the new Republican president sought. Determined to extricate the

United States from Vietnam as quickly as possible, Nixon was equally determined that it exit Vietnam in an honorable fashion. Otherwise, he told a
journalist in May 1969, there would be a "terrible" outcry at home. Even
worse, from his perspective, a precipitous withdrawal would lead other
nations to doubt America's resolution, thereby undermining its ability to
work both with allies and adversaries. "If we suddenly reneged on our earlier pledge of support," Nixon later emphasized, "because they had become
difficult or costly to carry out, or because they had become unpopular at
home, we would not be worthy of the trust of other nations and would not
receive it."[27]

Nixon's closest foreign policy adviser, Henry A. Kissinger, fully endorsed
that rationale for pursuing what the two men invariably termed "peace with
honor." In an article that appeared in the January 1969 issue of *Foreign
Affairs*, the former Harvard professor observed that while the initial intervention in Vietnam may well have been a strategic mistake, "the commitment of five hundred thousand Americans has settled the issue of the importance of Vietnam. For what is involved now is confidence in American
promises."[28] Kissinger later elaborated on that point in his memoirs. "We
could not simply walk away from an enterprise involving two administrations, five allied countries, and thirty-one thousand dead as if we were
switching a television channel," he insisted. "As the leader of democratic
alliances we had to remember that scores of countries and millions of people
relied for their security on our willingness to stand by allies, indeed on our
confidence in ourselves. No serious policymaker could allow himself to succumb to the fashionable debunking of 'prestige' or 'honor' or 'credibility.' "[29]

Kissinger subsequently recalled that when he assumed the soon-to-be-piv-
otal post of national security adviser in January 1969, "the increasing rage
of our domestic controversy" not only colored all foreign policy issues but
had begun to unravel the very fabric of American society. "The comity by
which a democratic society must live had broken down," he lamented. Moreover, "the consensus that had sustained our postwar foreign policy had evap-
orated." The most essential, yet most daunting, task Nixon and Kissinger
faced as they sought to construct a new grand design for American foreign
policy was to knit together that shattered domestic consensus. To do so, they
realized that the Vietnam time bomb had to be defused; the pain and anguish
caused by the war healed; and American foreign policy adjusted to meet
altered domestic and international conditions. With uncommon insight,
Kissinger put his finger on the core issue in his memoirs. "I was convinced,"
he explained, "that the deepest cause of our national unease was the realization—as yet dimly perceived—that we were becoming like other nations in

the need to recognize that our power, while vast, had limits. Our resources were no longer infinite in relation to our problems; instead we had to set priorities, both intellectual and material."[30]

Nixon and Kissinger moved quickly to set such priorities. In July 1969, during a trip to Guam, the president unveiled a fresh approach to allied relationships during an informal press conference. As subsequently refined by the White House, the so-called Nixon Doctrine contained three basic propositions: (1) that the United States would continue to honor all its treaty commitments; (2) that the United States would continue to provide a nuclear shield to allies menaced by any nuclear powers and to other nations so threatened "whose survival we consider vital to our security"; and (3) that "in cases involving other types of aggression, we shall furnish military and economic assistance when requested in accordance with our treaty commitments. But we shall look to the nation directly threatened to assume the primary responsibility of providing the manpower for its defense."[31]

The United States, in other words, would henceforth seek to avoid direct, Vietnam-type involvement in peripheral areas. Continuing a process begun haltingly by Johnson in the aftermath of the Tet offensive, Nixon was seeking to reverse the dangerous drift toward overextension by setting clear limits on America's international obligations. Equally important, the president was signaling to allied nations in Asia and elsewhere that American resources could no longer be viewed as inexhaustible. As Kissinger subsequently explained, the Nixon Doctrine meant "that the United States will participate in the defense and development of allies and friends, but that America cannot—and will not—conceive *all* the plans, design *all* the programs, execute *all* the decisions and undertake *all* the defense of the free nations of the world."[32]

With "Vietnamization"—its strategy for building up South Vietnamese forces while gradually withdrawing U.S. troops—the Nixon administration sought to demonstrate the practical application of this doctrine to what remained its most pressing foreign policy problem. In June 1969, just before the whirlwind Asian trip that took him to Bangkok, Manila, and Jakarta, as well as Guam, Nixon announced that 25,000 combat forces of the 550,000 stationed in South Vietnam would immediately be returning home. The process of troop withdrawals soon proved irreversible. By the end of the year, an additional 50,000 troops had been withdrawn from Vietnam; by the end of 1970, another 140,000 were sent home, reducing U.S. force levels to 335,000. The troop reductions proved extremely popular with the American public, enabling Nixon to distance his Vietnam policy from Johnson's while simultaneously deflating the appeal of the antiwar movement.

On the other hand, force reductions limited U.S. flexibility on the ground. North Vietnam proved no more willing to compromise now than it had in the past. Since Nixon's troop withdrawals were never made contingent on negotiating concessions from Hanoi, what incentive did the North Vietnamese have for compromising when they could presumably just wait until all U.S. troops had departed? And how could the United States exert meaningful pressure on Hanoi with a rapidly diminishing number of troops? Keenly aware that those problems were endemic to the disengagement strategy, Nixon and Kissinger calculated that periodic tactical escalation by the United States might keep the insurgents off balance while giving them the necessary incentive to negotiate in good faith. Nixon's decision to order the secret bombing of Viet Cong sanctuaries in Cambodia, made early in 1969, flowed from that general calculation, as would his subsequent moves into Cambodia in 1970 and Laos in 1971.[33]

The Southeast Asian regimes that had come to depend on U.S. support, aid, and protection understandably found the prospect of U.S. disengagement from the region disquieting. On May 14, 1969, the always outspoken Lee Kuan Yew of Singapore urged the United States not to withdraw from Vietnam too quickly "just because the burden has become too costly for you." He said that "every thinking person in Southeast Asia" recognized that it was the intent of the Nixon administration to remove U.S. combat forces from Vietnam, but urged that the disengagement proceed in a "gradual and orderly" fashion lest Southeast Asians lose confidence in America's commitment to the region.[34] Philippine President Marcos, following private talks with Nixon in July, warned that it would be a decade or more before Asian countries could mount an effective regional defense without strong American support. In a television interview, he went so far as to issue a blunt threat, warning that the Soviet Union might seek to fill the security vacuum left in Southeast Asia by a departing United States.[35] Even in still nonaligned Indonesia, where top officials privately expressed glee with the failure of an alien superpower to impose its will on a small Asian nation, President Suharto voiced oblique concern about how the "threat from the north" might increase if the United States withdrew from the region. Indonesia's traditional fear of Chinese power was not the only reason for its ambivalence about the changing American role in the region. The Suharto regime well appreciated its reliance on the United States for defense and development assistance and could not help but wonder if that support might wane as the United States recalibrated its regional commitments.[36]

Unease with and ambivalence about changing U.S. foreign policy priorities was particularly evident in Thailand, where nearly 50,000 U.S. servicemen were still stationed in 1969. Initially, Thai policymakers were jubilant at the ascendancy of so staunch an anticommunist as Nixon. They soon grew disillusioned, however, as the Paris peace talks continued, the new administration commenced troop withdrawals, and all signs pointed toward a diminished American commitment in Southeast Asia. In a candid interview published just before Nixon's Asian trip, Foreign Minister Thanat complained that the future direction of American foreign policy appeared highly uncertain. The veteran diplomat expressed exasperation with the mixed signals emanating from Washington. "Even for the American people themselves there is a question mark about future policies to Asia," he remarked, "so how can you expect us to be sure when the Americans are not even certain themselves?"[37]

Nixon's declaration in Bangkok, in July 1969, that "the US will stand proudly with Thailand against those who might threaten her from abroad or within," did little to ease Thai concerns, especially since the visiting American leader couched that pledge in terms of the largely moribund SEATO pact.[38] Thai misgivings about their ally's reliability were heightened by Senator Fulbright's blunt criticisms of U.S. commitments to Thailand and his repeated warnings about Thailand becoming "another Vietnam." In response, the Bangkok government began casting about for alternatives to its overdependence on the United States. Before the end of the year, the Thais had sent a trade mission to the Soviet Union, publicly declared a desire to begin face-to-face talks with China and North Vietnam, tried to repair long-strained relations with Cambodia, and opened ministerial talks with the United States aimed at reducing the number of U.S. military personnel stationed in Thailand. Such frenetic diplomatic activity bespoke Thailand's growing apprehension about the diminishing value of its American alliance—and its fledgling search for alternatives. "In a world of changing allegiances," prophesied Thanat, long the region's most vigorous proponent of a pro-American foreign policy, "enemies become the best of friends, and allies the worst of enemies."[39]

From the first, Nixon and Kissinger recognized that the success of the disengagement strategy depended in large measure upon their ability to ease the predictable doubts about American intentions issuing from many of Asia's noncommunist states. "In contrast to some of our domestic critics," Kissinger observed, "these threatened countries saw our withdrawal from Vietnam as irreversible. They feared that in the process the United States might shed *all* its responsibilities and turn its back on *all* its interests in the region." The doubts of nations such as Thailand, the Philippines, Singapore, and Indonesia could not be trivialized. Indeed, "if the United States was perceived to be abdicating its role in Asia," stressed Kissinger, "dramatic changes in the foreign policies and perhaps even the domestic evolution of key countries would be probable.[40] The Nixon administration plainly had no interest in achieving extrication from Vietnam at the expense of its relationships with friendly Asian states. Hence Nixon and Kissinger emphasized the need for gradual withdrawal and the attainment of an honorable peace, a strategy that would presumably leave American credibility intact and its position as an Asian-Pacific power undiminished. North Vietnamese obstinacy remained, from Nixon's perspective, the principal obstacle to the achievement of those objectives.

Widening the War

On April 30, 1970, in one of the most fateful decisions of his presidency, Nixon ordered a combined force of 20,000 U.S. and South Vietnamese troops to cross into Cambodian territory. The main targets of the invasion— or "incursion," in the president's preferred terminology—were some fourteen major North Vietnamese bases located in eastern Cambodia. The invading forces also aimed to capture the elusive headquarters of Viet Cong operations in South Vietnam, the so-called Central Office for South Vietnam (COSVN). Nixon was convinced that this sudden escalation and geographical extension of the war could advance each of the broader goals for which he had been working since his inauguration: it could presumably diminish the ability of the North Vietnamese and Viet Cong to conduct combat operations in South Vietnam; buy precious time for his Vietnamization strategy; demonstrate to South Vietnam that the United States remained a resolute ally; reassure Asia's other noncommunist states that the United States was still willing to use military force when necessary; and, above all, intimidate North Vietnam into accepting American terms for a negotiated settlement. "To protect our men who are in Viet-Nam and to guarantee the continued success of our withdrawal and Vietnamization programs," explained a pugnacious Nixon to a nationwide television audience, "I have concluded that the time has come for action." Framing the stakes in ridiculously apocalyptic terms, he added: "If, when the chips are down, the world's most powerful nation . . . acts like a pitiful, helpless giant, the forces of totalitarianism and anarchy will threaten free nations and free institutions throughout the world."[41]

Nixon's expansion of the war into technically neutral Cambodia had actually begun much earlier. In March 1969, just two months into his presidency, Nixon ordered secret B-52 strikes against North Vietnamese and Viet Cong sanctuaries located on Cambodian soil. Hoping not to antagonize Hanoi, Sihanouk had tacitly agreed back in 1963 to tolerate the existence of those sanctuaries. The Pentagon had long requested authority to take direct military action against them in order to limit Hanoi's ability to mount another offensive in South Vietnam. Nixon accepted that rationale while adding one of his own: by taking actions carefully avoided by Johnson, he believed he would signal to the North Vietnamese that they were now dealing with a more muscular and less restrained adversary than in the past, pushing them toward serious peace negotiations.

Although the ensuing saturation bombing of selected sites within eastern Cambodia did not make the North Vietnamese any more accommodating on the diplomatic front, it clearly had a devastating effect within Cambodia. During a fourteen-month period, American B-52s dropped 110,000 tons of bombs on Cambodia in 3,630 separate missions, some of which were followed by Special Forces ground operations against targeted base camps. Civilian casualties were unavoidably heavy during the bizarrely named Operation MENU, as was damage to property, livestock, and food supplies; and approximately 130,000 Cambodians were turned into refugees. The North Vietnamese and Viet Cong were driven deeper into Cambodian territory as they fled these punishing aerial and ground assaults. At the same time, Cambodia's home-grown insurgents, the communist Khmer Rouge, began to prosper, capitalizing upon local resentment with the havoc and destruction wrought by American bombing and benefiting from closer cooperation with their fellow communist revolutionaries from Vietnam.[42]

Nixon's bombing of Cambodia, kept secret by an intricate system of false bookkeeping so as to preclude public and congressional censure, also upset the delicate political balance Sihanouk had so valiantly sought to maintain within his country. With the intensification of the fighting, the prince's critics on the right called for an open tilt toward the United States and a concerted effort to rid the country once and for all of its unwelcome Vietnamese intruders. Sihanouk's leftist critics, many long committed to the overthrow of the prince's increasingly unpopular regime, found encouragement in the burgeoning Khmer Rouge movement. "We are a country caught between the hammer and the anvil," an anguished Sihanouk remarked, "a country that would very much like to remain the last haven of peace in Southeast Asia."[43] That hope daily grew more distant. Adapting, chameleon-like, to the rapidly changing political circumstances in his homeland, Sihanouk made a number of pro-American gestures: resuming diplomatic ties with Washington, acquiescing to the American bombing campaign, giving tacit assent to U.S. "hot pursuit" operations across the Vietnamese-Cambodian border, and naming the anticommunist Lon Nol prime minister in mid-1969. Those moves proved woefully insufficient, however. Sihanouk, the master tightrope walker, was now tottering, his country beset by massive economic problems, political intrigue, and open rebellion.

In March 1970, with Sihanouk out of the country on one of his periodic, weight-reduction visits to a high-priced European spa, Lon Nol opportunistically seized the reins of power. Whether he did so at the bequest of the United States remains uncertain. On one level, it hardly mattered. Delighted with the overthrow of the unpredictable Sihanouk—as the pro-American Lon Nol knew that it would be—the Nixon administration enthusiastically embraced the new government. The ouster of the prince also removed the principal obstacle to a cross-border invasion, thus setting the stage for Nixon's bold throw of the dice.[44]

The joint American–South Vietnamese incursion into Cambodia brought undeniable military gains for the United States, though considerably fewer than anticipated. The invading forces captured substantial quantities of weapons and supplies, destroyed some eight thousand bunkers, rendered the sanctuaries temporarily unusable, disrupted enemy military operations, and claimed to have killed at least two thousand enemy troops. The offensive probably bought some time as well for the U.S. strategy of Vietnamizing the war. But the United States and its South Vietnamese allies never inflicted a decisive defeat on the North Vietnamese. For the most part, enemy forces managed simply to flee deeper into Cambodia. Nor did the vaunted COSVN, a central target of the operation, turn out to be anything more imposing than a few huts. And the victory on the ground, such as it was, brought no commensurate breakthrough in the peace negotiations. Hanoi remained as uncompromising as ever; in fact, it boycotted the Paris peace negotiations for several months in protest against the Cambodian attack.[45]

The modest military gains achieved by the Nixon administration came at an exceedingly high political cost. Prior to the Cambodian incursion, the antiwar movement in the United States seemed to be losing ground, Nixon's regular troop withdrawals and his much-publicized efforts to gain a peace settlement having effectively defused it. All that changed with the announcement that U.S. and South Vietnamese forces were extending the war into Cambodia. Peace activists found Nixon's justification for the operation wholly unconvincing. How, they asked, could expanding the war advance the prospects for peace in Indochina? To antiwar critics, Nixon appeared bent not on making peace but on achieving military victory, an impression furthered by the president's bombastic justification of the invasion and his subsequent denunciation of peace activists as "bums." Angry demonstrations erupted across the country in response to the Cambodian invasion, especially on college campuses. On May 4, 1970, just five days after Nixon ordered the invasion, four students at Kent State University were killed by Ohio National Guardsmen. The guardsmen had been called by Gov. James Rhodes in an effort to restore order at an institution wracked by violent antiwar protests. The Kent State slayings just intensified the controversy surrounding the Cambodian invasion, a situation made worse by the murder of another two students at Jackson State University the same week. Fully one third of all American colleges and universities closed early that spring in one of the most explosive episodes of campus rebellion in American history. Before Cambodia, Nixon could justly claim that he was seeking to extricate the nation from a morass inherited from his predecessors. "With the Cambodian invasion," observed Sen. Lee Metcalf, "Nixon has made it his war."[46]

The move into Cambodia also sparked an uprising on Capitol Hill, culminating in the most far-reaching efforts to restrict presidential powers since the inception of the Vietnam conflict. Congress angrily revoked the Gulf of Tonkin Resolution in June 1970, stripping away—at least symbolically—the statutory basis for U.S. military intervention in Indochina. Then, in a far more fundamental challenge to the Nixon administration's freedom of action, Republican Sen. John Sherman Cooper of Kentucky joined with Democratic Sen. Frank Church of Idaho in offering an amendment to cut off all funds for U.S. military operations in Cambodia after June 30. Although it passed the Senate, the Cooper-Church amendment fell short of approval in the House. At the end of the year, Congress succeeded in passing a modified version of the Cooper-Church amendment, which prohibited U.S. armed forces from operating in either Cambodia or Laos. "The pattern was clear," complained Kissinger in his memoirs. "Senate opponents of the war would introduce one amendment after another, forcing the Administration into unending rearguard actions to preserve a minimum of flexibility. Hanoi could only be encouraged to stall, waiting to harvest the results of our domestic dissent."[47]

Stung by these efforts to tie his hands, Nixon began to see enemies everywhere—especially in the Congress, on the campuses, among the intelligentsia, and within the media. Enraged by the criticisms directed against him, the volatile and insecure Nixon vowed to seek vengeance against his political opponents. "Within the iron gates of the White House," recalled Charles Colson, one of the president's closest aides, "quite unknowingly, a siege mentality was setting in. It was now 'us' against 'them.' Gradually, as we drew the circle closer around us, the ranks of 'them' began to swell."[48]

On February 8, 1971, Nixon ordered another bold offensive action, this time across the Laotian border, and this time exclusively with South Vietnamese troops. As with the Cambodian operation, Nixon hoped this further extension of the war would bolster the confidence of the Saigon regime, gain additional time for his Vietnamization strategy, and help speed the departure of U.S. troops. More specifically, he hoped to destroy critical supply routes within Laos by severing the all-important Ho Chi Minh Trail. North Vietnamese and Viet Cong fighters in South Vietnam had become ever more dependent on Laos after their base camps in Cambodia had been incapacitated in the spring of 1970. Nixon and his chief military advisers believed that they could score, at minimal cost, a significant military and psychological victory with this action, demonstrating conclusively that Vietnamization was working.

Once again, however, the Nixon administration badly miscalculated. Approximately 21,000 South Vietnamese troops ultimately marched into Laos, backed by heavy U.S. air and artillery cover. Their prime objective: the North Vietnamese-controlled town of Tchepone, twenty miles from the border. By early March the South Vietnamese managed to capture Tchepone, which had been essentially reduced to rubble by the time of their arrival, thanks to withering U.S. aerial bombardment. Shortly thereafter, though, the invaders encountered heavy resistance from a superior force of North Vietnamese regulars, determined to protect their Laotian lifeline. Overwhelmed, the South Vietnamese beat a hasty retreat. Poor command decisions, compounded by the absence of U.S. advisers (prohibited under the Cooper-Church amendment), soon turned the retreat into a rout. After six weeks of hard fighting, some of the bloodiest of the war, the South Vietnamese limped back across the border. The toll was horrendous: ten thousand South Vietnamese and American soldiers had been killed or wounded in the operation, one hundred U.S. helicopters were destroyed, another 618 damaged, and thousands of trucks, armored vehicles, artillery pieces, and tanks were lost.[49]

Instead of demonstrating the success of Vietnamization, the Laos invasion underscored its limitations. The South Vietnamese, in the acid assessment of Ambassador William Sullivan, "got their tail beat off."[50] The North Vietnamese, for their part, not only battered South Vietnam's army divisions and dealt a body blow to the Vietnamization strategy—turning Vietnamization's "first test" into its "biggest failure," according to Foreign Minister Nguyen Co Thach—but were able to solidify and expand their presence in southern Laos.[51] Nixon's second effort at covering a strategic withdrawal with a sudden tactical escalation had come up even emptier than the first.

The Tortured Search for Peace

The failure of the Laotian operation, coupled with continuing domestic pressure to bring the interminable war to an end, led the Nixon administration to offer the North Vietnamese, in May 1971, its most comprehensive peace terms to date. Transmitted secretly by Kissinger to North Vietnamese negotiator Le Duc Tho, the new plan withdrew the long-standing American insistence on a mutual withdrawal of U.S. and North Vietnamese troops. Instead, it pledged the removal of all U.S. forces from South Vietnam within seven months of the signing of a peace agreement, provided that Hanoi immediately release all U.S. prisoners of war and agree to cease infiltrating additional forces into the south. The modification in the U.S. position led to the most serious peace talks yet, a flurry of diplomatic activity that extended over several hopeful months. By November 1971, however, the negotiations had once again broken down. The status of the Nguyen Van Thieu regime posed the most vexing obstacle to a settlement. The North Vietnamese wanted the United States to dissociate itself from a regime they considered illegitimate, whereas the Americans believed that to ditch an ally at the last minute, no matter how unsavory it might be, would just undermine the very credibility they were so doggedly seeking to preserve. Thieu's reelection in October 1971—facilitated not just by blatant fraud but by the South Vietnamese strongman's removal of his two leading opponents from the ballot— ensured that no diplomatic breakthrough would be forthcoming. In the largest sense, neither Washington nor Hanoi were willing at this time to modify basic positions; each clung to the conviction that it could ultimately achieve diplomatic success without making major concessions.[52]

Nixon's hopes in that regard stemmed especially from some of the broader geopolitical shifts his administration had set in motion. From the outset of their tenure, Nixon and Kissinger had been convinced that U.S. global interests would best be served by a relaxation of tensions with the Soviet Union and a simultaneous normalization of relations with China. The two geopoliticians believed that, despite continuing ideological differences, both communist powers were coming to share with the United States a parallel commitment to global peace and stability. Among other benefits of more businesslike relationships with the Soviet Union and China, Nixon and Kissinger calculated—in a classic bit of wishful thinking—that those new ties might even hasten peace in Vietnam. Moscow and Beijing, they imagined, could be induced to restrain their North Vietnamese allies, as great powers had traditionally acted to curb the disruptive ambitions of smaller states. Nixon's relative equanimity in the face of the latest breakdown of the Paris peace talks is thus partially explained by his increasing fixation on a great power condominium in Asia. Notably, at the very moment that the negotiations with North Vietnam were collapsing, the president was preparing for his breakthrough visit to China; a later summit meeting in the Soviet Union was already in the planning stages. With those essential elements of his new diplomatic grand strategy moving into place, an overconfident Nixon reasoned that a solution to the Vietnam settlement might now be found in Beijing or Moscow.[53]

Nixon's February 1972 trip to China clearly jolted the North Vietnamese every bit as much as it did the Soviets, the noncommunist nations of Asia, and the American public. A foreign policy coup of the first order, the visit and the normalization of Sino-American relations that it foreshadowed altered overnight the geopolitical equation within Asia. Nixon, after all, like most other prominent Cold Warriors in the United States, had long identified China as the true enemy in Vietnam. In 1965 he had described the Vietnam War as a "confrontation—not fundamentally between Vietnam and the Vietcong or between the United States and the Vietcong—but between the United States and Communist China." The critical question facing the United States, he added, was: "Do we stop Chinese Communist aggression in Vietnam now or wait until the odds and the risks are much greater?"[54] Not only did Nixon's historic trip to China represent a jarring repudiation of such widely shared convictions, but he was now, with massive irony, actually seeking Beijing's assistance in bringing Hanoi to terms. In other words, this lifelong anticommunist was *inviting* China to assume a major role in Southeast Asian politics, the very thing that every U.S. policy initiative in the region had, since the Truman administration, been designed to prevent. Deeply unsettled by Nixon's opening to China, and fearing that their principal allies might once again desert them as they had in 1954, the North Vietnamese chose one more time to seek a breakthrough on the battlefield.[55]

On March 30, 1972, a combined force of nearly 200,000 North Vietnamese regulars and Viet Cong guerrilla and main force units launched a sweeping offensive designed to cripple, if not completely topple, the Thieu regime. The attacks were mounted in three key areas: against South Vietnam's northern provinces—a conventional assault spearheaded by Soviet-made tanks and heavy artillery; in the central highlands; and in the strategic area northwest of Saigon. Several considerations lay behind this high-risk military gamble. Hanoi's rulers were emboldened by the recent success of their forces in Laos, by the continuing reduction of U.S. troops (only 95,000 remained in Vietnam at this time), and by their guess that the Nixon administration, in an election year, would find its military options severely circumscribed. North Vietnam, in addition, was already beginning to feel pressure from both China and the Soviet Union to accept a negotiated settlement—much as Nixon had hoped. "We were disgraced at Geneva," recalled one National Liberation Front official, "and we were not about to have our fate decided at the negotiating table again." General Giap, the guiding force behind the offensive, believed that a successful military strike would expose the bankruptcy of Vietnamization—and make the Vietnamese communists the masters of their own fate. Even if the offensive failed to achieve the maximum goal of bringing down the Thieu government, the North Vietnamese felt certain that it would, at a minimum, greatly strengthen their bargaining position at Paris and thus bring the goal of national unification one giant step closer to realization.[56]

Those may well rank among the war's more grievous miscalculations. After a series of stunning early successes, including the overrunning of Quang Tri province just south of the demilitarized zone, the North Vietnamese offensive stalled and the tide of battle began to turn. South Vietnamese troops fought harder and more effectively than ever before, much to the surprise of North Vietnam's strategists. More shocking still to the North Vietnamese, and almost certainly more decisive to the Easter offensive's final outcome, was the vigorous U.S. response. Nixon and Kissinger, after three and a half years of anguished attempts to gain what they invariably touted as a "peace with honor," were not about to permit the dismemberment of South Vietnam on their watch. "It's time," an angry Kissinger advised Nixon on May 2, "to send them an undeniable message, to deliver a shock, to let them know that things might get out of hand if the offensive doesn't stop." Nixon vowed that "the bastards have never been bombed like they're going to be bombed this time."[57] In a no-holds-barred effort to block a North Vietnamese victory, Nixon unleashed the most intensive bombing campaign of the war to date. Removing previous restraints, the president ordered the sustained bombing of Hanoi and Haiphong, the mining of Haiphong harbor, and a naval blockade of the entire North Vietnamese coast. By the summer, it was over, U.S. air power and a furious South Vietnamese counteroffensive having turned back the invasion.[58]

In the wake of the failed Easter offensive, North Vietnam's leaders suddenly saw wisdom in a renewed push for peace. With 100,000 battle deaths, their cities smoldering from merciless U.S. aerial bombardment, and their supply routes disrupted, the North Vietnamese were in no shape to launch any new military challenges to the status quo. The tepid protests issued by Moscow and Beijing in response to the renewed U.S. bombing campaign and mining of Haiphong left them feeling diplomatically isolated as well. The image of Soviet Party Secretary Leonid Brezhnev amiably hosting and toasting Nixon in the Kremlin that May while North Vietnam's cities were being blanketed by American bombs proved as galling as it was ominous. The Soviets, although greatly irritated by North Vietnam's failure to consult them in advance about the invasion, had agonized about whether to cancel the long-planned summit as a show of solidarity for "our ideological allies." According to Anatoly Dobrynin, Moscow's ambassador to the United States, "the final verdict of the Politboro was to go ahead with the summit, because its members recognized that the alternative would amount to giving Hanoi a veto over our relations with America."[59] Plainly, the changing shape of great power politics—in which the Soviet Union and China were each now competing for a closer relationship with the United States than that maintained by its arch-rival—was not working to North Vietnam's advantage.

Political developments within the United States during the summer and autumn of 1972 reinforced Hanoi's inclination to seek peace. Veteran America-watchers that they were, the North Vietnamese were dismayed by the rapidly diminishing strength of the antiwar movement and the increasingly dim presidential prospects of dovish Democratic nominee George McGovern. Left with little choice but to deal with Nixon, Hanoi's rulers reasoned that they could at least strike a better deal with U.S. negotiators before the election than after it.

When the secret talks resumed with Kissinger in Paris that July, the chief North Vietnamese negotiator demonstrated a conciliatory spirit startling to his American interlocutors. "Once Le Duc Tho started making concessions," Kissinger later quipped, "he proved as inventive as he had been obnoxious while stonewalling."[60] On October 8 the North Vietnamese dropped for the first time their insistence on the removal of the Thieu regime prior to a cease-fire. Kissinger exulted. The basic elements of a peace settlement now appeared within reach. After several more days of intensive negotiations, U.S. and North Vietnamese diplomats agreed to a draft plan that seemed to meet the needs of both parties. It provided for a cease-fire in place; the armies of each side were to remain in areas under their current control; and U.S. troops would fully be withdrawn within sixty days, at which time prisoners of war would be released. The future political shape of South Vietnam would then be settled in negotiations between the Saigon regime and the Provisional Revolutionary Government (as the National Liberation Front was now known), each recognized under the draft agreement as a legitimate "administrative entity."[61]

In mid-October a hopeful Kissinger flew to Saigon to secure Thieu's approval only to find that assignment far more daunting than he had anticipated. The South Vietnamese leader almost immediately balked at the American-negotiated agreement, raising a host of specific objections. "I see that those I regard as friends have failed me," Thieu sneered at the American envoy.[62] "What was success for us—the withdrawal of American forces—was a nightmare for our allies," Kissinger subsequently conceded. "The South Vietnamese, after eight years of American participation, simply did not feel ready to confront Hanoi without our direct involvement."[63] Upon Kissinger's return to Washington, Nixon exploded at the news of Thieu's recalcitrance. "Tell that little son of a bitch to sign or else," he snapped—then thought better of it.[64] Kissinger tried to put the best face on matters, even declaring at a celebrated press conference on October 26 that "peace is at hand." In truth, peace was anything but at hand.

Nixon's triumphant reelection several days later had little effect on the now-stalled peace talks between the Americans and the North Vietnamese. Kissinger gamely sought to gain Hanoi's acceptance of some sixty-nine specific changes in the draft agreement demanded by the South Vietnamese. The North Vietnamese, in turn, accused the Americans of bad faith for failing to secure Saigon's support for the agreement. It was certainly not for want of trying; on November 25, Nixon had instructed Kissinger to "settle and ram it down Saigon's throat."[65] But Thieu would not swallow. With another painful impasse looming, Nixon gambled that military force could compel Hanoi's cooperation while also demonstrating U.S. resolve to skeptical leaders in Saigon. Kissinger called it "jugular diplomacy."[66] Beginning on December 18 and continuing through early January, the United States dropped forty thousand tons of bombs on North Vietnam, most concentrated in the sixty-mile Hanoi-Haiphong corridor. This savage bombing, coming so quickly after Kissinger's "peace is at hand" declaration, sparked enormous controversy in the United States. Sen. Mike Mansfield decried the bombing as a "stone age tactic"; columnist Joseph Kraft called it an act "of senseless terror which stains the good name of America"; and the *Washington Post* editorialized that the latest air offensive caused Americans "to cringe in shame and to wonder at their President's very sanity."[67] The criticism took its toll on Nixon—and Kissinger—as did the surprisingly heavy loss of B-52s to North Vietnamese antiaircraft batteries.[68]

Finally, on January 8, talks resumed in Paris, each side determined this time to reach an acceptable agreement. After another week of marathon negotiating sessions, the Americans and North Vietnamese produced a document that managed to finesse previous disputes over details and phrasing. In truth, the final treaty, formally signed in Paris on January 27, 1973, made but cosmetic changes in the October 1972 draft agreement, belying Nixon's boastful claims that the Christmas bombing had forced Hanoi to make important concessions. The president's assurances to Thieu that the United States would "respond with full force" to any North Vietnamese violations of the agreement—coupled with his threat to go it alone if Saigon persisted in its obstructionism—helped gain the South Vietnamese leader's reluctant approval of the treaty.[69]

But "peace with honor" had come at a hefty cost for the United States. More than twenty thousand Americans perished during the four years that Nixon had labored to extricate the country from a war he recognized it could not win. Perhaps an additional one million Vietnamese died. His efforts to attain an honorable peace had, moreover, just prolonged and intensified the ugly divisions plaguing American society while doing little to refurbish the nation's tarnished global image. Some of Nixon's heavy-handed actions directed against opponents of his Vietnam policy had not only violated the law but fatally wounded his own administration, as the soon-to-break Watergate scandals would painfully reveal. All this for a deeply flawed agreement that left unresolved the key issue of the war: who would rule in South Vietnam?

A Resurgent Regionalism

Johnson's halting move toward disengagement, the Nixon Doctrine, the removal of U.S. forces from Vietnam, Nixon's China trip, the Paris peace accords—taken together, those actions portended a tectonic shift in U.S. interests and policies in Southeast Asia. America's diminished military presence in the area, in tandem with Nixon's sudden embrace of the once-hated Chinese as putative strategic partners, profoundly altered the geopolitical environment within which Southeast Asia's indigenous states operated. The American-imposed Cold War order appeared rapidly to be coming to a close. If it was to be relegated to history's dustbin, what then would take its place? Faced with the disturbing prospect of a regional power vacuum resulting from America's headlong retreat from empire, the ASEAN states cast about—individually and collectively—for alternatives.

In their own particular ways and at their own varied paces, Thailand, the Philippines, Indonesia, Malaysia, and Singapore each tentatively ventured forth with a series of diplomatic countermoves. Those various initiatives, following close on the heels of the major U.S. policy changes of the late 1960s and early 1970s that inspired them, encompassed two broad trends. First, nearly all of the ASEAN states engineered some form of detente with the communist powers during these years, most particularly with China. Second, they simultaneously sought to invigorate the Association of Southeast Asian Nations, seeing that fledgling organization as a potentially valuable forum for regional cooperation on a host of economic, political, security, and cultural matters. The latter trend culminated symbolically in November 1971 when all five of the ASEAN countries adopted a Malaysian proposal to work toward the creation of a neutralized Southeast Asia, "free from any form or manner of interference by outside powers." However halting and incomplete it might have been, this declarative commitment to a neutralized Southeast Asia offered a strikingly new vision of the region's future. It was one that bore no resemblance to the Cold War battleground image around which all U.S. actions of the past quarter century had revolved.[70]

Thailand, of all the Southeast Asian states outside Indochina, was most alarmed by the prospect of a diminished U.S. role in the region. The Thais feared that the Nixon administration, regardless of its own preferences, might well be forced by domestic pressures to withdraw entirely from the area, leaving Thailand's vulnerable borders more exposed than ever. In an unusually frank public address in New York in January 1970, long-serving Foreign Minister Thanat Khoman remarked sarcastically that a U.S. withdrawal "can hardly be taken as an indication of strength." With more than a trace of bitterness, he exclaimed: "We in Asia cannot sit idly by and wait for doomsday to come." The "relevant question" now, Thanat told his American audience, was "how Southeast Asia will fare when those who have for so long cast their shadows over the region will have gone from the scene."[71]

The Bangkok government enthusiastically supported the U.S. invasion of Cambodia in the spring of 1970 only to be disillusioned by the massive anti-war protests it triggered in the United States and the subsequent removal of U.S. forces. With Cambodia's neutral status a thing of the past, the Indochina war was moving ever closer to Thai soil. Prime Minister Thanom Kittikachorn offered to send Thai troops into Cambodia to replace U.S. forces, but the initiative fizzled when Nixon refused to foot the bill. Thai officials, in response, publicly vented their fury with a once-trusted ally now doing its best imitation of a superpower-in-retreat. Sounding much like an Asian Spiro Agnew, Thanat blamed everything on the "anti-war congress, the liberal press and the hippies and yippies." The Thai foreign minister offered his own venomous reading of the U.S. domestic scene in a luncheon address to the U.S. Chamber of Commerce. "In times of stress and strain," he snapped, "the scum come to the surface."[72]

Thailand had, of course, come to depend so heavily on its American ally for economic sustenance and basic security that this bitter reaction to shifting U.S. priorities could fairly easily have been predicted. A congressional committee revealed, during much-publicized hearings in November 1969, that the United States had over the past two decades poured about $2.2 billion in economic and military assistance into Thailand. It had invested another $702 million in the construction of military bases. The preference of R&R-bound GIs serving in Vietnam for the bright lights, nightclubs, and massage parlors of Bangkok had, moreover, in conjunction with the permanent U.S. military presence in the country, been pumping another $200 million per year into the Thai economy ever since the mid-1960s. That was a substantial sum in a land whose gross national product totaled only about $5 billion per year, and it had contributed to the impressive growth registered by the Thai economy throughout the 1960s. By the early years of the Nixon administration, those dollars were beginning to disappear, however, causing severe budgetary and unemployment problems within Thailand.[73]

Throughout 1970 and 1971, Bangkok sought with increasing urgency to hedge its diplomatic bets. With the pragmatic Thanat taking the lead, Thailand moved toward a modest rapprochement with North Vietnam, China, and the Soviet Union, the communist powers it had for so long aligned itself against. At the same time, the Thais continued to press for a concerted regional effort to help fill the vacuum being left by the departing Americans. Their interest in this regard focused especially on ASEAN, which the Thais wanted to transform into an instrument for region-wide collective security arrangements. What is needed is not Vietnamization, quipped Thanat, but "South-East Asianization."[74] The Thais redoubled those efforts following the shocking announcement, in July 1971, of Nixon's impending trip to China. The failure of their erstwhile ally to consult with them in advance about this major policy shift gave rise to renewed fears of a U.S. sellout. In August 1971 a Thai political cartoon acidly captured prevailing elite and popular feelings by portraying Nixon dropping a bomb on his Southeast Asian allies from a high-flying jet bound for China.[75]

Widespread popular disillusionment with the U.S. connection and the military regime that had staked so much on it sparked the most intense outburst of domestic dissent in Thailand in decades. In November 1971, Prime Minister Thanom cracked down, abrogating the two-year-old constitution, instituting press censorship, dissolving the national assembly, and reverting to strong-arm rule. He even sacked Foreign Minister Thanat, whose long public identification with Thailand's pro-American foreign policy had become a political liability. Yet the military-dominated regime, ironically, continued to pursue Thanat's more recent efforts to find common ground with former enemies. To that end, it dispatched a table tennis team and a trade mission to China in the fall of 1972. Thailand, it seemed clear, was reverting to its traditional penchant for bending to changing diplomatic winds.[76]

It was not alone. Although not quite so traumatized by the twin shocks of U.S. disengagement and the China opening as was Thailand, other Southeast Asian states also experienced profound political and diplomatic reverberations from America's about-face and made similar adjustments. In the Philippines, President Ferdinand Marcos, once lauded by Lyndon Johnson as his "right arm in Asia," announced in January 1971 that he intended to open trade and diplomatic relations with the Soviet Union and other Soviet bloc countries and to "review" U.S.-Philippine ties. His foreign minister, Carlos Romulo, long a reliable bellwether of official thinking, told the Philippine Congress in February that "with the rollback of the American presence in Asia," the Philippines needs to achieve "a more balanced set of alignments." No longer could Manila afford to place "all our eggs in one basket."[77]

Growing domestic opposition to American imperialism from radical and student groups, as in Thailand, also influenced the pace of change in Philippine foreign policy. The Marcos regime found itself under substantial domestic pressure to demonstrate a degree of independence from its superpower patron. By early 1972, Marcos had not only carried through his promised rapprochement with Moscow but had established trade links with Beijing and was inching closer to the normalization of diplomatic relations with both communist giants. Then, on September 8, 1972, he moved decisively against internal dissidents. Citing the threat posed by the New Peoples' Army (NPA), a Maoist-style insurgency that had first launched its violent challenge to the government several years earlier, Marcos declared martial law and sanctioned aggressive steps against the NPA and other opponents of his regime. Although more a ploy to ensure the continuance of his own corrupt and dictatorial rule than anything else, Marcos's preemptive action met with little disfavor from the Nixon administration—as the wily Philippine leader had anticipated. Recognizing that the Nixon administration prized order and the safeguarding of U.S. military bases far more than it prized democracy and social justice, and well aware of the Thai precedent, Marcos guessed correctly that an assault on democratic institutions would not undermine his relationship with Washington. In fact, it caused considerably less concern among U.S. policymakers than the Philippine leader's periodic demonstrations of a more independent-minded foreign policy.[78]

Malaysia and Singapore were also troubled by the potentially destabilizing effects of a complete American pullout. The former had by 1970 swapped its traditional pro-Western orientation for a more nonaligned foreign policy while moving to establish trade and diplomatic contacts with China. The architect of this new policy, Tun Abdul Razak, also sought a strengthened ASEAN and the adoption within ASEAN of Malaysia's pet proposal for the recognition of Southeast Asia as "a Zone of Peace, Freedom, and Neutrality." Although it moved much more slowly toward rapprochement with China, largely due to the bitter residue left by Beijing's suspected involvement in the abortive coup of 1965, Indonesia too worked for an enhanced regionalism and eagerly embraced Malaysia's neutralization scheme. In May 1970, Indonesia took the lead in convening an emergency meeting of twelve Asian nations to deal with the expansion of the war into Cambodia. President Suharto opened the gathering with a stirring expression of hope for the dawning of "a new Asia where primarily Asian countries will have the right and responsibility to solve their own problems."[79]

Such sentiments lay behind the rising importance attached to ASEAN by all five of its member states. Common security concerns and converging political outlooks made the unity-through-strength promise of ASEAN appear increasingly attractive during the late 1960s and early 1970s. It was these, after all, that prompted the association's creation in the first place. Adam Malik, Indonesia's foreign minister at the founding meeting at Bangkok in August 1967, has recalled that ASEAN was initially conceived as an instrument for economic, social, and cultural cooperation. Even so, the Indonesian diplomat quickly added, it was the "convergence in the political outlook of the five prospective member nations, both with regard to national priority objectives and on the question of how best to secure those objectives in the emergent strategic configuration of East Asia which provided the main stimulus to join together in ASEAN."[80]

Parallel security fears, in short, brought the five together—and held them together. Thailand, the Philippines, Indonesia, Malaysia, and Singapore each felt menaced by the military might and opaque regional aspirations of China. Each, in addition, sought to avoid another regional *konfrontasi* and the destabilizing effects sure to flow from such interstate conflicts, and each worried about internal insurgencies that could be stoked by outside powers. To meet those common concerns, the five states that founded ASEAN wanted to institutionalize mechanisms for resolving regional conflicts while gaining common support for the sanctity of territorial boundaries. An interest in economic growth coexisted with and reinforced those security concerns; by encouraging regional cooperation, the ASEAN states believed that they could minimize security problems and thus prevent scarce resources from being diverted from economic development priorities to military ones.[81]

An additional impetus for the sudden blossoming of ASEAN came from the mounting resentment among Southeast Asians with the widespread death and destruction that the Cold War's political and ideological struggles had brought to their shores. "The continuing tragedy of our time," groused Philippine Foreign Secretary Romulo in 1971, "is that our affairs are very much shaped by the ill-considered actions of the superpowers."[82] Seen in that light, as it must be, ASEAN represented an embryonic movement by Southeast Asians to steer clear of superpower involvement by devising indigenous solutions to indigenous problems. In that crucial sense, its emergence marks a watershed in the modern history of Southeast Asia. When the ASEAN foreign ministers, meeting in Kuala Lumpur in November 1971, declared a common commitment to establish Southeast Asia as a "Zone of Peace, Freedom, and Neutrality," they were seeking to bring peace and security to the region on their own terms. Differences continued to divide the ASEAN nations, to be sure. Malaysia and Indonesia wanted to eliminate all foreign bases, for example, while Thailand and the Philippines refused to sever military commitments to the United States that still brought significant economic and security benefits. ASEAN members differed on timing as well, with Thailand, in particular, viewing neutralization more as a distant than an immediate goal. Plans for implementing the Kuala Lumpur declaration, moreover, remained exceedingly fuzzy. Notwithstanding those obvious limitations, the neutralization initiative demonstrated that ASEAN was inching ever closer toward genuine regional unity.[83]

Denouement in Indochina

With all the blood, anguish, and treasure that the United States had shed in Indochina, it is perhaps understandable that the attention of Nixon, Kissinger, and their top associates would remain riveted there—and that the diplomatic gyrations of the ASEAN states would generate comparatively little concern or attention. It is certainly telling that in their lengthy memoirs covering this period neither Nixon nor Kissinger so much as mention ASEAN. During the period leading up to and that immediately following the signing of the Paris peace accords, the Nixon administration's interest in Southeast Asia revolved almost entirely around the prospects for peace in Indochina. Thailand, accordingly, generated much more concern for its possible military usefulness in the event of the settlement's breakdown than it did for its changing diplomatic priorities or lead role in ASEAN.

The Paris peace agreement, as already noted, settled little. It did provide for the final withdrawal of U.S. troops as well as the mutual return of prisoners of war, the fulfillment of the latter provision triggering emotional celebrations throughout the United States. Implementation of the agreement's elaborate procedures for determining the political future of South Vietnam—the crux of the conflict from the beginning—proved considerably more problematic. None of the contending Vietnamese parties exhibited any sign of the good faith and trust essential to the implementation of the provisions so tortuously hammered out by Kissinger and Le Duc Tho. The North and South Vietnamese, instead, almost immediately began jockeying for political and military advantage in what observers, with mordant irony, dubbed the cease-fire war.

The fighting, in fact, never stopped. The South Vietnamese army, ordered by Thieu to extend its authority wherever possible by aggressively contesting communist-controlled areas, suffered over 6,000 deaths in the first three months that followed the Paris peace accords alone. The first year of "peace" claimed 80,000 Vietnamese lives, including 14,000 civilians. The North Vietnamese, for their part, infiltrated about 100,000 troops into the south throughout 1973, bringing the combined strength of communist forces south of the seventeenth parallel up to 230,000 men. Each side, clearly, viewed the Paris agreement as an interruption rather than an end to the war; each recognized that the force of arms, not negotiations, would decide the future political coloration of South Vietnam.[84]

Nixon and Kissinger watched with dismay as the settlement they had staked so much on steadily unraveled. Whether the two American leaders truly believed that the jerry-built peace structure they had helped create could survive the removal of U.S. troops remains an open question. Most likely, they hoped it would, but, as consummate realists, were prepared to live with a "decent interval" between the final U.S. troop withdrawals and whatever solution the warring Vietnamese parties eventually wrought. The Nixon administration did everything it could to support the Thieu regime within the technical limits imposed by the Paris accords. It transferred title of U.S. bases to the Saigon regime, maintained high levels of military and economic assistance, and continued to provide a 9,000-man "civilian" advisory team to the South Vietnamese government. During a meeting in California in March 1973, Nixon once again reassured Thieu that "you can count on us" should the North Vietnamese openly violate the cease-fire.[85]

Those promises sounded increasingly hollow, however, as Nixon's authority progressively eroded during the year and a half bracketed by the Paris peace treaty and his forced resignation from office in August 1974. The spectacular revelations of illegal and unethical behavior by Nixon and his aides that constituted the Watergate scandals dominated headlines in the United States during that period, prompting televised congressional hearings and forcing the resignation and discrediting of some of Nixon's closest associates. The Democrat-dominated Congress, weary of a painful and unpopular war and eager to reassert its constitutional role in foreign affairs, moved at the same time to circumscribe Nixon's freedom of action in Indochina. In June 1973, right in the midst of the unfolding Watergate scandals, Congress passed legislation that terminated all U.S. military activity in and over Indochina by August 15. Then, on November 7, over Nixon's veto, Congress passed the War Powers Act to further limit the executive branch's power to deploy troops without formal congressional approval. The legislative branch also slashed the administration's aid requests for South Vietnam, reducing U.S. aid from about $2.3 billion in fiscal year 1973 to $1 billion in fiscal year 1974 to $700 million the next year.

Gerald R. Ford, named by Nixon to replace Agnew as vice president following the latter's resignation after the uncovering of yet another (unrelated) scandal, replaced Nixon as president in August 1974. Although popular with and respected by his former congressional colleagues, Ford proved no more able to check the legislature's newfound power than did his disgraced predecessor. Kissinger, who retained the positions of national security adviser and secretary of state under the new president (Nixon having added the State Department post to his bulging portfolio in September 1973), failed repeatedly in his lobbying with Congress for supplementary aid appropriations for South Vietnam.[86]

Those epochal developments in the United States almost certainly hastened the demise of the South Vietnamese regime. The continuing internal decay of the corrupt, faction-ridden Thieu regime, plagued by rampant inflation, rising unemployment, and a record number of army desertions, was already playing into Hanoi's hands. The North Vietnamese recognized that they could now move to exploit those manifest structural weaknesses without much fear of American retaliation. At the end of 1974, North Vietnamese Premier Pham Van Dong and his top military advisers decided that the time was ripe for a military probing action. They calculated—correctly—that the South Vietnamese army was overextended and far weaker than it appeared; and they sensed—incorrectly, it turned out—that by 1976 they could topple the Saigon regime once and for all. In fact, to everyone's surprise, ultimate victory came much sooner.

What became the final campaign of the war began with a modest probing action in December 1974 in the central highlands, an area that Thieu's ill-considered troop deployments had left especially vulnerable. Meeting little resistance, communist troops gained control over Phuc Long province by mid-January 1975. In early March, North Vietnamese and Viet Cong forces, emboldened by their easy success, next attacked and captured another central highlands outpost, the city of Ban Me Thout. The Ford administration, as Hanoi's strategists had predicted, made no move to bring American air or naval power back into the fray. A distraught Thieu, having presided over the gravest military defeat of the past decade, gave a fateful command on March 14 to abandon the central highlands and redeploy South Vietnamese troops to the major population centers. Hundreds of thousands of refugees fled along with the departing troops, creating hopelessly clogged roads and leaving the panicked civilians and soldiers an easy mark for enemy gunners. More than 100,000 civilians and 15,000 soldiers perished during the chaotic retreat from the central highlands. Thieu's disastrous order had dealt a crippling blow to the morale both of his armed forces and of his rapidly dwindling band of supporters.

North Vietnamese Gen. Van Tien Dung, sensing that victory was in sight, next seized control of the undefended cities of Pleiku and Kontum in a matter of days. South Vietnam had effectively been cut in half. Then, moving north with yet another offensive thrust, Dung's forces isolated Hue, leading Thieu on March 20 to abandon the former imperial capital. On March 24 communist forces marched unopposed into Hue; five days later, they took Danang. "Barely three weeks after the communists struck at the sleepy mountain city of Ban Me Thout," marveled a reporter on the scene, "the Army of the Republic of Vietnam (ARVN)—Southeast Asia's biggest war machine—lies in shambles."[87] Ford and Kissinger furiously lobbied Congress for emergency military assistance to prop up the tottering South Vietnamese regime. The appeals fell on deaf ears, however; realizing that the end was near, few legislators displayed any inclination to throw additional money at what seemed the most hopeless of causes. Senate Majority Leader Mike Mansfield declared that he was "sick and tired of pictures of Indochinese men, women, and children being slaughtered by American guns with American ammunition in countries in which we have no vital interests."[88] On April 17 a dejected Kissinger conceded that "the Vietnam debate has run its course."[89]

Four days later Thieu resigned, blaming the Americans for the military debacle spurred by his own incompetence. A desperate evacuation of U.S. and South Vietnamese military and civilian personnel followed, with Ambassador Graham Martin departing the U.S. Embassy on the morning of April 30. That same afternoon, a North Vietnamese tank column crashed through the gates of the presidential palace. The Vietnam War was over.[90]

The end came even sooner in Cambodia. The Nixon-ordered incursion in the spring of 1970 had set in motion a bloody five-year civil war between the Lon Nol government and the communist-led Khmer Rouge insurgents, a conflict that was reaching its grisly denouement at the very moment that the North Vietnamese were driving toward Saigon. The Lon Nol regime became so heavily dependent on U.S. military and economic support throughout those years that, like the Thieu regime across the border, it assumed all the trappings of a client state. Incessant U.S. bombing of Khmer Rouge and North Vietnamese positions within Cambodia propped up Lon Nol's government for a time—but rent the fabric of Cambodian society in the process. During the first half of 1973 alone, the United States dropped over 250,000 tons of bombs on Cambodian soil, a greater tonnage than it had dropped on Japan throughout the entire course of World War II. That bombing had a devastating effect on this once placid country and its traditionally gentle people, creating nearly two million refugees, grotesquely swelling the size of Phnom Penh and a handful of other urban areas, and contributing directly to the appeal of the communist rebels.

A ragged fighting force that numbered just a few thousand at the time of the April 1970 invasion, the Khmer Rouge blossomed within a few years into a dedicated, battle-hardened insurgency that proved more than a match for Lon Nol's corrupt and dispirited army. The exiled Sihanouk's support for the Khmer Rouge lent it legitimacy among ordinary Cambodians while North Vietnamese aid, equipment, and training gave it a fighting edge. Following the congressionally mandated termination of U.S. bombing in August 1973, the Khmer Rouge strengthened its hold on the countryside. By January 1975, as the insurgents laid siege to Phnom Penh, the fate of the Lon Nol regime was already sealed. By then, Cambodia's capital was populated largely by the war's victims: the poor, the uprooted, the malnourished, and the starving. Republican Congressman Paul N. McCloskey, Jr., witnessed firsthand the horrors of the Khmer Rouge siege of Phnom Penh. Upon his return to Washington that February, he angrily exclaimed to his congressional colleagues: "If I could have found the military or State Department leader who has been the architect of this policy, my instinct would be to string him up." In Cambodia, McCloskey charged, the United States has done "greater evil than we have done to any country in the world, and wholly without reason, except for our benefit to fight against the Vietnamese."[91] It is difficult to dispute that assessment, although Henry Kissinger has labored mightily—if unpersuasively—to disclaim any U.S. responsibility for the destruction of Cambodia.

With the situation plainly beyond hope, on April 1 Lon Nol abdicated, abandoning his country, as did Thieu, for a comfortable exile in Hawaii.

Those who remained would meet a very different fate. On April 10, President Ford ordered the evacuation of all remaining U.S. personnel; Ambassador John Gunther Dean, the last to leave, was photographed carrying at his side a neatly folded American flag, carefully emplaced in a plastic bag.[92] "The United States led Cambodia into this war," lamented Saukham Koy, the retired general who had assumed the presidency after Lon Nol's abdication. "But when the war became difficult the United States pulled out."[93] On April 17 the triumphant Khmer Rouge entered Phnom Penh. Pol Pot and his fellow revolutionaries, their fanaticism stoked by years of savage fighting in Cambodia's jungles, immediately commenced with the implementation of their horrific plans for the country's transformation. "Like a dying child struck by a speeding fire truck," recalled an American journalist who covered the final stages of the conflict, "Cambodia would come to the end of the war as it did to the start: a victim of blind forces it had not created or controlled or even understood."[94]

Indochina's third domino fell with considerably less drama, anguish, and bloodshed. That it, too, collapsed caught hardly anyone by surprise. Neither American nor Laotian observers expected that a noncommunist Laos could long survive the departure of U.S. troops and the termination of U.S. bombing. In February 1973, right after the initialing of the Paris peace settlement, Prime Minister Souvanna Phouma concluded a cease-fire agreement with the Pathet Lao that gave the communists a dominant position in Vientiane's coalition government. The withdrawal of U.S. troops from Vietnam and the termination of all U.S. bombing operations in Indochina further strengthened the hand of Souvanna's communist partners. Following the communist victories in Cambodia and Vietnam in April 1975, the five noncommunist members of the ruling cabinet resigned, fleeing to Thailand. Shortly thereafter, tens of thousands of Hmong who had fought for the United States joined them in exile in Thailand along with thousands of Royal Lao government officials and military officers. In December 1975 the Pathet Lao simply pulled the plug on what remained of the old regime, declaring an end to the monarchy and establishing a Lao People's Democratic Republic. All three states of what had been French Indochina were now firmly in communist hands.[95]

The ignominious defeats of U.S.-sponsored regimes in South Vietnam and Cambodia severely tarnished America's image among the remaining noncommunist states of Southeast Asia. The inability, or unwillingness, of the United States to bolster long-term allies in their moments of gravest need raised anew troubling questions about the power, resolve, and reliability of the United States. To what extent, the ASEAN countries wondered, could they any longer place trust in Washington? Did the United States truly intend to remain a Southeast Asian power? And, if not, what adjustments might they need to make to help safeguard the security of their own homelands? Equally vexing questions plagued American policymakers. Reduced to salvaging what they could from one of the greatest military and foreign policy disasters in American history, U.S. leaders debated how to treat the communist victors in Indochina. More fundamentally, they asked themselves whether Southeast Asia still held major importance for the United States and anguished about the kind of profile the United States should assume in postwar Southeast Asia.

After 1975, the dictates of commerce largely came to eclipse the imperatives of geopolitics, even as the Vietnam War's complex legacy continued to influence U.S. actions while circumscribing America's regional role. In the aftermath of the Vietnam debacle, the United States struggled both to redefine its foreign policy priorities and to rebuild a workable domestic consensus behind those priorities. Few tasks proved more essential—and none more difficult—for the presidential administrations of Gerald R. Ford, Jimmy Carter, and Ronald Reagan. Each leader tried, in his own way, to divine the appropriate lessons of the Vietnam experience, all the while seeking to minimize the debilitating impact of the physical, political, and psychic scars left by the nation's longest war.

"I think the lessons of the past in Vietnam have already been learned," Ford observed somewhat dismissively at a press conference of May 6, 1975. Though pressed by reporters, he would not specify what those lessons were. Instead, he urged the nation to look beyond the "sad and tragic" events in Indochina, since to "rehash allegations" or affix blame would just foster continued divisions within American society. "We should have our focus on the future," he said.[1]

Jimmy Carter, the former Democratic governor of Georgia, defeated Ford in the 1976 presidential election thanks in no small measure to the tide of post-Vietnam, post-Watergate revulsion that swept the American electorate. Adopting a neo-Wilsonian stance that appealed to the prevailing popular mood, the new president pledged not to succumb to the hubris, blunders, and excesses that had led his predecessors into Vietnam. "The Vietnamese war produced a profound moral crisis," preached Carter in the first major foreign policy speech of his presidency, "sapping world-wide faith in our own policy and our system of life." Calling the war the "best example" of the "intellectual and moral poverty" of the interventionist polices of the past, he expressed hope that "through failure we have now found our way back to our principles and values, and we have regained our lost confidence."[2] His administration's active promotion of human rights and social justice and its corresponding de-emphasis on military solutions to foreign policy problems stemmed directly from the lessons Carter found in the Indochina trauma.

Ronald Reagan took a very different tack toward the war. An unreconstructed Cold Warrior and unrepentant Vietnam hawk, the former governor of California overwhelmed the vulnerable Carter in the 1980 presidential election with a ringing defense of traditional American values and a clarion call for renewed military strength in order to meet a still-menacing Soviet Union. To the extent that the "Vietnam syndrome" had become a catch-phrase for America's post-Vietnam reluctance to use military force, Reagan believed it needed to be overcome. Thus, rather than trying to sidestep or seek atonement for American intervention in Indochina, he unapologetically embraced—even celebrated—it. During the 1980 political campaign, Reagan received thunderous applause when he told the Veterans of Foreign Wars that Vietnam had, in fact, been a "noble cause."[3] He returned to that theme during a Memorial Day address in 1988, his final year in office. Acknowledging the disturbing divisions that the war had opened in the United States, and the depth of feeling on all sides of the issue, the lame-duck president once again sought to reclaim the moral high ground. "Who can doubt that the cause for which our men fought was just?" Reagan asked. "It was, after all, however imperfectly pursued, the cause of freedom; and they showed uncommon courage in its service."[4]

Ford, Carter, and Reagan may each have pursued quite distinctive diplomatic—and rhetorical—strategies. But each plainly found himself laboring in the shadow of the nation's most controversial modern conflict, much as did the military, the foreign policy bureaucracy, and the public at large. Nor could George Bush or Bill Clinton, the nation's first post-Cold War presidents, escape that shadow. Following the American triumph against Iraq in the brief Persian Gulf War of early 1991, Bush exulted that the United States had finally "kicked the Vietnam syndrome."[5] It proved a premature boast, however, as subsequent national debates about the use of military force abroad would make powerfully evident.

If American leaders could not free themselves from the legacy, and shackles, of the Vietnam conflict, their postwar policies toward Southeast Asia had little chance of escaping history's grip. The aggressive behavior of Vietnam and the epochal human tragedy played out in Cambodia ensured that such would be the case. U.S. decision-makers strove, nonetheless, and with some marked success, to forge new relationships and fresh initiatives out of the wreckage of the past.

After 1975, Southeast Asia assumed a different kind of importance to the United States. American policymakers no longer considered it a region of vital national security import; wider threat perceptions had changed too fundamentally to permit such a distortion. In the more than two decades that have elapsed since North Vietnamese tanks first rumbled up to Saigon's presidential palace, it has been the economic dynamism of the region that has drawn the bulk of American attention and has been the fulcrum around which American policy has pivoted. Indeed, Southeast Asia's economic value to the United States has risen during that time almost as dramatically as its strategic stock has plummeted. Throughout the 1970s, 1980s, and 1990s, the noncommunist states of the area, so long caricactured by Americans as helpless dominoes, have achieved some of the most impressive growth rates in the world and have emerged as major trading partners of the United States.

Picking Up the Pieces

With the end of the Vietnam War, Southeast Asia for the first time in a generation ceased being a region of vital importance to the United States. In September 1976, during congressional hearings on U.S. policy toward the region, House Foreign Affairs Committee Chairman Lee Hamilton stated the obvious. "I certainly have the impression," the Indiana Democrat mused, that Southeast Asia has become "an area of more limited interest to the United States as a result of Vietnam and the changes that have occurred." Arthur W. Hummel, the assistant secretary of state for East Asian and Pacific affairs and the Ford administration's senior witness at the hearings, did not dispute Hamilton's blunt summation. "Yes," he replied, "I think surely our interests are more limited than they were at the time when we were overcommitted and overinvolved and we overstated our interest in terms of the Vietnam and Indochina situation."[6]

The veteran foreign service officer's almost casual admission that the United States had in the recent past been "overcommitted" and "overinvolved" in Southeast Asia is suggestive of the sea change that had occurred in U.S. thinking about the region with the end of the war. Not even in the most public of forums would a ranking American official any longer dare depict Southeast Asia as vital to the security of the United States—as had become so ritualistic a description ever since the late 1940s. The region seemed about to be relegated once again to its pre-Cold War status: essentially, as a peripheral area of interest to a superpower with more fundamental interests in Europe, the Middle East, Northeast Asia, and elsewhere. Southeast Asia's chief importance, in the post-Vietnam War era, seemed to rest more on mundane trade and investment indices—each of which, incidentally, were growing—than on the lofty geopolitical calculations that had driven past policy.

A large part of the reason for Southeast Asia's suddenly reduced importance stemmed, of course, from the great power realignments that preceded America's final withdrawal from Vietnam. Nixon's opening toward China during the early 1970s, a move quickly emulated by nearly all the noncommunist states of Southeast Asia, meant that the nation long identified as the greatest threat to the peace and stability of the region was now being cultivated as America's strategic partner. Similarly, the process of detente between Washington and Moscow, coupled with evidence that the Soviets were now acting to restrain the ambitions of their triumphant Vietnamese ally, served to further reduce American fears about the communist powers' intentions in Southeast Asia. A principal raison d'être for American intervention in the area was thus gone.

Since U.S. interests in Southeast Asia had largely been defined in terms of perceived threats throughout the 1950s and 1960s, the diminution of threats heralded by the reorientation of American foreign policy under Nixon and Ford brought a corresponding reduction in U.S. interests. "There seems to be a rough equilibrium among the interests of the major powers at the present time," observed Hummel in September 1976. Moscow and Beijing were competing for influence in Southeast Asia, to be sure, but they were doing so "through such traditional means as diplomatic relations, trade, and aid, rather than through any significantly increased support to insurgent movements or Communist parties." In a conclusion pregnant with meaning for American policy in postwar Southeast Asia, the assistant secretary of state emphasized that "at present, no major power is aggressively seeking a predominant role in the region."[7]

The more modest and circumscribed nature of U.S. interests in the area during the Ford and Carter administrations was primarily a consequence, then, of altered threat perceptions. If neither China nor the Soviet Union was seeking regional hegemony, as American planners now believed, and if the psychological weight attached to the region as a critical test case of America's global credibility had finally been lifted following a communist victory across Indochina that brought none of the dreaded consequences once imagined, then Southeast Asia no longer held a reasonable claim to the status of a major national security interest. Putting the best light possible on this transformation, Hummel told his congressional examiners that U.S. relations with the noncommunist states of Southeast Asia were now more balanced, more rational, and more equal than in the past. These "sounder" relationships, he averred, "are more mutual and less paternalistic on our part."[8]

Reduced interests did not, of course, mean no interests. Top officials in the Ford and Carter administrations insisted publicly and privately that the United States continued to value its relationships with the nations of Southeast Asia, and especially with the ASEAN states. In a landmark speech in Honolulu in December 1975, and during subsequent visits to the Philippines and Indonesia, President Ford insisted that the United States fully intended to remain a Pacific power and was determined to play an active role in promoting stability and equilibrium throughout the Asia-Pacific region. "American strength is basic to any stable balance of power in the Pacific," he declared.[9] In July 1976, Secretary of State Kissinger reiterated that commitment. Admitting that "the collapse of Viet-Nam [had] produced concern about a more general American retreat from Asia," he proclaimed that there should be no grounds for doubt about America's continuing commitment to the security of Asia. The United States remained committed to the preservation of an Asian balance of power, he said, a goal that necessitated "a strong and balanced U.S. military posture in the Pacific."[10] U.S. military bases in the Philippines formed a critical part of that Pacific defense posture. Any reduction in U.S. forces in the Philippines, U.S. officials insisted, would call into question American treaty commitments in the Pacific, with pernicious consequences for Japan, South Korea, Thailand, Australia, and other regional allies.[11]

But with no discernible threat to the security of Southeast Asia's noncommunist countries on the horizon, U.S. officials increasingly emphasized the economic basis of U.S. interests in the region. Even Kissinger, the consummate geopolitician, explicitly framed the case in this manner. "Our prosperity is inextricably linked to the economy of the Pacific Basin," he declared during a July 1976 address in Seattle. "Last year our trade with Asian nations exceeded our trade with Europe. Asian raw materials fuel our factories; Asian manufactures serve our consumers; Asian markets offer outlets for our exports and investment opportunities for our business community."[12] Richard N. Cooper, the under secretary of state for economic affairs in the Carter administration, was equally effusive about the growing economic value of Asia's noncommunist nations to the United States. Following consultations with representatives of the five ASEAN states in Manila in September 1977, Cooper described ASEAN as "a source of numerous commodities important for industrializing and industrialized nations alike" and "an area with unusual growth potential." The under secretary called attention, in particular, to the quadrupling in U.S. trade with the ASEAN countries between 1970 and 1976 and the tripling, within the same period, of the book value of U.S. investments there.[13]

As the Ford and Carter administrations strove to devise policies appropriate to the realization of Washington's more limited interests in postwar Southeast Asia, they focused much of their energy on ASEAN's potential as a force for regional stabilization. In doing so, they were building on the legacy of the Nixon Doctrine, which explicitly encouraged regional cooperation and self-reliance. "Asian regionalism has an essential role to play in the future structure of Asia," Nixon had declared in his annual foreign policy report of February 1971.[14] A year later he specifically praised ASEAN for demonstrating the "utility of periodic consultations on major regional issues" and for serving as a useful forum for the resolution of disputes among member-states. "A central purpose of the new partnership we are building with Asian states," he explained, "is to nurture a growing sense of regional identity and self-confidence."[15] As ASEAN gained strength in the aftermath of the Vietnam War, U.S. officials continued to hail it as a model to be emulated in other parts of the globe. "We welcome Southeast Asian regional cooperation," proclaimed Kissinger in 1976.[16]

Through the end of the Ford administration, however, U.S. support for ASEAN never moved much beyond the rhetorical stage. Washington continued to deal with the ASEAN states individually rather than collectively. With Jimmy Carter's ascendance to the presidency in January 1977, U.S. backing for ASEAN deepened appreciably; indeed, active American support for ASEAN emerged as the cornerstone of U.S. policy toward Southeast Asia. "One of the building blocks of our post-Vietnam policy, not only in East Asia but throughout the world," recalled Cyrus R. Vance, Carter's secretary of state, "was support of regional economic or political organizations that could bear an increasing role in maintaining stability in the world." Calling ASEAN "perhaps the outstanding example of such an organization," Vance applauded its growing economic and political effectiveness and the high, sustained growth rates achieved by its member-nations throughout the 1970s.[17]

Washington officialdom no longer regarded Southeast Asia's noncommunist states, in Vance's words, "as fragile dominoes that would topple one by one if the United States lost in Vietnam."[18] Rather, Carter administration planners began to see the ASEAN states as burgeoning economic powerhouses that were contributing positively to global prosperity and interdependence. In September 1977 a U.S. representative formally met for the first time with the ASEAN foreign ministers to discuss matters of mutual economic concern. Calling the sessions at Manila "historic," Under Secretary of

State Cooper said that they represented "an experiment aimed at determining whether a regional approach to matters of mutual interest can bring additional advantages to existing relationships." The "historic dialogue," as Philippine Foreign Secretary Carlos Romulo termed it, continued the next year in Washington, with Secretary of State Vance hosting a meeting that explored areas of common economic and political interest between the United States and the ASEAN states.[19] In July 1979, Vance traveled to Bali for the association's annual ministerial meeting. "We see our cooperation with ASEAN," he told the assembled delegates, "as vital to the peace, prosperity, and stability of Southeast Asia."[20]

The War's Continuing Fallout

The Carter administration's unwavering commitment to ASEAN went a long way toward easing the doubts and suspicions about the United States that had proliferated throughout the region in the wake of the humiliating U.S. defeats in Vietnam and Cambodia. Even before the collapse of the Saigon and Phnom Penh regimes, Southeast Asian diplomats and political leaders had routinely begun voicing serious reservations about U.S. power, resolve, and dependability. In the spring and summer of 1975, Thai Prime Minister Kukrit Pramoj, Philippine President Marcos, and Singaporean Prime Minister Lee Kuan Yew all openly questioned American credibility. They and other regional leaders confessed shock at the appalling spectacle of the Thieu and Lon Nol regimes' final days, and especially at the ineptitude and inflexibility of the United States in the face of defeat.[21]

Those countries that had long relied on the United States were particularly unsettled. "The tragedy in South Vietnam exposes the weakness of this country, which has been dependent largely on American assistance," observed the Manila *Daily Express*, a newspaper with close ties to the Marcos regime. "Other countries relying on any big power for their internal security and progress should learn and profit from the mistakes of South Vietnam," it cautioned. "The day may come when their benefactors have a change of heart and they will be left fending for themselves."[22]

Marcos and Pramoj took that sentiment to heart. The former threatened to reexamine U.S. base rights in the Philippines, a nationalist threat Filipinos often trotted out during times of stress. The latter, newly installed as head of a fragile coalition government in Thailand, called publicly for the removal from Thai soil of all 25,000 remaining U.S. servicemen. Both leaders were responding to domestic pressures for a reduced U.S. presence as well as to their own geopolitical instincts about America's waning regional influence. The ever-outspoken Lee Kuan Yew was, as usual, the most scathing in his public comments. The United States was no longer a "symbol of power and security" to Southeast Asians, Lee proclaimed during an April 7, 1975, speech in New Zealand. "An era has come to end," he observed; America, "the dominant power in Southeast Asia for 30 years since the end of World War II," now seemed fated to watch from the sidelines as the Soviet Union and China competed for influence. Under the circumstances, Singapore's premier commented acidly, Pramoj's request for the removal of U.S. troops made eminent sense. "Since American forces cannot help them on land or in the air," he said, "the Thais might as well make a virtue of requesting an American military withdrawal."[23]

The bonds of trust between the United States and its Southeast Asian allies and friends had become badly frayed as a result of the communist victories in Cambodia and South Vietnam. "Every time [the Americans] speak of honoring commitments," said one cynical Singaporean official, "I think of the Chancellors of the Exchequor in England who always used to insist that the pound would never be devalued. Five minutes later the B.B.C. would announce a devaluation."[24] Added an exasperated Tun Abdul Razak, prime minister of Malaysia, after returning in early May 1975 from an overseas trip: "The situation is changing so rapidly that the Southeast Asia I left three weeks ago is different from the one I am now returning to."[25] A high-ranking Indonesian official might as well have been speaking for the entire ASEAN diplomatic and defense community when he predicted that the United States would not be able to fashion a coherent regional policy for some time to come. The domino theory may have been "old hash," in Lee's pungent description, but concerns about Washington's trustworthiness and about its ability—and willingness—to play a constructive role in the region were most certainly not.[26]

Those doubts began to fade somewhat as first the Ford and then the Carter administrations managed to demonstrate that the United States intended to remain a Pacific power. All five of the ASEAN states very much *wanted* an American presence in the region. They no more longed for a wholesale U.S. withdrawal than they did for a return to the overinvolvement of the past. Instead, they preferred a middle ground: a United States that would play some kind of role in contributing to a regional balance of power, albeit a far more circumscribed role than that assumed during the 1960s and early 1970s. When Lee provocatively proclaimed the end of an era of American dominance and the onset of a new era of Soviet-Chinese hegemony, he was expressing his fears, not his hopes. He, along with the leaders of Thailand, the Philippines, Malaysia, and Indonesia, hoped against hope that the agonies of Indochina would not lead to the creation of a fortress America. If that occurred, the states of that region would be vulnerable to the influence of external powers they trusted much less than the United States; they could also prove badly outmatched militarily by the region's newly triumphant communist states. Despite the bitter legacy of the recent past, then, the United States and the ASEAN countries found themselves groping during the mid- and late 1970s toward a different kind of relationship. U.S. support for ASEAN's economic and political aspirations provided a necessary framework for such a relationship. Equally crucial were the new security fears unleashed by Vietnamese aggression.[27]

Despite congressional efforts to the contrary, U.S. relations with Vietnam remained frozen during the Ford administration. Ford insisted that any normalization of relations hinged on Vietnamese cooperation in providing a full accounting of all U.S. soldiers missing in action during the war. Until that occurred, he was determined to maintain an embargo on all prospective U.S. trade with Vietnam and to block Vietnam's admission to the United Nations. The Vietnamese, for their part, insisted that the United States had an obligation to fulfill Nixon's promise to provide upward of $3.5 billion in reconstruction aid to their war-ravaged country. A congressional committee headed by Democratic Rep. G. V. "Sonny" Montgomery of Mississippi took the initiative in an effort aimed at breaking the deadlock by holding a series of meetings with Vietnamese diplomats in Paris in December 1975. Those promising efforts were negated, however, by the overheated rhetoric produced by the 1976 presidential campaign.

Ford, engaged in a tough renomination battle with former California governor Ronald Reagan, called the Vietnamese "a bunch of international pirates" during one stump speech and pledged that he would never "capitulate to a government that has broken its word every time we have ever made an agreement with them." Reagan, for his part, falsely accused the president of seeking "friendly relations" with Vietnam, a charge Kissinger vehemently denied. Democratic nominee Jimmy Carter further politicized the issue, criticizing Ford during their presidential debates for not having created a commission to investigate the fate of all American MIAs.[28]

Upon assuming office, Carter backed away from his campaign rhetoric and almost immediately began exploring the prospects for a normalization of relations between Washington and Hanoi. He was eager to put Vietnam and several other "festering sores" behind the nation and to move forward with a set of fresh foreign policy initiatives and priorities.[29] To that end, the new chief executive set up a commission in February 1977 to explore and make recommendations about normalizing relations with Vietnam. The commission, under the chairmanship of United Auto Workers President Leonard Woodcock, traveled to Hanoi the next month. In preliminary negotiations with the Vietnamese, commission members made substantial headway by managing, at least partially, to separate the issue of improved relations from the more complex and emotional subjects of reconstruction assistance and America's MIAs. Upon Woodcock's return to Washington, Carter hinted publicly that the United States was now contemplating the formal recognition of Vietnam as well as an end to the trade embargo.[30]

The still-unhealed wounds of the war, however, prevented further progress. The Vietnamese, during subsequent negotiations in Paris, tried to make normalization contingent upon U.S. reconstruction assistance, assistance that loomed large in their economic rebuilding plans. The House of Representatives, in a quick and angry response to that proposed linkage, voted 266–131 to forbid postwar aid, reparations, or payments of any kind to Vietnam. The National League of Families of American Prisoners or Missing in Southeast Asia further tied Carter's hands by vigorously protesting any move to recognize Vietnam in the absence of a full accounting of American MIAs. By the end of 1977, Washington and Hanoi had reached an impasse, the domestic needs of each precluding any mutually acceptable arrangement. Plainly, Carter had overestimated his ability to satisfy the diverse domestic audiences whose support was required for normalization, just as the Vietnamese had overestimated the extent to which they could bring any pressure to bear on the nation they had so recently humbled in battle.[31]

There matters stood until December 1978 when Vietnam, in response to a series of border violations by the Khmer Rouge regime in Cambodia, invaded its troublesome neighbor. The Vietnamese invasion of Cambodia not only hammered the final nail into the coffin of Carter's normalization initiative but plunged Southeast Asia once again into the tangled thicket of great power rivalries. It also effectively blunted the human rights campaign that formed the other novel element of Carter's approach to Southeast Asia—and the world.

The Cold War Returns

Vietnam's decision to invade, and then occupy, Cambodia was the product of a combustible mix of historical enmity, national rivalry, and frustrated ambition involving Vietnam, Cambodia, and China. In the victorious afterglow of their prolonged wars against the French and the Americans, Vietnam's rulers assumed that they had earned the right to play a dominant political role throughout the Indochina peninsula. They expected to receive gratitude, support, and fealty—if not outright subservience—from fellow communist rulers in Cambodia and Laos whose victories they had done so much to bring to fruition. In much the same fashion, China expected to receive gratitude, support, and fealty—if not outright subservience—from a communist neighbor whose long struggle for national unification had been so substantially boosted by Chinese material and political support. Neither of those expectations were met. Instead, the Cambodians, like the Vietnamese, jealously guarded their hard-won independence and showed no inclination to follow the lead of any other power—ideological compatriot or not.

Meanwhile, tension among all three nations steadily mounted throughout the 1975–1978 period as each saw the other endangering its vital interests. The Chinese resented Vietnam's warm relationship with their principal rival, the Soviet Union; that relationship, cemented with a 1978 security treaty, served as a frustrating check on China's desire to reassert its historic hegemony over the Indochina peninsula. The Vietnamese, for their part, bristled at Chinese support for Pol Pot's regime in Cambodia. Democratic Kampuchea, as Pol Pot had renamed his country, was provocatively pursuing irredentist claims against border territory seized by Vietnam a century earlier.

Khmer Rouge border raids into Vietnam, combined with Pol Pot's savage annihilation of approximately 100,000 Cambodians alleged to be sympathetic to Vietnam, forced Hanoi's hand. In the fall of 1978 the Vietnamese decided to launch a full-scale invasion of Cambodia during the upcoming dry season. On Christmas Day, they struck. Offering little resistance to superior Vietnamese forces, defending Khmer Rouge troops quickly dispersed. The Pol Pot regime crumbled in a matter of weeks. By January 7, 1979, Phnom Penh had fallen to the invaders and Vietnam's 120,000-man force began to function as an army of occupation.[32]

At about the same time that Vietnam was planning its military incursion into Cambodia, China was preparing to teach Vietnam a comparable lesson in power politics. Infuriated by its southern neighbor's independent-mindedness, its close ties to Moscow, and its ill treatment of ethnic Chinese, Beijing opted for some muscle-flexing of its own. Deng Xiaping, China's paramount leader of the post-Mao era, publicly denounced the Vietnamese as "hooligans," privately castigating them as "dogs." The Chinese Politboro that Deng dominated decided in the summer of 1978 that the "ungrateful and arrogant" Vietnamese must be taught "a lesson."[33]

In late January 1979, Deng, during his first visit to the United States, confided to President Carter that China considered it "necessary to put a restraint on the wild ambitions of the Vietnamese and to give them an appropriate limited lesson."[34] The Chinese leader emphasized in his various talks with Carter and other top American representatives that he was gravely concerned about the Vietnamese occupation of Cambodia, fearing that the Soviets were attempting to expand their own influence throughout Southeast Asia by using Vietnam as a surrogate. Deng also thought it necessary to punish the Vietnamese for their outrageous affront to a Chinese ally. Carter, naturally, urged restraint. Yet, at the same time, he gave Deng the clear indication that America's reaction to any Chinese military move against Vietnam would be restrained. The recent announcement by Carter that the United States had formally recognized the Beijing regime, coupled with America's concern about Vietnam's sudden reversion to the force of arms, lay behind this muted response.[35]

In Feburary 1979, China launched its long-planned attack. After less than three weeks of heavy fighting, fighting that ravaged several of Vietnam's northern provinces and claimed an estimated twenty thousand Chinese and fifty thousand Vietnamese casualties, the invaders withdrew. China's first use of military force in postwar Southeast Asia had been directed, ironically, not against an American ally or a neutral state, as U.S. officials had for so long feared, but against a fellow communist regime. And, most ironic of all, it had taken place with the passive support of a United States now determined to deepen its burgeoning strategic partnership with China. Such support, National Security Adviser Zbigniew Brzezinski revealingly emphasized in his memoirs, was desirable because it "would convince the Chinese that we were not a 'paper tiger' and that the relationship with us had certain longer-range and reciprocal security benefits." The most important result of the brief Sino-Vietnamese conflict, Brzezinski added, was that "the new American-Chinese relationship had successfully weathered its baptism of fire."[36]

The Vietnamese invasion of Cambodia in December 1978, Vietnam's subsequent occupation of that country, and the brief Sino-Vietnamese conflict that followed left a deep imprint both on the United States and on the nations of Southeast Asia. Those events, as already noted, hardened the Carter administration's attitudes toward Vietnam, rendering the normalization initiative moribund for the foreseeable future. In addition, the renewal of open regional conflict so soon after the conclusion of the Vietnam War led the United States and ASEAN to strengthen their political, security, and economic ties to each other. Those developments, at the same time, invigorated ASEAN, imparting to its member-states a strong sense of common purpose. Finally, Vietnam's actions vis-à-vis Cambodia seemed to fit, according to many Carter administration insiders, a disturbing pattern of increasingly aggressive and adventuristic behavior by the Soviet Union and states closely allied with it. A reversion to traditional Cold War categories of thought was already evident within the upper reaches of the Carter administration by the time that Vietnam invaded and began occupying Cambodia. Vietnamese aggression thus served as a further impetus for the remilitarized, anti-Soviet foreign policies that dominated the latter part of the Carter administration, and for the even more militantly anti-Soviet policies that characterized the Reagan years that followed.

Like the United States, the ASEAN states were surprised and alarmed by Vietnam's extraterritorial aggression. Indeed, the invasion and accompanying occupation of Cambodia posed the greatest challenge to ASEAN since the association's birth as it violated two of ASEAN's most hallowed security principles: first, that no state within the region should interfere or intervene in the affairs of another state; and, second, that no state should seek to resolve a political dispute through force of arms. ASEAN, consequently, moved quickly to condemn Vietnam's occupation of another sovereign nation. It really had little choice; passivity in the face of Vietnamese aggression would have fatally compromised the association's commitment to its foundational principles.

Beyond an essential concurrence regarding the gravity of Vietnam's breach of a fundamental principle of regional order, however, lay significant differences in perspective on the part of the various ASEAN states. Thailand, for example, feared from the first—and with good reason—that a Vietnamese-occupied Cambodia would pose an imminent threat to its own national security. The Thais worried about the destabilizing implications of Vietnamese hegemony throughout Indochina and about the possibility that Hanoi might support insurgents and secessionists within Thailand, especially in the unsettled northeast corner of the country. Singapore and Malaysia were also apprehensive about Vietnamese expansionism. Indonesia, on the other hand, continued to see China as the principal long-term threat to regional security while viewing Vietnam as a potentially valuable buffer against a Chinese move southward.[37]

Despite those different perspectives and interests, the ASEAN states consciously strove to adopt a unified posture toward the dispute. Vietnam's frequent incursions into Thailand in search of Khmer Rouge guerrilla bases brought the matter to a head. In June 1980 the ASEAN foreign ministers condemned those incursions as a "grave and direct threat to the security of Thailand, affecting the security of ASEAN member-states and endangering peace and security in the whole region."[38] From that point forward, the association assumed a leading role in various international efforts to resolve the

Kampuchean crisis. ASEAN adopted an ultimately successful diplomatic strategy designed to contain Vietnamese expansion, to deny to Hanoi the fruits of its aggression, to keep the Cambodia problem at the forefront of international diplomacy, and to mobilize broad international support for the principle of Cambodian self-determination. This strategy gained its first tangible success during the International Conference on Kampuchea of July 1981, a conference initiated by ASEAN and supported by the United Nations—and the United States.[39]

Presidents Carter and Reagan wholeheartedly supported ASEAN's diplomatic campaign against Vietnam. Both administrations, in addition, stepped up U.S. military and economic aid to the ASEAN states and provided substantial humanitarian assistance aimed at facilitating the resettlement of the growing numbers of Indochinese refugees, the so-called "boat people." The most agonizing decision for the United States came early on, when the ASEAN powers implored the Carter administration to join with them in support of the Pol Pot regime's right to maintain Cambodia's UN seat. "We were being asked, recalled a conflicted Secretary of State Vance, "to vote for the continued seating in the UN of one of history's most barbaric regimes, one that had fought us and that now controlled none of the cities of Cambodia."[40] The Khmer Rouge may have killed as many as two million of its own people during its brief time in power, a horrific bloodletting of genocidal proportions. Yet, as abominable as the United States found the Khmer Rouge, it saw advantages to lining up with ASEAN—and China—on this vexing issue. Unwilling to isolate itself from its friends inside and outside the region, and not wanting to take any step that might "appear to legitimize a forcible takeover of one country by another," the United States voted, on self-described "narrow technical grounds," to support Democratic Kampuchea's place at the UN.[41]

The Reagan administration abided by that politically contentious decision while moving to intensify U.S. efforts to isolate and punish Vietnam for its aggression against Cambodia. That stance formed an essential part of the reinvigorated containment strategy that Reagan made the hallmark of his foreign policy. Despite ample evidence to the contrary, the conservative Republican president and his top foreign policy advisers genuinely believed that American power, along with American will, had declined precipitously during the 1970s. When the new administration assumed office in January 1981, claimed Secretary of State Alexander M. Haig, Jr., the Soviet Union "possessed greater military power than the United States, which had gone into a truly alarming military decline even before the withdrawal from Vietnam accelerated the weakening trend." According to the former general and self-styled geopolitician, the Kremlin "had been seduced by the weakness of the American will and extended itself far beyond the natural limits of its own apparent interests and influence."[42] Reagan, Haig, Secretary of Defense Casper Weinberger, and other top national security planners were determined to reverse this trend. To achieve that goal, the president authorized a major increase in U.S. defense spending, launched a vigorous rhetorical assault against both the Soviet state and the ideology that undergirded it, vowed to oppose Soviet-sponsored regimes and insurgencies across the globe, and endeavored to rebuild U.S. alliance relationships as counterweights against what the former actor once memorably referred to as "the evil empire."

This new policy orientation bore significant consequences for the American role in Southeast Asia, and for U.S.-ASEAN relations in particular. A region for which the Cold War appeared to have lost its relevance just a few years earlier was now being viewed by Washington once again as an important theater in its all-defining, global struggle with Moscow. "Our Asian security policy," explained a senior State Department official in April 1981, "is related to our larger task of coping with the strategic challenge posed by our principal adversary, the Soviet Union, and by the aggressive actions of nations which receive its backing and act as its proxies, such as Vietnam."[43] The Reagan administration made clear the importance it attached to Southeast Asia when Haig traveled to Manila in June 1981 to meet with the ASEAN foreign ministers to forge a common stance against Vietnam. The next month, the new secretary of state lent warm American support to the ASEAN-initiated International Conference on Kampuchea, held in New York under UN auspices. "The United States will not normalize relations with a Vietnam that occupies Kampuchea and remains a source of trouble to the entire region," vowed the combative Haig.[44]

Defending the administration's renewed interest in Southeast Asia to Congress, John H. Holdridge, the assistant secretary of state for East Asian and Pacific affairs, testified that Vietnam's continuing occupation of Cambodia posed a major threat to the peace and stability of Southeast Asia, and hence to U.S. interests. Since Hanoi was so obviously Moscow's stalking horse in Southeast Asia, Holdridge averred, the Soviet threat to the region must be recognized as "a very palpable and growing one." It represented, he added, "part and parcel of what we see in other parts of the world," including Afghanistan, Africa, the Middle East, and Central America.[45] Richard L. Armitage, the deputy assistant secretary of defense for international security affairs, got even more specific. He told the Senate Foreign Relations Committee, in July 1981, that the Soviets were currently pursuing three specific objectives in Southeast Asia, each of them dangerously destabilizing. "First, they seek to flank China; second, they seek a position astride the major sea lanes linking East Asia, and especially Japan, with petroleum source areas in Southwest Asia; third, they seek to parlay the economic ruin of Indochina into advantage." He emphasized, in addition, that the Soviets were developing air and naval bases at Da Nang and Cam Ranh Bay that posed not only "a growing menace to China's southern flank" but could over time challenge the critically important U.S. bases at Clark Field and Subic Bay.[46] Cooperation with ASEAN thus assumed increased salience in light of the Reagan administration's heightened alarm about Soviet intentions and capabilities in the area. "Our concern with Vietnam," explained Holdridge, "is a function of the threat which Vietnam poses to ASEAN through its aggression in Kampuchea and through its relationship with the Soviet Union."[47]

Yet ASEAN was far more, of course, than just a convenient counterweight to Vietnamese-Soviet expansion. Even the security-obsessed Reagan administration recognized that U.S. trade and investment with the ASEAN states was fast increasing and formed a compelling ingredient of U.S. interest in its own right. By 1981 trade between the United States and the ASEAN states amounted to over $21 billion per year, with direct U.S. investment totaling over $4.5 billion. Testifying before the Senate Foreign Relations Committee in July 1982, one State Department official noted that average annual growth rates of 7 percent over the past decade had "earned ASEAN the reputation as perhaps the most dynamic area in the world." Another called attention to a recent financial survey in the *New York Times* that had identified Southeast Asia as economically "the most upbeat area of the world." That representatives of the private sector, including leading members of the recently established ASEAN-U.S. Business Council, shared time with administration spokesmen during that, and subsequent, congressional hearings is indicative of America's deepening commercial stake in Southeast Asia.

During the annual ASEAN ministerial meeting in Singapore in June 1982, American representatives made it clear once again that the United States prized the region's economic vitality and considered ASEAN "the central element in our policies in Southeast Asia."[48] Several months later, during a White House welcoming ceremony for Indonesia's Suharto, Reagan remarked that "ASEAN now stands as a model for regional cooperation" and "regional resilience." American "support for ASEAN," the president added, "has been and will continue to be the keystone of American policy in Southeast Asia."[49] He repeated that message with equal vigor during a May 1986 visit to Indonesia. Addressing the annual ASEAN ministerial meeting, a first for an American president, Reagan proclaimed that "support for and cooperation with ASEAN is a linchpin of American Pacific policy."[50]

The Reagan administration applauded the ASEAN regimes on a number of counts: for their economic progress, for their relative political stability, for their pro-Western orientation, and for their willingness to work with the United States on regional security matters. That approval did not, to be sure, translate into sustained, high-level interest in the area; the Middle East, Central America, Western Europe, the Soviet Union—all commanded far more of the attention of President Reagan and his top diplomatic and defense personnel than did Southeast Asia. It is doubtless revealing in this regard that George P. Shultz, who replaced the fired Haig as secretary of state in July 1982, mentions ASEAN but once in a memoir about his six-and-a-half-year tenure at Foggy Bottom that runs over eleven hundred pages.[51]

But good news characteristically generates far less attention than bad; and on the scale of global hot spots of the 1980s, Southeast Asia hardly registered. The Vietnamese occupation of Cambodia excepted, and that situation appeared reasonably well contained by the early 1980s, Southeast Asia seemed one of the more placid and prosperous corners of the Third World. Hence the relative lack of time and energy devoted to the region by leading U.S. officials during the Reagan years reflected the relative absence of pressing policy problems there. Deputy Secretary of State Walter J. Stoessel embraced this theme directly at the ASEAN foreign ministers' meeting of June 1982. He assured the assembled statesmen that their "dynamic, well-tended societies" were no less important to the United States because they were "noncrisis areas." Paraphrasing Lee Kuan Yew, Stoessel added pointedly that "ASEAN is an exception in the Third World by reason of its success and its stability."[52]

The Human Rights Conundrum

Of course, many of the same ASEAN states that the Reagan administration ritualistically lauded for their economic vitality and political stability were highly repressive, authoritarian regimes with dreadful human rights records. Indonesia under Suharto, the Philippines under Marcos, Singapore under Lee Kuan Yew, Thailand under various military chieftains—all stood at considerable remove from America's oft-promulgated ideal of pluralistic, representative democracies that protected basic human rights. Of the ASEAN five (six after the admission of the tiny sultanate of Brunei in 1984), only Malaysia even came close to genuine democracy during Reagan's first term in office.

Yet the ardently anticommunist Reagan made it clear from the beginning of his tenure that imploring friendly countries to respect civil liberties and democratic freedoms would not be the priority that it had been for his predecessor. The Republican president was no more inclined to cajole friends and allies about protecting individual liberties than he was inclined to mount a crusade against human rights abuses—at least not anywhere outside the Soviet bloc. Reagan saw few advantages, and substantial disadvantages, in raising such sensitive issues with stable, noncommunist countries that were, for the most part, supportive of American foreign policy objectives. His ascension to power, consequently, was greeted warmly, and with a degree of relief, by ASEAN's authoritarian rulers. The pressure of the Carter years, as circumscribed as it might have been in practice, was now officially being jettisoned.

"Our commitment to human rights must be absolute," President Jimmy Carter had declared at his inauguration.[53] "Human rights is the soul of our foreign policy," he reiterated in 1978.[54] Although Carter made a strong declaratory commitment to human rights a centerpiece of his foreign policy, the issue by no means originated with him. A group of liberal Democratic activists in Congress, offended by the evident amorality of U.S. foreign policy during the Nixon and Ford presidencies, had begun pressing a human rights agenda on the White House several years before Carter's election. Indeed, forty hearings about international human rights violations were held on Capitol Hill during 1974 and 1975. Further, Congress passed several amendments to foreign aid legislation during the Ford administration that restricted military and economic assistance to countries engaged in "a consistent pattern of gross violations of internationally recognized human rights."[55] One law, passed in 1976, made it "a principal goal of the foreign policy of the United States to promote the increased observance of internationally recognized human rights by all countries." The bill required the secretary of state to submit an annual report on the human rights records of all countries receiving U.S. aid and prohibited assistance to any country guilty of a wholesale violation of such rights.[56]

Carter made this issue his own for a complementary set of moral, practical, and political reasons. A born-again Christian with deeply held religious convictions, the Georgian considered it an essential responsibility of the United States to do good in the world. That crusader impulse coexisted with a hunch that promoting human rights also made good diplomatic and political sense. Brzezinski, although cut out of the same realpolitik cloth as Kissinger, agreed with Carter that there was "a pressing need to reinvigorate the moral content of American foreign policy." Not only would such an approach help "revitalize an American image which had been tarnished by the Vietnam experience," but it "would advance America's global interests by demonstrating to the emerging nations of the Third World the reality of our democratic system, in sharp contrast to the political system and practices of our adversaries." The human rights emphasis neatly blended American idealism with American self-interest; it was "a humanitarian effort," in Brzezinski's words, "which we believed ultimately would also benefit the United States." The policy had the added benefit of drawing a sharp contrast between Carter's values and those of his predecessors, a politically useful distinction given public disgust with the sordid Vietnam and Watergate revelations of the recent past.[57] But how, precisely, could Carter, or any other American leader, translate such grand impulses into practical policies? How could a human rights campaign advance American interests without in the process alienating friendly regimes whose support the United States needed?

The situation in Southeast Asia encapsulated the basic dilemmas at the core of any human rights-oriented foreign policy. The behavior of the region's authoritarian regimes, especially Thailand, Indonesia, and the Philippines, had come in for withering criticism by congressional activists throughout the Nixon and Ford years. Carter was highly sensitive to such criticisms. Yet, as much as he wanted to promote greater respect for human freedoms and democratic practices in each of those countries, the president and his foreign policy team recognized from the outset that meddling in the internal affairs of friendly states carried risks. Official criticisms, as a result, were often toned down, mixed signals sent, and meaningful sanctions never applied. A wide gulf, in the end, separated the rhetoric from the reality of Carter's human rights orientation.

Thailand offers a clear case in point. On October 6, 1976, the military had snuffed out a rocky three-year experiment with democracy and civilian rule by seizing power in a bloodless coup d'état. The previous day, leftist students at Thammasat University had staged massive antigovernment rallies that inspired counterdemonstrations from rightist elements. The police intervened to restore order. "Savage violence" ensued, in the apt description of one U.S. government official, leaving forty dead and over three thousand jailed. The melee also gave the Thai military the pretext it needed to topple the civilian government of Seni Pramoj. The new regime, headed by Thanim Kraivichien and, after October 1977, Gen. Kriangsak Chomanand, imposed rigid censorship, cracked down on dissidents, disbanded all political parties, and jailed or forced into exile leading political opponents.[58] "The United States has made President Carter's views on human rights very clearly known to Thai Government officials, both here and in Thailand," a State Department representative assured Congress in June 1977, "including our view that a state of emergency cannot justify the commission of violations of human rights."[59] But the administration, in fact, soft-pedaled all such admonitions, an inclination just strengthened after the Vietnamese invasion of Cambodia renewed U.S. interest in Thailand's strategic salience.

Carter followed a similarly accommodating approach toward Suharto's repressive and corruption-riddled "New Order." In December 1975 the Indonesian strongman had dispatched troops to put down a revolt in neighboring East Timor, a former Portuguese possession that had recently declared its independence and become engulfed in civil war. A bloody repression followed that resulted in as many as 100,000 Timorese deaths. Yet the Indonesian takeover of East Timor, although a blatant affront to the long-professed American ideal of self-determination, occasioned no condemnation by Washington. Carter was content, as Ford had been, to accept the Indonesian annexation of the island as a fait accompli. To do otherwise, an administration legal adviser explained to a congressional investigating committee, "would not serve our best interests in light of the importance of our relations with Indonesia."[60]

Nor was Carter willing to threaten Indonesia with an aid reduction as punishment for the tens of thousands of political prisoners it had held without trial ever since the 1965–66 upheaval, for its heavy-handed press censorship, or for its suppression of any and all political voices that dared speak out against Suharto's autocratic rule. In October 1977 a State Department representative assured Congress that the administration had made known to Indonesian officials, "on numerous occasions," its "strong concern over the maintenance and fulfillment of human rights and individual liberties."[61] U.S. officials were quick to claim credit for Jakarta's release, by 1979, of most of the political prisoners and detainees it had been holding for more than a decade. What the administration failed to admit publicly, however, was that it had consistently subordinated its commitment to human rights in Indonesia, much as it had in Thailand, to its larger interest in maintaining friendly relations with an economically and strategically valuable partner.[62]

A comparably accommodating pattern obtained with regard to the Philippines, perhaps the most notorious human rights violator within ASEAN. An Amnesty International report, released late in 1976, harshly censured Marcos's regime for its systematic jailing of political opponents and for its widespread use of torture against political prisoners. Martial law procedures, in effect since 1972, stood as a further affront to the democratic freedoms and individual liberties Carter so frequently advocated. The new Democratic administration urged Marcos—albeit gently—to eschew torture, treat pris-

oners more humanely, restore basic human liberties, and return his country
to the rule of law. Richard C. Holbrooke, the assistant secretary of state for
East Asian and Pacific affairs, informed the Philippine leader early in 1977
that the violation of human rights in his country was a matter "of personal
importance to President Carter." Holbrooke said that the continued deten-
tion of Benigno Aquino, the leading opposition figure, constituted a matter
of particular concern in the United States.[63] Patricia Derian, head of the State
Department's newly established Bureau of Human Rights Affairs, was an
even more insistent advocate of political reform. During a visit to Manila in
January 1978, the outspoken Derian, a former civil rights activist in her
native Mississippi, not only chided Marcos for the human rights abuses his
regime was committing but had the effrontery to visit the jailed Aquino. Even
so, the Carter administration's signals to the Philippines, as with Thailand
and Indonesia, were at best mixed. When no sanctions followed Derian's
hectoring, Marcos surmised correctly that he could weather the human
rights storm with little more than cosmetic changes in his style of governance.[64]

As Marcos had suspected all along, the Carter administration's determination to maintain U.S. control over its Philippine bases took precedence
over its desire to reform a still-dependable ally. The Filipino ruler had, in
1976, broken off a Kissinger-directed effort to renegotiate the military bases
agreement between the two countries; not even the secretary of state's offer
of $1 billion in "rent" over the next five years could keep the talks on track.[65]
Carter made the formalization of a new agreement permitting continued U.S.
control over the valuable air and naval facilities a top priority, one that ultimately trumped human rights considerations. "We have certain specific
national security objectives, namely, the retention of our military bases,"
Ambassador David D. Newsom advised the State Department, "which we
can only achieve by reaching agreement with a leadership considered by
many in the United States—and in the Philippines—to be in violation of
accepted norms of human rights."[66] Vice President Walter Mondale visited
Manila in the spring of 1978 and, after the requisite conversations about
human rights, quickly got down to the real business at hand.

On January 1, 1979, the United States and the Philippines signed a new
bases agreement, with the Carter administration pledging $500 million per
year in military assistance as a quid for quo for continued American use of
the bases. "It is our strong view that you cannot use your leverage two ways
at once," a realistic Holbrooke told Congress in 1979. "And we had to
choose between using our bilateral relationship for human rights objectives
and using it first for putting our military facilities on a stable basis."[67] For

their part, opponents of the Marcos regime were disheartened by what seemed an egregious compromise of principle. On Christmas Day 1978, forty-two prominent members of the Philippine opposition, including former President Macapagal, condemned Marcos, the about-to-be-signed agreement, and the Carter administration. "We denounce the Carter administration," they said in a formal letter of protest, "for advocating respect for human rights while at the same time generously subsidizing a dictator and imposing the continued presence of its bases upon a people shackled by martial law, thereby denying them the most basic of all human rights, namely, their right to survival."[68]

If Carter's approach to the human rights conundrum could rightly be indicted as a capitulation to authoritarian regimes that bordered on the hypocritical, Reagan's approach was nothing if not consistent. From the first, the Republican president made it clear that his administration would not interfere in the internal affairs of friendly states. Reagan prized the political stability, geostrategic cooperation, and market-oriented economic policies that the ASEAN states featured; he was willing to live with their checkered human rights records as a more-than-acceptable trade-off. The new chief executive's determination to abandon Carter's human rights touchstone quickly became evident. His vice president, George Bush, went so far as to toast Marcos, during a 1981 visit to Manila, for his "adherence to democratic principles and democratic processes."[69] That comment, widely derided by administration critics in the United States and in the Philippines, spoke volumes about the even more accommodating mood now prevailing in Washington.

Marcos, ironically, proved his own worst enemy, taking actions so heavy-handed and so destabilizing that even the forgiving Reagan ultimately had little choice but to cut him loose. The president and his senior foreign policy advisers valued Marcos primarily because of his long record of cooperation with the United States. They feared, moreover, that any U.S. pressure on the regime to implement major reforms would just weaken Marcos, intensify the already serious threat posed by the 12,000–15,000 communist-oriented insurgents of the New Peoples' Army (NPA), and even jeopardize the security of U.S. military installations. "Our relationship with the Philippines is dominated by our interest in the maintenance of unhampered use of our military facilities at Subic Bay and Clark," Assistant Secretary of State Paul D. Wolfowitz reminded Secretary of State Shultz in June 1983. "These facilities are essential for our strategic posture in the Far East as well as the Indian Ocean areas."[70] Unambiguous support for Marcos, according to that logic, seemed the surest path to Philippine stability and the protection of U.S. interests. Other voices in the administration challenged that view. They contended that Marcos's autocratic manner, in concert with the dreadful performance of the Philippine economy and the world-class corruption that had created obscene fortunes for Ferdinand and Imelda Marcos and a small coterie of family members and friends, lay behind the acute socioeconomic tensions that produced and fed the NPA rebellion.[71]

The murder of Benigno Aquino in August 1983, just as he was stepping onto the airport tarmac in Manila, demonstrated that such skepticism was warranted. A popular symbol of the anti-Marcos opposition, who had finally been released from jail in 1980 and had been living in exile, "Ninoy" became in death a martyred, larger-than-life hero. Most Filipinos suspected—correctly, as it turned out—that someone close to Marcos had planned the Aquino assassination. A growing number of policy analysts in Washington began to doubt whether the beleaguered president could long survive in the face of widespread public revulsion with an act labeled "cowardly and despicable" by the U.S. government. "As in Nicaragua," observed an incisive State Department intelligence assessment, "a plundering of the country by the local oligarchy rather than foreign oppression or simple poverty has united the Philippine middle class, the business community, the church, and youth against the regime, while the decay of government institutions and a declining economy have sown the seeds of revolution in the countryside."[72]

Faced with the most serious challenge yet to his two-decade reign, Marcos called for a snap election, hoping evidently to demonstrate that the masses continued to adore him. The vote, held on February 7, 1986, had precisely the opposite effect. Widespread ballot fraud, witnessed firsthand by U.S. and other international election monitors, allowed Marcos to claim victory over Corazon Aquino, the widow of the slain Benigno Aquino and the consensus candidate of the anti-Marcos forces. The Philippine strongman claimed to have achieved 54 percent of the vote to Aquino's 46 percent. Privately, the CIA estimated the actual tally to be closer to 58 percent for Aquino to 42 percent for Marcos.[73] "The bottom line conclusion is inescapable," reported Ambassador Stephen Bosworth from Manila: "Mrs. Aquino would have won if there had been an even minimally fair count. . . . This election has effectively cost Ferdinand Marcos most of his remaining political legitimacy and credibility both in the Philippines and in the U.S."[74] On February 16, Aquino confidently declared herself the victor and announced to her followers a bold plan of nonviolent resistance aimed at toppling the imperious Marcos.

Impressed by the resultant "people power" campaign and convinced that Marcos had lost his ability to govern, Shultz urged Reagan to withdraw U.S.

support from the discredited dictator and to recognize Aquino as the legitimate president of the Philippines. Otherwise, Shultz feared, "we were headed for the worst outcome imaginable: an election perceived to be phony; a leader perceived to be a dictator; a reform movement supported by the people perceived to be defrauded; a Communist guerrilla force able to take advantage of these setbacks; a Congress demanding a cutoff of U.S. assistance to Marcos; and an American media that had tasted blood."[75] Reagan, albeit with great reluctance in lieu of his personal fondness for the Marcoses, bowed to the logic of Shultz's argument. On February 25, he formally recognized the Aquino government, the same day Ferdinand and Imelda departed their homeland.[76]

"The rise to power of Corazon Aquino and the fall of Ferdinand Marcos marked an important shift in American official thinking," exulted Shultz in his memoirs: "Support for authoritarian governments that opposed communism could not be taken for granted. The United States supported people who were themselves standing up for freedom and democracy, whether against communism or against another form of repressive government."[77] But the Philippine case was, in many respects, sui generis; it had little impact on the Reagan administration's continued inclination to support friendly, authoritarian regimes in Southeast Asia and elsewhere. So long as those regimes remained noncommunist, reasonably stable, and maintained a firm grip on power—as Marcos's had not—they could expect few problems from Washington.

The contrast with Indonesia is telling. Just before Reagan arrived on the picturesque island of Bali for his state visit of early May 1986, the Indonesian government expelled several Western and Australian journalists who had dared write honestly about the corrupt and repressive nature of the Suharto regime. U.S. officials "made plain our view of freedom of the press," Shultz remarked at a press conference following the arrival of the American party, a view he described delicately as "different from the view here." Yet the flap proved as minor as it was transitory. It did nothing to disturb the broader pattern of Indonesian-American cooperation. Nor did it put a dent in Reagan's support for an autocrat he lauded as "a long-time friend of the United States" and praised for bringing progress and economic growth to his country. Shultz's public reference to the ongoing "quiet dialogue" between Americans and Indonesians "on problems in the general human rights area" amounted to little more than pious rhetoric.[78]

As the Cold War receded by the end of the 1980s, and with it America's preoccupation with the threat posed by communist insurgencies, the human rights conundrum remained. To what extent would—or should—the United

States use whatever leverage it possessed to encourage greater respect for basic human rights, the rule of law, and democratic processes in friendly states? That dilemma proved no easier to resolve in the dramatically altered security environment of the 1990s. Indeed, the policies of Presidents Bush and Clinton on the human rights front suggest that, rhetoric aside, the compromises of the Cold War era are likely to persist well into the post-Cold War era.

The Dawning of a New Era: The Strategic Dimension

The late 1980s witnessed the most momentous changes in the overall architecture of world politics since the 1940s. Reagan's second term in office coincided, rather fortuitously for the American president, with the emergence at the top of the Kremlin leadership structure of Mikhail Gorbachev, the most imaginative and innovative Soviet ruler since Lenin. Together, that most unlikely pair initiated a series of moves that led to a dramatic relaxation in the Cold War tensions that had dominated international affairs since the end of World War II. Not only were nuclear stockpiles reduced, regional conflicts defused, and the Soviet reins of power loosened in Eastern Europe, but, most miraculously, the fervently anticommunist Reagan actually came to see Gorbachev and his rapidly liberalizing Soviet Union less as a threat and more as a partner.

President Bush presided over the breathtaking culmination of the changes set in motion under his predecessor's watch. He, and the American people as a whole, marveled as Gorbachev allowed Eastern Europe's democratic revolutions of 1989 to unfold without Soviet intervention, watched in wonderment as the Berlin Wall came down in November of that year, delighted in Gorbachev's removal of Soviet troops from Afghanistan, and exulted at his decision not to oppose the reunification of Germany within NATO. When, at the end of 1991, the Soviet Union itself dissolved, the United States suddenly found itself the sole remaining superpower. It would be difficult to imagine a set of developments more far reaching in their implications—or more beneficial to the global position of the United States.[79]

The end of the Cold War carried significant consequences for Southeast Asia, even if the resultant shock waves produced less of a fallout there than in many other corners of the planet. Vietnam's announcement, in April 1989, that it would immediately commence withdrawing its troops from Cambodia plainly owed much to the pressures emanating from a weakened Soviet Union. Gorbachev was determined to reduce drastically the Kremlin's financial and political commitments to allied states, which meant that Hanoi could no longer count on the $3 billion per year that it had been receiving from Moscow in military and financial aid. By September 1989, true to their word, the Vietnamese had withdrawn all their troops from Cambodia. Just over two years later, on October 23, 1991, a comprehensive Cambodian peace treaty was initialed in Paris, an agreement cobbled together by the UN Security Council's permanent members, with an able assist from the ASEAN states. Even though a tangled web of details still needed to be worked out, the settlement paved the way for a compromise political solution that aimed to bring into the governing structure in Phnom Penh elements from each of the major contending parties: the Hun Sen regime established by the Vietnamese, the Khmer Rouge, and an anticommunist resistance that included in its fold the indomitable Sihanouk. For the United States, the settlement marked another end-of-the-Cold War diplomatic victory, even if the need to accord a degree of legitimacy to the murderous Khmer Rouge caused more than a few moments of acute political embarrassment for the Bush administration.[80]

For ASEAN the Vietnamese withdrawal from Cambodia and the peace settlement that followed constituted politico-diplomatic triumphs of the highest order. Success had been made possible, of course, by a number of favorable external factors: Gorbachev's new foreign policy directions; the beginnings of a Sino-Soviet rapprochement that necessitated, for both communist powers, a resolution of this nagging trouble spot; the convergence of interests between the ASEAN states, the United States, and China; and the belated recognition by the Vietnamese that their intervention in Cambodia was isolating them internationally while hurting them financially. Even so, the peaceful resolution of this decade-long problem represented a crowning achievement for the regional association that had stood in solid opposition to Vietnam's blatant violation of the principle of territorial integrity and that had kept the issue at the forefront of international diplomacy. The settlement, as one astute observer put it, "endowed ASEAN with a unique sense of status."[81]

Paradoxically, the dizzying swirl of geopolitical changes that brought the Cold War to a close, and that made possible a resolution of the region's most vexing dispute, also triggered a new set of fears among Southeast Asians about the future. Throughout the late 1980s and early 1990s, ASEAN statesmen expressed apprehension that the United States, its principal enemy now defanged, might return to a pre-Cold War policy of isolation from the affairs of Southeast Asia. Without America's active engagement—and strong military presence—in the area, they worried that larger Asian nations might try to fill the resulting power vacuum. China, Japan, even India, could well revert to older patterns of behavior, striving for regional dominance at the expense of the far weaker nation-states of Southeast Asia. China's long-standing territorial claims in the South China Sea generated particular discomfort among ASEAN's strategic analysts. "The potential for conflict in the region," spelled out Indonesian Foreign Minister Mochtar Kusumaatmadja, "comes from regional powers with hegemonistic ambitions."[82] The ASEAN countries encouraged, consequently, a visible U.S. regional presence as a necessary check on the latent territorial and military ambitions of others. In April 1990, Lee Kuan Yew's hand-picked successor as Singapore's prime minister, Goh Chok Tong, publicly called upon Washington to maintain its position as the underpinner of Asian security. To that end, Singapore offered to provide the United States with a permanent berth for one of its naval vessels and to host up to one squadron of U.S. fighter aircraft, an offer the Americans gratefully accepted.[83]

The Reagan and Bush administrations tried on numerous occasions to reassure their skeptical partners across the Pacific about America's determination to remain active and engaged in Asian affairs. On July 21, 1988, Secretary of State Shultz declared that the United States would continue to be "the fundamental guarantor of the balance of power" in Asia. Following a valedictory trip to Asia that included stops in Thailand, Malaysia, Indonesia, and the Philippines, Shultz said that the United States not only could, but must, continue the role it had assumed with the end of World War II—as "the indispensable stabilizing influence in the region."[84] Bush administration officials, frequently accused by Asians of neglecting the Pacific, made a number of similar public pledges. Early in 1990, for example, Secretary of Defense Dick Cheney insisted during a whirlwind tour of the continent that the United States intended to remain the dominant military power in Asia. "If containing Soviet expansion was all we cared about, we might be tempted to withdraw," he conceded. "But that is not what we intend to do," Cheney quickly added. If the United States folded its tents, "a vacuum would quickly develop. There almost surely would be a series of destabilizing regional arms races, an increase in regional tensions and possibly conflict."[85] President Bush himself, in a November 1991 address to the New York-based Asia Society, pledged that he would not permit a "retreat into a kind of Fortress America, which will doom us to irrelevance and poverty."[86]

Perhaps the strongest indications of U.S. intentions in post-Cold War Asia came not in public pledges but in separate strategic blueprints produced by the Pentagon. The first, entitled "A Strategic Framework for Asia: Looking into the 21st Century," was released in April 1990. Paul Wolfowitz, now serving as Cheney's under secretary of defense for policy, succinctly summarized the thrust of the report to a congressional committee in the following manner: "We must maintain a credible presence in the region if we wish to remain a world power, to protect our national interest, and to preserve a secure environment in which democracies and free economies can prosper."[87] Then, in February 1992, the Defense Department issued a more sweeping planning document that again stressed the critical importance American strategists still attached to the whole Asia-Pacific region. "To buttress the vital political and economic relationships we have along the Pacific rim," it declared, "we must maintain our status as a military power of the first magnitude in the area." Doing so would enable the United States to shore up regional security "by acting as a balancing force" and "prevent[ing] the emergence of a vacuum or a regional hegemon."[88]

But how much longer, ASEAN leaders wondered, could the U.S. military presence remain at current levels in the absence of a palpable threat and in the face of America's severe budgetary problems and a public clamoring for a "peace dividend"? It was a reasonable question, and one whose astuteness was confirmed by events in the Philippines. With the U.S. lease on its military bases scheduled to expire in September 1991, Filipino nationalists demanded that the United States either depart entirely by that date or, at a minimum, pay much higher "rent" for the privilege of using the facilities. The Philippine bases, so essential a part of the U.S. defense posture throughout the entire Cold War era, had begun to lose their luster for American military planners with the collapse of the Soviet Union and virtual abandonment by Russia of the Cam Ranh Bay naval base. Why maintain expensive military facilities, in the face of substantial local opposition no less, when you could not even define with any degree of precision the threat they were supposed to protect against?

An unforeseen act of nature settled the issue. On June 25, 1991, Mount Pitatubo erupted, spewing forth volcanic ash and debris that soon blanketed Clark Air Force Base, ten miles to the east, rendering it unusable. "Clark is not irreplaceable," one U.S. official cracked, "especially if it's covered with volcanic sludge."[89] When the Philippine senate, three months later, voted down a new military bases agreement, it signified the end of an era. On November 24, 1992, the last U.S. warship departed Subic Bay. In January 1993, for the first time in this century, an American president was inaugurated without the Stars and Stripes flying over a Philippine military facility. As Bill Clinton assumed the reins of power, the sole remnant of the once-formidable U.S. military presence in Southeast Asia was a small logistics base in Singapore that housed about two hundred troops.[90]

The Dawning of a New Era: The Economic Dimension

"Commercial interests are now on an equal par with security in the world of foreign policy."[91] So proclaimed Ron Brown, Clinton's influential commerce secretary, at the outset of the new administration. With the drastic reduction in security fears that had accompanied the end of the Cold War, economic issues had indeed achieved parity with—even, in many parts of the world, begun to supplant—security concerns in the hierarchy of American overseas interests. Clinton was quite forthright about that fact, emphasizing throughout his first term that expanded and more open international trade created American jobs and promoted American prosperity, the highest priorities of his presidency. In a July 1995 interview, the president said that "building a new structure of opportunity and peace through trade, investment and commerce" stood as an overarching objective of U.S. foreign policy.[92]

Clinton's approach to Southeast Asia, and to the Asia-Pacific region as a whole, well reflected that broader priority. In one of his earliest diplomatic-cum-economic initiatives, the American leader hosted, at Seattle, a summit meeting of the recently formed Asia-Pacific Economic Cooperation Forum (APEC). Clinton invited each of the ASEAN heads of government, all APEC members, to attend the November 1993 convocation. Only Malaysia's Mahathir Mohammed declined. Marked by great conviviality and Clinton's famous informality, the Seattle summit turned out to be the largest gathering of Asian leaders since Lyndon Johnson's hastily arranged Manila summit of 1966. If the Manila meeting demonstrated the primacy of geopolitical fears to an earlier generation of U.S. policymakers, the Seattle gathering made clear the primacy of commercial opportunism to the current generation. Explained a senior State Department official just before the APEC summit opened: "The Asia-Pacific region, the fastest-growing, most economically dynamic region in the world, is critical to America's economic future."[93] Clinton hammered away at that theme throughout the formal and informal sessions. Describing the economic transformation of Asia over the past fifty years as "amazing and unprecedented," Clinton told the visiting dignitaries that commerce now occupied center stage in U.S. relations with its Pacific neighbors. Asian economies, he marveled, "are growing at three times the rate of the established industrial nations." Alluding specifically to the spectacular growth rates attained by the ASEAN nations, Clinton said: "In a short time, many of these economies have gone from being dominoes to dynamos."[94]

The Clinton administration's engagement with Southeast Asia was primarily a function, then, of its deep-seated appreciation for the region's rising economic value. Of course, commerce had begun to replace geopolitics as the principal basis of U.S. interest in the region as early as the mid-1970s, as this chapter has emphasized. That trend remained partially obscured, however, by the Cold War tensions and the Cold War habits of thought that persisted right up to the end of the 1980s, aided in no small measure by the behavior of Vietnam. With the advent of the Clinton administration, nothing was left to obscure the centrality of trade and investment considerations in U.S. policy-making.[95]

And with good reason. Clinton was keenly aware that Southeast Asia had, as the *New York Times* trumpeted in September 1993, become "the fastest-growing region on earth" over the past decade.[96] The president and his chief foreign policy advisers were convinced that the area's relevance to the United States derived almost entirely from that basic fact of economic life. The *Times* article appeared, appropriately enough, as the lead story in the newspaper's business section—not the place readers used to find news about Southeast Asia. Increasingly, though, that was precisely where the American media carried news about the region. The narrative of Southeast Asia as a capitalist showcase and wondrous success story had, by the 1990s, become the dominant one. So completely had it eclipsed the earlier narrative of Southeast Asia as a crucial cockpit of great power rivalry, that a Rip Van Winkle awakening during the Clinton years from a twenty-year sleep might well have thought himself in some distant century.

The breadth of contemporary Southeast Asia's economic metamorphosis has been nothing short of phenomenal. Between 1965 and 1990 the Gross Domestic Product (GDP) of the ASEAN states increased fourteenfold. In 1993 the combined GDP of those nations, plus Vietnam, stood at $440 million, with experts projecting that it would reach $1 trillion by 2010. The American stake in these expanding economies grew proportionately. U.S. trade with the ASEAN nations increased by more than 100 percent between 1985 and 1995 and was expected to double again by 2001. By 1996, U.S. two-way trade with ASEAN had reached $109 billion—57 percent greater than U.S. trade with China and greater than U.S. trade with either South America, the Middle East, or Africa. At the start of the Clinton administration, ASEAN ranked as America's fourth-largest regional trading partner, with 5 percent of all U.S. exports going to ASEAN markets. By then, according to a conservative Commerce Department estimate, the value of U.S. investments in the region stood at $32.2 billion.

The economic progress of individual ASEAN countries, and America's multiplying commercial links with those countries, proved no less impressive. Between 1986 and 1996, Thailand averaged annual growth rates of over 8 percent, virtually the highest in the world during those years. Malaysia was not far behind, recording average growth rates of nearly 8 percent per annum during that same time period. Along with those high growth rates came expanding markets for American goods. U.S. trade with Malaysia increased by 66 percent between 1992 and 1994. Indonesia, identified by the Clinton Commerce Department as one of the world's top ten "emerging markets," recorded a 113 percent leap in U.S. exports between 1989 and 1994. Singapore, with a population of only 2.9 million, boasted a higher per capita income than that of the United States and ranked as America's tenth-largest export market. Even the Philippines, long the economic laggard within ASEAN, has seen steady economic growth since Presidents Corazon Aquino and Fidel Ramos initiated long-overdue economic reforms in the early 1990s.[97]

Malaysia's decision to begin construction in 1995 of what would become the world's tallest building provided a fitting symbol of the growing wealth and soaring self-confidence of an entire region. The flow, a year later, of major financial contributions from wealthy Indonesian and Thai businessmen to Bill Clinton's reelection campaign provided a different kind of symbol of Southeast Asian assertiveness and newfound financial muscle.[98]

Not even the serious currency and banking problems that swept Southeast Asia in the summer and autumn of 1997, and that forced hard-hit Indonesia to accept a $33 billion bailout from the IMF in January 1998, seemed likely to do much more than slow temporarily the region's economic progress. Those difficulties did, however, call needed attention to major structural weaknesses plaguing many of the ASEAN states, weaknesses that had partially been obscured by the soaring growth rates they were recording up through the end of the 1990s. Fundamental problems included poor financial management, inadequate administrative oversight, the failure to develop highly skilled work forces, and pervasive environmental degradation. Perhaps most basic of all, Southeast Asia's capitalist states all suffered from continuing gross disparities in income distribution. Only time would tell whether those problems would be addressed forthrightly by Southeast Asian political leaders—or what the politico-economic consequences would be if they were not.[99]

For its part, the United States paid little heed to those structural problems before the currency crisis of 1997–98. Much of American policy toward Southeast Asia under Bush, and especially under Clinton, focused instead on how best to increase the U.S. share of Southeast Asia's rapidly growing markets. Several problems prevented the United States from capturing as large a share as it wanted. For one, Japan proved a formidable competitor. By the time its economic expansion hit a historic peak in 1989, Japan had become far and away the dominant economic power in Southeast Asia. In that year it bought over 20 percent of the ASEAN nations' exports, provided 64 percent of all nonmilitary aid to the region, and owned between one-fifth and one-half of foreign investments in Thailand, Malaysia, Singapore, and Indonesia. Although Japan's commercial stake in the region has declined somewhat in the 1990s, a consequence mainly of a general, recession-induced retrenchment, Tokyo remains the chief investor, trader, and aid dispenser in Southeast Asia.[100]

Greater American penetration of Southeast Asian markets has also been hampered by a lack of experience and aggressiveness on the part of U.S. businesspeople and an insufficient awareness of the new possibilities the region presented to American capital. "There needs to be a swift kick in the rear for American businesses," complained Robert D. Orr, the former U.S. ambassador to Singapore, in 1993. "I just don't think they understand what has happened in Southeast Asia."[101] There persists as well a fundamental cultural divide between Americans and Southeast Asians, a divide marked by the type of unfamiliarity, suspicion, and clash of business styles that militates against closer economic ties. The irritation expressed by Southeast Asian leaders with the periodic pressure exerted by American government officials and legislators on the human rights front—no matter how muted—serves as another nettlesome manifestation of that cultural gulf.

The Clinton administration's major Southeast Asian policy initiative came at the conjuncture between past legacies and current possibilities. In February 1994, Clinton announced that he was lifting the long-standing trade embargo against Vietnam. Then, in July 1995, twenty years after the last American helicopter fled the besieged Saigon Embassy, he announced that the two nations had finally agreed to establish formal diplomatic relations. The president tapped former Florida Congressman Pete Peterson to be the first U.S. ambassador to Hanoi. Thirty years earlier, as a young Air Force pilot, Peterson had been shot down over North Vietnam; he spent the next seven years as a prisoner of war, enduring torture, solitary confinement, and regular interrogations at the hands of his captors. The Peterson appointment proved a political masterstroke for Clinton, effectively defusing much of the lingering domestic opposition to normalization. If Peterson, a man who still carried so many physical and psychic scars from the war, could transcend the tragic events of the past and look to the future, how could others obdurately refuse to do the same? Conservative North Carolina Sen. Jesse Helms, chairman of the Senate Foreign Relations Committee, held up the Peterson nomination, to be sure, grumbling that Vietnam remained "an unrepentant communist dictatorship."[102] But, in the end, even the ideologically fixated Helms relented. On April 10, 1997, Peterson was confirmed overwhelmingly by the Senate as the first American envoy to unified Vietnam. A month later, the former prisoner of war returned to Hanoi, preaching the message of healing and pleading for the development of new, positive ties between the former enemies.[103]

The Vietnam that Peterson encountered was not only profoundly different from the country that he remembered, but profoundly different from the Vietnam he would have seen had he arrived just a few years earlier. Signs of Vietnam's belated embrace of the capitalist ethos were ubiquitous. On the highway connecting the Hanoi airport to the downtown area, visitors now were greeted by a blizzard of billboards advertising American products. Two signs, in the form of gigantic Coca-Cola bottles, carried the message: "Coke Welcomes You to Vietnam." Another billboard, featuring a smiling young Vietnamese woman in traditional dress, blared: "Welcome to the World of Visa." On April 30, 1997, the chief celebration in Ho Chi Minh City of the twenty-second anniversary of national unification took the form of a bicycle race. That the race, in the vicinity of the old presidential palace, was sponsored by Pepsi-Cola, with each of the contestants sporting bicycle helmets emblazoned with the Pepsi logo, spoke volumes about the new Vietnam.[104]

Long stagnant under the iron grip of the communist party and its stultifying, command-style economic policies, Vietnam in 1986 gingerly initiated an economic liberalization program. By the early 1990s, the campaign its rulers dubbed "doi moi" had begun to bear fruit. In 1996, Vietnam achieved a remarkable 9 percent growth rate, one of the strongest in the entire region. The fast-developing capitalist states of ASEAN served as Vietnam's models, even if the ruling Politboro members looked to China for a practical example of how private enterprise could be stimulated without the communist party relaxing its grip on political power.[105] Delighted with the economic changes sweeping Vietnam, the ASEAN countries in 1995 accepted Vietnam's request for admission to a club it once had shunned. The United States, significantly, did not oppose that decision.

The Clinton administration's normalization of relations with Vietnam owed much to the pro-business orientation of its Asian policy. The desire of the administration and of powerful elements within the American business community to gain a foothold in the region's latest fast-growing market probably contributed more to the recognition decision than anything else. The importance of the administration's publicly expressed desire to bind the wounds of war while gaining even greater cooperation from Hanoi in the search for the remains of American MIAs cannot be discounted, of course.

Still, business lobbyists eyeing a potentially lucrative new market proved the most active and most influential advocates of normalization. That Vietnam's industrious low-wage workforce had become a leading producer of the American Nike Corporation's world-famous athletic shoes suggests one of the many ways in which the relationship between Americans and Vietnamese is being reshaped by the dictates of a global economy. Peterson's arrival in Vietnam, proclaimed Vietnamese Prime Minister Vo Van Kiet, "affirms that both countries are interested in closing the chapter on the past in order to look towards the future."[106] That future will almost certainly revolve less around issues of power, ideology, and politics than around the pull of market forces.

Southeast Asia has experienced breathtaking changes in the more than two decades that have elapsed since the end of the Vietnam War. More are doubtless in store. Yet striking continuities persist as well, particularly in terms of the regional self-assertion, powerful nationalist currents, and abiding mistrust of outside powers that have been so evident since at least the early 1970s. ASEAN's historic announcement on May 31, 1997, that Myanmar (Burma), Laos, and Cambodia would be admitted to full membership in the association before the end of the year, provided ample evidence of all three. The decision, reached with typical ASEAN unanimity, shattered decisively Southeast Asia's artificial division into communist and noncommunist blocs, with isolationist Myanmar standing apart from both. ASEAN's policy of "constructive engagement" with the notoriously repressive military rulers of Myanmar was followed to its logical conclusion—despite American opposition. The association rejected the Clinton administration's plea that Myanmar be kept out of the association as punishment for a human rights record Washington characterized as atrocious. ASEAN, once again, marched to its own beat. "We have tried very hard to get the [ASEAN] countries to follow our steps," Secretary of State Madeleine K. Albright told Congress, "but they don't seem to be interested in it."[107]

That, indeed, was the point—as it had been the point for decades. The ASEAN states wanted a relationship with the United States, but on their own terms. They craved American products, valued the jobs produced by American investment dollars, sought wider entry for their goods into American markets, and actively solicited a modest American military presence as a helpful counterweight against the territorial ambitions of China and other regional powers. They did not want to hear sanctimonious American sermons about the virtues of Western-style political, or economic, openness. Nor were they willing to tolerate American interference in their internal affairs, any more than they themselves were inclined to interfere in the internal affairs of Myanmar or Cambodia.

"We are complete now," observed Indonesian Foreign Minister Ali Alatas about the decision to admit the outside three to the ASEAN fold. "And we are in a better position to contribute to peace and stability in our region."[108]

The Indonesian diplomat's prediction proved not just premature but wildly optimistic. Shortly after Ali Alatas uttered those confident remarks, Cambodia's second prime minister Hun Sen ousted his chief rival, first prime minister Norodom Ranariddh, in a violent coup. The ASEAN nations, in response, postponed indefinitely Phnom Penh's entrance into the club. Talk about the "ASEAN 10" abruptly ceased.

The thirtieth anniversary meeting of ASEAN, held in Kuala Lumpur at the end of July 1997, consequently proved far less triumphal than the association's member states had planned. If the problems surrounding Myanmar's admission and the renewal of civil strife in Cambodia were not sufficient to puncture the official bubble of optimism about the future, there was the rippling currency crisis in Thailand. A precipitous decline in the value of the Thai baht, well under way at the time of the Kuala Lumpur gathering, heralded Thailand's most serious economic crisis since World War II—and East Asia's.

That economic crisis soon engulfed Indonesia, Malaysia, and the Philippines, carrying the most profound of consequences both for ASEAN and for its individual member states. It exacted a heavy toll on the prestige and self-confidence of an association poorly equipped to deal with a region-wide financial implosion of such proportions. Thailand and Indonesia were each forced to seek bailout packages from the IMF in order to shore up their battered and depleted financial reserves. Indonesian President Suharto initially opposed the preconditions set by the IMF for an emergency loan since those struck too hard at the cronyism and nepotism long at the heart of his system of governance. When fiscal realities forced him to relent, the ensuing economic pain triggered widespread social upheaval throughout Indonesia. On May 21, 1998, facing massive popular unrest and the brazen occupation of parliament by 30,000 student protesters, the indomitable Suharto abruptly resigned, turning over the reins of power to his vice president, B. J. Habibie. The sudden and wholly unexpected collapse of the thirty-two-year-old Suharto regime sent shock waves throughout the region, and left an enormous political vaccuum in its largest nation.[109]

As the economic crisis dragged on, ASEAN leaders grumbled openly about external interference in their affairs, much as they had during the Myanmar contretemps. The United States, the IMF, and Western investors, all of whom were calling for greater economic liberalization in Southeast Asia, caught the brunt of the ensuing nationalistic attacks. Malaysian Prime Minister Mahathir Mohammed, the region's most vociferous critic of the West, adamantly refused IMF assistance, vowing that he would never permit Malaysia to be economically "colonized." During a speech before the ASEAN Regional Forum, the long-serving Malaysian ruler told his fellow ASEAN leaders that they should never again depend on foreign powers. Reopening an old wound, he even made a pointed reference to American behavior during the Vietnam War. Mahathir blamed the economic crisis, even the collapse of the Suharto regime, however illogically, on "callous" Western financial speculators. "When you take away our money and impoverish our people and take away our jobs, naturally you have to admit some responsibility for that," he sneered.[110]

Such attitudes suggest that the long-standing search for genuine national independence and for meaningful regional autonomy is likely to complicate Southeast Asia's relationship with the United States, and the external world, for a long time to come. The region remains highly vulnerable: not just to larger and more powerful states but to unforgiving global markets. Yet, for all its continuing vulnerability, and for all the uncertainties of the current economic turmoil, it bears emphasizing that Southeast Asia's future lies in the hands of Southeast Asians far more now than at any time in the modern era.

The United States became a full-fledged Southeast Asian power only in the aftermath of World War II. The strategic fears stirred by early Japanese and German military successes, together with the socioeconomic wreckage and destabilizing power vacuums that followed their eventual defeats, impelled the United States to assume a much more active posture in the postwar Pacific. No other option was really feasible for a nation determined to prevent future global conflicts through the creation of a more stable and prosperous world order.

The Truman administration's various Southeast Asian initiatives of the early postwar years—its retention of air and naval bases in the Philippines, its active promotion of revived regional trade and productivity, its diplomatic entreaties on behalf of an orderly devolution of power from European colonizers to local nationalists—all flowed from the same basic premise. Washington's civilian and military decision-makers were convinced that the United States needed to use its power actively, constructively, and imaginatively in order to bring about the kind of world most conducive to the preservation of American security and to the protection of the nation's domestic institutions and core values. The United States needed, in short, to assume the role of global hegemon.

That calculation alone probably guaranteed that, even if the Cold War had never occurred, Americans would have been far more directly engaged in the affairs of the Southeast Asian region than ever before in their history. But, absent the global confrontation with the Soviet Union and, after 1949, China, the United States almost certainly would not have carved its own Southeast Asian empire out of the carcass of Europe's rapidly decaying one. A complex mosaic of strategic, economic, psychological, and political factors, each related directly to the Cold War, propelled the United States, by the early 1950s, into a regional activism scarcely anyone could have conceived possible just a few years earlier.

Closely interrelated strategic and economic considerations proved paramount in the American embrace of empire in Southeast Asia. Between 1949 and 1950, the Truman administration fundamentally redefined the significance of Southeast Asia to broader American foreign policy goals, elevating the region to a position of hitherto unheard-of primacy. Concerned that its communist adversaries appeared to be fast gaining power and momentum at the expense of a dispirited and economically stagnant West, the Truman administration determined to thwart any additional communist breakthroughs. Top American strategists identified Southeast Asia as an especially vulnerable area, and hence an area where a major commitment of U.S. resources and prestige was warranted. The lingering economic dislocations caused by the Pacific War, widespread social upheavals, colonial rebellions ignited at war's end and made worse by the intransigence of French and Dutch colonialists, the menacing proximity of China's new communist regime, the positive appeal of communism's millennial vision to many of the region's aspiring nationalists—those forces together conspired to make Southeast Asia one of the world's most volatile and unpredictable places.

The region's resources and markets, viewed by American planners as essential to the economic recoveries of both Western Europe and Japan, and thus to the proper functioning of the global economic system, just deepened the appreciation that American strategists developed for Southeast Asia's critical significance. The important psychological underpinnings of America's global leadership served to reinforce that appreciation, as did the vicissitudes of American domestic politics. The latter factor stemmed especially from the political firestorm ignited by Truman's "loss" of China and the Republican Party's efforts to vilify the Democratic president for his presumed failures in meeting communism's challenge in Asia. Truman's strong stand in Southeast Asia thus made as much sense politically as it seemed to make sense in geopolitical, economic, and psychological terms.

Most of the same basic considerations that underlay the Truman administration's early commitments in Southeast Asia governed the dramatic expansion and extension of those commitments throughout the 1950s and 1960s. The economic rationale for U.S. involvement in Southeast Asia had lost much of its force by the end of the Eisenhower years, to be sure; the recoveries of the Western European and Japanese economies were, by then, well advanced. Yet that fact did little to alter American policymakers' convictions about the region's commanding importance both to the global balance of power and to America's exercise of world leadership. Eisenhower, Kennedy, and Johnson, along with their chief defense and diplomatic advisers, continued to see the Cold War struggle against the Soviet Union and

China as a zero-sum game in which a victory for communist forces anywhere would constitute a demoralizing defeat for the United States and the entire "Free World." Their abiding concern about the psychological dimensions of power—the credibility factor—remained high throughout the 1950s and 1960s, as did the domestic political fears first visible during Truman's embattled presidency. Each of Truman's successors worried, in their own distinctive fashion, about the permanent political scars likely to be left on any president found guilty of surrendering another piece of real estate to the communists.

Those interrelated national security and domestic fears conditioned the American response to all major Southeast Asian developments throughout this period. They led to the SEATO commitment, elevated base sites in Thailand and the Philippines into prominence in America's global defense network, justified hundreds of millions of dollars in military and economic assistance to Southeast Asia's noncommunist regimes, and led to ill-conceived covert operations aimed at overthrowing governments in Indonesia and Laos. Those fears reached their apotheosis, of course, with the dispatch of over half a million U.S. troops in a desperate effort to block the imminent triumph of the communist-led insurgency in South Vietnam.

Well before its ultimate defeat in Indochina, the United States had belatedly come to recognize how dangerously overextended it had become in Southeast Asia. Johnson initiated that reassessment in the wake of the illusion-shattering Tet offensive of 1968. Nixon completed the process. Convinced that his predecessors had foolishly exaggerated Southeast Asia's actual value to the national security and international prestige of the United States, as well as to the global balance of power that so preoccupied him, Nixon sought a sharply reduced regional role for the United States. The successful opening toward China of the early 1970s eased the transition, as it removed in a single stroke Asia's most unpredictable power from America's pantheon of enemies. Nixon's obsession with finding a graceful exit from Vietnam only partially disguised the deliberate policy of retrenchment and disengagement that his administration was pursuing in Southeast Asia.

Since the Nixon years, U.S. policymakers have rarely devoted sustained attention to Southeast Asia. The region has, in nearly all respects, been relegated once again to the status of a peripheral interest. America's more modest, and hence more realistic, posture in Southeast Asia has, along with the region's phenomenal economic upsurge over the past two decades, permitted issues of trade and investment to eclipse the geostrategic fixations of the postwar era's first quarter century.

In retrospect, it is difficult not to disparage the doomsday scenarios conjured up by American policymakers to justify the hyperinvolvement of that earlier period. It is impossible not to view with a jaundiced eye the exaggerated U.S. emphasis on Southeast Asia's presumed centrality to the global struggle for power. Neither the evidence available at the time, nor that which has surfaced since, has proven consistent with the common American image of China as an aggressive, expansionist power bent on establishing hegemony over Southeast Asia. Nor has the notion that revolutionary success in one country would inevitably beget success in adjacent countries stood the test of time. The domino theory appears never to have been based on anything other than illusory, worst-case projections. Moreover, the persistent worry about the disastrous political repercussions sure to follow retreat or defeat in Southeast Asia appear as equally fanciful now as they should have seemed at the time.

Yet, for all their distortions of prevailing domestic, regional, and international conditions, such concerns exerted an undeniably powerful impact on American perceptions and policies toward Southeast Asia. They derived from the same heightened sense of vulnerability that drove so many Cold War commitments, and that formed so instrumental an element of the American Cold War mindset. The deeper reasons for the American fixation with its presumed vulnerability—at a time when its power was, by any objective criteria, at a historic peak—probably lie more within the realm of social psychology than within the realms of geopolitics or political economy. Regardless of the precise origins of American fears, though, they were quite real to a whole generation of policymakers. In that regard, it bears emphasizing that the short-lived American empire in Southeast Asia did not derive from self-aggrandizing territorial or economic ambitions. It was, instead, largely a defensive empire. Built to contain Beijing, Moscow, and indigenous revolutionaries, it was the product of America's fears rather than its greed.

But it was an empire, nevertheless, replete with all the weaknesses and contradictions endemic to all modern empires. It was an external imposition, held together temporarily by superior military and economic power and by the occasional convergence of interests between Washington and certain indigenous regimes. Much like the European imperialists of the past, the stewards of the American empire frequently evidenced paternalistic, arrogant, culturally superior, and racist attitudes toward very same local peoples whose welfare they were championing. In the event, America's heavy-handed presence triggered deep resentment among indigenous peoples, thus sowing some of the seeds of its own destruction.

Nationalism proved the most formidable impediment to the achievement of America's regional goals throughout the postwar era. It was the rock on which the American empire ultimately foundered. Many of the region's newly emergent nations rejected American leadership for fear that an active American presence would compromise their hard-won independence. The nonaligned regimes of Indonesia, Burma, Cambodia, and Malaysia proved resistant, from the first, to American direction and obdurately refused to join the American alliance system or even to accept any American aid that might come with strings attached. Those nations that did ally themselves with the United States formally—the Philippines, Thailand, South Vietnam—did so principally for their own purposes. The resultant partnerships were invariably fraught with tensions. From the flap over the Brownell memorandum in the Philippines to the Saigon regime's periodic attempts to gain greater control over its own affairs to the popular efforts to drive U.S. forces from Thailand and the Philippines, nationalism kept wreaking havoc with the best-laid of American plans.

Ironically, those very same nationalist impulses proved, in the long run, the greatest impetus for regional order, cohesion, development, and stability. In that regard, ASEAN is best understood as an effort by Southeast Asians to forge a regional order on their own terms—free from the external dictation of the United States or any other great powers. Because the United States served for the ASEAN states as a negative reference point, it probably can, in a curious way, claim some credit for the association's emergence. In an equally unintended and indirect manner, America's Vietnam War-related spending probably contributed to the postwar surge in economic activity throughout Northeast and Southeast Asia—with Japan serving as the principal beneficiary. The precise economic, social, and political impact of American exertions in Southeast Asia do not, of course, lend themselves to precise measurement. Suffice it to say that American policies in post-World War II Southeast Asia serve as yet another example of how the unintended results of historical actions can often prove far more consequential than the intended ones.

Appendix 1

U.S. Trade and Investment, 1950–1995

(in millions of U.S. dollars)

	1950	1955	1960	1965	1970	1975	1980	1985	1990	1995
Burma/Myanmar										
Import (from U.S.)	0.8	1.0	9.8	16.6	8.9	19.8	31.7	17.0	19.0	18.0
xport (to U.S.)	0.9	4.4	0.7	0.8	0.3	0.6	8.3	2.3	9.0	79.0
U.S. Direct Investment	—	—	—	—	—	—	—	—	—	241[a]
Indonesia										
Imports	155.7	212	89.3	45.7	178.5	670.0	1,409	1,721	2,520	4,579
Exports	78.4	74.7	194.2	165.3	110.7	1,866	4,303	4,040	3,365	6,476
U.S. Direct Investment	58	86	178	106[c]	—	1,612	1,314	4,807	3,827	6,607
Malaysia										
Imports	310.0	235.1	29.1	50.2[b]	120.4	376.7	1,632	1,881	4,944	12,657
Exports	19.7	35.6	99.0	176.7[b]	219.1	612.3	2,119	1,970	4,986	15,313
U.S. Direct Investment	—	—	—	57[c]	—	—	632	1,217	1,425	4,200
Philippines										
Imports	236	253.1	256.7	311.7	354.9	816.6	1,958	1,344	2,538	5,225
Exports	235	340.1	268.5	348.7	433.3	663.1	1,594	1,658	3,104	6,217
U.S. Direct Investment	149	226	414	529	710	733	1,259	983	1,655	2,531
Singapore										
Imports	#	#	51.0	55.7[b]	266.2	1,279	3,389	3,988	9,801	18,725
Exports	#	#	79.1	15.2[b]	172.3	746.8	2,424	4,830	11,215	21,576
U.S. Direct Investment	—	—	—	30[c]	—	—	1,204	1,897	3,971	12,689
Thailand										
Imports	75.2	104.7	75.5	141.0	192.8	471.5	1,332	1,052	3,600	8,507
Exports	25.0	49.9	57.2	40.5	95.5	244.0	823.1	1,402	5,240	10,078
U.S. Direct Investment	—	—	—	51[c]	—	—	361	1,022	1,515	4,315

[a] = United Nations, *Myanmar: Trade and Investment Potential in Asia* (New York: UN, 1996), 9.
[b] = for 1966 (1965 is not listed).
[c] = for 1963.
# = included with Malaysia.

Sources: (a) Trade Statistics: IMF, *Direction of Trade Statistics Yearbook* for 1981–82, 1992, 1997; IMF, *Direction of Trade Annual* for 1960–1964, 1963–1967, 1971–1977, 1980; (b) Investment: U.S. Dept. of Commerce, *Survey of Current Business* for 1956 (Aug.), 1961 (Aug.), 1966 (Sept.), 1971 (Oct.), 1976 (Aug.), 1982 (Aug.), 1986 (June), 1991 (June); U.S. Dept. of Commerce, *U.S. Direct Investment Abroad* for 1966.

Note: *Survey of Current Business* does not differentiate Singapore, Malaysia, Thailand until 1980; Indonesia is not done so for 1965 and 1970 but is differentiated before and after; Burma is not listed.

Appendix 2

U.S. Economic Assistance to Southeast Asia, 1950–1975

(in millions of U.S. dollars)

	Burma	Indonesia	Malaysia	Philippines	Singapore	Thailand
1950	—	137.7	—	137.9	—	—
1951	10.4	8.0	—	138.8	—	8.9
1952	−0.2	−1.9	—	132.4	—	7.2
1953	12.8	13.2	—	20.8	—	6.5
1954	−1.8	4.5	<	14.8	—	8.8
1955	−1.0	7.2	0.3	30.0	—	46.8
1956	17.0	88.2	0.5	47.9	—	33.5
1957	1.3	12.3	0.4	42.8	—	35.0
1958	44.2	29.0	0.1	29.1	—	30.9
1959	8.9	67.6	20.2	145.2	—	45.7
1960	−2.6	70.2	0.3	23.4	—	24.6
1961	0.4	31.6	0.4	86.0	—	26.1
1962	−0.8	82.9	0.9	49.9	0.2	26.4
1963	20.9	40.8	3.2	91.6	0.3	26.8
1964	−7.5	12.1	3.5	16.9	0.4	12.3
1965	3.9	−3.1	4.3	26.5	<	19.5
1966	0.5	23.8	6.1	13.5	0.1	43.8
1967	0.5	57.5	22.6	43.3	19.0	55.3
1968	0.3	101.8	3.4	18.0	0.2	54.2
1969	0.9	242.4	5.9	39.3	<	40.4
1970	0.5	208.0	4.5	33.7	0.2	33.9
1971	1.1	177.1	3.6	40.5	0.2	24.0
1972	0.7	239.6	3.0	69.9	0.1	30.8
1973	0.3	240.6	3.3	124.0	—	34.9
1974	—	90.0	3.3	63.6	0.1	19.0
1975	—	89.8	2.9	68.5	<	12.9

< = less than $50,000

Sources: International Cooperation Administration, *Overseas Loans and Grants and Assistance to International Organizations* for 1945–1960; Agency for International Development, *Overseas Loans and Grants and Assistance to International Organizations* for 1945–1962, 1945–1970, 1945–1975. (This includes AID, *Food for Peace* (PL 480), Ex-Im Loans, Peace Corps, and other.) Thailand figures from Robert J. Muscat, *Thailand and the United States: Development, Security, and Foreign Aid* (New York: Columbia University Press, 1990).

Appendix 3

U.S. Military Assistance to Southeast Asia, 1950–1975

(in millions of U.S. dollars)

	Burma	Indonesia	Malaysia	Philippines	Singapore	Thailand
1950	—	51.0	—	1.5	—	9.7
1951	0.3	0.1	—	4.5	—	46.7
1952	10.0	5.9	—	12.0	—	31.6
1953	2.8	2.8	—	34.5	—	24.3
1954	5.3	5.3	—	12.0	—	42.5
1955	1.0	5.4	—	15.7	—	45.6
1956	0.2	7.4	—	33.3	—	45.6
1957	0.1	8.3	—	23.7	—	16.2
1958	0.3	10.2	—	21.1	—	14.3
1959	6.3	6.2	—	20.5	—	16.4
1960	3.9	10.9	—	19.5	—	40.4
1961	—	8.5[a]	—	23.6	—	60.9
1962	49.8[b]	16.3	—	21.5	—	78.4
	5.1[a]					
	6.1[a]					
1963		8.4	—	24.5	—	64.5
1964		7.1	—	10.7	—	36.0
1965		2.1	<	18.2	—	30.4
1966	3.5	—	4.2	25.2	—	51.6
1967	3.9	2.5	11.8	33.0	—	69.6
1968	2.8	4.8	0.2	29.9	13.0	89.8
1969	0.1	5.4	0.2	21.9	6.0	96.4
1970	0.1	8.1	0.2	27.3	—	110.0
1971	<	35.1	2.4	18.7	—	98.7
1972	—	32.7	10.6	21.1	1.9	122.1
1973	<	20.3	10.2	50.4	—	62.8
1974	—	19.7	19.0	27.0	—	35.4
1975	—	21.0	5.0	36.3	—	41.7

[a] = Figures drawn from DOD, *Foreign Military Sales and Military Assistance Facts* for 1966 and 1974; Thailand figures drawn from Robert J. Muscat, *Thailand and the United States: Development, Security, and Foreign Aid* (New York: Columbia University Press, 1990).

[b] = AID does not give military assistance for Burma in its 1945–1970 issue, but cites this figure for the 1962–1965 period in the 1945–1975 issue.

< = less than $50,000.

Sources: International Cooperation Administration, *Overseas Loans and Grants and Assistance to International Organizations* for 1945–1960, 1945–1961 (prelim); Agency for International Development, *Overseas Loans and Grants and Assistance to International Organizations* for 1945–1962, 1945–1970, 1945–1975.

Notes

1. The Colonial Order

1. D. R. SarDesai, *Southeast Asia: Past and Present*, 3d rev. ed. (Boulder, Colo.: Westview, 1994), 3.

2. Robert E. Elson, "International Commerce, the State, and Society: Economic and Social Change," in Nicholas Tarling, ed., *The Cambridge History of Southeast Asia*, vol. 2, *The Nineteenth and Twentieth Centuries* (New York: Cambridge University Press, 1992), 156.

3. Elson, "International Commerce, the State, and Society," 161.

4. This broad overview of the colonial order has been drawn especially from Nicholas Tarling, "The Establishment of the Colonial Regimes," in Tarling, ed., *Cambridge History* 2:5–78; Carl A. Trochi, "Political Structures in the Nineteenth and Early Twentieth Centuries," in ibid. 2:79–130; Elson, "International Commerce, the State, and Society," 131–95; SarDesai, *Southeast Asia*, 81–131; David J. Steinberg, ed., *In Search of Southeast Asia: A Modern History* (New York: Praeger, 1971), 211–32.

5. Quoted in Steinberg, ed., *In Search of Southeast Asia*, 251.

6. Mohammed Hatta, "The Anti-Colonial Congress in Brussels in the Light of World History," in *Portrait of a Patriot: Selected Writings by Mohammed Hatta* (The Hague: Mouton, 1972), 185–99.

7. This broad overview of the development of Southeast Asian nationalism has been drawn especially from Paul Kratoska and Ben Baston, "Nationalism and Modernist Reform," in Tarling, ed., *Cambridge History* 2:249–324; Steinberg, ed., *In Search of Southeast Asia*, 239–58; Clive J. Christie, *A Modern History of Southeast Asia: Decolonization, Nationalism, and Separatism* (London: Tauris, 1996). See also Benedict R. O'G. Anderson, *Imagined Communities: Reflections on the Origins and Spread of Nationalism* (London: Verso, 1983).

8. Welles, quoted in Robert J. McMahon, *Colonialism and Cold War: The United States and the Struggle for Indonesian Independence, 1945–49* (Ithaca, N.Y.: Cornell University Press, 1981), 55.

9. Hull, quoted in McMahon, *Colonialism and Cold War*, 55.

10. Roosevelt, quoted in Wm. Roger Louis, *Imperialism at Bay: The United States and the Decolonization of the British Empire, 1941–1945* (New York: Oxford University Press, 1978), 227, 356.

11. Roosevelt, quoted in Cordell Hull, *Memoirs* 2:1597 (New York: Macmillan, 1948).

12. Roosevelt, quoted in Elliot Roosevelt, *As He Saw It* (New York: Duel, Sloan, and Pearse, 1945), 74.

13. Hull, *Memoirs* 1:81.

14. Loudon, quoted in McMahon, *Colonialism and Cold War*, 66.

15. Hull, *Memoirs* 2:1559.

16. This account of Roosevelt's anticolonial policy has been drawn especially from McMahon, *Colonialism and Cold War*, 53–73; Louis, *Imperialism at Bay*; Gary R. Hess, *The United States' Emergence as a Southeast Asian Power, 1940–1950* (New York: Columbia University Press, 1987); Fred E. Pollock and Warren F. Kimball, " 'In Search of Monsters to Destroy': Roosevelt and Colonialism," in Warren F. Kimball, *The Juggler: Franklin Roosevelt as Wartime Statesman* (Princeton: Princeton University Press, 1991), 127–57.

2. The Roots of Intervention, 1945–1950

1. Jefferson, quoted in Reginald Horsman, *The Diplomacy of the New Republic, 1776–1815* (Arlington Heights, Ill.: Harlan Davidson, 1985), 82. In 1862, President Abraham Lincoln similarly referred to the United States as "the last, best hope of earth." Lincoln, quoted in Tony Smith, *America's Mission: The United States and the Worldwide Struggle for Democracy in the Twentieth Century* (Princeton: Princeton University Press, 1994), 22.

2. Wilson, quoted in Arthur Link, *Woodrow Wilson: Revolution, War, and Peace* (Arlington Heights, Ill.: Harlan Davidson, 1979), 7; Truman, quoted in Walter McDougall, *Promised Land, Crusader State: The American Encounter with the World Since 1776* (Boston: Houghton Mifflin, 1997), 169.

3. Acheson, quoted in Stephen E. Ambrose, *Rise to Globalism: American Foreign Policy, 1938–1970* (Baltimore: Penguin, 1971), 297.

4. Acheson, quoted in Gaddis Smith, *Dean Acheson* (New York: Cooper Square, 1972), 416.

5. Hull, *Memoirs* 1:81.

6. Alfred E. Eckes, Jr., *A Search for Solvency: Bretton Woods and the International Monetary System, 1941–1971* (Austin: University of Texas Press, 1975); Robert A. Pollard, *Economic Security and the Origins of the Cold War, 1945–1950* (New York: Columbia University Press, 1985); Michael J. Hogan, *The Marshall Plan: America, Britain, and the Reconstruction of Western Europe, 1947–1952* (New York: Cambridge University Press, 1987), 12–18; Warren I.

Cohen, *America in the Age of Soviet Power, 1945–1991* (New York: Cambridge University Press, 1993), 4–7.

7. Melvyn P. Leffler, "The American Conception of National Security and the Beginnings of the Cold War," *American Historical Review* 89 (April 1984): 346–80; Melvyn P. Leffler, *A Preponderance of Power: National Security, the Truman Administration, and the Cold War* (Stanford, Calif.: Stanford University Press, 1990), chs. 1–2; Robert A. Dallek, *Franklin D. Roosevelt and American Foreign Policy, 1932–1945* (New York: Oxford University Press, 1979).

8. McMahon, *Colonialism and Cold War* (Ithaca, N.Y.: Cornell University Press, 1981); Hess, *The United States' Emergence as a Southeast Asian Power* (New York: Columbia University Press, 1987).

9. U.S. Office of Strategic Services (OSS), "Effects of the Japanese Occupation," Research and Analysis Report no. 3293, September 1945, in U.S. Department of State Records (DSR), Record Group (RG) 59, National Archives (NA), Washington, D.C.

10. See, for example, Willard H. Elsbree, *Japan's Role in Southeast Asian Nationalist Movements, 1941–1945* (Cambridge: Harvard University Press, 1953); Alfred W. McCoy, ed., *Southeast Asia Under Japanese Occupation: Transition and Transformation* (New Haven: Yale University Press, 1980); Benedict R. O'G. Anderson, *Java in a Time of Revolution: Occupation and Resistance, 1944–1946* (Ithaca, N.Y.: Cornell University Press, 1972); Shigeru Sato, *War, Nationalism, and Peasants: Java Under the Japanese Occupation, 1942–1945* (Armonk, N.Y.: M. E. Sharpe, 1994); Josef Silverstein, *Burmese Politics: The Dilemma of National Unity* (New Brunswick, N.J.: Rutgers University Press, 1981), ch. 3; Christopher Thorne, *The Issue of War: States, Societies, and the Far Eastern Conflict of 1941–1945* (New York: Oxford University Press, 1984), 152–61; A. J. Stockwell, "Southeast Asia in War and Peace: The End of European Colonial Empires," in Tarling, ed., *Cambridge History of Southeast Asia* 2:333–36 (New York: Cambridge University Press, 1992).

11. Sato, *War, Nationalism, and Peasants*; Stanley Karnow, *Vietnam: A History* (New York: Viking, 1983), 144–45. On the "comfort women," see Ustinia Dolgopol, "Women's Voices, Women's Pain," *Human Rights Quarterly* 17 (1995): 127–54; George Hicks, *The Comfort Women: Japan's Brutal Regime of Enforced Prostitution in the Second World War* (New York: Norton, 1994).

12. Ba Maw, *Breakthrough in Burma: Memoirs of a Revolution, 1939–1946* (New Haven: Yale University Press, 1968), 272.

13. Quoted in Nick Cullather, *Illusions of Influence: The Political Economy of United States–Philippines Relations, 1942–1960* (Stanford, Calif.: Stanford University Press, 1994), 33–34. See also Stanley Karnow, *In Our Image: America's Empire in the Philippines* (New York: Ballantine, 1989), 333; Thomas G. Paterson, *On Every Front: The Making and Unmaking of the Cold War*, rev. ed. (New York: Norton, 1992), 11.

14. Lord Louis Mountbatten, *Post Surrender Tasks: Section E of the Report*

to the Combined Chiefs of Staff by the Supreme Allied Commander Southeast Asia, 1943–1945 (London: Her Majesty's Stationery Office, 1969), 282.

15. George McT. Kahin, *Nationalism and Revolution in Indonesia* (Ithaca, N.Y.: Cornell University Press, 1952), 138–40; Anderson, *Java in a Time of Revolution*, 87–91; John R. W. Smail, *Bandung in the Early Revolution, 1945–46: A Study in the Social History of the Indonesian Revolution* (Ithaca, N.Y.: Cornell University Modern Indonesia Project, 1964); Anthony Reid, *The Blood of the People: Revolution and the End of Traditional Rule in Northern Sumatra* (Kuala Lumpur: Oxford University Press, 1979).

16. Mountbatten to the British Chiefs of Staff, September 29, 1945, in box 90, Southeast Asia Command (SEAC) War Diaries, RG 331, Washington National Record Center (WNRC), Suitland, Md.

17. Extract from SEAC War Diary, September 30, 1945, ibid.

18. Gary R. Hess, *Vietnam and the United States: Origins and Legacy of War* (Boston: Twayne, 1990), 18–20; Karnow, *Vietnam: A History*, 145–49.

19. Bernard B. Fall, ed., *Ho Chi Minh: On Revolution* (New York: Praeger, 1967), 143; George C. Herring, *America's Longest War: The United States and Vietnam, 1950–1975*, 2d rev. ed. (New York: Knopf, 1986), 3; Lloyd C. Gardner, *Approaching Vietnam: From World War II through Dienbienphu* (New York: Norton, 1988), 64–65; Jean Lacouture, *Ho Chi Minh: A Political Biography* (New York: Vintage, 1968).

20. Hess, *Vietnam and the United States*, 34–36.

21. Silverstein, *Burmese Politics*, 71–92; Benedict J. Kerkvliet, *The Huk Rebellion: A Study of Peasant Revolt in the Philippines* (Berkeley: University of California Press, 1977); A. J. Stockwell, *British Policy and Malay Politics During the Malayan Union Experiment, 1942–1948* (Kuala Lumpur: Oxford University Press, 1979).

22. OSS, "Problems Arising from a Sudden Liberation of the N.E.I." Research and Analysis Report no. 3229, August 13, 1945, DSR.

23. Robert J. McMahon, "Toward a Post-Colonial Order: Truman Administration Policies Toward South and Southeast Asia," in Michael J. Lacey, ed., *The Truman Presidency* (New York: Cambridge University Press, 1989), 340–45.

24. Policy paper prepared in the Department of State, "An Estimate of Conditions in Asia and the Pacific at the Close of the War and the Objectives and Policies of the United States," June 22, 1945, *Foreign Relations of the United States* (1945): 6:557–58 (hereafter cited as *FRUS*).

25. Stanley K. Hornbeck, "The United States and the Netherlands East Indies," *Annals of the American Academy of Political and Social Science* 255 (January 1948): 132–33.

26. Ho, quoted in Gardner, *Approaching Vietnam*, 66; memorandum by John Carter Vincent (director of the State Department's Office of Far Eastern Affairs), October 22, 1945, *FRUS* (1945): 6:1167–68.

27. McMahon, "Toward a Post-Colonial Order."

28. MacArthur, quoted in Karnow, *In Our Image*, 324–25.

29. Cullather, *Illusions of Influence*, 36–43, 51–59; H. W. Brands, *Bound to Empire: The United States and the Philippines* (New York: Oxford University Press, 1992), 227–33; Stephen R. Shalom, *The United States and the Philippines: A Study of Neocolonialism* (Philadelphia: Institute for the Study of Human Issues, 1981).

30. Hess, *The United States' Emergence as a Southeast Asian Power*, 267–70.

31. Ibid., 193–202.

32. McMahon, *Colonialism and Cold War*, 137–67.

33. CIA, "Review of the World Situation as It Relates to the Security of the United States," CIA-1, September 26, 1947, President's Secretary's File (PSF), Harry S. Truman Papers, Harry S. Truman Library (HSTL), Independence, Mo.

34. For an extended discussion of these points, see McMahon, *Colonialism and Cold War*, 168–205; Alastair M. Taylor, *Indonesian Independence and the United Nations* (Ithaca, N.Y.: Cornell University Press, 1960).

35. See McMahon, *Colonialism and Cold War*, 206ff.

36. U.S. Department of State, Office of Intelligence and Research, Division of Research for the Far East, "Political Implications of E.C.A. Aid to Indonesia," October 29, 1948, DSR.

37. Robert Lovett (Acting Secretary of State) to Frank P. Graham (U.S. representative on the Good Offices Committee), December 31, 1947, *FRUS* (1947): 6:1099–1101.

38. Howard P. Jones, *Indonesia: The Possible Dream* (New York: Harcourt Brace Jovanovich, 1971), 111–12.

39. NSC 51, "U.S. Policy Toward Southeast Asia," March 29, 1949, NSC Records, RG 273, NA.

40. For a comparison of U.S. policy toward Indochina and Indonesia during these years, see Evelyn Colbert, "The Road Not Taken: Decolonization and Independence in Indonesia and Indochina," *Foreign Affairs* 51 (April 1973): 608–28; McMahon, *Colonialism and Cold War*, 313–15.

41. Marshall to the Embassy in France, February 3, 1947, *FRUS* (1947): 6:67–68.

42. Ibid.

43. Charles S. Reed II (Consul in Saigon) to the State Department, July 11, 1947, ibid., 114.

44. On the Asian Tito option, see esp. House Committee on Armed Services, *United States–Vietnam Relations, 1945–1967: Study Prepared by the Department of Defense* (Washington, D.C.: GPO, 1971), vol. 1, c1–c7; Robert M. Blum, *Drawing the Line: The Origin of the American Containment Policy in East Asia* (New York: Norton, 1982).

45. Department of State Policy Statement on Indochina, September 27, 1948, *FRUS* (1948): 6:48.

46. Reed to the State Department, July 11, 1947, *FRUS* (1947): 6:114.

47. Marshall to the Embassy in France, May 13, 1947, ibid., 97; Gary R. Hess, "The First American Commitment in Indochina: The Acceptance of the 'Bao Dai' Solution, 1950," *Diplomatic History* 2 (fall 1978): 331–50.

48. Department of State Policy Statement on Indochina, September 27, 1948, *FRUS* (1948): 6:43–49. For similar analyses, see CIA Report ORE 25-48, "The Break-up of the Colonial Empires and Its Implications for U.S. Security," September 3, 1948, PSF, Truman Papers, HSTL; Policy Planning Staff (PPS) Paper 51, "United States Policy toward Southeast Asia," March 29, 1949, in *The State Department Policy Planning Staff Papers*, 3 vols., introduction by Anna Kasten Nelson (New York: Garland, 1983), 3:32–53.

49. U.S. Department of State *Bulletin* 24 (February 20, 1950): 291–92. See also David K. E. Bruce to Acheson, December 11, 1949, and NSC 48/2, December 30, 1949, *FRUS* (1949): 7:105–10, 1215–20; and Acheson to Truman, February 2, 1950, *FRUS* (1950): 6:716–17.

50. PPS 51, March 29, 1949; NSC 48/2, December 30, 1949.

51. For the broader context of these challenges to U.S. foreign policy goals, see esp. Leffler, *A Preponderance of Power*, ch. 8; Thomas J. McCormick, *America's Half-Century: United States Foreign Policy in the Cold War* (Baltimore: Johns Hopkins University Press, 1989), 88–98.

52. Memorandum by Acheson, December 20, 1949, *FRUS* (1949): 1:612–17.

53. Acheson to British Ambassador Oliver Franks, December 24, 1949, *FRUS* (1949): 7:927.

54. The crucial link between Japan and Southeast Asia is emphasized in a number of important books, including William Borden, *The Pacific Alliance: United States Foreign Economic Policy and Japanese Trade Recovery, 1947–1955* (Madison: University of Wisconsin Press, 1984); Michael Schaller, *The American Occupation of Japan: The Origins of the Cold War in Asia* (New York: Oxford University Press, 1985); Andrew J. Rotter, *The Path to Vietnam: Origins of the American Commitment to Southeast Asia* (Ithaca, N.Y.: Cornell University Press, 1987); and Leffler, *A Preponderance of Power*.

55. Hogan, *The Marshall Plan*, ch. 6; Melvyn P. Leffler, "The United States and the Strategic Dimensions of the Marshall Plan," *Diplomatic History* 12 (summer 1988): 277–306.

56. PPS 61, "Policy Relating to the Financial Crisis of the United Kingdom and the Sterling Area," August 31, 1949, in *State Department Policy Planning Staff Papers* 3:150–56; Leffler, "Strategic Dimensions," 298.

57. Bevin, quoted in Rotter, *The Path to Vietnam*, 54.

58. Clayton, quoted in ibid., 141.

59. Rotter, *The Path to Vietnam*, chs. 3, 7, 8.

60. This argument is developed most fully in Blum, *Drawing the Line*.

61. Quoted in John Lewis Gaddis, *Strategies of Containment: A Criticial Appraisal of Postwar American National Security Policy* (New York: Oxford

University Press, 1982), 92. For the full text of NSC 68, see *FRUS* (1950): 1:237–92.

62. On this point, see Robert J. McMahon, "Credibility and World Power: Exploring the Psychological Dimension in Postwar American Diplomacy," *Diplomatic History* 15 (fall 1991): 455–71; and Gaddis, *Strategies of Containment*, 91–92.

63. Zhai Qiang, "Transplanting the Chinese Model: Chinese Military Advisers and the First Vietnam War, 1950–1954," *Journal of Military History* 57 (October 1993): 689–715 (quotations from 695); Chen Jian, "China and the First Indo-China War, 1950–54," *China Quarterly*, no. 133 (March 1993): 85–110; Sergei N. Goncharov, John W. Lewis, and Xue Litai, *Uncertain Partners: Stalin, Mao, and the Korean War* (Stanford, Calif.: Stanford University Press, 1993), 106–108. See also John Lewis Gaddis, *We Now Know: Rethinking Cold War History* (New York: Oxford University Press, 1997), 161; Vladislav Zubok and Constantine Pleshakov, *Inside the Kremlin's Cold War: From Stalin to Khrushchev* (Cambridge: Harvard University Press, 1996), 57.

64. Analysis prepared for the Joint Chiefs of Staff by the Joint Strategic Survey Committee, November 17, 1950, *FRUS* (1950): 6:949–50.

65. Ibid. See also Joint Chiefs of Staff to Secretary of Defense George C. Marshall, November 28, 1950, ibid., 945–48.

3. Searching for Stability, 1950–1954

1. Memorandum by Nitze, March 5, 1952, *Foreign Relations of the United States (FRUS)* (1952–1954): 12(pt. 1): 68.

2. Memorandum of discussion at State-JCS meeting, January 16, 1952, ibid., 32.

3. On the importance of these links, see Borden, *The Pacific Alliance* (Madison: University of Wisconsin Press, 1984); Rotter, *The Path to Vietnam* (Ithaca, N.Y.: Cornell University Press, 1987); Schaller, *The American Occupation of Japan* (New York: Oxford University Press, 1985); and Leffler, *A Preponderance of Power* (Stanford, Calif.: Stanford University Press, 1990).

4. Leffler, "The American Conception of National Security," *American Historical Review* 89 (April 1984): 346–80; Leffler, *A Preponderance of Power*.

5. See, for example, John Lewis Gaddis, "Drawing Lines: The Defensive Perimeter Strategy in East Asia, 1947–1951," in Gaddis, ed., *The Long Peace: Inquiries into the History of the Cold War* (New York: Oxford University Press, 1987), 72–103.

6. Acheson, quoted in Leffler, *A Preponderance of Power*, 341.

7. Ilya V. Gaiduk, *The Soviet Union and the Vietnam War* (Chicago: Ivan Dee, 1996), 5; Chen Jian, "China and the First Indo-China War," *China Quarterly*, no. 133 (March 1993): 85–110.

8. Zhai, "Transplanting the Chinese Model," *Journal of Military History* 57 (October 1993): 715.

9. Chen Jian, "China and the First Indo-China War"; Zhai, "Transplanting the Chinese Model"; King Chen, *Vietnam and China, 1938–1954* (Princeton: Princeton University Press, 1969). On Indonesia, see David Mozingo, *Chinese Policy Toward Indonesia, 1949–1965* (Ithaca, N.Y.: Cornell University Press, 1976). On the Chinese role in the Malayan insurrection, see Anthony Short, *The Communist Insurrection in Malaya, 1948–1960* (New York: Crane, Russack, 1975), 315–18.

10. Memorandum of discussion at NSC meeting, March 5, 1952, *FRUS* (1952–1954): 12(pt. 1): 70–74.

11. Memorandum of discussion between Acheson, Eden, and others, May 26, 1952, ibid., 96–97.

12. NSC 124/2, June 25, 1952, ibid., 127–32.

13. NSC 148, April 6, 1953, ibid., 288–89.

14. Final Report of the Joint MDAP Survey Mission to Southeast Asia, December 6, 1950, *FRUS* (1950): 6:165.

15. Acheson to Truman, January 9, 1950, ibid., 964–66.

16. Ibid., 914ff.

17. Acheson to Cochran, July 26, 1950, ibid., 1040.

18. *FRUS* (1951): 6(pt. 1): 729ff.; Herbert Feith, *The Decline of Constitutional Democracy in Indonesia* (Ithaca, N.Y.: Cornell University Press, 1962), 198–207; Paul F. Gardner, *Shared Hopes, Separate Fears: Fifty Years of U.S.-Indonesian Relations* (Boulder, Colo.: Westview, 1997), 105–109.

19. On the importance of this dispute to the Indonesian-American relationship, see esp. two revealing memoirs by former U.S. ambassadors: John M. Allison, *Ambassador from the Prairie or Allison in Wonderland* (Boston: Houghton Mifflin, 1973), 297–304; Jones, *Indonesia: The Possible Dream* (New York: Harcourt Brace Jovanovich, 1971), 174–82.

20. NIE-77, June 11, 1953, *FRUS* (1952–1954): 12(pt. 2): 362.

21. Ibid., 361–63; SE-51, September 18, 1953, ibid., 386–87; memorandum of discussion at NSC meeting, November 19, 1953, ibid., 388–89.

22. John F. Cady, *The United States and Burma* (Cambridge: Harvard University Press, 1976), 196–207; Silverstein, *Burmese Politics* (New Brunswick, N.J.: Rutgers University Press, 1981), 200–209; State Department Policy Statement on Burma, June 16, 1950, *FRUS* (1950): 6:232–44.

23. State Department Policy Statement on Burma, June 16, 1950, *FRUS* (1950): 6:232–44. The quote is from Ba Maw, *Breakthrough in Burma* (New Haven: Yale University Press, 1968), 34.

24. Day to the State Department, February 15, 1952, *FRUS* (1952–1954): 12(pt. 2): 13.

25. Key to the State Department, August 15, 1951, *FRUS* (1951): 6(pt. 1): 288–89.

26. Nu to Eisenhower, September 12, 1953, *FRUS* (1952–1954): 12(pt. 2): 135–38.

27. State Department Draft Position Paper on Burma, December 20, 1951, *FRUS* (1951): 6(pt. 1): 325–26.

28. NIE-36, "Prospects for Survival of a Non-Communist Regime in Burma," August 1, 1951, ibid., 279–85.

29. State Department paper, undated (attached to memorandum from Acheson to Truman, March 9, 1950), *FRUS* (1950): 6(pt. 1): 42–43.

30. State Department Policy Statement on Thailand, October 15, 1950, ibid., 1529.

31. Stanton to the State Department, March 15, 1951, *FRUS* (1951): 6(pt. 2): 1598–1600.

32. Daniel Fineman, *A Special Relationship: The United States and Military Government in Thailand, 1947–1958* (Honolulu: University of Hawaii Press, 1997), 88–125.

33. Dulles to Secretary of Defense Charles Wilson, May 5, 1953, *FRUS* (1952–1954): 12(pt. 2): 666.

34. Stanton to the State Department, January 23, 1953, ibid., 658–61.

35. Ibid., 661.

36. Cullather, *Illusions of Influence* (Stanford, Calif.: Stanford University Press, 1994), 72–80 (quote from 79–80); Brands, *Bound to Empire* (New York: Oxford University Press, 1992), 234–35; memorandum of conversation between Acheson and Quirino, *FRUS* (1949): 7:597–99.

37. Final Report of the Joint Mutual Defense Assistance Program Survey Mission to Southeast Asia (Melby Mission), December 6, 1950, *FRUS* (1950): 6(pt. 1): 171–72.

38. Cullather, *Illusions of Influence*, 80.

39. Report of the Bell Mission, October 9, 1950, *FRUS* (1950): 6:1497–1502.

40. Melby, quoted in Cullather, *Illusions of Influence*, 83.

41. Truman, quoted in ibid., 87.

42. Brands, *Bound to Empire*, 237–45; Cullather, *Illusions of Influence*, 89–92.

43. Nick Cullather, "America's Boy? Ramon Magsaysay and the Illusion of Influence," *Pacific Historical Review* 62 (August 1993): 305–38; Cullather, *Illusions of Influence*, 94–105.

44. Dulles to Acheson, November 30, 1950, *FRUS* (1950): 6:163.

45. NIE-5, "Indochina: Current Situation and Probable Developments," December 29, 1950, ibid., 958–63.

46. Progress Report on NSC 64, March 15, 1951, *FRUS* (1951): 6(pt. 1): 397–400; Under Secretary of State James E. Webb to Truman, September 13, 1951, ibid., 496–97.

47. Edmund Gullion (Chargé in Saigon) to the State Department, August 18, 1951, ibid., 480–84.

48. JCS to George C. Marshall, November 28, 1950, *FRUS* (1950): 6:946.

49. Bruce to the State Department, May 31, 1950, ibid., 819–20.

50. Heath to the State Department, February 24, 1951, *FRUS* (1951): 6(pt. 1): 385.

51. See, for example, memorandum of discussion at State-JCS meeting, December 21, 1951, ibid., 569–70.

52. Louis Johnson to Acheson, April 14, 1950, *FRUS* (1950): 6:780–85; JCS to Marshall, January 10, 1951, *FRUS* (1951): 6(pt. 1): 347–48. See also Robert Buzzanco, "Prologue to Tragedy: U.S. Military Opposition to Intervention in Vietnam, 1950–1954," *Diplomatic History* 17 (spring 1993): 201–22.

53. Ohly to Acheson, November 20, 1950, *FRUS* (1950): 6:929.

54. Memorandum of discussion at NSC meeting, March 5, 1952, *FRUS* (1952–1954): 12(pt. 1): 71–72.

55. Secretaries of the Army, Navy, and Air Force to Lovett, April 8, 1952, CD 092 (Indochina), 1952, Records of the Office of the Administrative Secretary, Office of the Secretary of Defense, Record Group 330, National Archives.

56. Eisenhower, quoted in David L. Anderson, "Dwight D. Eisenhower and Wholehearted Support of Ngo Dinh Diem," in Anderson, ed., *Shadow on the White House: Presidents and the Vietnam War, 1945–1975* (Lawrence: University of Kansas Press, 1993), 44–45.

57. Herring, *America's Longest War*, 2d rev. ed. (New York: Knopf, 1986), 25–29.

58. George C. Herring and Richard H. Immerman, "Eisenhower, Dulles, and Dienbienphu: 'The Day We Didn't Go to War' Revisited," *Journal of American History* 71 (September 1984): 343–63; Melanie Billings-Yun, *Decision Against War: Eisenhower and Dien Bien Phu, 1954* (New York: Columbia University Press, 1988).

59. Herring and Immerman, "Eisenhower, Dulles, and Dienbienphu," 343–63; Billings-Yun, *Decision Against War*.

60. U.S. Department of State *Bulletin* 30 (April 12, 1954): 539.

61. See, for example, memorandum of conversation between Dulles and the foreign ministers of Australia and New Zealand, May 2, 1954, *FRUS* (1952–1954): 12(pt. 1): 439–42; and memorandum of conversation between Dulles and Eisenhower, May 5, 1954, ibid., 446–50.

62. JCS to Wilson, April 9, 1954, ibid., 412–21; JCS to Dulles, March 12, 1954, *FRUS* (1952–1954): 16:472–75; Michael Schaller, *Altered States: The United States and Japan Since the Occupation* (New York: Oxford University Press, 1997), 96–100.

63. On the origins of SEATO, see esp. Gary R. Hess, "The American Search for Stability in Southeast Asia: The SEATO Structure of Containment," in Warren I. Cohen and Akira Iriye, eds., *The Great Powers in East Asia, 1953–1960* (New York: Columbia University Press, 1990), 272–95; Roger Dingman, "John Foster Dulles and the Creation of the South-East Asia Treaty

Organization in 1954," *International History Review* 11 (August 1989): 457–77.

64. Memorandum of conversation between Dulles and Eisenhower, August 17, 1954, *FRUS* (1952–1954): 16:735.

65. Memorandum of conversation between Dulles, Radford, and others, May 9, 1954, ibid., 463–65.

66. Memorandum of conversation between Eisenhower, Dulles, and others, May 28, 1954, ibid., 521–22.

67. Memorandum of discussion at NSC meeting, June 3, 1954, ibid., 534.

68. Memorandum of discussion at NSC meeting, July 22, 1954, (editorial note), ibid., 651.

69. Chen Jian, "China and the First Indo-China War," 106–110; George McT. Kahin, *Intervention: How America Became Involved in Vietnam* (New York: Knopf, 1986), 54–65; Zhai Qiang, "China and the Geneva Conference of 1954," *China Quarterly*, no. 129 (March 1992): 103–22.

70. NSC 5429, August 4, 1954, *FRUS* (1952–1954): 12(pt. 1): 698.

71. Memorandum of discussion at NSC meeting, August 12, 1954, ibid., 731–32.

72. Davis, quoted in Hess, "The American Search for Stability in Southeast Asia," 286.

4. The Deepening Crisis, 1954–1961

1. Eisenhower, quoted in Schaller, *Altered States* (New York: Oxford University Press, 1997), 100.

2. CIA, "Probable Consequences of the Death of Stalin and of the Elevation of Malenkov to Leadership in the USSR," SE-39, March 12, 1953, *FRUS* (1952–1954): 8(pt. 1): 125; NIE 11-5-54, "Soviet Capabilities and Main Lines of Policy through Mid-1959," June 7, 1954, ibid., 235–38; CIA, "Probable Long Term Development of the Soviet Bloc and Western Power Positions," SE-46, July 3, 1953, in Scott A. Koch, ed., *CIA Cold War Records: Selected Estimates on the Soviet Union, 1950–1959* (Washington: CIA History Staff, 1993), 155–62; Zubok and Pleshakov, *Inside the Kremlin's Cold War* (Cambridge: Harvard University Press, 1996), 138–40, 154–62. For an expanded treatment of the themes developed in this section, see Robert J. McMahon, "The Illusion of Vulnerability: American Reassessments of the Soviet Threat, 1955–1956," *International History Review* 18 (August 1996): 591–619.

3. NSC 5501, "Basic National Security Poicy," January 7, 1955, *FRUS* (1955–1957): 19:24–38.

4. NIE 100-7-55, "World Situation and Trends," November 1, 1955, ibid., 131–45.

5. Joseph L. Nogee and Robert H. Donaldson, *Soviet Foreign Policy Since*

World War II, 4th ed. (New York: Macmillan, 1992), 163–71; Francis Fukuyama, "Soviet Strategy in the Third World," in Andrzej Korbonski and Francis Fukuyama, eds., *The Soviet Union and the Third World: The Last Three Decades* (Ithaca, N.Y.: Cornell University Press), 25–28; Roger Kanet, "The Soviet Union and the Colonial Question, 1917–1953," in Kanet, ed., *The Soviet Union and the Developing Nations* (Baltimore: Johns Hopkins University Press, 1974); Nikita S. Khrushchev, *Khrushchev Remembers: The Last Testament*, ed. and trans. Strobe Talbot (Boston: Little, Brown, 1974); David J. Dallin, *Soviet Foreign Policy After Stalin* (Philadelphia: Lippincott, 1961), 286–306; R. Craig Nation, *Black Earth, Red Star: A History of Soviet Security Policy, 1917–1991* (Ithaca, N.Y.: Cornell University Press, 1992), 225–28.

6. Kuznetsov, quoted in Dallin, *Soviet Foreign Policy*, 299.

7. S. Neil MacFarlane, "Successes and Failures in Soviet Policy Toward the Third World, 1917–1985," in Mark N. Katz, ed., *The USSR and Marxist Revolutions in the Third World* (New York: Cambridge University Press, 1990), 60–61.

8. Memorandum of discussion at NSC meeting, November 15, 1955, *FRUS* (1955–1957): 10:28–31.

9. Nixon, quoted in ibid.

10. Memorandum of discussion at NSC meeting, November 21, 1955, ibid., 32–36.

11. See, for example, NSC 5429, August 12, 1954, Policy Papers Subseries, NSC series, Records of the Office of the Special Adviser for National Security Affairs, Eisenhower Library.

12. Quoted in William Duiker, *Sacred War* (New York: McGraw-Hill, 1995), 102–103; George McT. Kahin, *Intervention* (New York: Knopf, 1986), 66–92; David L. Anderson, *Trapped By Success: The Eisenhower Administration and Vietnam, 1953–61* (New York: Columbia University Press, 1991), 65–90.

13. Quoted in Hess, *Vietnam and the United States* (Boston: Twayne, 1990), 56.

14. Anderson, *Trapped By Success*, 91–119.

15. John F. Kennedy, "America's Stake in Vietnam," *Vital Speeches* 22 (August 1956): 617–19.

16. Kahin, *Intervention*, 93–99; Anthony Short, *The Origins of the Vietnam War* (London: Longman, 1989), 211–12.

17. Kahin, *Intervention*, 101–15; Duiker, *Sacred War*, 116–27.

18. Memorandum of discussion at NSC meeting, May 9, 1960, *FRUS* (1958–1960): 1:446–47.

19. Bernard B. Fall, *Anatomy of a Crisis: The Laotian Crisis of 1960–1961* (Garden City, N.Y.: Doubleday, 1969), 23.

20. Charles A. Stevenson, *The End of Nowhere: American Policy Toward Laos Since 1945* (Boston: Beacon, 1972), 9; Roger Warner, *Shooting at the*

Moon: The Story of America's Clandestine War in Laos (South Royalton, Vt.: Steerforth Press, 1996), 3, 6.

21. Nina S. Adams, "Patrons, Clients, and Revolutionaries: The Lao Search for Independence, 1945–1954," in Nina S. Adams and Alfred W. McCoy, eds., *Laos: War and Revolution* (New York: Harper and Row, 1970), 100–120; Timothy N. Castle, *At War in the Shadow of Vietnam: U.S. Military Aid to the Royal Lao Government, 1955–1975* (New York: Columbia University Press, 1993), 3–13.

22. Stevenson, *End of Nowhere*, 39–48.

23. Memorandum of discussion at NSC meeting, May 29, 1959, (editorial note), *FRUS* (1958–1960): 16:450; Horace H. Smith (Ambassador in Laos) to the State Department, May 19, 1959, ibid., 443–46; Acting Secretary of State Christian Herter to the Embassy in Laos, ibid., 448–50; Stevenson, *End of Nowhere*, 59–66.

24. *FRUS* (1958–1960): 16:478ff.; Len E. Ackland, "No Place for Neutralism: The Eisenhower Administration and Laos," in Adams and McCoy, eds., *Laos: War and Revolution*, 139–54.

25. Castle, *At War in the Shadow of Vietnam*, 17–25.

26. U.S. Department of State, *The Situation in Laos* (Washington: GPO, 1959), i.

27. Eisenhower, quoted in Castle, *At War in the Shadow of Vietnam*, 26.

28. Eisenhower, quoted in ibid., 27.

29. David P. Chandler, *The Tragedy of Cambodian History: Politics, War, and Revolution Since 1945* (New Haven: Yale University Press, 1991), chs. 1–2; Roger M. Smith, *Cambodia's Foreign Policy* (Ithaca, N.Y.: Cornell University Press, 1965), 38–86.

30. *FRUS* (1955–1957): 21:403ff.; Kenton Clymer, "The United States and Cambodian Neutralism, 1955–60," unpublished paper (in author's possession).

31. McClintock to Admiral Felix Stump, March 30, 1956, *FRUS* (1955–1957): 21:506–507.

32. McClintock to the State Department, May 11, 1956, ibid., 518–20. See also Ambassador Carl W. Strom to the State Department, February 14, 1957, ibid., 556–58; Clymer, "The United States and Cambodian Neutralism."

33. See, for example, Eisenhower to Sihanouk, May 7, 1959, *FRUS* (1958–1960): 26:313–15.

34. For Sihanouk's perspective, see esp. Norodom Sihanouk, *My War with the CIA* (New York: Pantheon, 1973); John Armstrong, ed., *Sihanouk Speaks* (New York: Walker, 1964).

35. Hugh S. Cumming, Jr. (Ambassador in Indonesia) to the State Department, January 19 and February 21, 1955, *FRUS* (1955–1957): 22:129 and 137; NIE 65–55, March 1, 1955, ibid., 140–41; NSC 5518, May 3, 1955, ibid., 154–55.

36. Cumming to the State Department, August 16, 1955, *FRUS* (1955–1957): 22:181.

37. Assistant Secretary of State Walter Robertson to Under Secretary of State Herbert Hoover, Jr., September 20, 1955, ibid., 194–95.

38. Cumming to the State Department, October 7, 1955, ibid., 201; memorandum of discussion at NSC meeting, October 6, 1955, ibid., 200.

39. Memorandum of discussion at NSC meeting, December 22, 1955, ibid., 218.

40. Dulles to Eisenhower, February 27, 1956, ibid., 236.

41. Robertson to Hoover, July 27, 1956, ibid., 287. On Sukarno's visit, see Paul F. Gardner, *Shared Hopes, Separate Fears* (Boulder, Colo.: Westview, 1997), 126–27.

42. Cumming to the State Department, June 30, 1956, *FRUS* (1955–1957): 22:282–84.

43. Cumming to the State Department, October 27, 1956, ibid., 316–19; Cumming to the State Department, February 23, 1957, ibid., 351–53.

44. For background to the rebellion, see esp. George McT. Kahin and Audrey R. Kahin, *Subversion as Foreign Policy: The Secret Eisenhower and Dulles Debacle in Indonesia* (New York: New Press, 1995); Daniel Lev, *The Transition to Guided Democracy: Indonesia Politics, 1957–1959* (Ithaca, N.Y.: Cornell University Modern Indonesia Project, 1966); Barbara S. Harvey, *Permesta: Half a Rebellion* (Ithaca, N.Y.: Cornell University Modern Indonesia Project, 1977).

45. Memorandum of discussion at NSC meeting, February 28, 1957, (editorial note), *FRUS* (1955–1957): 22:357–58.

46. Report by the Intelligence Advisory Committee, March 5, 1957, ibid., 362–64.

47. Memorandum of conversation between Dulles and Casey, March 13, 1957, ibid., 366–67.

48. Memorandum of discussion at NSC meeting, March 14, 1957, ibid., 370–71.

49. Memorandum of discussion at NSC meeting, August 1, 1957, ibid., 400–401.

50. NIE 65–57, August 27, 1957, ibid., 429–31.

51. Special Report on Indonesia, by the Ad Hoc Interdepartmental Committee on Indonesia for the NSC, September 3, 1957, ibid., 436–40.

52. Robertson to Dulles, September 19, 1957, ibid., 445–48.

53. State Department memorandum, January 2, 1958, *FRUS* (1958–1960): 22:1–3.

54. Ide Anak Agung Gde Agung, *Twenty Years of Indonesian Foreign Policy, 1945–1965* (The Hague: Mouton, 1973), 380–81. For the fullest accounts of the U.S. role in the colonels' revolt, see Kahin and Kahin, *Subversion*; Lu Soo Chun, "U.S. Policy Toward Indonesia, 1953–1961," (unpublished Ph.D. diss., Ohio University, 1997), ch. 4. Also valuable are John Prados, *Presidents' Secret Wars: CIA and Pentagon Covert Operations Since World War II* (New York: Morrow, 1987), 128–48; Gardner, *Shared Hopes, Separate Fears*, 133–62; Peter Grose,

Gentleman Spy: The Life of Allen Dulles (Boston: Houghton Mifflin, 1995), 452–54.

55. Jones, *Indonesia: The Possible Dream* (New York: Harcourt Brace Jovanovich, 1971).

56. Cullather, *Illusions of Influence* (Stanford, Calif.: Stanford University Press, 1994), 126–31.

57. Cullather, *Illusions of Influence*, 131–37.

58. Ibid., 137–38.

59. Dulles, quoted in ibid., 139. See also Dulles to the State Department, March 16, 1956, *FRUS* (1955–1957): 22:642–43.

60. Cullather, *Illusions of Influence*, 139–41; Brands, *Bound to Empire* (New York: Oxford University Press, 1992), 270–73.

61. Cullather, *Illusions of Influence*, 132–33.

62. Ibid., 142–43.

63. Acting Secretary of State Herbert Hoover, Jr., to Eisenhower, May 3, 1956, *FRUS* (1955–1957): 22:647–48.

64. Joint Chiefs of Staff to Secretary of Defense Wilson, February 27, 1957, ibid., 710–13; NIE 66/1–57, September 3, 1957, ibid., 725–26.

65. Memorandum of discussion at NSC meeting, with attachment, June 3, 1958, *FRUS* (1958–1960): 15:852–57; NSCS 5813/1 June 4, 1958, ibid., 859–69; State Department memorandum, January 27, 1960, ibid., 946–57.

66. Rockwood H. Foster (Acting Officer in Charge of Thai and Malayan Affairs) to John E. Peurifoy (Ambassador in Thailand), June 22, 1955, *FRUS* (1955–1957): 22:825–27; Staff Study prepared for the Operations Coordinating Board (OCB), January 4, 1956, ibid., 845–53. On the infusion of security-related economic aid from the United States after 1954, see Robert J. Muscat, *Thailand and the United States: Development, Security, and Foreign Aid* (New York: Columbia University Press, 1990), 92–93.

67. Dulles to Radford, November 18, 1955, *FRUS* (1955–1957): 22:840–41.

68. NIE 62–57, June 18, 1957, ibid., 926.

69. Fineman, *A Special Relationship* (Honolulu: University of Hawaii Press, 1997), 211–21.

70. Bishop to the State Department, September 20, 1957, *FRUS* (1955–1957): 22:933–34.

71. Dulles to the Embassy in Thailand, October 22, 1957, ibid., 942.

72. U. Alexis Johnson, with Jef Olivarius McAllister, *Right Hand of Power: The Memoirs of an American Diplomat* (Englewood Cliffs, N.J.: Prentice-Hall, 1974), 275.

73. William O. Walker III, *Opium and Foreign Poicy: The Anglo-American Search for Order in Asia, 1912–1954* (Chapel Hill: University of North Carolina Press, 1991), 200–207; Thomas Lobe, *United States National Security Policy and Aid to the Thailand Police* (Denver: University of Denver Monograph Series in World Affairs, 1977), 19–28; Warner, *Shooting at the Moon*, 16–19.

74. Johnson, *Right Hand of Power*, 287–88.

75. Johnson to the State Department, December 24, 1960, *FRUS* (1958–1960): 15:1173.

76. Cady, *The United States and Burma* (Cambridge: Harvard University Press, 1976), 210–11; Josef Silverstein, *Burma: Military Rule and the Politics of Stagnation* (Ithaca, N.Y.: Cornell University Press, 1977), 188–90.

77. OCB Paper, October 27, 1954, *FRUS* (1952–1954): 12(pt. 2): 237.

78. Ibid., 234–41.

79. Dulles to the Embassy in Burma, December 27, 1955, *FRUS* (1955–1957): 22:29–30. The quote is from Khrushchev speech, December 3, 1955, in "Statements of N. A. Bulganin and N. S. Khrushchev in India, Burma, and Afghanistan," *New Times* 226 (December 22, 1955): *Supplement*, 2, 7.

80. Robertson to Dulles, February 9, 1956, *FRUS* (1955–1957): 22:36.

81. Daniel M. Braddock (Chargé in Burma) to the State Department, April 2, 1956, ibid., 52.

82. Dulles to the Embassy in Burma, March 29, 1956, ibid., 48–50.

83. MacArthur to Dulles, June 15, 1956, ibid., 71–72.

84. Memorandum of discussion at NSC meeting, August 30, 1956, *FRUS* (1955–1957): 21:243.

85. Ibid.; editorial note, *FRUS* (1955–1957): 22:83–84.

86. Walter P. McConaughy (Ambassador in Burma) to the State Department, October 2 and December 12, 1957, ibid., 120–24.

87. OCB Outline Plan of Operations, February 27, 1957, *FRUS* (1955–1957): 22:91.

88. Memorandum by Frank Wisner, June 1, 1955, *FRUS* (1955–1957): 22:736.

89. Young to Robertson, February 17, 1956, ibid., 765.

90. Report of an Interdepartmental Committee for the OCB, December 14, 1955, ibid., 744–54.

91. Ibid., 752.

92. Joey Long Shi Ruey, "The United States Involvement in Singapore, 1953–1960" (master's thesis, Nanyang Technological University, Singapore, 1998) (quotations from 96 and 114); C. M. Turnbull, *A History of Singapore, 1819–1988*, 2d rev. ed. (New York: Oxford University Press, 1989), 251–65.

93. Ruey, "United States Involvement in Singapore"; Minutes, ANZUS meeting, October 29, 1959, *FRUS* (1958–1960): 16:156–58; NSC 6012, July 25, 1960, ibid., 214–15, 221–22.

5: At War in Southeast Asia, 1961–1968

1. Kennedy, quoted in Thomas G. Paterson, "Introduction: John F. Kennedy's Quest for Victory and Global Crisis," in Paterson, ed., *Kennedy's*

Quest for Victory: American Foreign Policy, 1961–1963, (New York: Oxford University Press, 1989), 10. On Peace Corps volunteers in Southeast Asia, see *Peace Corps Volunteers* 1, no. 4 (Washington: GPO, 1963): 23.

2. Schaller, *Altered States* (New York: Oxford University Press, 1997), 108–109, 113.

3. John F. Kennedy, "America's Stake in Vietnam," *Vital Speeches* 22 (August 1956): 617–19.

4. Lawrence J. Bassett and Stephen E. Pelz, "The Failed Search for Victory: Vietnam and the Politics of War," in *Kennedy's Search for Victory*, 223–52; Gary R. Hess, "Commitment in the Age of Counter-insurgency: Kennedy's Vietnam Options and Decisions, 1961–1963," in Anderson, ed., *Shadow on the White House* (Lawrence: University of Kansas Press, 1993), 63–83.

5. Fred I. Greenstein and Richard H. Immerman, "What Did Eisenhower Tell Kennedy about Indochina? The Politics of Misperception?" *Journal of American History* 79 (September 1992): 568–87; Robert S. McNamara, with Brian Van-DeMark, *In Retrospect: The Tragedy and Lessons of Vietnam* (New York: Times Books, 1995), 35–37.

6. Brief prepared for the JCS on NIE-50–61, *FRUS* (1961–1963): 23:2–4.

7. *Public Papers of the Presidents: John F. Kennedy* (1961): 212–20 (hereafter cited as *PPP*) (Washington: GPO, 1962).

8. Timothy N. Castle, *At War in the Shadow of Vietnam* (New York: Columbia University Press, 1993), 41.

9. Sullivan, quoted in ibid., 41; memorandum of meeting with Kennedy, April 26, 1961, *FRUS* (1961–1963): 24:142–44; notes on NSC meeting, May 1, 1961, ibid., 162–64.

10. Herring, *America's Longest War*, 2d rev. ed. (New York: Knopf, 1986), 80–82.

11. Hilsman-Forrestal report to Kennedy, January 25, 1963, *FRUS* (1961–1963): 3:49–62.

12. Lodge, quoted in Lloyd C. Gardner, *Pay Any Price: Lyndon Johnson and the Wars for Vietnam* (Chicago: Ivan Dee, 1995), 85.

13. George McT. Kahin, *Intervention* (New York: Knopf, 1986), 146–81; Ellen J. Hammer, *A Death in November: America in Vietnam, 1963* (New York: Oxford University Press, 1987); Ann E. Blair, *Lodge in Vietnam: A Patriot Abroad* (New Haven: Yale University Press, 1995).

14. Lyndon B. Johnson, *The Vantage Point: Perspectives on the Presidency, 1963–1969* (New York: Holt, Rinehart, and Winston, 1971), 61.

15. Johnson to Kennedy, May 23, 1961, U.S. Department of Defense, *The Pentagon Papers: The Defense Department History of United States Decision Making on Vietnam* 2:58–59, Senator Gravel edition (Boston: Beacon Press, 1971).

16. National Security Action Memorandum 288, March 17, 1964, in *The Pentagon Papers: Abridged Edition*, ed. George C. Herring (New York: McGraw-Hill, 1993), 93–94.

17. Valenti, in Ted Gittinger, ed., *The Johnson Years: A Vietnam Roundtable* (Austin: Lyndon Baines Johnson Library, University of Texas, 1993), 101.

18. Johnson, quoted in Doris Kearns, *Lyndon Johnson and the American Dream* (New York: Harper and Row, 1976), 252–53.

19. Johnson, quoted in ibid., 251, 259–60. On Johnson's decision-making, see esp. Larry Berman, *Planning a Tragedy: The Americanization of the War in Vietnam* (New York: Norton, 1982); and Brian VanDeMark, *Into the Quagmire: Lyndon Johnson and the Escalation of the Vietnam War* (New York: Oxford University Press, 1991).

20. Conversation between Johnson and Bundy, May 27, 1964, in Michael R. Beschloss, ed., *Taking Charge: The Johnson White House Tapes, 1963–1964* (New York: Simon and Schuster, 1997), 370–72.

21. Conversation between Johnson and John S. Knight (Chairman of the Board, *Miami Herald*), February 3, 1964, in ibid., 214.

22. Herring, *America's Longest War*, 113–17.

23. Bundy, in Gittinger, ed., *The Johnson Years*, 23. On the Tonkin Gulf episode, see esp. Edwin E. Möise, *Tonkin Gulf and the Escalation of the Vietnam War* (Chapel Hill: University of North Carolina Press, 1996).

24. *PPP: Lyndon B. Johnson (1963–1964)*: 2:1267.

25. *Ibid.*, 1126.

26. *Quoted in James S. Olson and Randy Roberts, Where the Domino Fell: America and Vietnam, 1945 to 1990* (New York: St. Martin's, 1991), 125.

27. Taylor, quoted in ibid., 126.

28. Herring, *America's Longest War*, 128–30.

29. Johnson, *The Vantage Point*, 147.

30. Ball to Johnson, July 1, 1965, in *The Pentagon Papers: Abridged Edition*, 122–28.

31. Johnson, quoted in Robert Buzzanco, *Masters of War: Military Dissent and Politics in the Vietnam Era* (New York: Cambridge University Press, 1996), 223.

32. On the Indonesian background to these events, see esp. Harold Crouch, *The Army and Politics in Indonesia* (Ithaca, N.Y.: Cornell University Press, 1978); Ulf Sundhaussen, *The Road to Power: Indonesian Military Politics, 1945–1967* (Kuala Lumpur: Oxford University Press, 1982).

33. Komer, quoted in H. W. Brands, *The Wages of Globalism: Lyndon Johnson and the Limits of American Power* (New York: Oxford University Press, 1995), 178.

34. McNamara, *In Retrospect*, 214.

35. Rusk, quoted in H. W. Brands, "The Limits of Manipulation: How the United States Didn't Topple Sukarno," *Journal of American History* 76 (December 1989): 798.

36. JCS to McNamara, October 13, 1961, *FRUS (1961–1963)*: 23:443–45.

37. Komer to Kennedy, September 11, 1961, ibid., 426.

38. Komer memorandum, November 30, 1961, ibid., 470.

39. Extensive documentation on the West Irian question can be found in ibid., 462–625ff. See also Roger Hilsman, *To Move a Nation: The Politics of Foreign Policy in the Administration of John F. Kennedy* (New York: Delta, 1967), 361–80; Jones, *Indonesia: The Possible Dream* (New York: Harcourt Brace Jovanovich, 1971), 202–14.

40. Komer memorandum, January 16, 1963, *FRUS* (1961–1963): 23:657.

41. Jones to the State Department, November 4, 1963, ibid., 692–94; Kennedy press conference, November 14, 1963, *PPP: John F. Kennedy* (1963): 845–53.

42. Brands, "The Limits of Manipulation," 794–95.

43. Ibid., 795–800; Rusk statement, January 16, 1964, Senate Foreign Relations Committee, *Executive Sessions* (1964): 16:5–7.

44. Quoted in Brands, "The Limits of Manipulation," 806.

45. Hugh Tovar, "The Indonesian Crisis of 1965–1967: A Retrospective," *International Journal of Intelligence and Counterintelligence* 7 (fall 1994): 324. See also Paul F. Gardner, *Shared Hopes, Separate Fears* (Boulder, Colo.: Westview, 1997), 213–29; Marshall Green, *Indonesia: Crisis and Transformation, 1965–1968* (Washington, D.C.: Compass, 1990).

46. Helms, quoted in Brands, "The Limits of Manipulation," 805.

47. Rusk to Kennedy, February 24, 1961, *FRUS* (1961–1963): 23:841; *New York Times*, May 11, 1961, 1, and May 13, 1961, 2.

48. Those and other critical comments by Philippine leaders are summarized in a memorandum from Lucius Battle (Executive Secretary, State Department) to Bundy, July 13, 1961, *FRUS* (1961–1963): 23:770–73.

49. Robert H. Johnson (NSC) to Walt Rostow, July 14, 1961, ibid., 775–76.

50. *New York Times*, May 11, 1962, 3; Macapagal to Kennedy, quoted in Brands, *Bound to Empire* (New York: Oxford University Press, 1992), 278.

51. *Washington Evening News*, June 8, 1962, 1; memorandum of conversation between Averell Harriman and the Philippine ambassador, June 8, 1962, *FRUS* (1961–1963): 23:799–800.

52. William E. Stevenson (U.S. Ambassador in the Philippines) to Hilsman, May 6, 1963, ibid., 818–821.

53. Memorandum, February 26, 1962, *FRUS* (1961–1963): 23:915. Although the author of this memorandum is not identified, indications in the published document make clear that he was a CIA agent, most likely the station chief in Bangkok.

54. Young to Maxwell Taylor, October 27, 1961, ibid., 28–29.

55. Rusk to Kennedy, February 28, 1961, ibid., 841–42; Embassy in Thailand to the State Department, April 3, 1961, ibid., 844–46. On the use of Thai paramilitary operatives in Laos, a group called the Police Aerial Resupply Unit (Paru), see Warner, *Shooting at the Moon* (South Royalton, Vt.: Steerforth Press, 1996), 13–23ff. On the Rusk-Thanat communique, see Muscat, *Thailand and the United States* (New York: Columbia University Press, 1990), 26.

56. Memorandum from Johnson to Rostow, June 26, 1961, *FRUS* (1961–1963): 23:870.

57. Rostow to Kennedy, October 2, 1961, ibid., 885–86.

58. Ibid., 926–39; Castle, *At War in the Shadow of Vietnam*, 45–46.

59. *New York Times*, June 8, 1962, 3.

60. Summary of Discussions at Honolulu Conference, October 8–9, 1962, *FRUS* (1961–1963): 23:973–74.

61. Brands, *Bound to Empire*, 281–82.

62. JCS Paper, August 27, 1965, *FRUS* (1964–1968): 3:363.

63. Memorandum of White House meeting, December 1, 1964, *FRUS* (1964–1968): 1:967.

64. Quoted in Brands, *Bound to Empire*, 281. See also remarks by Assistant Secretary of State William P. Bundy, January 15, 1965, Senate Foreign Relations Committee, *Executive Sessions* (1965): 17:228–29.

65. Herring, *America's Longest War*, 146–52; Mark Clodfelter, *The Limits of Air Power: The American Bombing of North Vietnam* (New York: Free Press, 1989), 8–9, 134–37.

66. Quoted in Herring, *America's Longest War*, 151. On the attrition strategy, see William Westmoreland, "The Military Strategy of Attrition," in W. Scott Thompson and Donaldson D. Frizzel, eds., *The Lessons of Vietnam* (New York: Crane, Russak, 1977), 57–71.

67. Herring, *America's Longest War*, 156.

68. Analyses that use Clausewitzian principles to critique American strategy in Vietnam include Harry G. Summers, Jr., *On Strategy: A Critical Analysis of the Vietnam War* (New York: Dell, 1984; first published in 1982); and Olson and Roberts, *Where the Domino Fell*.

69. McNamara, *In Retrospect*, 322.

70. Westmoreland, quoted in Olson and Roberts, *Where the Domino Fell*, 142.

71. See, for example, Duiker, *Sacred War* (New York: McGraw-Hill, 1995).

72. Ho, quoted in Olson and Roberts, *Where the Domino Fell*, 145.

73. Giap, quoted in ibid., 147.

74. Gaiduk, *The Soviet Union and the Vietnam War* (Chicago: Ivan Dee, 1996); Anatoly Dobrynin, *In Confidence* (New York: Times Books, 1995), 115–16, 143–44; Zhai Qiang, "Beijing and the Vietnam Conflict: New Chinese Evidence," *Cold War International History Project Bulletin* (winter 1995–1996): 233–50 (quotation from 235); Chen Jian, "China's Involvement with the Vietnam War, 1964–1969," *China Quarterly*, no. 142 (June 1995): 356–78; John W. Garver, "The Chinese Threat in the Vietnam War," *Parameters* 22 (spring 1992): 73–85.

75. On the appeal of the Viet Cong, see esp. Eric M. Bergerud, *The Dynamics of Defeat: The Vietnam War in Hau Nghia Province* (Boulder, Colo.: Westview, 1991); Jeffrey Race, *War Comes to Long An: Revolutionary Conflict in a*

Vietnamese Province (Berkeley: University of California Press, 1972); and Duiker, *Sacred War.*

76. McNamara, quoted in Larry Berman, *Lyndon Johnson's War: The Road to Stalemate in Vietnam* (New York: Norton, 1989), 51.

77. Philip Caputo, *A Rumor of War* (New York: Ballantine, 1977), xiv.

78. Hess, *Vietnam and the United States* (Boston: Twayne, 1990), 102–103. An excellent analysis of the destructive impact of U.S. actions on South Vietnamese society can be found in Gabriel Kolko, *Anatomy of a War: Vietnam, the United States, and the Modern Historical Experience* (New York: Pantheon, 1985).

79. Morse remarks, March 3, 1964, Senate Foreign Relations Committee, *Executive Sessions* (1964): 16:141.

80. Quoted in Buzzanco, *Masters of War,* 304.

81. *Newsweek* 70 (July 10, 1967): 16–17.

82. Castle, *At War in the Shadow of Vietnam,* 46–97; Stevenson, *The End of Nowhere* (Boston: Beacon, 1972), 180–221; Warner, *Shooting at the Moon;* William H. Sullivan, *Obbligato, 1939–1979: Notes on a Foreign Service Career* (New York: Norton, 1984), 210–33 (quotation from 210). See also Prados, *Presidents' Secret Wars* (New York: Morrow, 1987), 261–82.

83. Sihanouk, quoted in Chandler, *The Tragedy of Cambodian History* (New Haven: Yale University Press, 1991), 140.

84. Chandler, *The Tragedy of Cambodian History,* 130–58.

85. *New York Times,* March 23, 1967, 1; Kahin, *Intervention,* 335.

86. *New York Times,* April 26, 1965, 3.

87. *New York Times,* April 15, 1966, 38; Bundy comments, September 20, 1966, Senate Foreign Relations Committee, *Executive Sessions* (1966): 18:946.

88. See, for example, *New York Times,* December 12, 1965, 4; April 15, 1966, 38; July 11, 1966, 3; March 23, 1967, 1; and April 8, 1967, 3.

89. *New York Times,* August 11, 1966, 2; Muscat, *Thailand and the United States,* 25–26.

90. W. Scott Thompson, *Unequal Partners: Philippine and Thai Relations with the United States, 1965–75* (Lexington, Mass.: Lexington Books, 1975), 83–86; *New York Times,* April 16, 1967, sec. 4, p. 4, and November 10, 1967, 1; Robert M. Blackburn, *Mercenaries and Lyndon Johnson's "More Flags": The Hiring of Korean, Filipino, and Thai Soldiers in the Vietnam War* (Jefferson, N.C.: McFarland, 1994), 101–15.

91. *New York Times,* August 11, 1966, 2; Walt Rostow to Johnson, March 22, 1967, "Thailand, Memos, vol. VI," Thailand Country File, box 284, National Security File (NSF), Lyndon B. Johnson Library, Austin, TX (hereafter cited as LBJL).

92. Wright to Walt Rostow, August 2, 1967, "Memos(2), vol. IV," Philippine Country File, box 279, NSF, LBJL.

93. Valenti, quoted in Raymond Bonner, *Waltzing with a Dictator: The Mar-*

coses and the Making of American Policy (New York: Times Books, 1987), 49. See also Karnow, *In Our Image* (New York: Ballantine, 1989), 375–77; Blackburn, *Mercenaries*, 67–94.

94. *New York Times*, September 15, 1966, 1, 15, and September 16, 1966, 1, 3.

95. *New York Times*, October 29, 1966, 10.

96. *New York Times*, March 29, 1967, 10.

97. Thomas R. Havens, *Fire Across the Sea: The Vietnam War and Japan, 1965–1975* (Princeton: Princeton University Press, 1987), 84–102; Schaller, *Altered States*, 198–202; Muscat, *Thailand and the United States*, 45–46; Richard Stubbs, "Geopolitics and the Political Economy of Southeast Asia," *International Journal* 44 (summer 1989): 517–40.

98. *New York Times*, August 4, 1966, 1. Lee reflected those views during conversations with LBJ and other top U.S. officials in Washington in October 1967; see memorandum for the record by Francis J. Galbraith (U.S. Ambassador in Singapore), undated, "Singapore, Visit of PM Lee," Singapore Country File, box 282, NSF, LBJL.

99. *New York Times*, April 12, 1967, 6.

100. Michael Leifer, *ASEAN and the Security of South-East Asia* (London: Routledge, 1989), 19–21.

6. Disengagement, 1968–1975

1. Westmoreland, quoted in Herring, *America's Longest War*, 2d rev. ed. (New York: Knopf, 1986), 199; George C. Herring, *LBJ and Vietnam: A Different Kind of War* (Austin: University of Texas Press, 1994), 146–48.

2. Dave Richard Palmer, *Summons of the Trumpet: A History of the Vietnam War from a Military Man's Viewpoint* (New York: Ballantine, 1978), 217. The literature on the Tet offensive is voluminous. The above account draws especially from William S. Turley, *The Second Indochina War: A Short Political and Military History, 1954–1975* (Boulder, Colo.: Westview, 1986), 99–117; Don Oberdorfer, *Tet!* (Garden City, N.Y.: Doubleday, 1973); Hess, *Vietnam and the United States* (Boston: Twayne, 1990), 106–109; and Herring, *America's Longest War*, 186–94.

3. Duiker, *Sacred War* (New York: McGraw-Hill, 1995), 213–14, 218; Herring, *America's Longest War*, 191.

4. Quoted in Turley, *Second Indochina War*, 116.

5. Westmoreland, quoted in Buzzanco, *Masters of War* (New York: Cambridge University Press, 1996), 316.

6. Wheeler, quoted in Buzzanco, *Masters of War*, 323–24.

7. Johnson, quoted in ibid., 311.

8. Cronkite, quoted in Oberdorfer, *Tet!*, 158.

9. *New York Times*, February 9, 1968, 1.

10. Bundy, quoted in Marilyn B. Young, *The Vietnam Wars, 1945–1990* (New York: HarperCollins, 1991), 225.

11. Quoted in Olson and Roberts, *Where the Domino Fell* (New York: St. Martin's, 1991), 186.

12. The text of Cronkite's broadcast is reprinted in Peter Braestrup, *The Big Story: How the American Press and Television Reported and Interpreted the Crisis of Tet 1968 in Vietnam and Washington* 2:188–89 (Boulder, Colo.: Westview, 1977).

13. Young, *The Vietnam War*, 226.

14. For accounts of the Westmoreland troop request and the subsequent debate it stirred within the Johnson administration, see Clark M. Clifford, "A Viet Nam Reappraisal," *Foreign Affairs* 47 (July 1969): 601–22; Clark Clifford, with Richard Holbrooke, *Counsel to the President: A Memoir* (New York: Random House, 1991), 473–87; Herbert Y. Schandler, *The Unmaking of a President: Lyndon Johnson and Vietnam* (Princeton: Princeton University Press, 1979); Buzzanco, *Masters of War*, 311–14, 318–29.

15. Johnson, quoted in Kolko, *Anatomy of a War* (New York: Pantheon, 1985), 314. On the gold-dollar crisis, in addition to Kolko, see Robert M. Collins, "The Economic Crisis of 1968 and the Waning of the 'American Century,' " *American Historical Review* 101 (April 1996): 396–422; Lloyd C. Gardner, *Pay Any Price* (Chicago: Ivan Dee, 1995).

16. On the antiwar movement and the political turmoil of this period, see esp. Charles DeBenedetti, with Charles Chatfield, *An American Ordeal: The Antiwar Movement of the Vietnam Era* (Syracuse, N.Y.: Syracuse University Press, 1990); Melvin Small, *Johnson, Nixon, and the Doves* (New Brunswick, N.J.: Rutgers University Press, 1988); Robert D. Schulzinger, *A Time for War: The United States and Vietnam, 1941–1975* (New York: Oxford University Press, 1997); Gardner, *Pay Any Price*; Dan T. Carter, *The Politics of Rage: George Wallace, The Origins of the New Conservatism, and the Transformation of American Politics* (Baton Rouge: Louisiana State University Press, 1995).

17. Clifford, quoted in Kolko, *Anatomy of a War*, 317–18.

18. Clifford, *Counsel to the President*, 488–526; Kolko, *Anatomy of a War*, 312–22; Johnson, *The Vantage Point* (New York: Holt, Rinehart, and Winston, 1971), 417–24.

19. *New York Times*, January 7, 1968, 14, and April 6, 1968, 6.

20. *New York Times*, February 7, 1968, 13, and March 23, 1968, 2.

21. *New York Times*, April 14, 1968, 1, and May 8, 1968, 5.

22. State Department, Scope Paper for Thanom visit, May 3, 1968, "Thailand, PM Thanom Visit (1)," NSF Country File, Thailand, box 285, LBJL.

23. *New York Times Magazine*, April 28, 1968, 79ff.

24. Thieu, quoted in Herring, *America's Longest War*, 218. On the South

Vietnamese sense of betrayal, see Bui Diem and David Chanoff, *In the Jaws of History* (New York: Houghton Mifflin, 1987).

25. Nixon, quoted in H. R. Haldeman, *The Ends of Power* (New York: Times Books, 1978), 81. On the relationship between the Vietnam War and the 1968 election, see Stephen E. Ambrose, *Nixon*, vol. 2, *The Triumph of a Politician, 1962–1972* (New York: Simon and Schuster, 1989), 206–18; Clifford, *Counsel to the President*, 567–96.

26. Quoted in Gaddis, *Strategies of Containment* (New York: Oxford University Press, 1982), 284. For Nixon's perspective, see *RN: The Memoirs of Richard Nixon* (New York: Grosset and Dunlap, 1978), 343–47.

27. Nixon, *RN*, 347; Herring, *America's Longest War*, 223.

28. Henry A. Kissinger, "The Vietnam Negotiations," *Foreign Affairs* 47 (January 1969): 219.

29. Henry Kissinger, *White House Years* (Boston: Little, Brown, 1979), 227–28. See also Henry Kissinger, *Diplomacy* (New York: Simon and Schuster, 1994), 674–680. On Kissinger, see esp. Walter Isaacson, *Kissinger: A Biography* (New York: Simon and Schuster, 1992); Robert D. Schulzinger, *Henry Kissinger: Doctor of Diplomacy* (New York: Columbia University Press, 1989).

30. Kissinger, *White House Years*, 57–58, 226.

31. Gaddis, *Strategies of Containment*, 298; Raymond L. Garthoff, *Detente and Confrontation: American-Soviet Relations from Nixon to Reagan* (Washington, DC: Brookings Institution, 1985), 74–75; Kissinger, *White House Years*, 222–25.

32. Kissinger, quoted in Gaddis, *Strategies of Containment*, 298.

33. Herring, *America's Longest War*, 221–34.

34. *New York Times*, May 15, 1969, 14.

35. *Far Eastern Economic Review* 65 (August 7, 1969): 310; *New York Times*, August 5, 1969, 5.

36. *New York Times*, June 23, 1969, 6; *Far Eastern Economic Review* 65 (August 7, 1969): 310.

37. *Far Eastern Economic Review* 63 (June 12, 1969): 608.

38. *Far Eastern Economic Review* 65 (August 28, 1969): 520.

39. *Far Eastern Economic Review* 63 (June 12, 1969): 609. See also *United States Security Agreements and Commitments Abroad: Kingdom of Thailand*, Hearings Before the Subcommittee on United States Security Agreements and Commitments Abroad of the Committee on Foreign Relations, U.S. Senate, 91st Cong., 1st sess., part 3, November 10–17, 1969 (Washington: GPO, 1970); Randall Bennett Woods, *Fulbright: A Biography* (New York: Cambridge University Press, 1995), 506–509, 527–28.

40. Kissinger, *White House Years*, 222–23.

41. *Public Papers of the Presidents: Richard M. Nixon* (1970): 405–10.

42. Young, *The Vietnam Wars*, 238; Seymour M. Hersh, *The Price of Power:*

Kissinger in the Nixon White House (New York: Summit Books, 1983), 168–93; Herring, *America's Longest War*, 225, 234–37.

43. Sihanouk, quoted in Karnow, *Vietnam: A History* (New York: Viking, 1983), 590.

44. Chandler, *The Tragedy of Cambodian History* (New Haven: Yale University Press, 1991), 187–204.

45. Herring, *America's Longest War*, 236–37; Hersh, *Price of Power*, 200–202.

46. Metcalf, quoted in Olson and Roberts, *Where the Domino Fell*, 238. See also DeBenedetti, *An American Ordeal*, 277–87; Melvin Small, "Containing Domestic Enemies: Richard M. Nixon and the War at Home," in Anderson, ed., *Shadow on the White House* (Lawrence: University of Kansas Press, 1993), 139–43.

47. Kissinger, *White House Years*, 513; Ambrose, *Nixon* 2:358–59.

48. Colson, quoted in Herring, *America's Longest War*, 239. See also H. R. Haldeman diary entry, May 9, 1970, in Haldeman, ed., *The Haldeman Diaries: Inside the Nixon White House* (New York: Putnam's, 1994), 163–64.

49. Castle, *At War in the Shadow of Vietnam* (New York: Columbia University Press, 1993), 108–110; Turley, *Second Indochina War*, 141–43.

50. William Sullivan oral history interview, in Kim Willenson, ed., *The Bad War: An Oral History of the Vietnam War* (New York: New American Library, 1987), 158.

51. Quoted in Hersh, *Price of Power*, 311.

52. Herring, *America's Longest War*, 244–46; Young, *The Vietnam Wars*, 263–66.

53. Garthoff, *Detente and Confrontation*, 245–56.

54. Nixon, quoted in Young, *The Vietnam Wars*, 267.

55. On the tangled Vietnamese-Chinese relationship, see William J. Duiker, *China and Vietnam: The Roots of Conflict* (Berkeley: University of California Institute of East Asian Studies, 1987).

56. Turley, *Second Indochina War*, 142–44. The quote is from Robert K. Brigham, "Viet Nam at the Center: Patterns of Diplomacy and Resistance," in Lloyd C. Gardner, ed., *The Vietnam War: International Perspectives* (College Station: Texas A&M University Press, forthcoming).

57. Kissinger and Nixon, quoted in Olson and Roberts, *Where the Domino Fell*, 248. See also Haldeman diary entry, April 10, 1972, *Haldeman Diaries*, 438.

58. Turley, *Second Indochina War*, 144–49; Young, *The Vietnam War*, 269–72.

59. Dobrynin, *In Confidence* (New York: Times Books, 1995), 246–48.

60. Kissinger, *White House Years*, 1316.

61. Young, *The Vietnam Wars*, 272–74.

62. Thieu, quoted in Alexander M. Haig, Jr., *Inner Circles: How America Changed the World. A Memoir* (New York: Warner Books, 1992), 301.

63. Kissinger, *White House Years*, 1372, 1375.

64. Nixon, quoted in Olson and Roberts, *Where the Domino Fell*, 249.

65. Haldeman diary entry, November 25, 1972, *Haldeman Diaries*, 543.

66. Kissinger, quoted in Herring, *America's Longest War*, 253. See also Haig, *Inner Circles*, 304–307.

67. Nixon, *RN*, 738.

68. Turley, *Second Indochina War*, 151–56; Young, *The Vietnam Wars*, 277–80.

69. Turley, *Second Indochina War*, 151–56; Young, *The Vietnam Wars*, 277–80; Herring, *America's Longest War*, 254–56.

70. *Far Eastern Economic Review* 74 (December 4, 1971): 5–6; Leifer, *ASEAN and the Security of South-East Asia* (London: Routledge, 1989), 52–59.

71. *Far Eastern Economic Review* 67 (March 26, 1970): 25–26; *New York Times*, February 26, 1970, 3.

72. *Far Eastern Economic Review* 70 (August 13, 1970): 23–25.

73. *New York Times*, June 8, 1970, 13, and June 14, 1970, sec. 4, pp. 2–3; U.S. Senate Committee on Foreign Relations, *United States Security Agreements: Kingdom of Thailand*.

74. *New York Times*, August 30, 1970, 1.

75. *Far Eastern Economic Review* 73 (August 14, 1971): 14; *Washington Post*, May 5, 1972, 1.

76. John L. S. Girling, *Thailand: Society and Politics* (Ithaca, N.Y.: Cornell University Press, 1981), 114–16, 187–88.

77. *Far Eastern Economic Review* 72 (June 12, 1971): 28.

78. *Far Eastern Economic Review* 75 (March 4, 1972): 17. For the Marcos coup and the U.S. response, see esp. Bonner, *Waltzing with a Dictator* (New York: Times Books, 1987), 112–28.

79. *New York Times*, May 17, 1970, 1. On Indonesian and Malaysian foreign policy, see esp. Franklin B. Weinstein, *Indonesian Foreign Policy and the Dilemma of Dependence: From Sukarno to Suharto* (Ithaca, N.Y.: Cornell University Press, 1976); Chin Kin Wah, *The Defence of Malaysia and Singapore: The Transformation of A Security System, 1957–1971* (Cambridge: Cambridge University Press, 1983).

80. Malik, quoted in Leifer, *ASEAN*, 20–21.

81. For the origins and early years of ASEAN, see esp. Michael Antolik, *ASEAN and the Diplomacy of Accommodation* (Armonk, N.Y.: Sharpe, 1990); Ronald D. Palmer and Thomas J. Reckford, *Building ASEAN: Twenty Years of Southeast Asian Cooperation* (New York: Praeger, 1987); and Leifer, *ASEAN*.

82. *Far Eastern Economic Review* 74 (December 11, 1971): 18.

83. *Far Eastern Economic Review* 74 (December 4, 1971): 5–6; Leifer, *ASEAN*, 1–6.

84. Young, *The Vietnam Wars*, 289–91; Hess, *Vietnam and the United States*, 135–38; Allan E. Goodman, *The Lost Peace: America's Search for a*

Negotiated Settlement of the Vietnam War (Stanford, Calif.: Hoover Institution Press, 1978).

85. Nixon, quoted in Herring, *America's Longest War*, 259. On the Thieu-Nixon relationship, see also Henry Kissinger, *Years of Upheaval* (Boston: Little Brown, 1982), 309–35; Nguyen Tien Hung and Jerold L. Schecter, *The Palace File* (New York: Harper and Row, 1986).

86. Olson and Roberts, *Where the Domino Fell*, 253–54; Herring, *America's Longest War*, 259–60.

87. *Far Eastern Economic Review* 88 (April 11, 1975): 13.

88. Mansfield, quoted in Olson and Roberts, *Where the Domino Fell*, 258.

89. Kissinger, quoted in Herring, *America's Longest War*, 266.

90. This account of the final campaign of the Vietnam War has been drawn especially from William J. Duiker, *The Communist Road to Power in Vietnam* (Boulder, Colo.: Westview, 1981), 314–29; Alan Dawson, *55 Days: The Fall of South Vietnam* (Englewood Cliffs, N.J.: Prentice-Hall, 1977); Arnold R. Isaacs, *Without Honor: Defeat in Vietnam and Cambodia* (Baltimore: Johns Hopkins University Press, 1983); Van Tien Dung, *Our Great Spring Victory: An Account of the Liberation of South Vietnam* (New York: Monthly Review Press, 1977); and Larry Engelman, *Tears Before the Rain: An Oral History of the Fall of South Vietnam* (New York: Oxford University Press, 1980).

91. McCloskey, quoted in Isaacs, *Without Honor*, 271.

92. This account of the final stages of the war in Cambodia has been drawn especially from Isaacs, *Without Honor*; Chandler, *The Tragedy of Cambodian History*, 202–46.

93. Quoted in Isaacs, *Without Honor*, 273.

94. Ibid., 270.

95. Castle, *At War in the Shadow of Vietnam*, 116–27.

7: Toward a New Regional Order, 1975–1998

1. *New York Times*, May 7, 1975, 1.

2. *Public Papers of the Presidents: Jimmy Carter* (1977): 955–62.

3. *New York Times*, August 19, 1980, 1.

4. *PPP: Ronald Reagan* (1988–89): 2:1495–96.

5. *New York Times*, March 4, 1991, 1.

6. Hearings Before the Special Subcommittee on Investigations of the House Committee on International Relations, *U.S. Policies in Southeast Asia*, 94th Cong., 2d sess., September 28, 1976 (Washington: GPO, 1976), 10.

7. House Committee on International Relations, *U.S. Policies in Southeast Asia*, 10.

8. Ibid., 27.

9. *PPP: Gerald R. Ford* (1975): 2:1951.

10. U.S. Department of State *Bulletin* 75 (August 16, 1976): 219–20. Kissinger made a similar pronouncement in a speech of June 18, 1975. For the text, see *New York Times*, June 19, 1975, 8.

11. House Committee on International Relations, *U.S. Policies in Southeast Asia* (Hummel testimony), 25.

12. U.S. Department of State *Bulletin* 75 (August 16, 1976): 218.

13. U.S. Department of State *Bulletin* 77 (October 31, 1977): 595–97.

14. U.S. Department of State *Bulletin* 64 (March 22, 1971): 380.

15. Third Annual Report to the Congress on United States Foreign Policy, February 9, 1972, *PPP: Richard M. Nixon* (1972): 256.

16. U.S. Department of State *Bulletin* 75 (August 16, 1976): 221.

17. Cyrus R. Vance, *Hard Choices: Critical Years in America's Foreign Policy* (New York: Simon and Schuster, 1983), 125.

18. Vance, *Hard Choices*, 123.

19. U.S. Department of State *Bulletin* 77 (October 31, 1977): 598–600; U.S. Department of State *Bulletin* 78 (September 1978): 19–25.

20. U.S. Department of State *Bulletin* 79 (September 1979): 35.

21. *Washington Post*, April 9, 1975, 13, and April 12, 1975, 9; *New York Times*, June 29, 1975, 3; *Far Eastern Economic Review* 88 (April 25, 1975): 36–40; *Far Eastern Economic Review* 88 (May 16, 1975): 39–40.

22. Quoted in *Washington Post*, April 9, 1975, 13. See also *Far Eastern Economic Review* 88 (June 13, 1975): 3–7.

23. Lee speech, reprinted in *Washington Post*, April 13, 1975, C6.

24. Quoted in *New York Times*, June 29, 1975, 3.

25. Quoted in *Far Eastern Economic Review* 88 (May 16, 1975): 39.

26. *New York Times*, June 29, 1975, 3; *Far Eastern Economic Review* 88 (April 25, 1975): 36.

27. *Far Eastern Economic Review* 88 (June 13, 1975): 3–7.

28. T. Christopher Jesperson, "The Politics and Culture of Nonrecognition: The Carter Administration and Vietnam," *Journal of American–East Asian Relations* 4 (winter 1995): 397–412. The quotes are from 400–401.

29. The "festering sores" comment was made by Vance in an interview. See *New York Times*, May 4, 1977, 12.

30. Jesperson, "Politics and Culture of Nonrecognition," 398–406; Report of the Presidential Commission on Americans Missing and Unaccounted for in Southeast Asia, March 23, 1977, *American Foreign Policy: Basic Documents, 1977–1981* (Washington: GPO, 1983), 1100.

31. Jesperson, "Politics and Culture of Nonrecognition," 407–10.

32. William J. Duiker, "China and Vietnam and the Struggle for Indochina," in Joseph J. Zasloff, ed., *Postwar Indochina: Old Enemies and New Allies* (Washington: Foreign Service Institute, 1988), 147–89; Marilyn B. Young, *The Vietnam Wars* (New York: HarperCollins, 1991), 305–308.

33. Quoted in Young, *The Vietnam Wars*, 308.

34. Zbigniew Brzezinski, *Power and Principle: Memoirs of the National Security Adviser, 1977–1981* (New York: Farrar, Straus, Giroux, 1985), 409.

35. Jimmy Carter, *Keeping Faith* (New York: Bantam, 1982), 204–09; Brzezinski, *Power and Principle*, 409–10; Robert M. Gates, *From the Shadows: The Ultimate Insider's Story of Five Presidents and How They Won the Cold War* (New York: Simon and Schuster, 1996), 120–22.

36. Brzezinski, *Power and Principle*, 414.

37. Donald E. Weatherbee, ed., *Southeast Asia Divided: The ASEAN Indochina Crisis* (Boulder, Colo.: Westview, 1989).

38. Quoted in Muthiah Alagappa, "Regionalism and the Quest for Security: ASEAN and the Cambodian Conflict," *Journal of International Affairs* (winter 1993): 452.

39. Weatherbee, ed., *Southeast Asia Divided*.

40. Vance, *Hard Choices*, 126.

41. Ibid., 126–27.

42. Alexander M. Haig, Jr., *Caveat: Realism, Reagan, and Foreign Policy* (New York: Macmillan, 1984), 26–27.

43. Address by Walter J. Stoessel, Under Secretary of State for Political Affairs, April 24, 1981, U.S. Department of State *Bulletin* 81 (June 1981): 33–35.

44. U.S. Department of State *Bulletin* 81 (August 1981): 40.

45. Hearings Before the Subcommittee on East Asian and Pacific Affairs of the Senate Committee on Foreign Relations, *U.S. Policy Objectives in Southeast Asia and the Factors which Shape These Objectives*, 97th Cong., 1st sess., July 15, 21, and 22, 1981 (Washington: GPO, 1981), 3.

46. Senate Committee on Foreign Relations, *U.S. Policy Objectives in Southeast Asia*, 33.

47. Ibid., 4–6.

48. Hearings Before the Subcommittee on East Asian and Pacific Affairs of the Committee on Foreign Relations, *U.S. Policies and Programs in Southeast Asia*, U.S. Senate, 97th Cong., 2d sess., June 8, 10, and 18, and July 15, 1982 (Washington: GPO, 1982), 70, 148–50. See also statement by Deputy Secretary of State Walter J. Stoessel, March 9, 1982, U.S. Department of State *Bulletin* 82 (May 1982): 45–48; and testimony by Stoessel, June 10, 1982, U.S. Department of State *Bulletin* 82 (August 1982): 55–58.

49. *PPP: Ronald Reagan* (1982): 2:1297.

50. *PPP: Ronald Reagan* (1986): 1:541.

51. George P. Shultz, *Turmoil and Triumph: My Years as Secretary of State* (New York: Scribner's, 1993).

52. U.S. Department of State *Bulletin* 82 (October 1982): 27.

53. *PPP: Jimmy Carter* (1977): 2.

54. Carter speech, December 6, 1978, U.S. Department of State *Bulletin* 79 (January 1979): 2. On Carter's human rights policy, see esp. Gaddis Smith, *Morality, Reason, and Power: American Diplomacy in the Carter Years* (New York: Hill

and Wang, 1986), 49–55; Tony Smith, *America's Mission* (Princeton: Princeton University Press, 1994), 239–65; and Sandy Vogelgesang, *American Dream, Global Nightmare: The Dilemma of U.S. Human Rights Policy* (New York: Norton, 1980).

55. Quoted in Tony Smith, *America's Mission*, 241.

56. Quoted in Gaddis Smith, *Moralty, Reason, and Power*, 50.

57. Brzezinski, *Power and Principle*, 49, 123–24.

58. U.S. Department of State *Bulletin* 77 (August 15, 1977): 210–13; David K. Wyatt, *Thailand: A Short History* (New Haven: Yale University Press, 1984), 301–304.

59. U.S. Department of State *Bulletin* 77 (August 15, 1977): 210–13.

60. Quoted in Gaddis Smith, *Morality, Reason, and Power*, 103. See also Robert Pringle, *Indonesia and the Philippines: American Interests in Island Southeast Asia* (New York: Columbia University Press, 1980), 101–103, 106–107.

61. Testimony of Robert B. Oakley, Deputy Assistant Secretary of State for East Asian and Pacific Affairs, U.S. Department of State *Bulletin* 77 (December 12, 1977): 848–52.

62. Testimony of Richard C. Holbrooke, Assistant Secretary of State for East Asian and Pacific Affairs, U.S. Department of State *Bulletin* 80 (May 1980): 30; Brzezinski, *Power and Principle*, 129.

63. Holbrooke, quoted in Brands, *Bound to Empire* (New York: Oxford University Press, 1992), 308.

64. Bonner, *Waltzing with a Dictator* (New York: Times Books, 1987), 225–26; Pringle, *Indonesia and the Philippines*, 95–101.

65. Bonner, *Waltzing with a Dictator*, 209–10.

66. Newsom, quoted in Brands, *Bound to Empire*, 312.

67. Holbrooke, quoted in Bonner, *Waltzing with a Dictator*, 223.

68. Quoted in ibid., 251.

69. Bush, quoted in Shultz, *Turmoil and Triumph*, 624.

70. Wolfowitz, quoted in Brands, *Bound to Empire*, 321.

71. Brands, *Bound to Empire*, 321–24; Karnow, *In Our Image* (New York: Ballantine, 1989), 406–409. Shultz also refers to these divisions within the administration, and notes his own doubts about Marcos, in his memoirs. See Shultz, *Turmoil and Triumph*, 609–12.

72. Quoted in Brands, *Bound to Empire*, 327.

73. Ibid., 332–34; Karnow, *In Our Image*, 413–15; Shultz, *Turmoil and Triumph*, 623–28.

74. Bosworth, quoted in Shultz, *Turmoil and Triumph*, 627–28.

75. Shultz, *Turmoil and Triumph*, 627.

76. Ibid., 631–39.

77. Ibid., 642.

78. Reagan radio address, April 26, 1986, *PPP: Ronald Reagan* (1986): 1:526; Shultz news briefing, May 1, 1986, U.S. Department of State *Bulletin* 86 (July 1986): 17; *New York Times*, April 29, 1986, 3. On Indonesia's banishment

of certain reporters, see *Washington Post*, April 25, 1986, 29; *New York Times*, April 26, 1986, 3; Raymond Bonner, "A Reporter at Large: The New Order—1," *New Yorker*, June 6, 1988, 45–46, 78–79.

79. For the American perspective on these developments, see Shultz, *Turmoil and Triumph*; James A. Baker, III, *The Politics of Diplomacy: Revolution, War, and Peace, 1989–1992* (New York: Putnam's, 1995).

80. Frederick Z. Brown, "Cambodia in 1991: An Uncertain Peace," *Asian Survey* 32 (January 1992): 88–96.

81. Leszek Buszynski, "Southeast Asia in the Post Cold War Era: Regionalism and Security," *Asian Security* 32 (September 1992): 830. See also Amitav Acharya, "Regional Military Security Cooperation in the Third World: The ASEAN Model," *Journal of Peace Research* 29 (February 1992): 7–22.

82. Quoted in *Far Eastern Economic Review* 150 (December 30, 1990): 30; Rosemary Foot, "Thinking Globally from a Regional Perspective: Chinese, Indonesian, and Malaysian Reflections on the Post-Cold War Era," *Contemporary Southeast Asia* 18 (June 1996): 17–35; Robert S. Ross, ed., *East Asia in Transition: Toward a New Regional Order* (Armonk, N.Y.: Sharpe, 1995).

83. *Far Eastern Economic Review* 150 (May 3, 1990): 10–11; *Far Eastern Economic Review* 148 (December 30, 1990): 30–32; *New York Times*, May 12, 1991, sec. 4, p. 2.

84. *Washington Post*, July 22, 1988, 18.

85. *New York Times*, February 25, 1990, sec. 4, p. 3; Paul H. Kreisberg, "The U.S. and Asia in 1990," *Asian Survey* 31 (January 1991): 7–8.

86. Bush, quoted in *Far Eastern Economic Review* 154 (November 21, 1991): 12; Allen S. Whiting, "ASEAN Eyes China: The Security Dimension," *Asian Survey* 37 (April 1997): 299–322.

87. Department of Defense Report, April 18, 1990, in *American Foreign Policy: Current Documents* (1990) (Washington: GPO, 1991), 649–54; Wolfowitz, quoted in *Far Eastern Economic Review* 148 (May 3, 1990): 10.

88. *New York Times*, March 8, 1992, 4, and May 24, 1992, 1, 5.

89. Quoted in *New York Times*, June 21, 1991, 3.

90. Cullather, *Illusions of Influence* (Stanford, Calif.: Stanford University Press, 1994), 1–2, 181–82.

91. Brown, quoted in *New York Times*, April 5, 1996, 7.

92. Clinton, quoted in *New York Times*, July 29, 1996, 17.

93. Testimony of Joan E. Spero, Under Secretary of State for Economic and Agricultural Affairs, November 15, 1993, Hearing Before the House Committee on Foreign Affairs, 103rd Cong., 1st sess., *Asia Pacific Economic Cooperation (APEC) and U.S. Policy Toward Asia* (Washington: GPO, 1993), 4.

94. Clinton, quoted in *New York Times*, November 19, 1993, 1; *New York Times*, November 21, 1993, 1; *Far Eastern Economic Review* 156 (November 18, 1993): 16–17.

95. See, for example, testimony of Winston Lord, Assistant Secretary of State

for East Asian and Pacific Affairs, February 9, 1995, Hearings Before the House Committee on International Relations, 104th Cong., 1st sess., *The Future of U.S. Foreign Policy in Asia and the Pacific* (Washington: GPO, 1996).

96. *New York Times*, September 12, 1993, sec. 3, p. 1.

97. These figures have been culled from the following: *Direction of Trade Statistics Yearbook* (Washington: IMF, 1997); U.S. Department of Commerce, *The Big Emerging Markets* (Washington: GPO, 1996); John Bresnan, *From Dominoes to Dynamos: The Economic Transformation of Southeast Asia* (New York: Council on Foreign Relations, 1994), 14–28; *New York Times*, February 2, 1996, C1, and March 9, 1996, sec. 3, p. 7; *Asian Wall Street Journal*, March 10, 1997, 5.

98. *New York Times*, February 2, 1996, C1.

99. See esp. Benedict Anderson, "From Miracle to Crash," *London Review of Books* 20 (April 16, 1998): 3–7; *Far Eastern Economic Review, Asia Handbook, 1998*, 7–12.

100. Bresnan, *From Dominoes to Dynamos*, 29–37; Mark Z. Taylor, "Dominance Through Technology: Is Japan Creating a Yen Bloc in Southeast Asia?" *Foreign Affairs* 74 (November-December 1995): 14–20; *New York Times*, July 2, 1989, sec. 4, p. 2.

101. *New York Times*, September 12, 1993, sec. 3, p. 6.

102. Helms, quoted in *Far Eastern Economic Review* 158 (July 24, 1995): 50; *New York Times*, July 12, 1995, 1.

103. *Far Eastern Economic Review* 158 (June 8, 1995): 14–15; *Far Eastern Economic Review* 158 (July 24, 1995): 50; *Far Eastern Economic Review* 159 (May 23, 1996): 36.

104. *New York Times*, December 17, 1995, sec. 4, p. 9. I am indebted to Phil Catton of Ohio University, who was in Ho Chi Minh City at the time, for the bicycle race story.

105. Brantley Womack, "Vietnam in 1996: Reform Immobilism," *Asian Survey* 37 (January 1997): 88–96; *New York Times*, April 8, 1996, 3; James W. Morley and Nasashi Nishihara, eds., *Vietnam Joins the World* (Armonk, N.Y.: Sharpe, 1997.

106. Quoted in *Gainesville Sun*, May 9, 1997, 3; *New York Times*, July 12, 1995, 1; *Los Angeles Times*, July 12, 1995, 1.

107. Albright, quoted in *New York Times*, June 1, 1997, 6; *Economist* 343 (June 7, 1997): 37–38; *Asian Wall Street Journal*, June 16, 1997, 12.

108. Quoted in *New York Times*, June 1, 1997, 6.

109. John Funston, "ASEAN: Out of Its Depth?" *Contemporary Southeast Asia* 20 (April 1998): 22–37; Suchitra Punyaratabandhu, "Thailand in 1997: Financial Crisis and Constitutional Reform," *Asian Survey* 38 (February 1998): 161–67; *Far Eastern Economic Review* 161 (June 4, 1998): 21–26.

110. *Far Eastern Economic Review* 161 (July 2, 1998), 10–11 (the quote is from p. 11); James Chin, "Malaysia in 1997," *Asian Survey* 38 (February 1998), 186–89; Donald K. Emmerson, "Americanizing Asia?" *Foreign Affairs* 77 (May-June 1998): 46–56.

Bibliographic Essay

Works on the United States and Southeast Asia that take a broad, regional focus are surprisingly sparse. That has been a result, in large measure, of the overshadowing impact that the Vietnam War has exerted on scholarship. Among those books that have adopted a region-wide focus are two older studies by Russell H. Fifield: *Southeast Asia in United States Policy* (New York: Praeger, 1965), and *Americans in Southeast Asia: The Roots of Commitment* (New York: Crowell, 1973). Also useful is Evelyn Colbert, *Southeast Asia in International Politics, 1941–1956* (Ithaca, N.Y.: Cornell University Press, 1977). For the early period, Gary R. Hess, *The United States' Emergence as a Southeast Asian Power, 1940–1950* (New York: Columbia University Press, 1987) is essential, as is Andrew J. Rotter, *The Path to Vietnam: Origins of the American Commitment to Southeast Asia* (Ithaca, N.Y.: Cornell University Press, 1987). A useful study focused on the more recent period is John Bresnan, *From Dominoes to Dynamos: The Transformation of Southeast Asia* (New York: Council on Foreign Relations, 1994).

The literature on the Vietnam War is dauntingly voluminous and tends to overwhelm virtually all other regional issues. For recent overviews of this substantial body of scholarship, see Gary R. Hess, "The Unending Debate: Historians and the Vietnam War," *Diplomatic History* 18 (spring 1994): 339–64; and Robert J. McMahon, "U.S.-Vietnamese Relations: A Historiographical Survey," in Warren I. Cohen, ed., *Pacific Passage: The Study of American–East Asian Relations on the Eve of the Twenty-First Century* (New York: Columbia University Press, 1995), 313–36. For the most recent and most comprehensive bibliographical guide to Vietnam War scholarship, see Lester Brune and Richard Dean Burns, *America and the Indochina Wars, 1945–1990: A Bibliographic Guide* (Claremont, Calif.: Regina, 1992). See also James S. Olson, *The Vietnam War: Handbook of Literature and Research* (Westport, Conn.: Greenwood, 1993).

On U.S.-Indonesian relations, see Robert J. McMahon, *Colo-*

nialism and Cold War: The United States and the Struggle for Indonesian Independence, 1945–49 (Ithaca, N.Y.: Cornell University Press, 1981); George McT. and Audrey R. Kahin, *Subversion as Foreign Policy: The Secret Eisenhower and Dulles Debacle in Indonesia* (New York: New Press, 1995); Lu Soo Chun, "U.S. Policy Toward Indonesia, 1953–1961" (unpublished Ph.D. diss., Ohio University, 1997); and Paul F. Gardner, *Shared Hopes, Separate Fears: Fifty Years of U.S.-Indonesian Relations* (Boulder, Colo.: Westview, 1997). Three memoirs written by former U.S. ambassadors are valuable: John M. Allison, *Ambassador from the Prairie or Allison in Wonderland* (Boston: Houghton Mifflin, 1973); Howard P. Jones, *Indonesia: The Possible Dream* (New York: Harcourt Brace Jovanovich, 1971); and Marshall Green, *Indonesia: Crisis and Transformation, 1965–1968* (Washington, D.C.: Compass, 1990). On the U.S. response to the 1965 coup, see H. W. Brands, "The Limits of Manipulation: How the United States Didn't Topple Sukarno," *Journal of American History* 76 (December 1989): 785–808. For the 1970s, see Robert Pringle, *Indonesia and the Philippines: American Interests in Island Southeast Asia* (New York: Columbia University Press, 1980).

On Thai-American relations, see especially the superb study by Daniel Fineman, *A Special Relationship: The United States and Military Government in Thailand, 1947–1958* (Honolulu: University of Hawaii Press, 1997). Also useful are Robert J. Muscat, *Thailand and the United States: Development, Security, and Foreign Aid* (New York: Columbia University Press, 1990); W. Scott Thompson, *Unequal Partners: Philippine and Thai Relations with the United States, 1965–75* (Lexington, Mass.: Lexington Books, 1975); Robert M. Blackburn, *Mercenaries and Lyndon Johnson's "More Flags": The Hiring of Korean, Filipino, and Thai Soliders in the Vietnam War* (Jefferson, N.C.: McFarland, 1994); and Thomas Lobe, *United States National Security Policy and Aid to the Thailand Police* (Denver: University of Denver Monograph Series in World Affairs, 1977).

On the Philippines, Nick Cullather's *Illusions of Influence: The Political Economy of United States–Philippines Relations, 1942–1960* (Stanford, Calif.: Stanford University Press, 1994) is incisive. Also noteworthy is Stephen R. Shalom, *The United States and the Philippines: A Study of Neocolonialism* (Philadelphia: Institute for the Study of Human Issues, 1981). Two excellent overviews that trace the story back to the American colonial era are Stanley Karnow, *In Our Image: America's Empire in the Philippines* (New York: Ballantine, 1989); and H. W. Brands, *Bound to Empire: The United States and the Philippines* (New York: Oxford University Press, 1992). See also Thompson, *Unequal Partners*; Blackburn, *Mercenaries and*

Lyndon Johnson's "More Flags" for the Vietnam War period. A colorful, journalistic account of the Marcos era is Raymond Bonner, *Waltzing with a Dictator: The Marcoses and the Making of American Policy* (New York: Times Books, 1987). For an incisive review of the literature on Philippine-American relations, see Glenn Anthony May, "The Unfathomable Other: Historical Studies of U.S.-Philippine Relations," in *Pacific Passage*, 279–312.

The literature on U.S. relations with Burma, Malaysia, and Singapore is disappointingly slim. For the former, John F. Cady's *The United States and Burma* (Cambridge: Harvard University Press, 1976) is helpful. For Malaysia, see Pamela Sodhy, *The US-Malaysian Nexus: Themes in Superpower–Small State Relations* (Kuala Lumpur: Institute of Strategic and International Studies, 1991).

Much of the literature on Laos has focused on that nation's connection to the Vietnam War. Especially valuable for U.S.-Laotian relations are the following: Charles A. Stevenson, *The End of Nowhere: American Policy Toward Laos Since 1954* (Boston: Beacon, 1972); Nina S. Adams and Alfred W. McCoy, eds., *Laos: War and Revolution* (New York: Harper and Row, 1970); Timothy N. Castle, *At War in the Shadow of Vietnam: U.S. Military Aid to the Royal Lao Government, 1955–1975* (New York: Columbia University Press, 1993); Roger Warner, *Shooting at the Moon: The Story of America's Clandestine War in Laos* (South Royalton, Vt.: Steerforth Press, 1996); and Sandra C. Taylor, "Laos: The Escalation of a Secret War," in Jane Errington and B. J. C. McKerchner, eds., *The Vietnam War as History* (New York: Praeger, 1990), 73–90.

Studies of U.S.-Cambodian relations, too, have been overshadowed by the Vietnam War. A devastating critique of U.S. policy can be found in William Shawcross, *Sideshow: Kissinger, Nixon, and the Destruction of Cambodia* (New York: Simon and Schuster, 1979). The case for the defense can be found in the relevant chapters of Henry Kissinger, *White House Years* (Boston: Little, Brown, 1979). For a more balanced perspective on Cambodian developments and U.S.-Cambodian relations, see especially David P. Chandler, *The Tragedy of Cambodian History: Politics, War, and Revolution Since 1945* (New Haven: Yale University Press, 1991); and Ben Kiernan, *How Pol Pot Came to Power* (London: Verso, 1985). See also Michael Haas, *Cambodia, Pol Pot, and the United States: The Faustian Pact* (New York: Praeger, 1991). For Sihanouk's perspective, see Norodom Sihanouk, *My War with the CIA* (New York: Pantheon, 1973).

On ASEAN, see especially Michael Leifer, *ASEAN and the Security of South-East Asia* (London: Routledge, 1989); Michael Antolik, *ASEAN and the Diplomacy of Accommodation* (Armonk, N.Y.: Sharpe, 1990); Ronald D. Palmer and Thomas J. Reckford, *Building ASEAN: Twenty Years of Southeast Asia Cooperation* (New York: Praeger, 1987); and W. W. Rostow, *The United States and the Regional Organization of Asia and the Pacific, 1965–1985* (Austin: University of Texas Press, 1986).

Index